Linux® Firewalls

Fourth Edition

D1126933

Linux® Firewalls

Enhancing Security with nftables and Beyond

Fourth Edition

Steve Suehring

✦✦ Addison-Wesley

Upper Saddle River, NJ • Boston • Indianapolis • San Francisco
New York • Toronto • Montreal • London • Munich • Paris • Madrid
Capetown • Sydney • Tokyo • Singapore • Mexico City

AURORA PUBLIC LIBRARY

Many of the designations used by manufacturers and sellers to distinguish their products are claimed as trademarks. Where those designations appear in this book, and the publisher was aware of a trademark claim, the designations have been printed with initial capital letters or in all capitals.

The author and publisher have taken care in the preparation of this book, but make no expressed or implied warranty of any kind and assume no responsibility for errors or omissions. No liability is assumed for incidental or consequential damages in connection with or arising out of the use of the information or programs contained herein.

For information about buying this title in bulk quantities, or for special sales opportunities (which may include electronic versions; custom cover designs; and content particular to your business, training goals, marketing focus, or branding interests), please contact our corporate sales department at corpsales@pearsoned.com or (800) 382-3419.

For government sales inquiries, please contact governmentsales@pearsoned.com.

For questions about sales outside the U.S., please contact international@pearsoned.com.

Visit us on the Web: informit.com/aw

Library of Congress Cataloging-in-Publication Data

Suehring, Steve.
  Linux firewalls : enhancing security with nftables and beyond.—Fourth edition / Steve Suehring.
      pages   cm
  Earlier ed. authored by Robert L. Ziegler.
  Includes bibliographical references and index.
  ISBN 978-0-13-400002-2 (pbk. : alk. paper)—ISBN 0-13-400002-1 (pbk. : alk. paper)
  1. Computers—Access control. 2. Firewalls (Computer security) 3. Linux. 4. Operating systems (Computers) I. Title.
  QA76.9.A25Z54 2015
  005.8—dc2

                                                                          2014043643

Copyright © 2015 Pearson Education, Inc.

All rights reserved. Printed in the United States of America. This publication is protected by copyright, and permission must be obtained from the publisher prior to any prohibited reproduction, storage in a retrieval system, or transmission in any form or by any means, electronic, mechanical, photocopying, recording, or likewise. To obtain permission to use material from this work, please submit a written request to Pearson Education, Inc., Permissions Department, One Lake Street, Upper Saddle River, New Jersey 07458, or you may fax your request to (201) 236-3290.

Permission is granted to copy, distribute, and/or modify Figures 3.1 through 3.4 under the terms of the GNU Free Documentation License, Version 1.3, or any later version published by the Free Software Foundation; with no Invariant Sections, no Front-Cover Texts, and no Back-Cover Texts. A copy of the license is included in Appendix D, "GNU Free Documentation License."

ISBN-13: 978-0-13-400002-2
ISBN-10: 0-13-400002-1
Text printed in the United States on recycled paper at R.R. Donnelley in Crawfordsville, Indiana.
First printing, January 2015

AURORA PUBLIC LIBRARY

❖

This book is dedicated to Jim Leu,
without whom I couldn't have written a book on Linux.

❖

Contents at a Glance

Contents

Preface

Welcome to the fourth edition of *Linux® Firewalls*. The book looks at what it takes to build a firewall using a computer running Linux. The material covered includes some basics of networking, IP, and security before jumping into `iptables` and `nftables`, the latest firewall software in Linux.

A reader of this book should be running a Linux computer, whether standalone or as a firewall or Internet gateway. The book shows how to build a firewall for a single client computer such as a desktop and also shows how to build a firewall behind which multiple computers can be hosted on a local network.

The final part of the book shows aspects of computer and network security beyond `iptables` and `nftables`. This includes intrusion detection, filesystem monitoring, and listening to network traffic. The book is largely Linux agnostic, meaning that just about any popular flavor of Linux will work with the material with little or no adaptation.

Acknowledgments

I'd like to thank my wife, family, and friends for their unending support. Thanks also to Robert P.J. Day and Andrew Prowant for reviewing the manuscript.

About the Author

Steve Suehring is a technology architect specializing in Linux and Windows systems and development. Steve has written several books and magazine articles on a wide range of technologies. During his tenure as an editor at *LinuxWorld* magazine, Steve wrote and edited articles and reviews on Linux security and advocacy including a feature story on the use of Linux in Formula One auto racing.

Packet Filtering and Basic Security Measures

1

Preliminary Concepts Underlying Packet-Filtering Firewalls

A small site may have Internet access through various means such as a T1 line, a cable modem, DSL, wireless, a PPP or ISDN connection, or any number of other means. The computer connected directly to the Internet is a point of focus for security issues. Whether you have one computer or a local area network (LAN) of linked computers, the initial focus for a small site will be on the machine with the direct Internet connection. This machine will be the firewall machine.

The term *firewall* has various meanings depending on its implementation and purpose. At this opening point in the book, firewall means the Internet-connected machine. This is where your primary security policies for Internet access will be implemented. The firewall machine's external network interface card is the connection point, or gateway, to the Internet. The purpose of a firewall is to protect what's on your side of this gateway from what's on the other side.

A simple firewall setup is sometimes called a *bastion firewall* because it's the main line of defense against attack from the outside. Many of your security measures are mounted from this one defender of your realm. Consequently, everything possible is done to protect this system.

Behind this line of defense is your single computer or your group of computers. The purpose of the firewall machine might simply be to serve as the connection point to the Internet for other machines on your LAN. You might be running local, private services behind this firewall, such as a shared printer or shared filesystems. Or you might want all of your computers to have access to the Internet. One of your machines might host your private financial records. You might want to have Internet access from this machine, but you don't want anyone getting in. At some point, you might want to offer your own services to the Internet. One of the machines might be hosting your own website for the Internet. Another might function as your mail server or gateway. Your setup and goals will determine your security policies.

The firewall's purpose is to enforce the security policies you define. These policies reflect the decisions you've made about which Internet services you want to be accessible to your computers, which services you want to offer the world from your computers, which services you want to offer to specific remote users or sites, and which services and programs you want to run locally for your own private use. Security policies are all about access control and authenticated use of private or protected services, programs, and files on your computers.

Home and small-business systems don't face all the security issues of a larger corporate site, but the basic ideas and steps are the same. There just aren't as many factors to consider, and security policies often are less stringent than those of a corporate site. The emphasis is on protecting your site from unwelcome access from the Internet. A packet-filtering firewall is one common approach to, and one piece of, network security and controlling access to and from the outside.

Of course, having a firewall doesn't mean you are fully protected. Security is a process, not a piece of hardware. For example, even with a firewall in place it's possible to download spyware or adware or click on a maliciously crafted email, thereby opening up the computer and thus the network to the attack. It's just as important to have measures in place to mitigate successful attacks as it is to spend resources on a firewall. Using best practices inside of your network will help to lessen the chance of a successful exploit and give your network resiliency.

Something to keep in mind is that the Internet paradigm is based on the premise of end-to-end transparency. The networks between the two communicating machines are intended to be invisible. In fact, if a network device somewhere along the path fails, the idea is that traffic between the two endpoint machines will be silently rerouted.

Ideally, firewalls should be transparent. Nevertheless, they break the Internet paradigm by introducing a single point of failure within the networks between the two endpoint machines. Additionally, not all network applications use communication protocols that are easily passed through a simple packet-filtering firewall. It isn't possible to pass certain traffic through a firewall without additional application support or more sophisticated firewall technology.

Further complicating the issue has been the introduction of Network Address Translation (NAT, or "masquerading" in Linux parlance). NAT enables one computer to act on behalf of many other computers by translating their requests and forwarding them on to their destination. The use of NAT along with RFC 1918 private IP addresses has effectively prevented a looming shortage of IPv4 addresses. The combination of NAT and RFC 1918 address space makes the transmission of some types of network traffic difficult, impossible, complex, or expensive.

> **Note**
>
> Many router devices, especially those for DSL, cable modems, and wireless, are being sold as firewalls but are nothing more than NAT-enabled routers. They don't perform many of the functions of a true firewall, but they do separate internal from external. Be wary when purchasing a router that claims to be a firewall but only provides NAT. Although some of these products have some good features, the more advanced configurations are sometimes not possible.

A final complication has been the proliferation of multimedia and peer-to-peer (P2P) protocols used in both real-time communication software and popular networked games. These protocols are antithetical to today's firewall technology. Today, specific software solutions must be built and deployed for each application protocol. The firewall architectures for easily and economically handling these protocols are in process in the standards committees' working groups.

It's important to keep in mind that the combination of firewalling, DHCP, and NAT introduces complexities that cause sites to have to compromise system security to some extent in order to use the network services that the users want. Small businesses often have to deploy multiple LANs and more complex network configurations to meet the varying security needs of the individual local hosts.

Before going into the details of developing a firewall, this chapter introduces the basic underlying concepts and mechanisms on which a packet-filtering firewall is based. These concepts include a general frame of reference for what network communication is, how network-based services are identified, what a packet is, and the types of messages and information sent between computers on a network.

The OSI Networking Model

The OSI (Open System Interconnection) model represents a network framework based on layers. Each layer in the OSI model provides distinct functionality in relation to the other layers. The OSI model contains seven layers, as shown in Figure 1.1.

The layers are sometimes referred to by number, with the lowest layer (Physical) being Layer 1 and the highest layer (Application) being Layer 7. If you hear someone refer to a

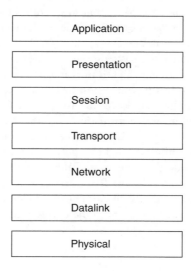

Figure 1.1　The seven layers of the OSI model

"Layer 3 switch," he or she is referring to the third layer of the OSI model. As a person interested in security and intrusion detection, you must know the layers of the OSI model to fully understand the attack paths that could compromise your systems.

Each layer in the OSI model is important. The protocols you use every day, such as IP, TCP, ARP, and others, reside on the various layers of the model. Each layer has its own distinct function and role in the communication process.

The Physical layer of the OSI model is occupied by the media itself, such as the cabling and related signaling protocols; in other words, transferring the bits. For the most part, the Physical layer is of less concern to the network intrusion analyst beyond securing the devices and cabling themselves. Because this book doesn't really talk much about physical security (how interesting are door locks?), I won't be devoting more time to the Physical layer of the OSI model either. Naturally, the steps you take to secure physical wires are different from those you would take to attempt to secure wireless devices.

The next layer above Physical is the Datalink layer. The Datalink layer transfers the data over the given medium and is responsible for things such as detection and recovery from errors in transmission. The Datalink layer is also the layer where physical hardware addresses are defined, such as an Ethernet card's Media Access Control (MAC) address.

Above the Datalink layer, the Network layer is the all-important third layer in IP networks. This layer is responsible for the logical addressing and routing of data. IP is a Network-layer protocol, which means that the Network layer is the layer on which IP addresses and subnet masks are used. Routers and some switches operate at Layer 3, moving data between both logically and physically divided networks.

The fourth layer, the Transport layer, is the primary layer on which reliability can be built. Protocols that exist at the Transport layer include TCP and UDP. The fifth layer is the Session layer, within which sessions are built between endpoints. The sixth layer, Presentation, is primarily responsible for communication with the Application layer above it, and it also defines such things as encryption to be used. Finally, the Application layer is responsible for displaying data to the user or application.

Aside from the OSI model, there exists another model, the DARPA model, sometimes called the TCP/IP reference model, which is only four layers. The OSI model has become the traditional or de facto model on which most network discussions take place.

As data moves from an application down the layers of the OSI model, the protocol at the next lower layer may add its own information onto the data. This data usually consists of a header that is prepended onto the data from the next highest level, though sometimes a trailer is added as well. This process, called *encapsulation*, continues until the data is transmitted across the physical medium. In the case of Ethernet, the data is known as a *frame* when it is transmitted. When the Ethernet frame arrives at its destination, the frame then begins the process of moving up the layers of the OSI model, with each layer reading the header (and possibly trailer) information from the corresponding layer of the sender. This process is called *demultiplexing*.

Connectionless versus Connection-Oriented Protocols

At some layers of the OSI model, protocols can be defined in terms of one of their properties, connectionless or connection oriented. This definition refers to the methods that the protocol contains for providing such things as error control, flow control, data segmentation, and data reassembly.

Think of connection-oriented protocols in terms of a telephone call. Generally there is an acceptable protocol for making a phone call and having a conversation. The person making the call, the initiator of the communication, opens the communication by dialing a telephone number. The person (or machine, as is the ever-increasing case) at the other end receives the request to begin a telephone conversation. The request to initiate a telephone conversation is frequently indicated by the ringing of the telephone on the receiver's end. The receiver picks up the telephone and says "Hello" or some other form of greeting. The initiator then acknowledges this greeting by responding in kind. At this point, it's safe to say that the conversation or call setup has been initiated. From this point forward, the conversation ensues. During the conversation if something goes wrong such as noise on the line, one of the parties may ask the other to repeat his or her last statement. Most of the time when a call is complete, both sides will indicate that they are done with the conversation by saying "Goodbye." The call ends shortly thereafter.

The example just given provides a semi-reasonable picture of a connection-oriented protocol such as TCP. There are exceptions to the rule, just as there can be exceptions or errors with the TCP protocol. For example, sometimes the initial call fails for technological reasons beyond the control of the caller or receiver.

On the other hand, a connectionless protocol is more akin to a postcard sent through the mail. After the sender writes a message on the postcard and drops it into the mailbox, the sender (presumably) loses control over that message. The sender receives no direct acknowledgment that the postcard was ever delivered successfully. Examples of connectionless protocols include UDP and IP itself.

Next Steps

From here, I'm going to jump into a more detailed look at the Internet Protocol (IP). However, I strongly recommend that you spend some additional time learning about the OSI model and the protocols themselves. Knowledge of the protocols and the OSI model is vital to a security professional. I highly recommend the book *TCP/IP Illustrated, Volume 1, Second Edition,* by Kevin R. Fall and W. Richard Stevens as a book that is indispensable on any computer professional's desk.

The Internet Protocol

The Internet Protocol is the basis on which the Internet operates. Together with protocols at other layers, the IP layer provides communications for countless applications. IP is a connectionless protocol providing Layer 3 routing functions.

IP Addressing and Subnetting

As you already know, but I feel compelled to write, IP addresses for version 4 of IP (IPv4) consist of four 8-bit numbers separated by periods, known as the "dotted quad" or "dotted decimal" notation. For IP version 6 (IPv6), addresses are 128-bit and are shown as eight groups of hexadecimal digits each separated by a colon. Although seemingly everyone understands or at least has seen an IP address, it certainly seems as though fewer and fewer understand subnetting and the subnet masks that are an important part of the IP addressing scheme. This section briefly looks at IP addressing and subnetting.

IPv4 addresses are divided into different classes rather than being an entirely flat address space. The classes for IPv4 addresses are shown in Table 1.1.

In practice, only addresses in Classes A through C are for general Internet use. However, some readers may have experience with Class D addresses, frequently used for multicast. Class E is the experimental and unallocated range.

Special IP Addresses

There are three major special cases of IP addresses:

- **Network address 0**—As noted under Class A addresses, network address 0 is not used as part of a routable address for IPv4. It is represented as `::/0` for IPv6. When used as a source address, its only legal use is during initialization when a host is attempting to have its IP address dynamically assigned by a server. When used as a destination, only address `0.0.0.0` has meaning, and then only to the local machine as referring to itself, or as a convention to refer to a default route.

- **Loopback network address 127**—As noted under Class A addresses, network address `127` is not used as part of a routable address. The IPv6 loopback address is represented as `0:0:0:0:0:0:0:1` or, more typically, reduced to `::1`. Loopback addresses refer to a private network interface supported by the operating system. The interface is used as the addressing mechanism for local network-based services. In other words, local network clients use it to address local servers. Loopback traffic remains entirely within the operating system. It is never passed to a physical network interface. Typically, `127.0.0.1` is the only loopback address used for IPv4 and `::1` for IPv6, referring to the local host.

- **Broadcast addresses**—Broadcast addresses are special addresses applying to all hosts on a network. There are two major categories of broadcast addresses. Limited broadcasts are not routed but are delivered to all hosts connected to the same physical network segment. All the bits in both the network and the host fields of the IP address are set to one, as `255.255.255.255`. Network-directed broadcasts are routed, being delivered to all hosts on a specified network. The IP address's network field specifies a network. The host field is usually all ones, as in `192.168.10.255`. Alternatively, you might sometimes see the address specified as the network address, as in `192.168.10.0`. IPv6 doesn't use broadcast addresses in this sense but rather uses multicasting to communicate with groups of hosts.

Table 1.1 **Internet Addresses**

Class	Address Range
A	`0.0.0.0` to `127.255.255.255`
B	`128.0.0.0` to `191.255.255.255`
C	`192.0.0.0` to `223.255.255.255`
D	`224.0.0.0` to `239.255.255.255`
E and unallocated	`240.0.0.0` to `255.255.255.255`

The IPv4 header consists of a number of fields and totals 20 bytes, not including optional option fields that can be included as part of the header. The IPv6 header is a 320-bit header. The IPv4 header is shown in Figure 1.2.

The IPv4 header begins with 4 bits indicating the version, currently version 4, followed by 4 bits indicating the length of the header. The header itself is normally 20 bytes plus optional options. The maximum length of the IPv4 header is 60 bytes. The next field, Differentiated Services Code Point (DSCP), is 6 bits in length followed by 2 bits for Explicit Congestion Notification (ECN).

The first number of an IP address indicates the class of the address. Because each number within the dotted decimal notation is 8 bits, the possible values for each number are 0 through 255. The class indicates the default number of bits devoted to the network portion of the address versus the number of bits devoted to the host identification with a given address. The division between the network portion of the address and the host portion of the address is important because it is the basis of subnet addressing.

Aside from classes, there are three types of addresses available on the Internet: unicast, multicast, and broadcast. Unicast addresses correspond to a single network interface on the Internet. Multicast addresses correspond to a group of hosts that ask to be included within

Version	Hdr Len	TOS	Total Datagram Len	
Packet ID			FI	Fragment Offset
TTL		Protocol	Header Checksum	
Source Address				
Destination Address				
(IP Options)				(Padding)

Figure 1.2   The IPv4 header

Table 1.2 **Default Subnet Masks**

Class	Default Subnet Mask
A	255.0.0.0
B	255.255.0.0
C	255.255.255.0

that group. Broadcast addresses are used by hosts that want to send data to every host on a given subnet.

Each class of address has a default subnet mask that indicates the division between the network and host portions of a given address. That's quite a mouthful, so I'll give examples and then there will be a quiz later. Kidding!

The default subnet masks for Classes A through C are given in Table 1.2.

You've undoubtedly seen and typed these numbers when configuring network settings. As previously stated, the subnet mask indicates the division between the network and the host portions of an IP address. The unmasked portion, known as the host portion, of the address comprises the logical network on which a given host resides. In other words, with a Class C subnet mask of 255.255.255.0, there can be a total of 254 hosts on the network. An astute reader might notice that there are really 256 addresses but only 254 hosts. Within a given logical IP network there are two special addresses, the network address and the broadcast address. This is true regardless of the size of the network. In the case of the Class C subnet example, the network address ends with .0 and the broadcast address ends with .255.

As Table 1.2 illustrates, of the total 32 bits in an IPv4 address, a Class A subnet mask uses 8 bits, a Class B subnet mask uses 16 bits, and a Class C subnet mask uses 24 bits. When a network is divided along traditional address class boundaries using the default subnet mask, it is said to be a *classful* network. As you might expect, there are times when it would be beneficial to use a much smaller network. For example, two IP routers that only need to transmit between each other would use an entire Class C network using traditional classful subnetting. Luckily, classless subnetting is also possible.

Using *classless* subnetting, officially called Classless Inter Domain Routing (CIDR), you can divide networks according to need by adding or subtracting bits from the subnet mask. This is useful for conservation of addresses because it enables the network administrator to customize the size of the network based more on need and convenience than on the classful boundaries. Jumping back to the example with two routers that communicate solely with each other, using CIDR a network administrator can create a network of just two hosts with the resulting subnet mask being 255.255.255.252.

I'll carry that example a little further. The two routers only need to talk to each other within this network so that they can route traffic between two different IP networks. The network administrator assigns one router the address 192.168.0.1 and the other router the address 192.168.0.2 and gives both a subnet mask of 255.255.255.252. Given that subnet mask, there are two available IP addresses with which a host could be addressed. The network address for this logical network is 192.168.0.0 and the broadcast address is

192.168.0.3. Using CIDR, the network administrator can now use the remainder of the 192.168.0 network, following CIDR rules, for other hosts.

You'll frequently see subnet notation referred to with a /NN with NN being the number of bits to be masked. For example, a Class C has 24 bits for the network portion of the address, which means that it could be referred to as /24. A Class B would be /16 and a Class A would be /8. Going back to the two-router example, the CIDR notation for this address is /30 because 30 bits of the address are consumed by the subnet.

Why is subnetting important? The simple answer is that a subnet defines the largest possible broadcast space for a given network. Within a given subnet a host can send a broadcast to all other hosts in that subnet. In practice, though, broadcasts are limited more by physical limitations than by the logical limitations presented by subnet masks. You can connect only so many devices to a switch before you may (I repeat, may) start to see performance degradation and would likely divide the network into smaller logical sections. Without subnetting we would have a very large, flat address space, which would be much slower than the hierarchical addressing currently used.

IP Fragmentation

There are times when an IP datagram is larger than the maximum allowed size for the physical medium on which it will be traveling. This maximum allowed size is known as the Maximum Transmission Unit, or MTU. If an IP datagram is larger than the MTU for the medium, the datagram will need to be split into smaller chunks before being transmitted. For Ethernet, the MTU is 1500 bytes. The process of splitting an IP datagram into smaller pieces is called *fragmentation*.

Fragmentation is handled at the IP layer of the OSI model and is thus transparent to higher-layer protocols such as TCP and UDP. As an administrator, you should care about fragmentation insofar as it can affect application performance if one of the fragments of a large segment gets lost. In addition, as a security administrator, you should understand fragmentation because it has been a path for attack in the past. Realize, however, that any intermediary router or other devices within the communication path may cause fragmentation and you may not even know it.

Broadcasting and Multicasting

When a device wants to send data to other devices on the same network segment, it can send the data to a special address known as a broadcast address to accomplish this task. On the other hand, a multicast is sent to the devices that belong to the multicast group, sometimes called *subscribers*.

Imagine a large, flat network in which every computer and device is connected to the others. In such an environment every network device sees every other network device's traffic. In this type of network, each device sees the traffic and determines whether it cares about the traffic in question. In other words, it looks to see whether the data is addressed to it or to another device. If the data is addressed to the device, it passes the data up to the layers of the OSI model. At the interface level for Ethernet, the device looks for its MAC address or the hardware address associated with the network interface itself. Remember that IP addresses are relevant only to protocols at higher layers on the OSI model.

Aside from frames addressed to the device itself, two special cases exist that might cause an interface to accept data and pass it up to higher layers. These two special cases are multicast and broadcast. Multicast is a method for transmitting data to a subset of devices that are said to be subscribed to that multicast.

On the other hand, broadcasts are meant to be processed by every device that receives them. Primarily two types of broadcasts are available: directed broadcast and limited broadcast. By far, directed broadcasts are the more common. Limited broadcasts are used by devices attempting to configure themselves through DHCP, BOOTP, or another configuration protocol. A limited broadcast is sent to the address 255.255.255.255 and should never pass through a router. This is a key hint for anyone who controls a router or other routing device such as a routing firewall. If you receive a packet on your external, Internet-facing router interface addressed to 255.255.255.255, chances are that there is a misconfigured device or, more likely, that a potential attacker is attempting to probe your network. You may see a limited broadcast on an internal interface for a router if you have devices that configure themselves on boot using DHCP.

Directed broadcasts are the most common form of broadcast you'll see on any given network. This is because broadcasts are used by the Address Resolution Protocol (ARP, discussed later) to determine the MAC address for an IP address on a given subnet. A directed broadcast is a broadcast that is limited by the network or subnet in which the sending device resides. By default, when a router interface encounters a directed broadcast, it does not pass it along to other subnets through the router. Most routers can be configured to allow this behavior; however, one should be careful so as not to create a broadcast storm by forwarding broadcasts through a router. A subnet broadcast is a data frame addressed to the broadcast address in a given subnet. This broadcast address varies depending on the subnet mask for the given subnet. In a Class C subnet (255.255.255.0 or /24), the default broadcast address is the highest available address, thus the one ending in .255. For example, in the 192.168.1.0/24 network, the broadcast address is 192.168.1.255.

ICMP

Holding a special place, some say, within the IP layer is ICMP. You're probably familiar with ICMP because ping uses ICMP. ICMP, or Internet Control Message Protocol, has several uses, including being the underlying protocol for the ping command. There are 15 functions within ICMP, each denoted by a type code. For instance, the type for an ICMP echo request (think: ping) is 8; the reply to that request, aptly titled an echo reply, is type 0. Within the different types there can also exist codes to specify the condition for the given type. The types and codes for ICMP messages are shown in Table 1.3.

The type and the code of an ICMP message are contained in the ICMP header, shown in Figure 1.3.

Table 1.3 **ICMP Message Types and Codes**

Type	Code	Description
0	0	Echo Reply
3		Destination Unreachable
	0	Network Unreachable
	1	Host Unreachable
	2	Protocol Unreachable
	3	Port Unreachable
	4	Fragmentation Needed and DF Set
	5	Source Route Failed
	6	Destination Network Unknown
	7	Destination Host Unknown
	8	Source Host Isolated
	9	Destination Network Administratively Prohibited
	10	Destination Host Administratively Prohibited
	11	Network Unreachable for Type of Service
	12	Host Unreachable for Type of Service
	13	Communication Administratively Prohibited
	14	Host Precedence Violation
	15	Precedence Cutoff in Effect
4		Source Quench (deprecated)
5		Redirect
	0	Network Redirect
	1	Host Redirect
	2	Type of Service and Network Redirect
	3	Type of Service and Host Redirect
8	0	Echo Request
9	0	Router Advertisement
10	0	Router Selection
11		Time Exceeded
	0	TTL (Time to Live) Exceeded in Transit
	1	Fragment Reassembly Time Exceeded
12	0	Parameter Problem
13	0	Timestamp Request
14	0	Timestamp Reply
15	0	Information Request (deprecated)
16	0	Information Reply (deprecated)
17	0	Address Mask Request (deprecated)
18	0	Address Mask Reply (deprecated)

Message Type	Sub Type Code	Checksum
Message ID		Sequence Number
(Optional ICMP Data Structure)		

Figure 1.3   The ICMP header

Transport Mechanisms

Internet Protocol defines a Network-layer protocol of the OSI model. There are also other Network-layer protocols, but I will be concentrating solely on IP because it is by far the most popular Network-layer protocol in use today. Above the Network layer on the OSI model is the Transport layer. As you might expect, the Transport layer has its own set of protocols. Two of the Transport-layer protocols are of interest: UDP and TCP. This section examines each of these protocols.

UDP

UDP, or User Datagram Protocol, is a connectionless protocol used for such services as DNS queries, SNMP, and RADIUS. Being connectionless, UDP is akin to a "fire and forget" type of protocol. The client sends a UDP packet, sometimes referred to as a datagram, and assumes that the server will receive the packet. It's up to a higher-layer protocol to assemble the packets in order. The UDP header, shown in Figure 1.4, is 8 bytes in length.

The UDP header begins with the source port number and the destination port number. Next up is the length of the entire packet, including data. Obviously because the header itself is 8 bytes in length, the minimum value for this portion of the header is 8. The final portion of the UDP header is the checksum, which includes both the header and the data.

TCP

TCP, an abbreviation for Transmission Control Protocol, is a connection–oriented protocol that is frequently used with IP. Referring to TCP as connection oriented means that it provides reliable service to the layers above it. Recall the telephone conversation analogy

Source Port	Destination Port
UDP Packet Length	Checksum

Figure 1.4   The UDP header

Source Port			Destination Port	
Sequence Number				
Acknowledgment Number				
Data Offset	Unused	Flags	Window	
Checksum			Urgent Pointer	

Figure 1.5   The TCP header

given earlier in this chapter. As in that analogy, two applications wanting to communicate using TCP must also establish a connection (sometimes referred to as a session). The TCP header is shown in Figure 1.5.

As you can see from Figure 1.5, the 20-byte TCP header is significantly more complicated than the other protocol headers shown in this chapter. Like the UDP header, the TCP header begins with both the source and the destination ports. The combination of the source and destination ports along with the IP addresses of the sender and receiver identifies the connection. The TCP header has a 32-bit sequence number and a 32-bit acknowledgment. Remember that TCP is a connection-oriented protocol and provides reliable service. The sequence and acknowledgment numbers are the primary (but not the only) mechanisms used to provide that reliability. As data is passed down to the Transport layer, TCP divides the data into what it believes to be the most appropriate size. These pieces are known as *TCP segments*. As TCP sends data down the protocol stack, it creates a sequence number that indicates the first byte of data for the given segment. On the opposite end of the communication, the receiver sends an acknowledgment indicating that the segment has been received. The sender keeps a timer running, and if an acknowledgment isn't received in a timely fashion, the segment will be resent.

Another mechanism for reliability that TCP provides is a checksum on both the header and the data. If the checksum set within the header by the sender does not match the checksum as computed by the receiver, the receiver will not send an acknowledgment. If an acknowledgment gets lost in transit, the sender will likely send another segment with the same sequence number. In such an event, the receiver will simply discard the repeated segment.

A 4-bit field is used for header length, including any options provided as part of the header. There are several individual bit flags within the TCP header: URG, ACK, PSH, RST, SYN, FIN, NS, CWR, and ECE. A description of these flags is contained in Table 1.4.

The 16-bit Window field is used to provide a sliding window mechanism. The receiver sets the window number to indicate the size that the receiver is ready to receive, beginning with the acknowledgment number. This is a form of flow control for TCP.

Table 1.4 **TCP Header Flags**

Flag	Description
URG	Indicates that the urgent pointer portion of the header should be examined.
ACK	Indicates that the acknowledgment number should be examined.
PSH	Indicates that the receiver should hand this data up to the next layer as soon as possible.
RST	Indicates that the connection should be reset.
SYN	Initiates a connection.
NS	ECN nonce concealment protection.
CWR	Congestion Window Reduced to indicate that a packet with the ECE flag was set and congestion control responded.
ECE	If the SYN flag is set to 1, this flag indicates that the TCP peer is ECN capable. If SYN is set to 0, this flag indicates that a Congestion Experienced flag was set in an IP header.
FIN	Indicates that the sender (could be either side of the connection) is done sending data.

The 16-bit urgent pointer indicates the offset from the sequence number where urgent data ends. This enables the sender to indicate that there is data that should be handled in an urgent manner. This pointer can be used in conjunction with the PSH flag as well.

Now that you have a feeling for the TCP header, it's time to examine how TCP connections are established and ended.

TCP Connections

Whereas UDP is a connectionless protocol, TCP is a connection-oriented protocol. With UDP there is no concept of a connection; there is only a sender and a receiver of a UDP datagram. With TCP, on the other hand, either side of the connection can send or receive data, possibly doing both at the same time. This is what makes TCP a full-duplex protocol. The process of establishing a TCP connection is sometimes called the *three-way handshake*—you'll see why shortly.

With a connection-oriented protocol, there is a specific set of procedures that takes place in order to establish a TCP connection. During this process, various states exist for the TCP connection. The connection establishment procedures and their corresponding states are detailed next.

The side of the communication wanting to initiate the connection (client) sends a TCP segment with the SYN flag set, as well as an Initial Sequence Number (ISN) and the port number for the connection to the other side, normally referred to as the server side of the connection. This is frequently referred to as a SYN packet or SYN segment, and the connection is said to be in the SYN_SENT state.

The server side of the connection responds with a TCP segment with the SYN flag set as well as the ACK flag set. In addition, the server sets the ISN with a value one higher than the ISN sent by the client. This is frequently referred to as a SYN-ACK packet or SYN-ACK segment, and the connection is said to be in the SYN_RCVD state.

The client then acknowledges the SYN-ACK by sending another segment with the ACK flag set and by incrementing the ISN by one. This completes the three-way handshake and the connection is said to be in an ESTABLISHED state.

As with the protocol for connection initiation, there is also a protocol for connection termination. The protocol for terminating a TCP connection is four steps as opposed to the three for connection establishment. The additional step is due to the full-duplex nature of a TCP connection insofar as either side may be sending data at any given time.

Closing a connection on one side is accomplished by that side sending a TCP segment with the FIN flag set. Either side of the connection can send a FIN to indicate that it is done sending data. The other side can still send data. However, in practice, after a FIN is received, the connection termination sequence will normally begin. For this discussion I'll call the side wanting to terminate the connection the client side.

The termination process begins with the client sending a segment with the FIN flag set, known as the CLOSE_WAIT state on the server side and FIN_WAIT_1 on the client side. After the FIN is received by the server, the server sends an ACK back to the client, incrementing the sequence number by one. At this point the client goes into the FIN_WAIT_2 state. The server also indicates to its own higher-layer protocols that the connection is terminated. Next, the server closes the connection, which causes a segment with the FIN flag to be sent to the client, which in turn causes the server to go into a LAST_ACK state while the client goes into a TIME_WAIT state. Finally, the client acknowledges this FIN with an ACK and increments the sequence number by one, which causes the connection to go into a CLOSED state. Because TCP connections can be terminated by either side, a TCP connection can exist in a half-closed mode in which one end has initiated the FIN sequence but the other side has not done so.

TCP connections can also be terminated by one end sending a segment with the reset (RST) flag set. This tells the other side to use an abortive release method. This is as opposed to the normal termination of a TCP connection, sometimes referred to as an orderly release.

An optional part of the TCP connection sequence is the establishment of the Maximum Segment Size (MSS). The MSS is the maximum chunk of data that the respective end of communication is able to receive. Because the MSS is the maximum size that a given end of the connection can receive, it's perfectly fine to send a chunk of data smaller than the MSS. In general, you should consider a larger MSS to be good, keeping in mind that fragmentation should be avoided because it adds overhead (the additional bytes for each IP and TCP header required for fragmented packets).

Don't Forget Address Resolution Protocol

Address Resolution Protocol, or ARP, is the protocol used to link a physical device such as a network card to an IP address. Network devices use a 48-bit address (known as a MAC address) that is unique across all devices in a given segment. Although sometimes devices have the same MAC address, this is quite rare within the same network segment.

When capturing traffic in a network, you will encounter ARP packets at varying frequencies as devices locate one another as they pass traffic. ARP requests are broadcast so that all devices will see them. However, most ARP replies are unicast so that only the requesting device will see the reply. ARP traffic is not normally passed between network segments. Therefore, a router can be configured to provide proxy ARP service so that it can answer for ARP requests in multiple network segments.

Hostnames and IP Addresses

People like to use words to name things, such as giving computers names like `mycomputer.mydomain.example.com`. Technically, it's not the computer that's being named, but the network interface in the computer. If the computer has multiple network cards, each card will typically have a different name and address and will most likely be on a different network in a different subdomain.

Hostname elements are separated by dots. In the case of `mycomputer.mydomain.example.com`, the leftmost element, `mycomputer`, is the hostname. The `.mydomain`, `.example`, and `.com` are elements of the domains this network card is a member of. Network domains are hierarchical trees. What is a domain? It's a naming convention. The hierarchical domain tree represents the hierarchical nature of the global Domain Name Service (DNS) database. DNS maps between the symbolic names people give to computers and networks and the numeric addresses the IP layer uses to uniquely identify network interfaces.

DNS maps in both directions: IP address to name and name to IP address. When you click on a URL in your web browser, the DNS database is consulted to find the unique IP address associated with that hostname. The IP address is passed to the IP layer to use as the destination address in the packet.

IP Addresses and Ethernet Addresses

Whereas the IP layer identifies network hosts by their 32- or 128-bit IP address, the subnet or link layer identifies the Ethernet card by its unique 48-bit Ethernet address, or MAC address, which the manufacturer burns into the card and can also be set by the user. IP addresses are passed between the endpoint hosts to identify themselves. Ethernet addresses are passed between adjacent hosts and routers.

Ordinarily, the Ethernet address could be ignored in a firewall discussion. The Layer 2 hardware Ethernet address is not visible to the Layer 3 IP level or Layer 4 Transport level. As you'll see in later chapters, the Linux firewall administration program has the extended capability to access and filter on the MAC address. There are specialized uses for this firewall functionality, but it's important to remember that Ethernet addresses do not pass end-to-end across the network. Ethernet addresses are passed between adjacent network interfaces, or hosts and routers. They are not passed through a router unchanged.

Routing: Getting a Packet from Here to There

Neither a residential site nor most businesses are likely to run routing protocols such as RIP or OSPF. In these cases, routing tables are set up statically, by hand. There's a hint in there. If you're running a routing protocol such as RIP, chances are that you don't need to be; you could operate a more efficient network without that unnecessary overhead. Typically, most sites have a default gateway device, which is the network that interface packets are sent out on when the destination address's route is unknown. The service provider usually provides a single router address, which is the default Internet gateway for the site's local network.

Service Ports: The Door to the Programs on Your System

Network-based services are programs running on a machine that other computers on the network can access. The service ports identify the programs and individual sessions or connections taking place. Service ports are the numeric names for the different network-based services. They are also used as numeric identifiers for the endpoints of a particular connection between two programs. Service port numbers range from 0 to 65535.

Server programs (that is, *daemons*) listen for incoming connections on a service port assigned to them. By historical convention, major network services are assigned well-known, or famous, port numbers in the lower range from 1 to 1023. These port number–to–service mappings are coordinated by the Internet Assigned Numbers Authority (IANA) as a set of universally agreed-on conventions or standards.

An advertised service is simply a service available over the Internet from its assigned port. If your machine isn't offering a particular service, and someone tries to connect to the port associated with that service, nothing will happen. Someone is knocking on the door, but no one lives there to answer. For example, HTTP is assigned to port 80 (though, again, there's no reason why you couldn't run it on port 8080, 20943, or any other available port). If your machine isn't running an HTTP-based web server and someone tries to connect to port 80, the client program receives a connection shutdown message as an error message from your machine indicating that the service isn't offered.

The higher port numbers from 1024 to 65535 are called *unprivileged ports*. They serve a dual purpose. For the most part, these ports are dynamically assigned to the client end of a connection. The combination of client and server port number pairs, along with their respective IP host addresses, and the transport protocol used, uniquely identifies the connection.

Additionally, ports in the 1024 through 49151 range are registered with the IANA. These ports can be used as part of the general unprivileged pool, but they are also associated with particular services such as SOCKS or X Window servers. Originally, the idea was that services offered on the higher ports were not running with root privilege. They were for use by user-level, nonprivileged programs. The convention may or may not hold in any individual case.

Service Name–to–Port Number Mappings

Linux distributions are supplied with a list of common service port numbers. The list is found in the `/etc/services` file.

Each entry consists of a symbolic name for a service, the port number assigned to it, the protocol (TCP or UDP) the service runs over, and any optional nicknames for the service. Table 1.5 lists some common service name–to–port number mappings, taken from Red Hat Linux.

Table 1.5 **Common Service Name–to–Port Number Mappings**

Port Name	Port Number/Protocol	Alias
ftp	21/tcp	- -
ssh	22/tcp	- -
smtp	25/tcp	mail
domain	53/tcp	nameserver
domain	53/udp	nameserver
http	80/tcp	www www-http
pop3	110/tcp	pop-3
nntp	119/tcp	readnews untp
ntp	123/udp	- -
https	443/tcp	- -

Note that the symbolic names associated with the port numbers vary by Linux distribution and release. Names and aliases differ; port numbers do not.

Also note that port numbers are associated with a protocol. The IANA has attempted to assign the same service port number to both the TCP and the UDP protocols, regardless of whether a particular service uses both transport modes. Most services use one protocol or the other. The Domain Name Service uses both.

A Typical TCP Connection: Visiting a Remote Website

As an illustration, a common TCP connection is going to a website through your browser (connecting to a web server). This section illustrates the aspects of connection establishment and ongoing communication that will be relevant to IP packet filtering in later chapters.

What happens? As shown in Figure 1.6, a web server is running on a machine somewhere, waiting for a connection request on TCP service port 80. You click on the link for a URL in your web browser. Part of the URL is parsed into a hostname; the hostname is translated into the web server's IP address; and your browser is assigned an unprivileged port (for example, TCP port 14000) for the connection. An HTTP message for the web server is constructed. It's encapsulated in a TCP message, wrapped in an IP packet header, and sent out. For our purposes, the header contains the fields shown in Figure 1.6.

Additional information is included in the header that isn't visible at the packet-filtering level. Nevertheless, describing the sequence numbers associated with the SYN and ACK flags helps clarify what's happening during the three-way handshake. When the client program sends its first connection request message, the SYN flag is accompanied by a synchronization sequence number. The client is requesting a connection with the server and passes along a sequence number it will use as the starting point to number all the rest of the data bytes the client will send.

The packet is received at the server machine. It's sent to service port 80. The server is listening to port 80, so it's notified of an incoming connection request (the SYN connection synchronization request flag) from the source IP address and port socket pair (*your IP address*, 14000). The server allocates a new socket on its end (*web server IP address*, 80) and associates it with the client socket.

The web server responds with an acknowledgment (ACK) to the SYN message, along with its own synchronization request (SYN), as shown in Figure 1.7. The connection is now half open.

Two fields not visible to the packet-filtering level are included in the SYN-ACK header. Along with the ACK flag, the server includes the client's sequence number incremented by

Web Browser   Web Server
Port 14000   Port 80
Address 192.168.10.30   Address 10.10.22.85

Protocol: TCP
Source Address: 192.168.10.30
Source Port: 14000
Destination Address: 10.10.22.85
Destination Port: 80 (www)
Flags: SYN (Connection Synchronization Request)

Figure 1.6   A TCP client connection request

Protocol: TCP
Source Address: 10.10.22.85
Source Port: 80 (www)
Destination Address: 192.168.10.30
Destination Port: 14000
Flags: ACK (SYN Acknowledgment)
       SYN (Connection Synchronization Request)

Figure 1.7   A TCP server connection request acknowledgment

the number of contiguous data bytes received. The purpose of the acknowledgment is to acknowledge the data the client referred to by its sequence number. The server acknowledges this by incrementing the client's sequence number, effectively saying it received the data, and sequence number plus one is the next data byte the server expects to receive. The client is free to throw its copy of the original SYN message away now that the server has acknowledged receipt of it.

The server also sets the SYN flag in its first message. As with the client's first message, the SYN flag is accompanied by a synchronization sequence number. The server is passing along its own starting sequence number for its half of the connection.

This first message is the only message the server will send with the SYN flag set. This and all subsequent messages have the ACK flag set. The presence of the ACK flag in all server messages, as compared to the lack of an ACK flag in the client's first message, will be a critical difference when we get to the information available for constructing a firewall.

Your machine receives this message and replies with its own acknowledgment, after which the connection is established. Figure 1.8 shows a graphic representation of this. From here on, both the client and the server set the ACK flag. The SYN flag won't be set again by either program.

With each acknowledgment, the client and server programs increment their partner process's sequence number by the number of contiguous data bytes received, plus one, indicating receipt of that many bytes of data, and indicating the next data byte in the stream the program expects to receive.

As your browser receives the web page, your machine receives data messages from the web server with packet headers, as shown in Figure 1.9.

Protocol: TCP
Source Address: 192.168.10.30
Source Port: 14000
Destination Address: 10.10.22.85
Destination Port: 80 (www)
Flags: ACK (Acknowledgment)

Figure 1.8   TCP connection establishment

Protocol: TCP
Source Address: 10.10.22.85
Source Port: 80 (www)
Destination Address: 192.168.10.30
Destination Port: 14000
Flags: ACK (Acknowledgment)

Figure 1.9   An ongoing TCP server-to-client connection

Summary

The simple examples in this chapter illustrate the information that IP packet-filtering firewalls are based on. Chapter 2, "Packet-Filtering Concepts," builds on this introduction, describing how the ICMP, UDP, and TCP message types and service port numbers are used to define a packet-filtering firewall.

2

Packet-Filtering Concepts

What is a firewall? Over the years, the term has changed in meaning. According to RFC 2647, "Benchmarking Terminology for Firewall Performance," a firewall is "a device or group of devices that enforces an access control policy between networks." This definition is very broad, purposefully so in fact. A firewall can encompass many layers of the OSI model and may refer to a device that does packet filtering, performs packet inspection and filtering, implements a policy on an application at a higher layer, or does any of these and more.

A nonstateful, or stateless, firewall usually performs some packet filtering based solely on the IP layer (Layer 3) of the OSI model, though sometimes higher-layer protocols are involved in this type of firewall. An example of this type of device might include a border router that sits at the edge of a network and implements one or more access lists to prevent various types of malicious traffic from entering the network. Some might argue that this type of device isn't a firewall at all. However, it certainly appears to fit within the RFC definition.

A border router access list might implement many different policies depending on which interface the packet was received on. It's typical to filter certain packets at the edge of the network connecting to the Internet. These packets are discussed later in this chapter.

As opposed to a stateless firewall, a stateful firewall is one that keeps track of the packets previously seen within a given session and applies the access policy to packets based on what has already been seen for the given connection. A stateful firewall implies the basic packet-filtering capabilities of a stateless firewall as well. A stateful firewall will, for example, keep track of the stages of the TCP three-way handshake and reject packets that appear out of sequence for that handshake. Being connectionless, UDP is somewhat trickier to handle for a stateful firewall because there's no state to speak of. However, a stateful firewall tracks recent UDP exchanges to ensure that a packet that has been received relates to a recent outgoing packet.

An *Application-level gateway* (ALG), sometimes referred to an as an *Application-layer gateway*, is yet another form of firewall. Unlike the stateless firewall, which has knowledge of the Network and possibly Transport layers, an ALG primarily handles Layer 7, the Application layer of the OSI model. ALGs typically have deep knowledge of the application data being passed and can thus look for any deviation from the normal traffic for the application in question.

An ALG will typically reside between the client and the real server and will, for all intents and purposes, mimic the behavior of the real server to the client. In effect, local traffic never leaves the LAN, and remote traffic never enters the LAN.

ALG sometimes also refers to a module, or piece of software that assists another firewall. Many firewalls come with an FTP ALG to support FTP's port mode data channel, where the client tells the server what local port to connect to so that it can open the data channel. The server initiates the incoming data channel connection (whereas, usually, the client initiates all connections). ALGs are frequently required to pass multimedia protocols through a firewall because multimedia sessions often use multiple connections initiated from both ends and generally use TCP and UDP together.

ALG is a proxy. Another form of proxy is a *circuit-level proxy*. Circuit-level proxies don't usually have application-specific knowledge, but they can enforce access and authorization policies, and they serve as termination points in what would otherwise be an end-to-end connection. SOCKS is an example of a circuit-level proxy. The proxy server acts as a termination point for both sides of the connection, but the server doesn't have any application-specific knowledge.

In each of these cases, the firewall's purpose is to enforce the access control or security policies that you define. Security policies are essentially about access control—who is and is not allowed to perform which actions on the servers and networks under your control.

Though not necessarily specific to a firewall, firewalls many times find themselves performing additional tasks, some of which might include Network Address Translation (NAT), antivirus checking, event notification, URL filtering, user authentication, and Network-layer encryption.

This book covers the ideas behind a packet-filtering firewall, both static and dynamic, or stateless and stateful. Each of the approaches mentioned controls which services can be accessed and by whom. Each approach has its strengths and advantages based on the differing information available at the various OSI reference model layers.

Chapter 1, "Preliminary Concepts Underlying Packet-Filtering Firewalls," introduced the concepts and information a firewall is based on. This chapter introduces how this information is used to implement firewall rules.

A Packet-Filtering Firewall

At its most basic level, a packet-filtering firewall consists of a list of acceptance and denial rules. These rules explicitly define which packets will and will not be allowed through the network interface. The firewall rules use the packet header fields described in Chapter 1 to decide whether to forward a packet to its destination, to silently throw away the packet, or to block the packet and return an error condition to the sending machine. These rules can be based on a wide array of factors, including the source or destination IP addresses, the source and (more commonly) destination ports, and portions of individual packets such as the TCP header flags, the types of protocol, the MAC address, and more.

MAC address filtering is not common on Internet-connected firewalls. Using MAC filtering, the firewall blocks or allows only certain MAC addresses. However, in all likelihood you see only one MAC address, the one from the router just upstream from your firewall. This means that every host on the Internet will appear to have the same MAC address as far as your firewall can see. A common error among new firewall administrators is to attempt to use MAC filtering on an Internet firewall.

Using a hybrid of the TCP/IP reference model, a packet-filtering firewall functions at the Network and Transport layers, as shown in Figure 2.1.

The overall idea is that you need to very carefully control what passes between the Internet and the machine that you have connected directly to the Internet. On the external interface to the Internet, you individually filter what's coming in from the outside and what's going out from the machine as exactly and explicitly as possible.

For a single-machine setup, it might be helpful to think of the network interface as an I/O pair. The firewall independently filters what comes in and what goes out through the interface. The input filtering and the output filtering can, and likely do, have completely different rules. Figure 2.2 depicts processing for rules in a flowchart.

This sounds pretty powerful, and it is; but it isn't a surefire security mechanism. It's only part of the story, just one layer in the multilayered approach to data security. Not all application communication protocols lend themselves to packet filtering. This type of

Figure 2.1   Firewall placement in the TCP/IP reference model

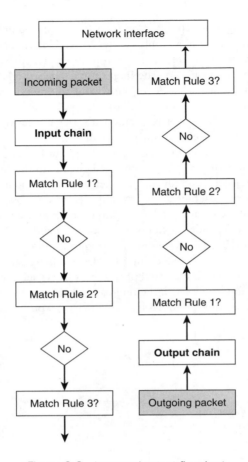

Figure 2.2   Input and output flowchart

filtering is too low-level to allow fine-grained authentication and access control. These security services must be furnished at higher levels. IP doesn't have the capability to verify that the sender is who he or she claims to be. The only identifying information available at this level is the source address in the IP packet header. The source address can be modified with little difficulty. One level up, neither the Network layer nor the Transport layer can verify that the application data is correct. Nevertheless, the packet level allows greater, simpler control over direct port access, packet contents, and correct communication protocols than can easily or conveniently be done at higher levels.

Without packet-level filtering, higher-level filtering and proxy security measures are either crippled or potentially ineffective. To some extent, at least, they must rely on the correctness of the underlying communication protocol. Each layer in the security protocol stack adds another piece that other layers can't easily provide.

Choosing a Default Packet-Filtering Policy

As stated earlier in this chapter, a firewall is a device to implement an access control policy. A large part of this policy is the decision on a default firewall policy.

There are two basic approaches to a default firewall policy:

- Deny everything by default, and explicitly allow selected packets through.
- Accept everything by default, and explicitly deny selected packets from passing through.

Without question, the deny–everything policy is the recommended approach. This approach makes it easier to set up a secure firewall, but each service and related protocol transaction that you want must be enabled explicitly (see Figure 2.3). This means that you

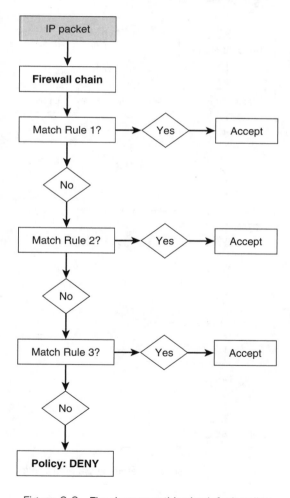

Figure 2.3   The deny-everything-by-default policy

must understand the communication protocol for each service you enable. The deny-everything approach requires more work up front to enable Internet access. Some commercial firewall products support only the deny-everything policy.

The accept-everything policy makes it much easier to get up and running right away, but it forces you to anticipate every conceivable access type that you might want to disable (see Figure 2.4). The danger is that you won't anticipate a dangerous access type until it's too late, or you'll later enable an insecure service without first blocking external access to it. In the end, developing a secure accept-everything firewall is much more work, much more difficult, almost always much less secure, and, therefore, much more error-prone.

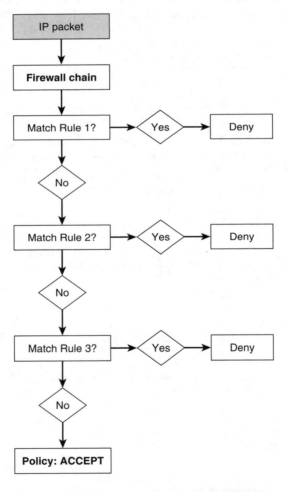

Figure 2.4   The accept-everything-by-default policy

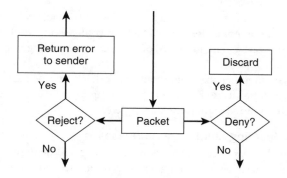

Figure 2.5   Rejecting versus denying a packet

Rejecting versus Denying a Packet

The Netfilter firewall mechanism in `iptables` and `nftables` gives you the option of either rejecting or dropping packets. What's the difference? As shown in Figure 2.5, when a packet is rejected, the packet is thrown away and an ICMP error message is returned to the sender. When a packet is dropped, the packet is simply thrown away without any notification to the sender.

Silently dropping the packet is almost always the better choice, for three reasons. First, sending an error response doubles the network traffic. The majority of dropped packets are dropped because they are malevolent, not because they represent an innocent attempt to access a service you don't happen to offer. Second, a packet that you respond to can be used in a denial-of-service (DoS) attack. Third, any response, even an error message, gives the would-be attacker potentially useful information.

Filtering Incoming Packets

The input side of the external interface I/O pair, the input rule set, is the more interesting in terms of securing your site. As mentioned earlier, you can filter based on source address, destination address, source port, destination port, TCP status flags, and other criteria. You'll learn about all these pieces of information at one point or another in the following sections.

Remote Source Address Filtering

At the packet level, the only means of identifying the IP packet's sender is the source address in the packet header. This fact allows for the possibility of source address spoofing, in which the sender places an incorrect address rather than his or her own address in the source field. The address might be a nonexistent address, or it might be a legitimate address belonging to someone else. This can allow unsavory types to break into your system by appearing as local, trusted traffic; appearing to be you while attacking other sites; pretending to be someone else while attacking you; keeping your system bogged down responding to nonexistent addresses; or otherwise misleading you as to the source of incoming messages.

It's important to remember that you usually can't detect spoofed addresses. The address might be legitimate and routable but might not belong to the packet's sender. The next section describes the spoofed addresses you can detect.

Source Address Spoofing and Illegal Addresses

There are several major classes of source addresses you should deny on your external interface in all cases. These are incoming packets claiming to be from the following:

- **Your IP address**—You will never see legal incoming packets claiming to be from your machine. Because the source address is the only information available and it can be modified, this is one of the forms of legitimate address spoofing you can detect at the packet-filtering level. Incoming packets claiming to be from your machine are spoofed. You can't be certain whether other incoming packets are coming from where they claim to be. (Note that some operating systems crash if they receive a packet in which both the source and the destination addresses belong to the host's network interface.)

- **Your LAN addresses**—You will rarely see legal incoming packets on the external, Internet interface claiming to be *from* your LAN. It's possible to see such packets if the LAN has multiple access points to the Internet, but it would probably be a sign of a misconfigured local network. In most cases, such a packet would be part of an attempt to gain access to your site by exploiting your local trust relationships.

- **Class A, B, and C private IP addresses**—These three sets of addresses in the historical Class A, B, and C ranges are reserved for use in private LANs. They aren't intended for use on the Internet. As such, these addresses can be used by any site internally without the need to purchase registered IP addresses. Your machine should never see incoming packets from these source addresses:
  - Class A private addresses are assigned the range from 10.0.0.0 to 10.255.255.255.
  - Class B private addresses are assigned the range from 172.16.0.0 to 172.31.255.255.
  - Class C private addresses are assigned the range from 192.168.0.0 to 192.168.255.255.

- **Class D multicast IP addresses**—IP addresses in the Class D range are set aside for use as destination addresses when participating in a multicast network broadcast, such as an audiocast or a videocast. They range from 224.0.0.0 to 239.255.255.255. Your machine should never see packets from these source addresses.

- **Class E reserved IP addresses**—IP addresses in the Class E range were set aside for future and experimental use and are not assigned publicly. They range from 240.0.0.0 to 247.255.255.255. Your machine should never see packets from these source addresses—and mostly likely won't. (Because the entire address range is permanently reserved up through 255.255.255.255, the Class E range can realistically be defined as 240.0.0.0 to 255.255.255.255. In fact, some sources define the Class E address range to be exactly that.)

- **Loopback interface addresses**—The loopback interface is a private network interface used by the Linux system for local, network-based services. Rather than sending local traffic through the network interface driver, the operating system takes a shortcut through the loopback interface as a performance improvement. By definition, loopback traffic is targeted for the system generating it. It doesn't go out on the network. The loopback address range is 127.0.0.0 to 127.255.255.255. You'll usually see it referred to as 127.0.0.1, localhost, or the loopback interface, lo.

- **Malformed broadcast addresses**—Broadcast addresses are special addresses applying to all machines on a network. Address 0.0.0.0 is a special broadcast source address. A legitimate broadcast source address will be either 0.0.0.0 or a regular IP address. DHCP clients and servers will see incoming broadcast packets from source address 0.0.0.0. This is the only legal use of this source address. It is not a legitimate point-to-point, unicast source address. When seen as the source address in a regular, point-to-point, nonbroadcast packet, the address is forged, or the sender isn't fully configured.

- **Class A network 0 addresses**—As suggested previously, any source address in the 0.0.0.0 through 0.255.255.255 range is illegal as a unicast address.

- **Link local network addresses**—DHCP clients sometimes assign themselves a link local address when they can't get an address from a server. These addresses range from 169.254.0.0 to 169.254.255.255.

- **Carrier-grade NAT**—There are IPs that are marked for use by Internet providers that should never appear on a public network, the public Internet. These addresses can, however, be used in cloud scenarios, and therefore, if your server is hosted at a cloud provider, you may see these addresses. The carrier-grade NAT addresses range from 100.64.0.0 to 100.127.255.255.

- **TEST-NET addresses**—The address space from 192.0.2.0 to 192.0.2.255 is reserved for test networks.

Blocking Problem Sites

Another common, but less frequently used, source address–filtering scheme is to block all access from a selected machine or, more typically, from an entire network's IP address block. This is how the Internet community tends to deal with problem sites and ISPs that don't police their users. If a site develops a reputation as a bad Internet neighbor, other sites tend to block it across the board.

On the individual level, blocking all access from selected networks is convenient when individuals in the remote network are habitually making a nuisance of themselves. This has historically been used as a means to fight unsolicited email, with some people going so far as to block an entire country's range of IP addresses.

Limiting Incoming Packets to Selected Remote Hosts

You might want to accept certain kinds of incoming packets from only specific external sites or individuals. In these cases, the firewall rules will define either specific IP addresses or a limited range of IP source addresses that these packets will be accepted from.

The first class of incoming packets is from remote servers responding to your requests. Although some services, such as web or FTP services, can be expected to be coming from anywhere, other services will legitimately be coming from only your ISP or specially chosen trusted hosts. Examples of servers that are probably offered only through your ISP are POP mail service, Domain Name Service (DNS) name server responses, and possible DHCP or dynamic IP address assignments.

The second class of incoming packets is from remote clients accessing services offered from your site. Again, although some incoming service connections, such as connections to your web server, can be expected to be coming from anywhere, other local services will be offered to only a few trusted remote users or friends. Examples of restricted local services might be ssh and ping.

Local Destination Address Filtering

Filtering incoming packets based on the destination address is not much of an issue. Under normal operation, your network interface card ignores regular packets that aren't addressed to it. The exception is broadcast packets, which are broadcast to all hosts on the network.

The IPv4 address 255.255.255.255 is the general broadcast destination address. It refers to all hosts on the immediate physical network segment, and it is called a *limited broadcast*. A broadcast address can be defined more explicitly as the highest address in a given subnet of IP addresses. For example, if your ISP's network address is 192.168.10.0 with a 24-bit subnet mask (255.255.255.0) and your IP address is 192.168.10.30, you would see broadcast packets addressed to 192.168.10.255 from your ISP. On the other hand, if you have a smaller range of IP addresses, say a /30 (255.255.255.252), then you have a total of four addresses: one network, two for hosts, and the broadcast. For example, consider the network 10.3.7.4/30. In this network, 10.3.7.4 is the network address, the two hosts would be 10.3.7.5 and 10.3.7.6, and the broadcast address would be 10.3.7.7. This /30 subnet configuration type is typically used between routers, though the actual addresses themselves may vary. The only way to know what the broadcast address will be for a given subnet is to know both an IP address within the subnet and the subnet mask. These types of broadcasts are called *directed subnet broadcasts* and are delivered to all hosts on that network.

Broadcast-to-destination address 0.0.0.0 is similar to the situation of point-to-point packets claiming to be from the broadcast source address mentioned earlier, in the section "Source Address Spoofing and Illegal Addresses." Here, broadcast packets are directed to source address 0.0.0.0 rather than to the destination address, 255.255.255.255. In this case, there is little question about the packet's intent. This is an attempt to identify your system as a Linux machine. For historical reasons, networking code derived from BSD UNIX returns an ICMP Type 3 error message in response to 0.0.0.0 being used as the broadcast destination address. Other operating systems silently discard the packet. As such, this is a good example of why dropping versus rejecting a packet makes a difference. In this case, the error message itself is what the probe is looking for.

Remote Source Port Filtering

Incoming requests and connections from remote clients to your local servers will have a source port in the unprivileged range. If you are hosting a web server, all incoming connections to your web server should have a source port between 1024 and 65535. (That the server port identifies the service is the intention but not the guarantee. You cannot be certain that the server you expect is running at the port you expect.)

Incoming responses and connections from remote servers that you contacted will have the source port that is assigned to the particular service. If you connect to a remote website, all incoming messages from the remote server will have the source port set to 80 (or whatever port the local client specified), the http service port number.

Local Destination Port Filtering

The destination port in incoming packets identifies the program or service on your computer that the packet is intended for. As with the source port, all incoming requests from remote clients to your services generally follow the same pattern, and all incoming responses from remote services to your local clients follow a different pattern.

Incoming requests and connections from remote clients to your local servers will set the destination port to the service number that you assigned to the particular service. For example, an incoming packet destined for your local web server would normally have the destination port set to 80, the http service port number.

Incoming responses from remote servers that you contacted will have a destination port in the unprivileged range. If you connect to a remote website, all incoming messages from the remote server will have a destination port between 1024 and 65535.

Incoming TCP Connection State Filtering

Incoming TCP packet acceptance rules can make use of the connection state flags associated with TCP connections. All TCP connections adhere to the same set of connection states. These states differ between client and server because of the three-way handshake during connection establishment. As such, the firewall can distinguish between incoming traffic from remote clients and incoming traffic from remote servers.

Incoming TCP packets from remote clients will have the SYN flag set in the first packet received as part of the three-way connection establishment handshake. The first connection request will have the SYN flag set, but not the ACK flag.

Incoming packets from remote servers will always be responses to the initial connection request initiated from your local client program. Every TCP packet received from a remote server will have the ACK flag set. Your local client firewall rules will require all incoming packets from remote servers to have the ACK flag set. Servers do not normally attempt to initiate connections to client programs.

Probes and Scans

A *probe* is an attempt to connect to or get a response from an individual service port. A *scan* is a series of probes to a set of different service ports. Scans are often automated.

Unfortunately, probes and scans are rarely innocent anymore. They are most likely the initial information-gathering phase, looking for interesting vulnerabilities before launching an attack. Automated scan tools are widespread, and coordinated efforts by groups of hackers are common. The security, or lack thereof, of many hosts on the Internet, along with the proliferation of worms, viruses, and zombied machines, makes scans a constant issue on the Internet.

General Port Scans

General port scans are indiscriminate probes across a large block of service ports, possibly the entire range (see Figure 2.6). These scans are somewhat less frequent—or, at least, less obvious—as more sophisticated, targeted stealth tools become available.

Targeted Port Scans

Targeted port scans look for specific vulnerabilities (see Figure 2.7). The newer, more sophisticated tools attempt to identify the hardware, operating system, and software versions. These tools are designed to identify targets that might be prone to a specific vulnerability.

Common Service Port Targets

Common targets often are individually probed as well as scanned. The attacker might be looking for a specific vulnerability, such as an insecure mail server, an unpatched web server, or an open remote procedure call (RPC) portmap daemon.

A more extensive list of ports can be found at http://www.iana.org/assignments/port-numbers. Only a few common ports are mentioned here, to give you the idea:

- Incoming packets from reserved port 0 are always bogus. This port isn't used legitimately.
- Probes of TCP ports 0 to 5 are a signature of the sscan program.
- ssh (22/tcp), smtp (25/tcp), dns (53/tcp/udp), pop-3 (110/tcp), imap (143/tcp), and snmp (161/udp), are favorite target ports. They represent some of the most potentially vulnerable openings to a system, whether intrinsically, due to

Figure 2.6   A general port scan

Figure 2.7   A targeted port scan

common configuration errors, or due to known flaws in the software. Because these services are so common, they are good examples of why you want to either not offer them to the outside world, or very carefully offer them with controlled outside access. NetBIOS (137-139/tcp/udp) and Server Message Block (SMB) on Windows (445/tcp) probes are tediously common. They typically pose no threat to a Linux system unless Samba is used on the system. The typical target is a Windows system, in this case, but the scans are all too common.

Stealth Scans

Stealth port scans, by definition, aren't meant to be detectable. They are based on how the TCP protocol stack responds to unexpected packets, or packets with illegal state flag combinations. For example, consider an incoming packet that has the ACK flag set but has no related connection. If the ACK were sent to a port with a listening server attached, the TCP stack wouldn't find a related connection and would return a TCP RST message to tell the sender to reset the connection. If the ACK were sent to an unused port, the system would simply return a TCP RST message as an error indication, just as the firewall might return an ICMP error message by default.

The issue is further complicated because some firewalls test only for the SYN flag or the ACK flag. If neither is set, or if the packet contains some other combination of flags, the firewall implementation might pass the packet up to the TCP code. Depending on the TCP state flag combination and the operating system receiving the packet, the system will respond with an RST or with silence. This mechanism can be used to help identify the operating system that the target system is running. In any of these cases, the receiving system isn't likely to log the event.

Inducing a target host to generate an RST packet in this manner also can be used to map a network, determining the IP addresses of systems listening on the network. This is especially helpful if the target system isn't a server and its firewall has been set to silently drop unwanted packets.

Avoiding Paranoia: Responding to Port Scans

Firewall logs normally show all kinds of failed connection attempts. Probes are the most common thing you'll see reported in your logs.

Are people probing your system this often? Yes, they are. Is your system compromised? No, it isn't. Well, not necessarily. The ports are blocked. The firewall is doing its job. These are failed connection attempts that the firewall denied.

At what point do you personally decide to report a probe? At what point is it important enough to take the time to report it? At what point do you say that enough is enough and get on with your life, or should you be writing abuse@some.system each time? There are no "right" answers. How you respond is a personal judgment call and depends in part on the resources available to you, how sensitive the information at your site is, and how critical the Internet connection is to your site. For obvious probes and scans, there is no clear-cut answer. It depends on your own personality and comfort level how you personally define a serious probe, and your social conscience.

With that in mind, these are some workable guidelines.

The most common attempts are a combination of automated probing, mistakes, legitimate attempts based on the history of the Internet, ignorance, curiosity, and misbehaving software.

You can almost always safely ignore individual, isolated, single connection attempts to `telnet`, `ssh`, `ftp`, `finger`, or any other port for a common service that you're not providing. Probes and scans are a fact of life on the Internet, are all too frequent, and usually don't pose a risk. They are kind of like door-to-door salespeople, commercial phone calls, wrong phone numbers, and junk postal mail. For me, at least, there isn't enough time in the day to respond to each one.

On the other hand, some probers are more persistent. You might decide to add firewall rules to block them completely, or possibly even their entire IP address space.

Scans of a subset of the ports known to be potential security holes are typically the precursor to an attack if an open port is found. More inclusive scans are usually part of a broader scan for openings throughout a domain or subnet. Current hacking tools probe a subset of these ports one after the other.

Occasionally, you'll see serious hacking attempts. This is unquestionably a time to take action. Write them. Report them. Double-check your security. Observe what they're doing. Block them. Block their IP address block.

Some system administrators take every occurrence seriously because, even if *their* machine is secure, other people's machines might not be. The next person might not even have the capability of knowing that he or she is being probed. Reporting probes is the socially responsible thing to do, for everyone's sake.

How should you respond to port scans? If you write these people, their postmaster, their uplink service provider network operations center (NOC), or the network address block coordinator, try to be polite. Give them the benefit of the doubt. Overreactions are misplaced more often than not. What might appear as a serious hacking attempt to you is often a curious kid playing with a new program. A polite word to the abuser, `root`, or postmaster can sometimes take care of the problem. More people need to be educated about Netiquette than need their network accounts rescinded. And they might be innocent of anything. Just as often, the person's system is compromised and that person has no idea what's going on and will be grateful for the information.

Probes aren't the only hostile traffic you'll see, however. Although probes are harmless in and of themselves, DoS attacks are not.

Denial-of-Service Attacks

DoS attacks are based on the idea of flooding your system with packets to disrupt or seriously degrade your Internet connection, tying up local servers to the extent that legitimate requests can't be honored or, in the worst case, crashing your system altogether. The two most common results are keeping the system too busy to do anything useful and tying up critical system resources.

You can't protect against DoS attacks completely. They can take as many different forms as the attacker's imagination allows. Anything that results in a response from your system, anything that results in your system allocating resources (including logging of the attack), anything that induces a remote site to stop communicating with you—all can be used in a DoS attack.

> ### More on Denial-of-Service Attacks
> For further information on DoS attacks, see the "Denial of Service" paper available at http://www.cert.org.

These attacks usually involve one of several classic patterns, including TCP SYN flooding, ping flooding, UDP flooding, fragmentation bombs, buffer overflows, and ICMP routing redirect bombs.

TCP SYN Flooding

A TCP SYN flood attack consumes your system resources until no more incoming TCP connections are possible (see Figure 2.8). The attack makes use of the basic TCP three-way handshaking protocol during connection establishment, in conjunction with IP source address spoofing.

The attacker spoofs his or her source address as a private address and initiates a connection to one of your TCP-based services. Appearing to be a client attempting to open a TCP connection, the attacker sends you an artificially generated SYN message. Your machine responds by sending an acknowledgment, a SYN-ACK. However, in this case, the

Figure 2.8   A TCP SYN flood

address that you're replying to isn't the attacker's address. In fact, because the address is private, there is no one out there to respond. The spoofed host won't return an RST message to tear down the half-opened connection.

The final stage of TCP connection establishment, receiving an ACK in response, will never happen. Consequently, finite network connection resources are consumed. The connection remains in a half-opened state until the connection attempt times out. The attacker floods your port with connection request after connection request, faster than the TCP timeouts release the resources. If this continues, all resources will be in use and no more incoming connection requests can be accepted. This applies not only to the service being probed, but to all new connections as well.

Several aids are available to Linux users. The first is source address filtering, described previously. This filters out the most commonly used spoofed source addresses, but there is no guarantee that the spoofed address falls within the categories you can anticipate and filter against.

The second is to enable your kernel's SYN cookie module, a specific retardant to the resource starvation caused by SYN flooding. When the connection queue begins to get full, the system starts responding to SYN requests with SYN cookies rather than SYN-ACKs, and it frees the queue slot. Thus, the queue never fills completely. The cookie has a short timeout; the client must respond to it within a short period before the serving host will respond with the expected SYN-ACK. The cookie is a sequence number that is generated based on the original sequence number in the SYN, the source and destination addresses and ports, and a secret value. If the response to the cookie matches the result of the hashing algorithm, the server is reasonably well assured that the SYN is valid.

Depending on the particular release, you may or may not need to enable the SYN cookie protection within the kernel by using the command echo 1 > /proc/sys/net/ ipv4/tcp_syncookies. Some distributions and kernel versions require you to explicitly configure the option into the kernel using make config, make menuconfig, or make xconfig and then recompile and install the new kernel.

SYN Flooding and IP Spoofing

For more information on SYN flooding and IP spoofing, see CERT Advisory CA-96.21, "TCP SYN Flooding and IP Spoofing Attacks," at http://www.cert.org.

---

ping Flooding

Any message that elicits a response from your machine can be used to degrade your network connection by forcing the system to spend most of its time responding. The ICMP echo request message sent by ping is a common culprit. An attack called *Smurf*, and its variants, forces a system to expend its resources processing echo replies. One method of accomplishing this is to spoof the victim's source address and broadcast an echo request to an entire network of hosts. A single spoofed request message can result in hundreds or thousands of resulting replies being sent to the victim. Another way of accomplishing a similar result is to install trojans on compromised hosts across the Internet and time them to each send echo requests to the same host simultaneously. Finally, a simple `ping` flood in which the attacker sends more echo requests and floods the data connection is another method for a DoS, though it's becoming less common. A typical `ping` flood is shown in Figure 2.9.

Ping of Death

An older exploit called the *Ping of Death* involved sending very large `ping` packets. Vulnerable systems could crash as a result. Linux is not vulnerable to this exploit, nor are many other current UNIX operating systems. If your firewall is protecting older systems or personal computers, those systems could be vulnerable.

The Ping of Death exploit gives an idea of how the simplest protocols and message interactions can be used by the creative hacker. Not all attacks are attempts to break into your computer. Some are merely destructive. In this case, the goal is to crash the machine. (System crashes also might be an indicator that you need to check your system for installed trojan programs. You might have been duped into loading a trojan program, but the program itself might require a system reboot to activate.)

`ping` is a very useful basic networking tool. You might not want to disable `ping` altogether. In today's Internet environment, conservative folks recommend disabling incoming `ping` or at least severely limiting from whom you accept echo requests. Because of `ping`'s history of involvement in DoS attacks, many sites no longer respond to external `ping` requests from any but selected sources. This has always seemed to be an overreaction to the relatively small threat of a DoS based on ICMP when compared to the more ubiquitous and dangerous threats against applications and other protocols within the stack.

Figure 2.9   A `ping` flood

Dropping `ping` requests isn't a solution for the victim host, however. Regardless of how the recipient of the flood reacts to the packets, the system (or network) can still be overwhelmed in the process of inspecting and dropping a flood of requests.

UDP Flooding

The UDP protocol is especially useful as a DoS tool. Unlike TCP, UDP is stateless. Flow-control mechanisms aren't included. There are no connection state flags. Datagram sequence numbers aren't used. No information is maintained on which packet is expected next. There is not always a way to differentiate client traffic from server traffic based on port numbers. Without state, there is no way to distinguish an expected incoming response from an unsolicited packet arriving unexpectedly. It's relatively easy to keep a system so busy responding to incoming UDP probes that no bandwidth is left for legitimate network traffic.

Because UDP services are susceptible to these types of attacks (as opposed to connection-oriented TCP services), many sites disable all UDP ports that aren't absolutely necessary. As mentioned earlier, almost all common Internet services are TCP based. The firewall we'll build in Chapter 5, "Building and Installing a Standalone Firewall," carefully limits UDP traffic to only those remote hosts providing necessary UDP services.

The classic UDP flood attack either involves two victim machines or works in the same way the Smurf `ping` flood does (see Figure 2.10). A single spoofed packet from the attacker's UDP `echo` port, directed to a host's UDP `chargen` port, can result in an infinite loop of network traffic. The `echo` and `chargen` services are network test services. `chargen` generates an ASCII string. `echo` returns the data sent to the port.

Source Address: Intermediary
Destination Address: Victim
Source Port: UDP 7- chargen

Source Address: Victim
Destination Address: Intermediary
Source Port: UDP 7 - echo
Destination Port: UDP 19 - chargen

Source Address: Victim
Destination Address: Intermediary
Source Port: UDP 7 - echo
Destination Port: UDP 19 - chargen

Figure 2.10   A UDP flood

> **UDP Port Denial-of-Service Attacks**
> For a fuller description of a DoS exploit using these UDP services, see CERT Advisory CA-96.01, "UDP Port Denial-of-Service Attack," at http://www.cert.org.

Fragmentation Bombs

Different underlying network technologies (such as Ethernet, Asynchronous Transfer Mode [ATM], and token ring) define different limits on the size of the Layer 2 frame. As a packet is passed on from one router to the next along the path from the source machine to the destination machine, network gateway routers might need to cut the packet into smaller pieces, called *fragments*, before passing them on to the next network. In a legitimate fragmentation, the first fragment contains the usual source and destination port numbers contained in the UDP or TCP transport header. The following fragments do not.

For example, although the maximum theoretical packet length is 65,535 bytes, the maximum Ethernet frame size (Maximum Transmission Unit, or MTU) is 1500 bytes.

When a packet is fragmented, intermediate routers do not reassemble the packet. The packets are reassembled either at the destination host or by its adjacent router.

Because intermediate fragmentation is ultimately more costly than sending smaller, nonfragmented packets, current systems often do MTU discovery with the target host at the beginning of a connection. This is done by sending a packet with the `Don't Fragment` option set in the IP header options field (the only generally legitimate current use of the IP options field). If an intermediate router must fragment the packet, it drops the packet and returns an ICMP 3 error, `fragmentation-required`.

One type of fragmentation attack involves artificially constructing very small packets. One-byte packets crash some operating systems. Current operating systems usually test for this condition.

Another use of small fragments is constructing the initial fragment so that the UDP or TCP source and destination ports are contained in the second fragment. (All networks' MTU sizes are large enough to carry a standard 40-byte IP and transport header.) Packet-filtering firewalls often allow these fragments through because the information that they filter on is not present. This form of attack is useful to get packets through the firewall that would not otherwise be allowed.

The Ping of Death exploit mentioned earlier is an example of using fragmentation to carry an illegally large ICMP message. When the `ping` request is reconstructed, the entire packet size is larger than 65,535 bytes, causing some systems to crash.

A classic example of a fragmentation exploit is the Teardrop attack. The method can be used to bypass a firewall or to crash a system. The first fragment is constructed to go to an allowed service. (Many firewalls don't inspect fragments after the first packet.) If it is allowed, the subsequent fragments will be passed through and reassembled by the target host. If the first packet is dropped, the subsequent packets will pass through the firewall, but the end host will have nothing to reconstruct and eventually will discard the partial packet.

The data offset fields in the subsequent fragments can be altered to overwrite the port information in the first fragment to access a disallowed service. The offset also can be altered so that offsets used in packet reassembly turn out to be negative numbers. Because kernel byte-copy routines usually use unsigned numbers, the negative value is treated as a very large positive number; the resulting copy trashes kernel memory and the system crashes.

Firewall machines and machines that do NAT for other local hosts should be configured to reassemble the packets before delivering them to the local target. Some of the `iptables` features require the system to reassemble packets before forwarding the packet to the destination host, and reassembly is done automatically.

Buffer Overflows

Buffer overflow exploits can't be protected against by a filtering firewall. The exploits fall into two main categories. The first is simply to cause a system or server to crash by overwriting its data space or runtime stack. The second requires technical expertise and knowledge of the hardware and system software or server version being attacked. The purpose of the overflow is to overwrite the program's runtime stack so that the call return stack contains a program and a jump to it. This program usually starts up a shell with `root` privilege.

Many of the current vulnerabilities in servers are a result of buffer overflows. It's important to install and keep up-to-date all the newest patches and software revisions.

ICMP Redirect Bombs

ICMP redirect message Type 5 tells the target system to change its in-memory routing tables in favor of a shorter route. Redirects are sent by routers to their adjacent hosts. Their intention is to inform the host that a shorter path is available (that is, the host and new router are on the same network, and the new router is the router that the original would route the packet to as its next hop).

Redirects arrive on an almost-daily basis. They rarely originate from the adjacent router. For residential or business sites connected to an ISP, it's very unlikely that your adjacent router will generate a redirect message.

If your host uses static routing and honors redirect messages, it's possible for someone to fool your system into thinking that a remote machine is one of your local machines or one of your ISP's machines, or even to fool your system into forwarding all traffic to some other remote host.

Denial-of-Service Attacks and Other System Resources

Network connectivity isn't the only concern in DoS attacks. Here are some examples of other areas to keep in mind while configuring your system:

- Your filesystem can overflow if your system is forced to write enormous numbers of messages to the error logs, or if your system is flooded with many copies of large email messages. You might want to configure resource limits and set up a separate partition for rapidly growing or changing filesystems.

> **Email Denial-of-Service Exploits**
> For a description of a DoS exploit using email, see "Email Bombing and Spamming" at http://www.cert.org.

- System memory, process table slots, CPU cycles, and other resources can be exhausted by repeated, rapid invocations of network services. You can do little about this other than setting any configurable limits for each individual service, enabling SYN cookies, and denying rather than rejecting packets sent to unsupported service ports.

Source-Routed Packets

Source-routed packets employ a rarely used IP option that allows the originator to define the route taken between two machines, rather than letting the intermediate routers determine the path. As with ICMP redirects, this feature can allow someone to fool your system into thinking that it's talking to a local machine, an ISP machine, or some other trusted host, or to create the necessary packet flow for a man-in-the-middle attack.

Source routing has few legitimate uses in current networks. Some routers ignore the option. Some firewalls discard packets containing the option.

Filtering Outgoing Packets

If your environment represents a trusted environment, filtering outgoing packets might not appear to be as critical as filtering incoming packets. Your system won't respond to incoming messages that the firewall doesn't pass through. Residential sites often take this approach. Nevertheless, even for residential sites, symmetric filtering is important, particularly if the firewall protects Microsoft Windows machines. For commercial sites, outgoing filtering is inarguably important.

If your firewall protects a LAN of Microsoft Windows systems, controlling outgoing traffic becomes much more important. Compromised Windows machines have historically been (and continue to be) used in coordinated DoS attacks and other outbound attacks. For this reason especially, it's important to filter what leaves your network.

Filtering outgoing messages also allows you to run LAN services without leaking into the Internet, where these packets don't belong. It's not only a question of disallowing external access to local LAN services. It's also a question of not broadcasting local system information onto the Internet. Examples of this would be if you were running a local DHCPD, NTP, SMB, or other server for internal use. Other obnoxious services might be broadcasting wall or syslogd messages.

A related source is some of the personal computer software, which sometimes ignores the Internet service port protocols and reserved assignments. This is the personal computer equivalent of running a program designed for LAN use on an Internet-connected machine.

A final reason is simply to keep local traffic local that isn't intended to leave the LAN but that conceivably could. Keeping local traffic local is a good idea from a security standpoint but also as a means for bandwidth conservation.

Local Source Address Filtering

Filtering outgoing packets based on the source address is easy. For a small site or a single computer connected to the Internet, the source address is always your computer's IP address during normal operation. There is no reason to allow an outgoing packet to have any other source address, and the firewall should enforce this.

For people whose IP address is dynamically assigned by their ISP, a brief exception exists during address assignment. This exception is specific to DHCP and is the one case in which a host broadcasts messages using 0.0.0.0 as its source address.

For people with a LAN whose firewall machine has a dynamically assigned IP address, limiting outgoing packets to contain the source address of the firewall machine's IP address is mandatory. It protects you from several fairly common configuration mistakes that appear as cases of source address spoofing or illegal source addresses to remote hosts.

If your users or their software aren't 100% trustworthy, it's important to ensure that local traffic contains legitimate, local addresses only, to avoid participating in DoS attacks using source address spoofing.

This last point is especially important. RFC 2827, "Network Ingress Filtering: Defeating Denial of Service Attacks Which Employ IP Source Address Spoofing" (updated by RFC 3704, "Ingress Filtering for Multihomed Networks"), is a current "best practices" document speaking to exactly this point. Ideally, every router should filter out the obvious illegal source addresses and ensure that traffic leaving the local network contains only routable source addresses belonging to that network.

Remote Destination Address Filtering

As with incoming packets, you might want to allow certain kinds of outgoing packets to be addressed only to specific remote networks or individual machines. In these cases, the firewall rules will define either specific IP addresses or a limited range of IP destination addresses to which these packets will be allowed.

The first class of outgoing packets to filter by destination address is packets destined to remote servers that you've contacted. Although some packets, such as those going to web or FTP servers, can be expected to be destined to anywhere on the Internet, other remote services will legitimately be offered from only your ISP or specially chosen trusted hosts. Examples of services that are probably offered only through your ISP are mail services such as SMTP or POP3, DNS services, DHCP dynamic IP address assignment, and the Usenet news service.

The second class of outgoing packets to filter by destination address is packets destined to remote clients who are accessing a service offered from your site. Again, although some outgoing service connections, such as responses from your local web server, can be expected to be going anywhere, other local services will be offered to only a few trusted remote sites or friends. Examples of restricted local services might be telnet, SSH, Samba-based services, and RPC services accessed via portmap. Not only will the firewall rules deny general incoming connections to these services, but the rules also won't allow outgoing responses from these services to just anyone.

Local Source Port Filtering

Explicitly defining which service ports on your network can be used for outgoing connections serves two purposes—one for your client programs and one for your server programs. Specifying the source ports allowed for your outgoing connections helps ensure that your programs are behaving correctly, and it protects other people from any local network traffic that doesn't belong on the Internet.

Outgoing connections from your local clients will almost always originate from an unprivileged source port. Limiting your clients to the unprivileged ports in the firewall rules helps protect other people from potential mistakes on your end by ensuring that your client programs are behaving as expected.

Outgoing packets from your local server programs will always originate from their assigned service port and will be in response to a request received. Limiting your servers to their assigned ports at the firewall level ensures that your server programs are functioning correctly at the protocol level. More important, it helps protect any private, local network services that you might be running from outside access. It also helps protect remote sites from being bothered by network traffic that should remain confined to your local systems.

Remote Destination Port Filtering

Your local client programs are designed to connect to network servers offering their services from their assigned service ports. From this perspective, limiting your local clients to connect only to their associated server's service port ensures protocol correctness. Limiting your client connections to specific destination ports serves a couple of other purposes as well. First, it helps guard against local, private network client programs inadvertently attempting to access servers on the Internet. Second, it does much to disallow outgoing mistakes, port scans, and other mischief potentially originating from your site.

Your local server programs will almost always participate in connections originating from unprivileged ports. The firewall rules limit your servers' outgoing traffic to only unprivileged destination ports.

Outgoing TCP Connection State Filtering

Outgoing TCP packet acceptance rules can make use of the connection state flags associated with TCP connections, just as the incoming rules do. All TCP connections adhere to the same set of connection states, which differs between client and server.

Outgoing TCP packets from local clients will have the SYN flag set in the first packet sent as part of the three-way connection establishment handshake. The initial connection request will have the SYN flag set, but not the ACK flag. Your local client firewall rules will allow outgoing packets with either the SYN or the ACK flag set.

Outgoing packets from local servers will always be responses to an initial connection request initiated from a remote client program. Every packet sent from your servers will have the ACK flag set. Your local server firewall rules will require all outgoing packets from your servers to have the ACK flag set.

Private versus Public Network Services

One of the easiest ways to inadvertently allow uninvited intrusions is to allow outside access to local services that are designed only for LAN use. Some services, if offered locally, should never cross the boundary between your LAN and the Internet beyond. Some of these services annoy your neighbors, some provide information you'd be better off keeping to yourself, and some represent glaring security holes if they're available outside your LAN.

Some of the earliest network services, the r-*-based commands in particular, were designed for local sharing and ease of access across multiple lab machines in a trusted environment. Some of the later services were intended for Internet access, but they were designed at a time when the Internet was basically an extended community of academicians and researchers. The Internet was a relatively open, safe place. As the Internet grew into a global network including general public access, it developed into a completely untrusted environment.

Lots of Linux network services are designed to provide local information about user accounts on the system, which programs are running and which resources are in use, system status, network status, and similar information from other machines connected over the network. Not all of these informational services represent security holes in and of themselves. It's not that someone can use them directly to gain unauthorized access to your system. It's that they provide information about your system and user accounts that can be useful to someone who is looking for known vulnerabilities. They might also supply information such as usernames, addresses, phone numbers, and so forth, which you don't want to be readily available to everyone who asks.

Some of the more dangerous network services are designed to provide LAN access to shared filesystems and devices, such as a networked printer or fax machine.

Some services are difficult to configure correctly and some are difficult to configure securely. Entire books are devoted to configuring some of the more complicated Linux services. Specific service configuration is beyond the scope of this book.

Some services just don't make sense in a home or small-office setting. Some are intended to manage large networks, provide Internet routing service, provide large database informational services, support two-way encryption and authentication, and so forth.

Protecting Nonsecure Local Services

The easiest way to protect yourself is to not offer the service. But what if you need one of these services locally? Not all services can be protected adequately at the packet-filtering level. File-sharing software, instant messaging services, and UDP-based RPC services are notoriously difficult to secure at the packet-filtering level.

One way to safeguard your computer is to not host network services on the firewall machine that you don't intend for public use. If the service isn't available, there's nothing for a remote client to connect to. Let firewalls be firewalls.

A packet-filtering firewall doesn't offer complete security. Some programs require higher-level security measures than can be provided at the packet-filtering level. Some programs are too problematic to risk running on a firewall machine, even on a less secure residential host.

Small sites such as those in the home often won't have a supply of computers available to enforce access security policies by running private services on other machines. Compromises must be made, particularly for required services that are provided solely by Linux. Nevertheless, small sites with a LAN should not be running file-sharing or other private LAN services on the firewall, such as Samba. The machine should not have unnecessary user accounts. Unneeded system software should be removed from the system. The machine should have no function other than that of a security gateway.

Selecting Services to Run

When all is said and done, only you can decide which services you need or want. The first step in securing your system is to decide which services and daemons you intend to run on the firewall machine, as well as behind the firewall in the private LAN. Each service has its own security considerations. When it comes to selecting services to run under Linux or any other operating system, the general rule of thumb is to run only network services that you need and understand. It's important to understand a network service, what it does and who it's intended for, before you run it—especially on a machine connected directly to the Internet.

Summary

Between this and the preceding chapter, the basics of networking and firewalls have been laid out. The next chapter digs deeper into `iptables` itself.

`iptables`: The Legacy Linux Firewall Administration Program

Chapter 2, "Packet-Filtering Concepts," covered the background ideas and concepts behind a packet-filtering firewall. Each built-in list of rules, sometimes called a *rule chain*, has its own default policy. Each rule can apply not only to an individual chain, but also to a specific network interface, message protocol type (such as TCP, UDP, or ICMP), and service port or ICMP message type number. Individual acceptance, denial, and rejection rules are defined for the INPUT chain and the OUTPUT chain, as well as for the FORWARD chain, which you'll learn about at the end of this chapter and in Chapter 7, "Packet Forwarding."

This chapter covers the `iptables` firewall administration program used to build a Netfilter firewall. The `iptables` administration program is part of the legacy firewall code in the Linux kernel. Beginning with version 3.13 of the kernel, a new filtering mechanism was added called `nftables`. The next chapter looks at `nftables`. This chapter focuses on the legacy `iptables` administration program because it is still widely used across Linux systems. For those of you who are familiar with or accustomed to the older `ipfwadm` and `ipchains` programs used with the IPFW technology, `iptables` will look very similar to those programs. However, it is much more feature-rich and flexible, and it is very different on subtle levels.

There is indeed a difference between `iptables` and Netfilter, though you'll often hear the terms used interchangeably. Netfilter is the Linux kernel-space program code to implement a firewall within the Linux kernel, either compiled directly into the kernel or included as a set of modules. On the other hand, `iptables` is the userland program used for administration of the Netfilter firewall. Throughout this text, I will refer to `iptables` as being inclusive of both Netfilter and `iptables`, unless otherwise noted.

Differences between IPFW and Netfilter Firewall Mechanisms

Because `iptables` is so different from the previous `ipchains`, this book won't attempt to cover the older implementation.

The next section is written for the reader who is familiar with or is currently using `ipchains`. If `iptables` is your first introduction to Linux firewalling, you can skip ahead to the section "Netfilter Packet Traversal."

If you are converting from `ipchains`, you'll notice several minor differences in the `iptables` syntax, most notably that the input and output network interfaces are identified separately. Other differences include:

- `iptables` is highly modularized, and the individual modules must occasionally be loaded explicitly.

- Logging is a rule target rather than a command option.

- Connection state tracking can be maintained. Address and Port Translation are logically separate functions from packet filtering.

- Full Source and Destination Address Translation are implemented.

- Masquerading is a term used to refer to a specialized form of source address NAT.

- Port forwarding and Destination Address Translation are supported directly without the need for third-party software support such as `ipmasqadm`.

Masquerading in Earlier Versions of Linux

For those of you who are new to Linux, Network Address Translation (NAT) is fully implemented in `iptables`. Before this, NAT was called *masquerading* in Linux. A simple, partial implementation of Source Address Translation, masquerading was used by site owners who had a single public IP address and who wanted other hosts on their private network to be capable of accessing the Internet. Outgoing packets from these internal hosts had their source address masqueraded to that of the public, routable IP address.

The most important difference is in how packets are routed or forwarded through the operating system, making for subtle differences in how the firewall rule set is constructed.

For `ipchains` users, understanding the differences in packet traversal that are discussed in the next two sections is very important. `iptables` and `ipchains` look very much alike on the surface, but they are very different in practice. It's very easy to write syntactically correct `iptables` rules that have a different effect from what a similar rule would have done in `ipchains`. It can be confusing. If you already know `ipchains`, you must keep the differences in mind.

IPFW Packet Traversal

Under IPFW (`ipfwadm` and `ipchains`), three built-in filter chains were used. All packets arriving on an interface were filtered against the INPUT chain. If the packet was accepted, it was passed to the routing module. The routing function determined whether the packet was to be delivered locally or forwarded to another outgoing interface. IPFW packet flow is pictured in Figure 3.1.

If forwarded, the packet was filtered a second time against the FORWARD chain. If the packet was accepted, it was passed to the OUTPUT chain.

Both locally generated outgoing packets and forwarded packets were passed to the OUTPUT chain. If the packet was accepted, it was sent out the interface.

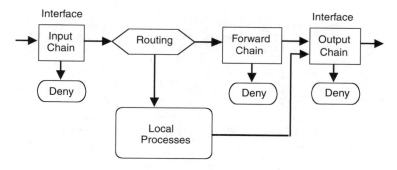

Figure 3.1   IPFW packet traversal

(Figure based on "Linux IPCHAINS-HOWTO," by Rusty Russel, v1.0.8.)

Received and sent local (loopback) packets passed through two filters. Forwarded packets passed through three filters.

The loopback path involved two chains. As shown in Figure 3.2, each loopback packet passed through the output filter before going "out" the loopback interface, where it was then delivered to the loopback's input interface. Then the input filter was applied.

Note that the loopback path demonstrates why an X Window session hangs when starting a firewall script that either doesn't allow loopback traffic or fails before doing so when a deny-by-default policy is used.

In the case of response packets being demasqueraded before forwarding them on to the LAN, the input filters were applied. Rather than passing through the routing function, the packet was handed directly to the OUTPUT filter chain. Thus, demasqueraded incoming packets were filtered twice. Outgoing masqueraded packets were filtered three times.

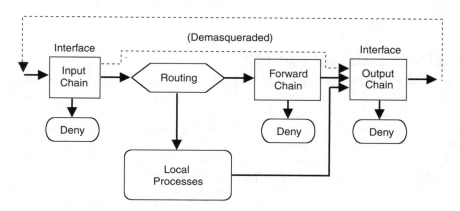

Figure 3.2   IPFW loopback and masqueraded packet traversal

(Figure based on "Linux IPCHAINS-HOWTO," by Rusty Russel, v1.0.8.)

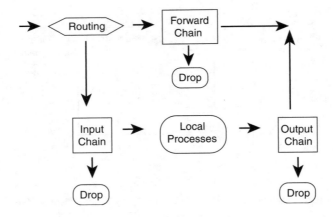

Figure 3.3   Netfilter packet traversal

(Figure based on "Linux 2.4 Packet Filtering HOWTO," by Rusty Russel, v1.0.1.)

Netfilter Packet Traversal

Under Netfilter (`iptables`), built-in INPUT, OUTPUT, and FORWARD filter chains are used. Incoming packets pass through the routing function, which determines whether to deliver the packet to the local host's INPUT chain or on to the FORWARD chain. Netfilter packet flow is pictured in Figure 3.3.

If a locally destined packet is accepted by the INPUT chain's rules, the packet is delivered locally. If a remotely destined packet is accepted by the FORWARD chain's rules, the packet is sent out the appropriate interface.

Outgoing packets from local processes are passed to the OUTPUT chain's rules. If the packet is accepted, it is sent out the appropriate interface. Thus, each packet is filtered once (except for loopback packets, which are filtered twice).

Basic `iptables` Syntax

Firewalls built with Netfilter are built through the `iptables` firewall administration command. The `iptables` command implements the firewall policies that you create and manages the behavior of the firewall. Netfilter firewalls have three individual tables: `filter`, `nat`, and `mangle`. Within these tables, firewalls are built through chains, with each individual link in the chain being an individual `iptables` command.

Within the default `filter` table there is a chain for input or data coming into the firewall, a chain for output or data leaving the firewall, a chain for forwarding or data being sent through the firewall, and other chains including chains named and configured by the user, commonly (and appropriately) called *user-defined chains*. The `nat` and `mangle` tables have specialty chains that will be discussed later. For now, it's sufficient to know that the filter table is the default table for implementing a basic firewall, the nat table is used to provide NAT and related functions, and the mangle table is used when the packet will be altered by the firewall.

iptables commands are issued with very specific syntax. Many times, the ordering of the options given to iptables makes the difference between a successful command and a syntax error. The commands issued to iptables fall through, so a command that allows certain packets that follows a command that denies those same packets will cause the data to be dropped by the firewall.

The basic syntax for an iptables command begins with the iptables command itself, followed by one or more options, a chain, a set of match criteria, and a target or disposition. The layout of the command largely depends on the action to be performed. Consider this syntax:

```
iptables <option> <chain> <matching criteria> <target>
```

In building a firewall, the option is usually -A to append a rule onto the end of the rule set. Naturally, there are several options depending on the target and the operation being performed. This chapter covers most of those options.

As previously stated, the chain can be an INPUT chain, an OUTPUT chain, a FORWARD chain, or a user-defined chain. In addition, the chain might also be a specialty chain contained in the nat or mangle tables.

The matching criteria in an iptables command set the conditions for the rule to be applied. For example, the matching criteria would be used to tell iptables that all TCP traffic destined for port 80 is allowed into the firewall.

Finally, the target sets the action to perform on a matching packet. The target can be something as simple as DROP to silently discard the packet, or it can send the matching packet to a user-defined chain, or it can perform any other configured action in iptables.

The following sections of this chapter show hands-on examples using iptables to implement real-world rules for various tasks. Some of the examples include syntax and options that haven't yet been introduced. If you get lost, refer to this section or the iptables man page for more information on the syntax being used.

iptables Features

iptables uses the concept of separate rule tables for different kinds of packet-processing functionality. These rule tables are implemented as functionally separate table modules. The three primary modules are the rule filter table, the NAT nat table, and the specialized packet-handling mangle table. Each of these three table modules has its own associated module extensions that are dynamically loaded when first referenced, unless you've built them directly into the kernel. Other tables include raw and security, which have specialty uses.

The `filter` table is the default table. The other tables are specified by a command-line option. The basic `filter` table features include these:

- Chain-related operations on the three built-in chains (INPUT, OUTPUT, and FORWARD) and on user-defined chains
- Help
- Target disposition (ACCEPT or DROP)
- IP header field match operations for protocol, source and destination address, input and output interfaces, and fragment handling
- Match operations on the TCP, UDP, and ICMP header fields

The `filter` table has two kinds of feature extensions: *target* extensions and *match* extensions. The target extensions include the REJECT packet disposition; the BALANCE, MIRROR, TEE, IDLETIMER, AUDIT, CLASSIFY, and CLUSTERIP targets; and the CONNMARK, TRACE, and LOG and ULOG functionalities, among others. The match extensions support matching on the following:

- The current connection state
- Port lists (supported by the multiport module)
- The hardware Ethernet MAC source address or physical device
- The type of address, link-layer packet type, or range of IP addresses
- Various parts of IPsec packets or the IPsec policy
- The ICMP type
- The length of the packet
- The time the packet arrived
- Every *n*th packet or random packets
- The packet sender's user, group, process, or process group ID
- The IP header Type of Service (TOS) field (possibly set by the `mangle` table)
- The TTL section of the IP header
- The `iptables` mark field (set by the `mangle` table)
- Rate-limited packet matching

The `mangle` table has two target extensions. The MARK module supports assigning a value to the packet's mark field that `iptables` maintains. The TOS module supports setting the value of the TOS field in the IP header.

The `nat` table has target extension modules for Source and Destination Address Translation and for Port Translation. These modules support these forms of NAT:

- **SNAT**—Source NAT
- **DNAT**—Destination NAT

- **MASQUERADE**—A specialized form of source NAT for connections that are assigned a temporary, changeable, dynamically assigned IP address (such as a phone dial-up connection)
- **REDIRECT**—A specialized form of destination NAT that redirects the packet to the local host, regardless of the address in the IP header's destination field

All TCP state flags can be inspected, and filtering decisions can be made based on the results. iptables can check for stealth scans, for example.

TCP can optionally specify the maximum segment size that the sender is willing to accept in return. Filtering on this one, single TCP option is a very specialized case. The TTL section of the IP header can also be matched and is a specialized case as well.

TCP connection state and ongoing UDP exchange information can be maintained, allowing packet recognition on an ongoing basis rather than on a stateless, packet-by-packet basis. Accepting packets recognized as being part of an established connection allows bypassing the overhead of checking the rule list for each packet. When the initial connection is accepted, subsequent packets can be recognized and allowed.

Generally, the TOS field is of historical interest only. The TOS field is either ignored or used with the newer Differentiated Services (DS) definitions by intermediate routers. IP TOS filtering has uses for local packet prioritizing—routing and forwarding among local hosts and the local router.

Incoming packets can be filtered by the MAC source address. This has limited, specialized uses for local authentication because MAC addresses are passed only between adjacent hosts and routers.

Individual filter log messages can be prefixed with user-defined strings. Messages can be assigned kernel logging levels as defined in the system log daemon configuration. This allows logging to be turned on and off, and for the log output files to be defined for a given system. In addition, there is a ULOG option that sends logging to a user-space daemon, ulogd, to enable further detail to be logged about the packet.

Packet matches can be limited to an initial burst rate, after which a limit is imposed by the number of allowed matches per second. If match limiting is enabled, the default is that, after an initial burst of five matched packets, a rate limit of three matches per hour is imposed. In other words, if the system were flooded with ping packets, for example, the first five pings would match. After that, a single ping packet could be matched 20 minutes later, and another one could be matched 20 minutes after that, regardless of how many echo-requests were received. The disposition of the packets, whether logged or not, would depend on any subsequent rules regarding the packets.

The REJECT target can optionally specify which ICMP (or RST for TCP) error message to return. The IPv4 standard requires TCP to accept either RST or ICMP as an error indication, although RST is the default TCP behavior. iptables' default is to return nothing (DROP) or else to return an ICMP error (REJECT).

Along with REJECT, another special-purpose target is QUEUE. Its purpose is to hand off the packet via the netlink device to a user-space program for handling. If there is no waiting program, the packet is dropped.

RETURN is another special-purpose target. Its purpose is to return from a user-defined chain before rule matching on that chain has completed.

Locally generated outgoing packets can be filtered based on the user, group, process, or process group ID of the program generating the packet. Thus, access to remote services can be authorized at the packet-filtering level on a per-user basis. This is a specialized option for multiuser, multipurpose hosts because firewall routers shouldn't have normal user accounts.

Matching can be performed on various pieces of the IPsec header, including the SPIs (security parameter indices) of the AH (Authentication Header) and ESP (Encapsulating Security Ppayload).

The type of packet, be it broadcast, unicast, or multicast, is another form of match. This is done at the link layer.

A range of ports as well as a range of addresses are also valid matches with `iptables`. The type of address is another valid match as well. Related to type matching is the ICMP packet type. Recall that there are a number of valid types of ICMP packets. `iptables` can match against these types.

The length of the packet is a valid match, as is the time a packet arrived. This time matching is interesting. Using the time matches, you could configure the firewall to reject certain traffic after business hours or allow it only during certain times of day.

A good match for auditing, a random packet match is also available with `iptables`. Using this match, you can capture every *n*th packet and log it. This would be a method for auditing the firewall rules without logging too much information.

NAT Table Features

There are three general forms of NAT:

- **Traditional, unidirectional outbound NAT**—Used for networks using private addresses.
  - **Basic NAT**—Address Translation only. Usually used to map local private source addresses to one of a block of public addresses.
  - **NAPT (Network Address and Port Translation)**—Usually used to map local private source addresses to a single public address (for example, Linux masquerading).

- **Bidirectional NAT**—Two-way Address Translation allows both outbound and inbound connections. A use of this is bidirectional address mapping between IPv4 and IPv6 address spaces.

- **Twice NAT**—Two-way Source and Destination Address Translation allows both outbound and inbound connections. Twice NAT can be used when the source and destination networks' address spaces collide. This could be the result of one site mistakenly using public addresses assigned to someone else. Twice NAT also can be used as a convenience when a site was renumbered or assigned to a new public address block and the site administrator didn't want to administer the new address assignments locally at that time.

iptables NAT supports source NAT (SNAT) and destination NAT (DNAT). The nat table allows for modifying a packet's source address or destination address and port. It has three built-in chains:

- The PREROUTING chain specifies destination changes to incoming packets before passing the packet to the routing function (DNAT). Changes to the destination address can be to the local host (transparent proxying, port redirection) or to a different host for host forwarding (ipmasqadm functionality, *port forwarding* in Linux parlance) or load sharing.

- The OUTPUT chain specifies destination changes to locally generated outgoing packets before the routing decision has been made (DNAT, REDIRECT). This is usually done to transparently redirect an outgoing packet to a local proxy, but it can also be used to port-forward to a different host.

- The POSTROUTING chain specifies source changes to outgoing packets being routed through the box (SNAT, MASQUERADE). The changes are applied after the routing decision has been made.

Masquerading in iptables

In iptables, masquerading is a specialized case of source NAT in the sense that the masqueraded connection state is forgotten immediately if the connection is lost. It's intended for use with connections in which the IP address is assigned temporarily (for example, dial-up). A user who reconnects immediately would probably be assigned a different IP address from the previous connection. (This is often not the case with many cable modem and ADSL service providers. Often, after a connection loss, the same IP address is assigned upon reconnection.)

With regular SNAT, connection state is maintained for the duration of a timeout period. If a connection were reestablished quickly enough, any current network-related programs could continue undisturbed because the IP address hasn't changed, and interrupted TCP traffic would be retransmitted.

The distinction between MASQUERADE and SNAT is an attempt to avoid a situation that occurred in previous Linux NAT/MASQUERADE implementations. When a dial-up connection was lost and the user reconnected immediately, the user was assigned a new IP address. The new address couldn't be used immediately because the old IP address and NAT information were still in memory until the timeout period expired.

Figure 3.4 shows the NAT chains in relation to the routing function and INPUT, OUTPUT, and FORWARD chains.

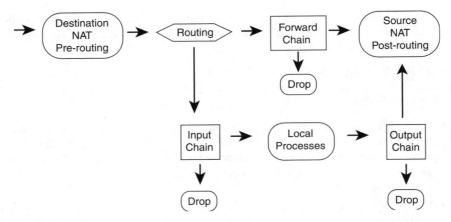

Figure 3.4   NAT packet traversal

(Figure based on "Linux 2.4 Packet Filtering HOWTO," v1.0.1,
and "Linux 2.4 NAT HOWTO," v1.0.1.)

Note that, for outgoing packets, the routing function is implied between the local process and the OUTPUT chain. Static routing is used to determine which interface the packet will go out on, before the OUTPUT chain's filter rules are applied.

`mangle` Table Features

The `mangle` table allows *marking*, or associating a Netfilter-maintained value with the packet, as well as making changes to the packet before sending the packet on to its destination. The `mangle` table has five built-in chains:

- The PREROUTING chain specifies changes to incoming packets as they arrive at an interface, before any routing or local delivery decision has been made.
- The INPUT chain specifies changes to packets as they are processed, but after the PREROUTING chain is traversed.
- The POSTROUTING chain specifies changes to packets as they are exiting the firewall, after the OUTPUT chain is traversed.
- The FORWARD chain specifies changes to packets that are forwarded through the firewall.
- The OUTPUT chain specifies changes to locally generated outgoing packets.

For the TOS field, the local Linux router can be configured to honor the TOS flags set by the `mangle` table or as set by the local hosts.

Little information is available about packet marking in the `iptables` documentation, beyond that it's used by the Linux Quality of Service (QoS) implementation and that it's intended as a communication flag between `iptables` modules.

The preceding sections provided an overview of the features available in `iptables` and the general structure and functionality of the individual table modules. The following sections present the syntax used to invoke these features.

iptables Syntax

As presented earlier, `iptables` uses the concept of separate rule tables for different packet-processing functionality. Nondefault tables are specified by a command-line option. Three primary tables are available, with others such as `security` and `raw` serving a specialized purpose. The three primary tables are:

- **filter**—The `filter` table is the default table. It contains the actual firewall filtering rules. The built-in chains include these:
  - INPUT
  - OUTPUT
  - FORWARD

- **nat**—The `nat` table contains the rules for Source and Destination Address and Port Translation. These rules are functionally distinct from the firewall filter rules. The built-in chains include these:
  - **PREROUTING**—DNAT/REDIRECT
  - **OUTPUT**—DNAT/REDIRECT
  - **POSTROUTING**—SNAT/MASQUERADE

- **mangle**—The `mangle` table contains rules for setting specialized packet-routing flags. These flags are then inspected later by rules in the `filter` table. The built-in chains include these:
  - **PREROUTING**—Routed packets
  - **INPUT**—Packets arriving at the firewall but after the PREROUTING chain
  - **FORWARD**—Changes packets being routed through the firewall
  - **POSTROUTING**—Changes packets just before they leave the firewall, after the OUTPUT chain
  - **OUTPUT**—Locally generated packets

Syntax Format Conventions

The conventions used to present command-line syntax options are fairly standard in the computer world. For those of you who are new to Linux or to computer documentation in general, Table 3.1 shows the conventions used in the upcoming syntax descriptions.

Table 3.1 **Conventions Representing Command-Line Syntax Options**

Element	Description
|	A bar or pipe symbol separates alternative syntax options. For example, most of the `iptables` commands have both a short and a long form, such as `-L` and `--list`, and so they would be listed as alternative options because you would use one or the other of `-L` or `--list`.
<value>	Angle brackets indicate a user-supplied value, such as a string or numeric value.
[ ]	Square brackets indicate that the enclosed command, option, or value is optional. For example, most match operators can take a negation operator, `!`, which matches anything other than the value specified in the match. The negation operator is usually placed between the match operator and the value to be matched.
<value>:<value>	A colon indicates a range of values. The two values define the minimum and maximum values within the range. Because ranges themselves are optional, the convention is more often presented as `<value>[:<value>]`.

`filter` Table Commands

The `filter` table commands are provided by the `ip_tables` module. The functionality is enabled by loading the module, which is done automatically with the first invocation of the `iptables` command, or it could be compiled into the kernel itself, which means you don't need to worry about modules being loaded at all.

`filter` Table Operations on Entire Chains

Table 3.2 shows the `iptables` operations on entire chains.

The `-h` help command is obviously not an operation on a chain, nor is `--modprobe=<command>`, but I didn't know where else to list the commands.

The `list` command takes additional options, as shown in Table 3.3.

`filter` Table Operations on a Rule

The most frequently used commands to create or delete rules within a chain are shown in Table 3.4.

Basic `filter` Table Match Operations

The basic `filter` match operations supported in the default `iptables` `filter` table are listed in Table 3.5.

Table 3.2 **iptables** Operations on Entire Chains

Option	Description
-N | --new-chain <chain>	Creates a user-defined chain.
-F | --flush [<chain>]	Flushes the chain, or all chains if none is specified.
-X | --delete-chain [<chain>]	Deletes the user-defined chain, or all chains if none is specified.
-P | --policy <chain> <policy>	Defines the default policy for one of the built-in chains, INPUT, OUTPUT, or FORWARD. The policy is either ACCEPT or DROP.
-L | --list [<chain>]	Lists the rules in the chain, or all chains if none is specified.
-S | --list-rules [<chain>]	Prints the rules in the specified chain in iptables save format.
-Z | --zero	Resets the packet and byte counters associated with each chain.
-h | <some command> -h	Lists the iptables commands and options, or if preceded by an iptables command, lists the syntax and options for that command.
--modprobe=<command>	Use <command> to load the necessary module(s) when adding or inserting a rule into a chain.
-E | --rename-chain <old chain>	Renames the user-defined chain <old chain> to the user-defined chain <new chain>.

Table 3.3 **Options to the list Chain Command**

Option	Description
-L -n | --numeric	Lists the IP addresses and port numbers numerically, rather than by name
-L -v | --verbose	Lists additional information about each rule, such as the byte and packet counters, rule options, and relevant network interface
-L -x | --exact	Lists the exact values of the counter, rather than the rounded-off values
-L --line-numbers	Lists the rule's position within its chain

Table 3.4 **Chain Commands on Individual Rules**

Command	Description
`-A | --append <chain> <rule specification>`	Appends a rule to the end of a chain
`-I | --insert <chain> [<rule number>] <rule specification>`	Inserts a rule at the beginning of the chain
`-R | --replace <chain> <rule number> <rule specification>`	Replaces a rule in the chain
`-D | --delete <chain> <rule number> | <rule specification>`	Deletes the rule at position `<rule number>` within a chain or the rule matching the specified rule
`-C | --check <chain> <rule specification>`	Examines the chain to see if a rule matches the specification

Table 3.5 **`filter` Table Rule Operations**

Option	Description
`-i | --in-interface [!] [<interface>]`	For incoming packets on either the `INPUT` or the `FORWARD` chains, or their user-defined subchains, specifies the interface name that the rule applies to. If no interface is specified, all interfaces are implied.
`-o | --out-interface [!] [<interface>]`	For outgoing packets on either the `OUTPUT` or the `FORWARD` chains, or their user-defined subchains, specifies the interface name that the rule applies to. If no interface is specified, all interfaces are implied.
`-p | --protocol [!] [<protocol>]`	Specifies the IP protocol that the rule applies to. The built-in protocols are `tcp`, `udp`, `icmp`, and all. The protocol value can be either the name or the numeric value, as listed in `/etc/protocols`.
`-s | --source | --src [!] <address>[</mask>]`	Specifies the host or network source address in the IP header.
`-d | --destination | --dst [!] <address>[</mask>]`	Specifies the host or network destination address in the IP header.

Table 3.5 **filter** Table Rule Operations (*Continued*)

Option	Description
`-j | --jump <target>`	Specifies the target disposition for the packet if it matches the rule. The default targets include the built-in targets, an extension, or a user-defined chain.
`-g | --goto <chain>`	Specifies that processing should continue in the specified chain but doesn't send processing back (like the `jump` option does).
`-m | --match <match>`	Uses an extension to test for a match.
`[!] -f | --fragment`	Specifies second and additional fragmented packets. The negated version of this specifies unfragmented packets.
`-c | --set-counters <packets> <bytes>`	Initializes the packet and byte counters.

Rule Targets Are Optional

If the packet matches a rule that doesn't have a target disposition, the packet counters are updated, but list traversal continues.

---

tcp filter Table Match Operations

TCP header match options are listed in Table 3.6. You can also see these options by adding the -h flag after the -p tcp option, as in iptables -p tcp -h.

Table 3.6 **tcp filter** Table Match Operations

-p tcp Option	Description
`--source-port | --sport [[!] <port>[:<port>]]`	This command specifies the source ports.
`--destination-port | --dport <port>[:<port>]`	This command specifies the destination [!] ports.
`--tcp-flags [!] <mask> [,<mask>] <set>[,<set>]`	This command tests the bits in the mask list, out of which the following bits must be set in order to match.
`[!] -syn`	The SYN flag must be set as an initial connection request.
`--tcp-option [!] <number>`	The only legal tcp option is the maximum packet size that the sending host is willing to accept.

Table 3.7 **`udp filter`** Table Match Operations

-p udp Option	**Description**
`--source-port	--sport [!] <port>[:<port>]`	Specifies the source ports
`--destination-port	--dport [!] <port>[:<port>]`	Specifies the destination ports

Table 3.8 **`icmp filter`** Table Match Operation

Option	**Description**
`--icmp-type [!] <type>`	Specifies the ICMP type name or number. The ICMP type is used in place of a source port.

`udp filter` Table Match Operations

UDP header match options are listed in Table 3.7. You can also see these options by adding the -h flag after the -p udp option, as in `iptables -p udp -h`.

`icmp filter` Table Match Operation

The ICMP header match option is listed in Table 3.8.

The major supported ICMP type names and numeric values are the following:

- `echo-reply (0)`
- `destination-unreachable (3)`
  - `network-unreachable`
  - `host-unreachable`
  - `protocol-unreachable`
  - `port-unreachable`
  - `fragmentation-needed`
  - `network-unknown`
  - `host-unknown`
  - `network-prohibited`
  - `host-prohibited`
- `source-quench (4)`
- `redirect (5)`
- `echo-request (8)`
- `time-exceeded (10)`
- `parameter-problem (11)`

> **Additional ICMP and ICMP6 Support**
>
> `iptables` supports a number of additional, less common or router-specific ICMP message types and subtypes and can also work with IPv6 ICMP packets through the icmp6 extension. To see the entire list, use the following `iptables` help commands:
>
> ```
> iptables -p icmp -h
> iptables -p ipv6-icmp -h
> ```

`filter` Table Target Extensions

The `filter` table target extensions include logging functionality and the capability to reject a packet rather than dropping it.

Table 3.9 lists the options available to the LOG target. Table 3.10 lists the single option available to the REJECT target. As with other options, you can add the -h flag after the -j <TARGET> to see more options, like so: `iptables -j <TARGET> -h`.

The ULOG Table Target Extension

Related to the LOG target is the ULOG target, which sends the log message to a user-space program for logging. Behind the scenes for ULOG, the packet gets multicast by the kernel

Table 3.9 **LOG Target Extension**

`-j LOG` Option	Description
`--log-level <syslog level>`	Log level is either the numeric or the symbolic login priority, as listed in /usr/include/sys/syslog.h. These are the same log levels used in /etc/syslog.conf. The levels are emerg (0), alert (1), crit (2), err (3), warn (4), notice (5), info (6), memerg (0), alert (1), crit (2), err (3), warn (4), notice (5), info (6), and debug (7).
`--log-prefix <"descriptive string">`	The prefix is a quoted string that will be printed at the start of the log message for the rule.
`--log-ip-options`	This command includes any IP header options in the log output.
`--log-tcp-sequence`	This command includes the TCP packet's sequence number in the log output.
`--log-tcp-option`	This command includes any TCP header options in the log output.
`--log-uid`	This command includes the user ID that generated the packet in the log output.

Table 3.10 **REJECT** Target Extension

`-j REJECT` Option	Description
`--reject-with <ICMP type 3>`	By default, a rejected packet results in an ICMP Type 3 `icmp-port-unreachable` message being returned to the sender. Other Type 3 error messages can be returned instead, including `icmp-net-unreachable`, `icmp-host-unreachable`, `icmp-proto-unreachable`, `icmp-net-prohibited`, and `icmp-host-prohibited`.
`--reject-with tcp-reset`	Incoming TCP packets can be rejected with the more standard TCP RST message, rather than an ICMP error message.

through a netlink socket of your choosing (the default is socket 1). The user-space daemon would then read the message from the socket and do with it what it pleases. The ULOG target is typically used to provide more extensive logging than is possible with the standard LOG target.

As with the LOG target, processing continues after matches on a ULOG targeted rule. The ULOG target has four configuration options, as described in Table 3.11.

`filter` Table Match Extensions

The `filter` table match extensions provide access to the fields in the TCP, UDP, and ICMP headers, as well as the match features available in `iptables`, such as maintaining connection state, port lists, access to the hardware MAC source address, and access to the IP TOS field.

Table 3.11 **ULOG** Target Extension

Option	Description
`--ulog-nlgroup <group>`	Defines the netlink group that will receive the packet. The default group is 1.
`--ulog-prefix <prefix>`	Messages will be prefixed by this value, up to 32 characters in length.
`--ulog-cprange <size>`	The size in bytes to send to the netlink socket. The default is 0, which sends the entire packet.
`--ulog-qthreshold <size>`	The size in packets to queue within the kernel. The default is 1, which means that one packet is sent per message to the netlink socket.

> **Match Syntax**
> The match extensions require the -m or --match command to load the module, followed by any relevant match options.

`multiport filter` Table Match Extension

`multiport` port lists can include up to 15 ports per list. Whitespace isn't allowed. There can be no blank spaces between the commas and the port values. Port ranges cannot be interspersed in the list. Also, the -m multiport command must exactly follow the -p <protocol> specifier.

Table 3.12 lists the options available to the `multiport` match extension.

The `multiport` syntax can be a bit tricky. Some examples and cautions are included here. The following rule blocks incoming packets arriving on interface eth0 destined for the UDP ports associated with NetBIOS and SMB, common ports that are exploited on Microsoft Windows computers and targets for worms:

```
iptables -A INPUT -i eth0 -p udp\
        -m multiport --destination-port 135,136,137,138,139 -j DROP
```

The next rule blocks outgoing connection requests sent through the eth0 interface to high ports associated with the TCP services NFS, SOCKS, and squid:

```
iptables -A OUTPUT -o eth0 -p tcp\
        -m multiport --destination-port 2049,1080,3128 --syn -j REJECT
```

What is important to note in this example is that the `multiport` command must exactly follow the protocol specification. A syntax error would have resulted if the --syn were placed between the -p tcp and the -m multiport.

To show a similar example of --syn placement, the following is correct:

```
iptables -A INPUT -i <interface> -p tcp \
        -m multiport --source-port 80,443 ! --syn -j ACCEPT
```

However, this causes a syntax error:

```
iptables -A INPUT -i <interface> -p tcp ! --syn \
        -m multiport --source-port 80,443 -j ACCEPT
```

Table 3.12 **`multiport`** Match Extension

m | --match multiport Option	Description
--source-port <port>[,<port>]	Specifies the source port(s).
--destination-port <port>[,<port>]	Specifies the destination port(s).
--port <port>[,<port>]	Source and destination ports are equal, and they match a port in the list.

Furthermore, the placement of source and destination parameters is not obvious. The following two variations are correct:

```
iptables -A INPUT -i <interface> -p tcp -m multiport \
        --source-port 80,443 \
        ! --syn -d $IPADDR --dport 1024:65535 -j ACCEPT
```

and

```
iptables -A INPUT -i <interface> -p tcp -m multiport \
        --source-port 80,443 \
        -d $IPADDR ! --syn --dport 1024:65535 -j ACCEPT
```

However, this causes a syntax error:

```
iptables -A INPUT -i <interface> -p tcp -m multiport \
        --source-port 80,443 \
        -d $IPADDR --dport 1024:65535 ! --syn -j ACCEPT
```

This module has some surprising syntax side effects. Either of the two preceding correct rules produces a syntax error if the reference to the SYN flag is removed:

```
iptables -A INPUT -i <interface> -p tcp -m multiport \
        --source-port 80,443 \
        -d $IPADDR --dport 1024:65535 -j ACCEPT
```

The following pair of rules, however, does not:

```
iptables -A OUTPUT -o <interface> \
        -p tcp -m multiport --destination-port 80,443 \
        ! --syn -s $IPADDR --sport 1024:65535 -j ACCEPT

iptables -A OUTPUT -o <interface> \
        -p tcp -m multiport --destination-port 80,443 \
        --syn -s $IPADDR --sport 1024:65535 -j ACCEPT
```

Note that the `--destination-port` argument to the `multiport` module is not the same as the `--destination-port` or `--dport` argument to the module that performs matching for the `-p tcp` arguments.

`limit filter` Table Match Extension

Rate-limited matching is useful for choking back the number of log messages that would be generated during a flood of logged packets.

Table 3.13 lists the options available to the `limit` match extension.

The burst rate defines the number of initial matches to be accepted. The default value is five matches. When the limit has been reached, further matches are limited to the rate limit. The default limit is three matches per hour. Optional time frame specifiers include `/second`, `/minute`, `/hour`, and `/day`.

In other words, by default, when the initial burst rate of five matches is reached within the time limit, at most three more packets will match over the next hour, one every 20 minutes, regardless of how many packets are received. If a match doesn't occur within the rate limit, the burst is recharged by one.

Table 3.13 **limit** Match Extension

**-m	--match limit** Option	Description
--limit <rate>	Maximum number of packets to match within the given time frame
--limit-burst <number>	Maximum number of initial packets to match before applying the limit

It's easier to demonstrate rate-limited matching than it is to describe it in words. The following rule will limit logging of incoming ping message matches to one per second when an initial five echo-requests are received within a given second:

```
iptables -A INPUT -i eth0 \
        -p icmp --icmp-type echo-request \
        -m limit --limit 1/second -j LOG
```

It's also possible to do rate-limited packet acceptance. The following two rules, in combination, will limit acceptance of incoming ping messages to one per second when an initial five echo-requests are received within a given second:

```
iptables -A INPUT -i eth0 \
        -p icmp --icmp-type echo-request \
        -m limit --limit 1/second -j ACCEPT

iptables -A INPUT -i eth0 \
        -p icmp --icmp-type echo-request -j DROP
```

The next rule limits the number of log messages generated in response to dropped ICMP redirect messages. When an initial five messages have been logged within a 20-minute time frame, at most three more log messages will be generated over the next hour, one every 20 minutes:

```
iptables -A INPUT -i eth0 \
        -p icmp --icmp-type redirect \
        -m limit -j LOG
```

The assumption in the final example is that the packet and any additional unmatched redirect packets are silently dropped by the default DROP policy for the INPUT chain.

state filter Table Match Extension

Static filters look at traffic on a packet-by-packet basis alone. Each packet's particular combination of source and destination addresses and ports, the transport protocol, and the current TCP state flag combination is examined without reference to any ongoing context. ICMP messages are treated as unrelated, out-of-band IP Layer 3 events.

The state extension provides additional monitoring and recording technology to augment the stateless, static packet-filter technology. State information is recorded when a TCP connection or UDP exchange is initiated. Subsequent packets are examined not only based on the static tuple information, but also within the context of the ongoing exchange. In other words, some of the contextual knowledge usually associated with the upper TCP Transport layer, or the UDP Application layer, is brought down to the filter layer.

After the exchange is initiated and accepted, subsequent packets are identified as part of the established exchange. Associated ICMP messages are identified as being related to a particular exchange.

> **Note**
>
> In computer terminology, a collection of values or attributes that together uniquely identify an event or object is called a *tuple*. A UDP or TCP packet is uniquely identified by the tuple combination of its protocol, UDP or TCP, the source and destination addresses, and the source and destination ports.

For session monitoring, the advantages of maintaining state information are less obvious for TCP because TCP maintains state information by definition. For UDP, the immediate advantage is the capability to distinguish responses from other datagrams. In the case of an outgoing DNS request, which represents a new UDP exchange, the concept of an established session allows an incoming UDP response datagram from the host and port the original message was sent to, within a certain time-limited window. Incoming UDP datagrams from other hosts or ports are not allowed. They are not part of the established state for this particular exchange. When applied to TCP and UDP, ICMP error messages are accepted if the error message is related to the particular session.

In considering packet flow performance and firewall complexity, the advantages are more obvious for TCP flows. Flows are primarily a firewall performance and optimization technology. The main goal of flows is to allow bypassing the firewall inspection path for a packet. Much faster TCP packet handling is obtained in some cases because the remaining firewall filters can be skipped if the TCP packet is immediately recognized as part of an allowed, ongoing connection. For TCP connections, flow state can be a major win in terms of filtering performance. Also, standard TCP application protocol rules can be collapsed into a single initial allow rule. The number of filter rules is reduced (theoretically, but not necessarily in practice, as you'll see later in the book).

The main disadvantage is that maintaining a state table requires more memory than standard firewall rules alone. Routers with 70,000 simultaneous connections, for example, would require tremendous amounts of memory to maintain state table entries for each connection. State maintenance is often done in hardware for performance reasons, where associative table lookups can be done simultaneously or in parallel. Whether implemented in hardware or software, state engines must be capable of reverting a packet to the traditional path if memory isn't available for the state table entry.

Also, table creation, lookup, and teardown take time in software. The additional processing overhead is a loss in many cases. State maintenance is a win for ongoing exchanges such as an FTP transfer or a UDP streaming multimedia session. Both types of data flow represent potentially large numbers of packets (and filter rule match tests). State maintenance is not a firewall performance win for a simple DNS or NTP client/server exchange, however. State buildup and teardown can easily require as much processing—and more memory—than simply traversing the filter rules for these packets.

The advantages are also questionable for firewalls that filter primarily web traffic. Web client/server exchanges tend to be brief and ephemeral.

Telnet and SSH sessions are in a gray area. On heavily trafficked routers with many such sessions, the state maintenance overhead may be a win by bypassing the firewall inspection. For fairly quiescent sessions, however, it's likely that the connection state entry will time out and be thrown away. The state table entry will be re-created when the next packet comes along, after it has passed the traditional firewall rules.

Table 3.14 lists the option available to the `state` match extension.

TCP connection state and ongoing UDP exchange information can be maintained, allowing network exchanges to be filtered as NEW, ESTABLISHED, RELATED, or INVALID:

- NEW is equivalent to the initial TCP SYN request, or to the first UDP packet.

- ESTABLISHED refers to the ongoing TCP ACK messages after the connection is initiated, to subsequent UDP datagrams exchanged between the same hosts and ports, and to ICMP `echo-reply` messages sent in response to a previous `echo-request`.

- RELATED currently refers only to ICMP error messages. FTP secondary connections are managed by the additional FTP connection tracking support module. With the addition of that module, the meaning of RELATED is extended to include the secondary FTP connection.

- An example of an INVALID packet is an incoming ICMP error message that wasn't a response to a current session, or an `echo-reply` that wasn't a response to a previous `echo-request`.

Ideally, using the ESTABLISHED match allows the firewall rule pair for a service to be collapsed into a single rule that allows the first request packet. For example, using the ESTABLISHED match, a web client rule requires allowing only the initial outgoing SYN request. A DNS client request requires only the rule allowing the initial UDP outgoing request packet.

Table 3.14 **state** Match Extension

-m | --match state Option	Description
--state <state>[,<state>]	Matches if the connection state is one in the list. Legal values are NEW, ESTABLISHED, RELATED, and INVALID.

With a deny-by-default input policy, connection tracking can be used (theoretically) to replace all protocol-specific filters with two general rules that allow incoming and outgoing packets that are part of an established connection, or packets related to the connection. Application-specific rules are required for the initial packet alone.

Although such a firewall setup might very well work for a small or residential site in most cases, it is unlikely to perform adequately for a larger site or a firewall that handles many connections simultaneously. The reason goes back to the case of state table entry timeouts, in which a state entry for a quiescent connection is replaced because of table size and memory constraints. The next packet that would have been accepted by the deleted state entry requires a rule to allow the packet, and the state table entry must be rebuilt.

A simple example of this is a rule pair for a local DNS server operating as a cache-and-forward name server. A DNS forwarding name server uses server-to-server communication. DNS traffic is exchanged between source and destination ports 53 on both hosts. The UDP client/server relationship can be made explicit. The following rules explicitly allow outgoing (NEW) requests, incoming (ESTABLISHED) responses, and any (RELATED) ICMP error messages:

```
iptables -A INPUT -m state \
        --state ESTABLISHED,RELATED -j ACCEPT

iptables -A OUTPUT --out-interface <interface> -p udp \
        -s $IPADDR --source-port 53 -d $NAME_SERVER --destination-port 53 \
        -m state --state NEW,RELATED -j ACCEPT
```

DNS uses a simple query-and-response protocol. But what about an application that can maintain an ongoing connection for extended periods, such as an FTP control session or a telnet or SSH session? If the state table entry is cleared out prematurely for some reason, future packets won't have a state entry to be matched against to be identified as part of an ESTABLISHED exchange.

The following rules for an SSH connection allow for that possibility:

```
iptables -A INPUT -m state \
        --state ESTABLISHED,RELATED -j ACCEPT

iptables -A OUTPUT -m state \
        --state ESTABLISHED,RELATED -j ACCEPT

iptables -A OUTPUT --out-interface <interface> -p tcp \
        -s $IPADDR --source-port $UNPRIVPORTS \
        -d $REMOTE_SSH_SERVER --destination-port 22 \
        -m state --state NEW, -j ACCEPT

iptables -A OUTPUT --out-interface <interface> -p tcp ! --syn \
        -s $IPADDR --source-port $UNPRIVPORTS \
        -d $REMOTE_SSH_SERVER --destination-port 22 \
        -j ACCEPT
```

```
iptables -A INPUT --in-interface <interface> -p tcp ! --syn \
        -s $REMOTE_SSH_SERVER --source-port 22 \
        -d $IPADDR --destination-port $UNPRIVPORTS \
        -j ACCEPT
```

`mac filter` Table Match Extension

Table 3.15 lists the option available to the `mac` match extension.

Remember that MAC addresses do not cross router borders (or network segments). Also remember that only source addresses can be specified. The `mac` extension can be used only on an `in-interface`, such as the `INPUT`, `PREROUTING`, and `FORWARD` chains.

The following rule allows incoming SSH connections from a single local host:

```
iptables -A INPUT -i <local interface> -p tcp \
        -m mac --mac-source xx:xx:xx:xx:xx:xx \
        --source-port 1024:65535 \
        -d <IPADDR> --dport 22 -j ACCEPT
```

`owner filter` Table Match Extension

Table 3.16 lists the options available to the `owner` match extension.

The match refers to the packet's creator. The extension can be used on the `OUTPUT` chain only.

These match options don't make much sense on a firewall router; they make more sense on an end host.

So, let's say that you have a firewall gateway with a monitor, perhaps, but no keyboard. Administration is done from a local, multiuser host. A single user account is allowed to log

Table 3.15 **mac** Match Extension

-m | --match mac Option	Description
--mac-source [!] <address>	Matches the Layer 2 Ethernet hardware source address, specified as xx:xx:xx:xx:xx:xx:, in the incoming Ethernet frame

Table 3.16 **owner** Match Extension

-m | --match owner Option	Description
--uid-owner <userid>	Matches on the creator's UID
--gid-owner <groupid>	Matches on the creator's GID
--pid-owner <processid>	Matches on the creator's PID
--sid-owner <sessionid>	Matches on the creator's SID or PPID
--cmd-owner <name>	Matches on a packet created by a process with command name <name>

in to the firewall from this host. On the multiuser host, administrative access to the firewall could be locally filtered as shown here:

```
iptables -A OUTPUT -o eth0 -p tcp \
        -s <IPADDR> --sport 1024:65535 \
        -d <fw IPADDR> --dport 22 \
        -m owner --uid-owner <admin userid> \
        --gid-owner <admin groupid> -j ACCEPT
```

`mark filter` Table Match Extension

Table 3.17 lists the option available to the `mark` match extension.

The `mark` value and the mask are unsigned long values. If a mask is specified, the value and the mask are ANDed together.

In the example, assume that an incoming telnet client packet between a specific source and destination had been marked previously:

```
iptables -A FORWARD -i eth0 -o eth1 -p tcp \
        -s <some src address> --sport 1024:65535 \
        -d <some destination address> --dport 23 \
        -m mark --mark 0x00010070 \
        -j ACCEPT
```

The `mark` value being tested for here was set at some earlier point in the packet processing. The `mark` value is a flag indicating that this packet is to be handled differently from other packets.

`tos filter` Table Match Extension

Table 3.18 lists the option available to the `tos` match extension.

The `tos` value can be one of either the string or numeric values:

- `minimize-delay, 16, 0x10`
- `maximize-throughput, 8, 0x08`
- `maximize-reliability, 4, 0x04`
- `minimize-cost, 2, 0x02`
- `normal-service, 0, 0x00`

Table 3.17 **`mark`** Match Extension

`-m	--match mark` Option	Description
`--mark <value>[/<mask>]`	Matches packets having the Netfilter-assigned `mark` value

Table 3.18 **`tos`** Match Extension

`-m	--match tos` Option	Description
`--tos <value>`	Matches on the IP TOS setting

The TOS field has been redefined as the Differentiated Services (DS) field for use by the Differentiated Services Code Point (DSCP).

For more information on Differentiated Services, see these sources:

- RFC 2474, "Definition of the Differentiated Services Field (DS Field) in the IPv4 and IPv6 Headers"
- RFC 2475, "An Architecture for Differentiated Services"
- RFC 2990, "Next Steps for the IP QoS Architecture"
- RFC 3168, "The Addition of Explicit Congestion Notification (ECN) to IP"
- RFC 3260, "New Terminology and Clarifications for Diffserv"

unclean filter Table Match Extension

The unclean module are not documented. The module is considered to be experimental.

The following line shows the unclean module syntax. The module takes no arguments:

```
-m | --match unclean
```

The unclean extension might be "blessed" by the time this book is published. In the meantime, the module lends itself to an example of the LOG options:

```
iptables -A INPUT -p ! tcp -m unclean \
        -j LOG --log-prefix "UNCLEAN packet: " \
        --log-ip-options

iptables -A INPUT -p tcp -m unclean \
        -j LOG --log-prefix "UNCLEAN TCP: " \
        --log-ip-options \
        --log-tcp-sequence --log-tcp-options

iptables -A INPUT -m unclean -j DROP
```

addrtype filter Table Match Extension

The addrtype match extension is used to match packets based on the type of address used, such as unicast, broadcast, and multicast. The types of addresses include those listed in Table 3.19.

Two commands are used with the addrtype match, as listed in Table 3.20.

iprange filter Table Match

Sometimes defining a range of IP addresses using CIDR notation is insufficient for your needs. For example, if you need to limit a certain range of IPs that don't fall on a subnet boundary or cross that boundary by only a couple of addresses, the iprange match type will do the job.

Table 3.19 **Address Types Used with the `addrtype` Match**

Name	Description
ANYCAST	An anycast packet
BLACKHOLE	A blackhole address
BROADCAST	A broadcast address
LOCAL	A local address
MULTICAST	A multicast address
PROHIBIT	A prohibited address
UNICAST	A unicast address
UNREACHABLE	An unreachable address
UNSPEC	An unspecified address

Table 3.20 **`addrtype` Match Commands**

Option	Description
--src-type <type>	Matches for addresses with a source of type <type>
--dst-type <type>	Matches for addresses with a destination of type <type>

Table 3.21 **`iprange` Match Commands**

Command	Description
[!] --src-range <ip address-ip address>	Specifies (or negates) the range of IP addresses to match. The range is given with a single hyphen and no spaces.
[!] --dst-range <ip address-ip address>	Specifies (or negates) the range of IP addresses to match. The range is given with a single hyphen and no spaces.

Using the `iprange` match, you specify an arbitrary range of IP addresses for the match to take effect. The `iprange` match can also be negated. Table 3.21 lists the commands for the `iprange` match.

`length filter` Table Match

The `length filter` table match examines the length of the packet. If the packet's length matches the value given or optionally falls within the range given, the rule is invoked. Table 3.22 lists the one and only command related to the `length` match.

Table 3.22 **length** Match Command

Command	Description
--length <length>[:<length>]	Matches a packet of <length> or within the range <length:length>

nat Table Target Extensions

As mentioned earlier, iptables supports four general kinds of NAT: source NAT (SNAT); destination NAT (DNAT); masquerading (MASQUERADE), which is a specialized case of the SNAT implementation; and local port direction (REDIRECT) to the local host. As part of the nat table, each of these targets is available when a rule specifies the nat table by using the -t nat table specifier.

SNAT nat Table Target Extension

Network Address and Port Translation (NAPT) is the kind of NAT people are most commonly familiar with. As shown in Figure 3.5, Source Address Translation is done after the routing decision is made. SNAT is a legal target only in the POSTROUTING chain. Because SNAT is applied immediately before the packet is sent out, only an outgoing interface can be specified.

Some documents refer to this form of source NAT (the most common form) as NAPT, to acknowledge the port number modification. The other form of traditional, unidirectional NAT is basic NAT, which doesn't touch the source port. That form is used when you are translating between the private LAN and a pool of public addresses.

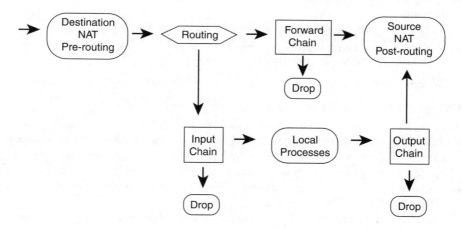

Figure 3.5   NAT packet traversal

NAPT is used when you have a single public address. The source port is changed to a free port on the firewall/NAT machine because it's translating for any number of internal computers, and the port that the internal machine is using might already be in use by the NAT machine. When the responses come back, the port is all that the NAT machine has to determine that the packet is really meant for an internal computer rather than itself and then to determine which internal computer the packet is meant for.

The general syntax for SNAT is as follows:

```
iptables -t nat -A POSTROUTING --out-interface <interface>  ...  \
        -j SNAT --to-source <address>[-<address>][:<port>-<port>]
```

The source address can be mapped to a range of possible IP addresses, if more than one is available.

The source port can be mapped to a specific range of source ports on the router.

MASQUERADE nat Table Target Extension

Source Address Translation has been implemented in two different ways in `iptables`, as SNAT and as MASQUERADE. The difference is that the MASQUERADE target extension is intended for use with connections on interfaces with dynamically assigned IP addresses, particularly in the case in which the connection is temporary and the IP address assignment is likely to be different at each new connection. As discussed previously, in the section "NAT Table Features," MASQUERADE can be useful for dynamic IP or mobile connections in particular.

Because masquerading is a specialized case of SNAT, it is likewise a legal target only in the POSTROUTING chain, and the rule can refer to the outgoing interface only. Unlike the more generalized SNAT, MASQUERADE does not take an argument specifying the source address to apply to the packet. The IP address of the outgoing interface is used automatically.

The general syntax for MASQUERADE is as follows:

```
iptables -t nat -A POSTROUTING --out-interface <interface>  ...  \
        -j MASQUERADE [--to-ports <port>[-<port>]]
```

The source port can be mapped to a specific range of source ports on the router.

DNAT nat Table Target Extension

Destination Address and Port Translation is a highly specialized form of NAT. A residential or small business site is most likely to find this feature useful if its public IP address is dynamically assigned or if the site has a single IP address, and the site administrator wants to forward incoming connections to internal servers that aren't publicly visible. In other words, the DNAT features can be used to replace the previously required third-party port-forwarding software, such as `ipmasqadm`.

Referring back to Figure 3.5, Destination Address and Port Translation is done before the routing decision is made. DNAT is a legal target in the PREROUTING and OUTPUT chains. On the PREROUTING chain, DNAT can be a target when the incoming interface is specified. On the OUTPUT chain, DNAT can be a target when the outgoing interface is specified.

The general syntax for DNAT is as follows:

```
iptables -t nat -A PREROUTING --in-interface <interface>  ...  \
       -j DNAT --to-destination <address>[-<address>][:<port>-<port>]
iptables -t nat -A OUTPUT --out-interface <interface>  ...  \
       -j DNAT --to-destination <address>[-<address>][:<port>-<port>]
```

The destination address can be mapped to a range of possible IP addresses, if more than one is available.

The destination port can be mapped to a specific range of alternative ports on the destination host.

REDIRECT nat Table Target Extension

Port redirection is a specialized case of DNAT. The packet is redirected to a port on the local host. Incoming packets that would otherwise be forwarded on are redirected to the incoming interface's INPUT chain. Outgoing packets generated by the local host are redirected to a port on the local host's loopback interface.

REDIRECT is simply an alias, a convenience, for the specialized case of redirecting a packet to *this* host. It offers no additional functional value. DNAT could just as easily be used to cause the same effect.

REDIRECT is likewise a legal target only in the PREROUTING and OUTPUT chains. On the PREROUTING chain, REDIRECT can be a target when the incoming interface is specified. On the OUTPUT chain, REDIRECT can be a target when the outgoing interface is specified.

The general syntax for REDIRECT is as follows:

```
iptables -t nat -A PREROUTING --in-interface <interface>  ...  \
       -j REDIRECT [--to-ports <port>[-<port>]]
iptables -t nat -A OUTPUT --out-interface <interface>  ...  \
       -j REDIRECT [--to-ports <port>[-<port>]]
```

The destination port can be mapped to a different port or to a specific range of alternative ports on the local host.

mangle Table Commands

The mangle table targets and extensions apply to the OUTPUT and PREROUTING chains. Remember, the filter table is implied by default. To use the mangle table features, you must specify the mangle table with the -t mangle directive.

mark mangle Table Target Extension

Table 3.23 lists the target extensions available to the mangle table.

Table 3.23 **mangle** Target Extensions

-t mangle Option	Description
-j MARK --set-mark <value>	Sets the value of the Netfilter mark value for this packet
-j TOS --set-tos <value>	Sets the TOS value in the IP header

There are two `mangle` table target extensions: MARK and TOS. MARK contains the functionality to set the unsigned long `mark` value for the packet maintained by the `iptables` `mangle` table.

An example of usage follows:

```
iptables -t mangle -A PREROUTING --in-interface eth0 -p tcp \
        -s <some src address> --sport 1024:65535 \
        -d <some destination address> --dport 23 \
        -j MARK --set-mark 0x00010070
```

TOS contains the functionality to set the TOS bits in the IP header. An example of usage follows:

```
iptables -t mangle -A OUTPUT ...   -j TOS --set-tos <tos>
```

The possible `tos` values are the same values available in the `filter` table's TOS match extension module.

Summary

This chapter covered many features available in `iptables`—certainly, the features most commonly used. I've tried to give a general sense of the differences between Netfilter and IPFW, if for no other reason than to give you a "heads up" for the implementation differences that will appear in the following chapters. The modular implementation divisions of three separate major tables—`filter`, `mangle`, and `nat`—were presented. Within each of these major divisions, features were further broken down into modules that provide target extensions and modules that provide match extensions.

Chapter 5, "Building and Installing a Standalone Firewall," goes through a simple, standalone firewall example. Basic antispoofing, denial of service, and other fundamental rules are presented. The purpose of the chapter isn't to present a general firewall for people to cut and paste for practical use, as much as to demonstrate the syntax presented in this chapter in a functional way. The next chapter, Chapter 4, "`nftables`: The Linux Firewall Administration Program," introduces the new Netfilter Tables system that will serve as a replacement for `iptables`. Later chapters cover more specifics such as user-defined chains, firewall optimization, LAN, NAT, and multihomed hosts.

4

`nftables`: The Linux Firewall Administration Program

Chapter 3, "`iptables`: The Legacy Linux Firewall Administration Program," examined `iptables`, the longtime administration program for Linux firewalls. The syntax and many of the options within `iptables` were covered there. This chapter examines the new Netfilter Tables (`nftables`) program. The `nftables` program became available as part of the mainline Linux kernel beginning with version 3.13.

Differences between `iptables` and `nftables`

Within the kernel, `nftables` represents a significant departure from the `iptables` system of filtering. `nftables` replaces the functionality in not only `iptables` but also ip6tables for IPv6, arptables for ARP filtering, and ebtables for Ethernet bridge filtering. The syntax of commands for `nftables` and `iptables` is different, with `nftables` enabling the use of additional scripting capabilities. The administration program for `nftables` is called `nft`, and it's from that command that firewalls are built.

Unlike `iptables`, `nftables` does not include any built-in tables. It's up to the administrator to determine which tables are needed and to add those tables followed by the rules for processing. The remainder of this chapter looks at the syntax of `nftables` and its usage to create a firewall.

Basic `nftables` Syntax

The `nft` command provides the administrative program that is used to build a firewall. The basic syntax of an `nftables` command begins with the `nft` program itself, followed by a command and subcommand and various arguments and expressions. Here's an example:

```
nft <command> <subcommand> <chain> <rule definition>
```

The typical commands are

- `add`
- `list`

- `insert`
- `delete`
- `flush`

Typical subcommands are

- `table`
- `chain`
- `rule`

`nftables` Features

`nftables` includes some higher-level programming language–like capabilities such as the ability to define variables and include external files. `nftables` can also be used for filtering and processing of various address families. These address families include

- **ip**—IPv4 addresses
- **ip6**—IPv6 addresses
- **inet**—Both IPv4 and IPv6 addresses
- **arp**—Address Resolution Protocol (ARP) addresses
- **bridge**—Processing for bridged packets

When not specified, the default address family is IP. The capability to process different families means that `nftables` is intended to replace other filtering mechanisms such as `ebtables` and `arptables`.

The overall processing architecture for `nftables` is to determine the address family to which the rule will apply. `nftables` then uses one or more tables, which contain one or more chains, which in turn contain the processing rules. Processing rules for `nftables` are made up of expressions such as the address, interface, ports, or other data contained in the packet currently being processed and statements such as `drop`, `queue`, and `continue`.

> **Tip**
> Tables contain chains; chains contain rules.

Certain address families contain hooks that enable `nftables` to get access to packets as they traverse the network stack in Linux. This means that you can perform an operation on a packet prior to it being passed for routing or after it's been processed. For the ip, ip6, and inet families the following hooks apply:

- **prerouting**—Packets that have just arrived and haven't yet been routed or processed by other parts of `nftables`.
- **input**—Incoming packets that have been received and sent through the `prerouting` hook.

- **forward**—If the packet will be sent to a different device, it will be available through the forward hook.
- **output**—Packets outbound from processes on the local system.
- **postrouting**—Just prior to leaving the system, the postrouting hook makes the packet available for further processing.

The ARP address family uses only the input and output hooks.

nftables Syntax

The nft command itself has a few options that are available from the command line and not directly related to defining filtering rules. These command-line options include:

- **--debug <level, [level]>**—Add debugging at <level> such as scanner, parser, eval, netlink, mnl, segtree, proto-ctx, or all.
- **-h | --help**—Show basic help.
- **-v | --version**—Show the version number of nft.
- **-n | --numeric**—Display address and port information using numbers rather than performing name resolution.
- **-a | --handle**—Display rule handles.
- **-I | --includepath <directory>**—Add <directory> to the search path for included files.
- **-f | --file <filename>**—Include the contents of <filename>.
- **-i | --interactive**—Read input from the command line.

As previously stated, there are no predefined tables in nftables. As such, it's up to you to define the tables that you want to use in an nftables system. The commands available to define a given rule depend on whether you're working with a table, chain, or rule.

Table Syntax

There are four commands available when working with a table:

- **add**—Add a table.
- **delete**—Delete a table.
- **list**—Display all of the chains and rules for a table.
- **flush**—Clear all chains and rules in a table.

You can list which tables are available with the following command (run as root):

```
nft list tables
```

Remember, there are no default tables for nftables as there were for iptables. Therefore, the list tables command can return nothing if no tables have been defined.

This would be the expected behavior if you just set up `nftables` and haven't yet defined a firewall with it. You can define a table that will hold normal firewall chains and rules like so:

```
nft add table filter
```

Once the firewall table has been added, the `list tables` command will return the table name:

```
table filter
```

Further information about the table can be gleaned with this command:

```
nft list table filter
```

Doing so will show information about the table, including any chains defined in the table:

```
table ip filter{
}
```

As the example shows, the `filter` table uses the IP family and is currently empty.

The table in this example is called `filter`, but it could be named anything, such as `firewall`, instead. However, the common usage and the one shown in the `nftables` documentation and examples is to call this table `filter` as shown here.

When listing rules, adding the `-a` option to show handle numbers is quite helpful. The handle can be used to modify or delete a rule rather easily. This usage will be demonstrated later in this chapter when rules are added to the firewall.

When listing firewall rules, `nftables` will perform address and port resolution. This behavior is modified with the `-n` option. Two `-n` options can be added in order to prevent both address and port resolution, as in the following:

```
nft list table filter -nn
```

Chain Syntax

When operating on a chain, there are six commands available:

- **add**—Add a chain to a table.
- **create**—Create a chain within a table unless a chain with the same name already exists.
- **delete**—Delete a chain.
- **flush**—Clear all rules in a chain.
- **list**—Display all rules in a chain.
- **rename**—Change the name of a chain.

When adding a chain, the hook, discussed previously, can be defined. Additionally, an optional priority can be added to the chain definition.

There are three base chain types that can contain rules and also have the previously described hooks connected to them. The chain type and hook type need to be defined during chain creation and are vital to the chain operation in a normal firewall scenario. If the chain type and hook type aren't defined, packets will not be routed to the chain.

The three base chain types are:

- **filter**—Used for packet filtering
- **route**—Used for packet routing
- **nat**–Used for Network Address Translation (NAT)

Other chains can be added and used to group similar rules. As packets traverse a base chain, processing can be routed toward one or more of the user-defined chains for additional processing.

When adding a chain, the table within which the chain will be defined must be specified. For example, this command adds an input chain to the filter table (defined in the previous section):

```
nft add chain filter input { type filter hook input priority 0 \; }
```

The command states that a chain called input will be added to the table called filter. The type of chain will be a filter base chain and it will be attached to the input hook with a priority of 0. When this command is entered from the command line, a single space followed by a semicolon needs to be added between the braces. When this command is used within a native nft script, the space and backslash can be omitted.

Adding an output chain looks similar, just swapping input for output where appropriate:

```
nft add chain filter output { type filter hook output priority 0 \; }
```

Rule Syntax

Rules are where the action of filtering takes place. There are three commands when working with rules:

- **add**—Add a rule.
- **insert**—Prepend a rule on the chain, either at the beginning or at the location specified.
- **delete**—Delete a rule.

Within rules you specify the matching criteria for a given rule and a verdict or decision on what should happen to a packet matching that rule. nftables and the rules created therein use various statements and expressions to create the definition.

nftables statements are similar to the statements for iptables and usually affect how the packet will be processed, either stopping processing, sending processing to another chain, or simply logging the packet. Statements and verdicts include the following:

- **accept**–Accept the packet and stop processing.
- **continue**—Continue processing the packet.

- **drop**—Stop processing and silently drop the packet.
- **goto**—Send processing to the specified chain but don't return to the calling chain.
- **jump**—Send processing to the specified chain and return to the calling chain when done or when a return statement is executed.
- **limit**—Process the packet according to the rule if the limit of matching received packets has been reached.
- **log**—Log the packet and continue processing.
- **queue**—Stop processing and send the packet to the user-space process.
- **reject**—Stop processing and reject the packet.
- **return**—Send processing back to the calling chain.

nftables expressions can be specific to an address family or type of packet being processed. nftables uses payload expressions and meta expressions. Payload expressions are those that are gathered from packet information. For instance, there are certain header expressions such as sport and dport (source port and destination port, respectively) that apply to TCP and UDP packets and don't make sense at the IPv4 and IPv6 layer since those layers don't use ports. Meta expressions can be used for rules that apply broadly or are tied to common packet or interface properties.

Table 4.1 describes the available meta expressions.

Connection tracking (sometimes called conntrack) expressions work with the metadata from the packet to provide information for further rule processing. Conntrack expressions are included with the keyword ct followed by one of these options:

- daddr
- direction
- expiration
- helper
- l3proto
- mark
- protocol
- proto-src
- proto-dst
- saddr
- state
- status

The state expression is an important one in firewall usage. Normal packet inspection and rule processing are stateless, meaning that the processing knows nothing about the packet previously processed. Each packet is inspected according to its unique

Table 4.1 **Meta Expressions in `nftables`**

Expression	Description
iif	Index of the interface that received the packet
iifname	Name of the interface on which the packet was received
iiftype	Type of interface on which the packet was received
length	Length of the packet in bytes
mark	The packet mark
oif	Index of the interface that will output the packet
oifname	Name of the interface on which the packet will be sent
oiftype	Type of interface on which the packet will be sent
priority	The TC packet priority
protocol	The EtherType protocol
rtclassid	Routing realm for the packet
skgid	Group identifier of the originating socket
skuid	User identifier of the originating socket

characteristics of source and destination addresses, ports, and other criteria. The state expression, listed below, enables information about the packet to be recorded so that the processing rule will have context about the ongoing exchange of related traffic.

- **new**—A new packet arriving at the firewall, a TCP packet with the SYN flag set, for example
- **established**—A packet that's part of a connection that's already being processed or tracked
- **invalid**—A packet that doesn't conform to protocol rules
- **related**—A packet that's related to a connection for a protocol that doesn't use other means to track its state, such as ICMP or passive FTP
- **untracked**—An administrative state used for bypassing connection tracking, typically used in special cases only

In practice, the new, related, and established states are used frequently, and the invalid state is used where appropriate. For example, following is a rule to allow established and related SSH connections. Allowing related connections is important in case the state memory is flushed, thereby negating any established connection states.

```
nft add rule filter input tcp dport 22 ct state established,related accept
```

The section titled "state filter Table Match Extension" in Chapter 3, "iptables: The Legacy Linux Firewall Administration Program," discussed the state mechanism in detail.

Payload expressions are used to build rules that match certain specific criteria and are closely related to the type of packet being processed.

Table 4.2 describes the expressions for IPv4 headers.

Table 4.3 describes the expressions for IPv6 headers.

Table 4.4 describes the expressions for TCP headers.

UDP is generally a simpler protocol, and as such there are fewer expressions for UDP headers, as described in Table 4.5.

Table 4.6 shows the header expressions available for ARP.

Table 4.2 **Payload Expressions for IPv4**

Expression	Description
checksum	Checksum of the IP header
daddr	Destination IP address
frag-off	Fragmentation offset
hdrlength	Length of the IP header, including options
id	IP identifier
length	Total length of the packet
protocol	Protocol in use at the layer above IP
saddr	Source IP address
tos	Type of Service value
ttl	Time to Live value
version	IP header version, which will always be 4 for IPv4 expressions

Table 4.3 **IPv6 Header Expressions**

Expression	Description
daddr	Destination IP address
flowlabel	Flow label
hoplimit	Hop limit
length	Length of the payload
nexthdr	Nexthdr protocol
priority	Priority value
saddr	Source IP address
version	IP header version, which will always be 6 for IPv6 expressions

Table 4.4 **TCP Header Expressions**

Expression	Description
ackseq	Acknowledgment number
checksum	Checksum of the packet
doff	Data offset
dport	Port to which the packet is destined
flags	TCP flags
sequence	Sequence number
sport	Port from which the packet originated
urgptr	Urgent pointer value
window	TCP window value

Table 4.5 **UDP Header Expressions**

Expression	Description
checksum	Checksum of the packet
dport	Port to which the packet is destined
length	Total length of the packet
sport	Port from which the packet originated

Table 4.6 **ARP Header Expressions**

Expression	Description
hlen	Hardware address length
htype	ARP hardware type
op	Operation
plen	Protocol address length
ptype	EtherType

Basic `nftables` Operations

When adding a rule, the table and chain are specified along with the matching criteria. For example, adding a rule to accept SSH connections from a specific host would look like the following. This rule is being added to the previously created input chain of the filter table:

```
nft add filter input tcp dport 22 accept
```

The various statements such as accept, drop, reject, log, and others (listed earlier in this section) were called *extensions* in iptables. Many of the same options and modes of operation that worked for those extensions also now work with `nftables`. For example, to log incoming connections, the `log` statement is used. This statement can be combined with connection tracking such that only new connections to port 22 are logged. Further, a limit can be added so that the logging mechanism isn't overwhelmed.

Logging in `nftables` requires the `nfnetlink_log` or the `xt_LOG` kernel modules or kernel support. Additionally, you need to enable logging by echoing `"ipt_LOG"` to the `nf_log` proc entry:

```
echo "ipt_LOG" > /proc/sys/net/netfilter/nf_log/2
```

The final `nftables` command to log new SSH connections (rate limited) looks like this:

```
nft add filter input tcp dport 22 ct state new limit rate 3/second log
```

The meta expressions, such as those that select the incoming or outgoing interface, are used as further selectors within a rule. For example, to log new connections arriving at the `eth0` interface, the command looks like this:

```
nft add filter input iif eth0 ct state new limit rate 10/minute log
```

Chapter 3 contains syntax rules and options for the various expressions.

`nftables` File Syntax

One of the best features of `nftables` is the capability to read external files containing `nftables` rules. These files enable saved rule sets to be imported and used without needing to create long and complex shell scripts. That said, a shell script is still helpful as the main container for the firewall rule files, importing them at the right time.

Files are imported with the `-f` option to `nftables`. For example, this file creates a basic filtering firewall that logs new SSH packets (rate limited):

```
table filter {
        chain input {
                type filter hook input priority 0;
                tcp dport 22 ct state new limit rate 3/second log prefix "NEW
                ↪packet: "
        }

        chain output {
                type filter hook input priority 0;
        }
}
```

Assuming the file was saved with the name `firewall.nft`, it could be loaded with the following command:

```
nft -f firewall.nft
```

Summary

nftables is similar to iptables insofar as the rules and options typically translate well when building a firewall. nftables utilizes tables, which contain chains, which in turn contain rules. The rules tell nftables what to do with the packet being processed. Like iptables, nftables can accept, drop, reject, log, and perform similar actions on a packet. nftables can also include state-based processing. nftables replaces arptables, iptables, and ebtables.

Because many of the rules and much of the operation of nftables are similar to iptables, you can use Chapter 3 as a reference for those expressions that weren't covered explicitly in this chapter.

5

Building and Installing a Standalone Firewall

Chapter 2, "Packet-Filtering Concepts," covered the background ideas and concepts behind a packet-filtering firewall. Each firewall rule chain has its own default policy. Each rule not only applies to an individual INPUT or OUTPUT chain but also can apply to a specific network interface, message protocol type (such as TCP, UDP, or ICMP), and service port number. Individual acceptance, denial, and rejection rules are defined for the INPUT chain and the OUTPUT chain, as well as for the FORWARD chain, which you'll learn about in Chapter 7, "Packet Forwarding." This chapter pulls together those ideas to demonstrate how to build a simple, single-system firewall for your site.

The firewall that you'll build in this chapter is based on a deny-everything-by-default policy. All network traffic is blocked by default. Services are individually enabled as exceptions to the policy.

After the single-system firewall is built, Chapter 7 and Chapter 8, "NAT—Network Address Translation," demonstrate how to extend the standalone firewall to a dual-homed firewall. A multihomed firewall has at least two network interfaces. It insulates an internal LAN from direct communication with the Internet. It protects your internal LAN by applying packet-filtering rules at the two forwarding interfaces and, with the addition of Network Address Translation (NAT), by acting as a proxying gateway between the LAN and the Internet. NAT is not a proxy service, in the sense that it does not provide an intermediate termination point for the connection. NAT is proxylike in the sense that the local hosts are hidden from the public Internet.

The single-system and dual-homed firewalls are the least secure forms of firewall architectures. If the firewall host were compromised, any local machines would be open to attack. As a standalone firewall, it's an all-or-nothing proposition. A single-homed host is found most often in a demilitarized zone (DMZ) hosting a public Internet service or in a residential setting.

In the case of the single-system home or small-business setting, the assumption is that the majority of users have a single computer or device connected to the Internet or a single firewall machine protecting a small, private LAN. The assumption is that these sites simply don't have the resources to extend the model to an architecture with additional levels of firewalls.

The term *least secure* does not necessarily imply an insecure firewall, however. These firewalls are less secure than more complicated architectures involving multiple machines. Security is a compromise between available resources and diminishing returns on the next dollar spent. Chapter 7 introduces alternative configurations that allow for additional internal security protecting more complicated LAN and server configurations than a single-system firewall can.

The Linux Firewall Administration Programs

This book is based on the 3.14 Linux kernel series. Most current distributions of Linux come supplied with the Netfilter firewall mechanism introduced in Chapter 3, "iptables: The Legacy Linux Firewall Administration Program." This mechanism is usually referred to as iptables, its administration program's name. Older Linux distributions used the earlier IPFW mechanism. That firewall mechanism is usually referred to as ipfwadm or ipchains, the earlier version's administration program names. As distributions are updated to kernels later than 3.13, the new Netfilter firewall mechanism, nftables or nft (as its administration program is called) will likely be included.

As a firewall administration program, iptables creates the individual packet-filtering rules for the INPUT and OUTPUT chains composing the firewall. nftables does not create default tables, chains, or rules, so tables to filter packets containing chains that are connected to the INPUT and OUTPUT hooks must be created manually.

One of the most important aspects of defining firewall rules is the order in which the rules are defined. Generally, packet-filtering rules are stored in a kernel filter table or tables, within INPUT, OUTPUT, or FORWARD chains, in the order in which they are defined. Individual rules are inserted at the beginning of the chain or are appended to the end of the chain. All rules are appended in the examples in this chapter (with one exception at the end of the chapter). The order in which you define the rules is the order in which they'll be added to the kernel tables and, thereby, the order in which the rules will be compared against each packet.

As each externally originating packet arrives at the network interface, its header fields are compared against each rule in the interface's INPUT chain until a match is found. Conversely, as each locally generated packet is sent out, its header fields are compared against each rule in the interface's OUTPUT chain until a match is found. In either direction, when a match is found, the comparison stops and the rule's packet disposition is applied: ACCEPT, DROP, or, optionally, REJECT. If the packet doesn't match any rule on the chain, the default policy for that chain is applied. The bottom line is that the first matching rule wins.

The numeric service port numbers, rather than their symbolic names, as listed in /etc/services, are used in all the filter examples in this chapter. iptables and nftables support the symbolic service port names. The examples in this chapter use the numeric values because the symbolic names are not consistent across Linux distributions—or even from one release to the next. You could use the symbolic names for clarity in your own rules, but remember that your firewall could break with the next system upgrade. I've found it much more reliable to use the port numbers themselves. The last thing you want in a firewall is ambiguity, which is just what is introduced by using names instead of numbers for ports.

Most Linux distributions implement `iptables` as a set of loadable program modules. Most or all of the modules are dynamically and automatically loaded on first use. If you choose to build your own kernel, which I nearly always do, and which you'll need to do if your distribution doesn't yet have `nftables` support, you'll need to compile in support for Netfilter, either as modules or directly into the kernel.

When working with `iptables`, the `iptables` command must be invoked once for each individual firewall rule you define. This is initially done from a shell script. This chapter will create and use a script called `rc.firewall` for a firewall. The location in which this script should be placed is dependent on the flavor of Linux where the script will be used. On most systems, including Red Hat/CentOS/Fedora and Debian, the correct location would be within `/etc/init.d/`. In cases in which shell semantics differ, the examples are written in Bourne (`sh`) or Bourne Again (`bash`) shell semantics.

The `iptables` shell script sets a number of variables. Chief among these is the location of the `iptables` command itself. It's important to set this in a variable so that it is explicitly located. There's no excuse for ambiguity with a firewall script. The variable used to represent the `iptables` command in this chapter is `$IPT`. If you see `$IPT`, it is a substitute for the `iptables` command. You could just as easily execute the commands from the shell by typing `iptables` instead of `$IPT`. However, for use in a script (which is the intention in this chapter), setting this variable is a good idea.

The script should begin with the "shebang" line invoking the shell as the interpreter for the script. In other words, put this as the first line of the script:

```
#!/bin/sh
```

The examples are not optimized. They are spelled out for clarity. Firewall optimization and user-defined chains are discussed separately in Chapter 6, "Firewall Optimization."

The `nftables` firewall script begins as a shell script but also includes various direct `nftables` rules as separate and included files. These files will be called out when used later in this chapter.

The remainder of the chapter looks at building a firewall and shows examples of both `iptables` and `nftables` usage for each item.

Build versus Buy: The Linux Kernel

There is great debate over whether it is advisable to compile a custom kernel or stick with the "stock" kernel that comes with a given Linux distribution. The debate also includes whether it is inherently better to compile a monolithic kernel (in which everything is compiled into the kernel) or use a modular kernel. As with any debate, there are pros and cons to each method. On the one hand there are those who always (or almost always) build their own kernel, sometimes called "rolling their own." On the other hand, there are those who rarely or never roll their own kernel. There are those who always build monolithic kernels and others who use modular kernels.

Building a custom kernel has a few advantages. First is the capability to compile in only the exact drivers and options necessary for the computer to run. This is great for a server such as a firewall because the hardware rarely, if ever, changes. Another advantage to compiling a custom kernel, if you choose a monolithic kernel, is the capability to completely prevent some types of attacks against the computer. Although attacks against monolithic kernels are possible, they are less common than attacks against modular kernels. Further, when you roll your own kernel, you're not confined to the kernel version used by the distribution. This enables you to use the latest and greatest kernel, which may include bug fixes for your hardware. Finally, with a custom kernel you can apply additional security enhancements to the kernel itself.

Building a custom kernel is not without its own set of pitfalls. After you roll your own kernel, you can no longer use the distribution's kernel updates. Actually, you can revert to the distribution's kernel and use the updates, but it's likely that the distribution uses an earlier version of the kernel that may reintroduce bugs that were fixed in your custom version. Using a stock kernel also makes it easier to obtain support from the vendor for kernel issues.

As alluded to earlier, I nearly always roll my own kernel for production server machines. The situations in which direct support is an absolute requirement are the only exceptions. These are few and far between. I believe the capability to customize the kernel to the computer and add greater security through additional patches far outweighs the need to use official kernel updates from the distribution.

Source and Destination Addressing Options

A packet's source address and destination address can both be specified in a firewall rule. Only packets with that specific source and/or destination address match the rule. Addresses may be a specific IP address, a fully qualified hostname, a network (domain) name or address, a limited range of addresses, or all-inclusive.

IP Addresses Expressed as Symbolic Names

Remote hosts and networks may be specified as fully qualified hostnames or network names. Using a hostname is especially convenient for firewall rules that apply to an individual remote host. This is particularly true for hosts whose IP address can change or that invisibly represent multiple IP addresses, as ISP mail servers sometimes do. In general, however, remote addresses are better expressed in dotted quad notation because of the possibility of DNS hostname spoofing.

Symbolic hostnames can't be resolved until DNS traffic is enabled in the firewall rules. If hostnames are used in the firewall rules, those rules must follow the rules enabling DNS traffic, unless /etc/hosts contains entries for the hostnames.

Furthermore, some distributions use a boot environment that installs the firewall rules before starting the network or any other services, including BIND. If symbolic host and network names are used in the firewall script, those names must have entries in /etc/hosts to be resolved.

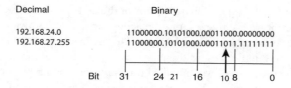

Figure 5.1   The matching first 22 bits in the masked IP address
range `192.168.24.0/22`

Both `iptables` and `nftables` allow addresses to be suffixed with a bit mask specifier.
The mask's value can range from 0 through 32, indicating the number of bits to mask. As
discussed in Chapter 1, "Preliminary Concepts Underlying Packet-Filtering Firewalls," bits
are counted from the left, or most significant, bit. This mask specifier indicates how many
of the leading bits in the address must exactly match the IP address specified.

A mask of 32, /32, means that all the bits must match. The address must exactly match
what you've defined in the rule. Specifying an address as `192.168.10.30` is the same as
specifying the address as `192.168.10.30/32`. The /32 mask is implied by default; you
don't need to specify it.

An example using masking is to allow connections to a particular service to be made
only between your machine and your ISP's server machines. Let's say that your ISP uses
addresses in the range of `192.168.24.0` through `192.168.27.255` for its server address
space. In this case, the address/mask pair would be `192.168.24/22`. As shown in Figure 5.1, the first 22 bits of all addresses in this range are identical, so any address matching
on the first 22 bits will match. Effectively, you are saying that you will allow connections
to the service only when offered from machines in the address range `192.168.24.0`
through `192.168.27.255`.

A mask of 0, /0, means that no bits in the address are required to match. In other
words, because no bits need to match, using /0 is the same as not specifying an address.
Any unicast address matches. `iptables` has a built-in alias for `0.0.0.0/0`, `any/0`. Note
that `any/0`, whether implied or stated, does not include broadcast addresses.

Initializing the Firewall

A firewall is implemented as a series of packet-filtering rules defined by options given on
the `iptables` or `nftables` command line.

The rule invocations should be made from an executable shell script, not directly from
the command line. You should invoke the complete firewall shell script. Do not attempt
to invoke specific rules from the command line because this could cause your firewall to
accept or drop packets inappropriately. When the chains are initialized and the default
drop policy is enabled, all network services are blocked until acceptance filters are defined
to allow the individual service.

Ideally, you should execute the shell script from the console. Only the brave execute the firewall shell script from either a remote machine or an X Window `xterm` session. Not only is remote network traffic blocked, but access to the local loopback interface used by X Windows is blocked until access to the interface is explicitly reenabled. Ideally, X Windows should not be running or even installed on a firewall. It is a typical example of software that is not necessary and has been used as a means to exploit servers in the past.

As someone who manages Linux computers that are geographically hundreds to thousands of miles away, I can activate a firewall script only from a remote location. In these instances, it's advisable to do two things. First, change the default policy to `ACCEPT` for the first or first few executions of the firewall script. Do this to debug the syntax of the script itself, not the rules. After the script is syntactically correct, change that policy back to `DROP`.

A second and just as important tip for working with firewall scripts from remote locations is to create a cron job to stop the firewall at some point in the near future. Doing so will effectively allow you to enable the firewall and perform some testing but will also enable you to get back into the computer if you lock yourself out through misplaced (or missing) rules. For example, when debugging a firewall script, I'll create a cron entry to disable the firewall every 2 minutes. I can then safely run the firewall script and find out whether I've locked out my SSH session. If indeed I have locked myself out, I merely wait a few minutes for the firewall script to run and shut the firewall down, giving me the opportunity to fix the script and try again.

Furthermore, remember that firewall filters are applied in the order in which you've defined them. The rules are appended to the end of their chain in the order in which you define them. The first matching rule wins. Because of this, firewall rules must be defined in the proper order from most specific to more general rules.

Firewall initialization is used to cover a lot of ground, including defining global constants used in the shell script, enabling kernel support services (when necessary), clearing out any existing rules in the firewall chains, defining default policies for the `INPUT` and `OUTPUT` chains, reenabling the loopback interface for normal system operation, denying access from any specific hosts or networks you've decided to block, and defining some basic rules to protect against bad addresses and to protect certain services running on unprivileged ports.

Symbolic Constants Used in the Firewall Examples

A firewall shell script is easiest to read and maintain if symbolic constants are used for recurring names and addresses. The following constants either are used throughout the examples in this chapter or are universal constants defined in the networking standards. This example also includes the "shebang" interpreter line from above as a friendly reminder:

```
#!/bin/sh
INTERNET="eth0"                    # Internet-connected interface
LOOPBACK_INTERFACE="lo"            # However your system names it
IPADDR="my.ip.address"             # Your IP address
```

```
MY_ISP="my.isp.address.range"        # ISP server & NOC address range
SUBNET_BASE="my.subnet.network"      # Your subnet's network address
SUBNET_BROADCAST="my.subnet.bcast"   # Your subnet's broadcast address
LOOPBACK="127.0.0.0/8"               # Reserved loopback address range
CLASS_A="10.0.0.0/8"                 # Class A private networks
CLASS_B="172.16.0.0/12"              # Class B private networks
CLASS_C="192.168.0.0/16"             # Class C private networks
CLASS_D_MULTICAST="224.0.0.0/4"      # Class D multicast addresses
CLASS_E_RESERVED_NET="240.0.0.0/5"   # Class E reserved addresses
BROADCAST_SRC="0.0.0.0"              # Broadcast source address
BROADCAST_DEST="255.255.255.255"     # Broadcast destination address
PRIVPORTS="0:1023"                   # Well-known, privileged port range
UNPRIVPORTS="1024:65535"             # Unprivileged port range
```

nftables and iptables define port ranges differently. Therefore, the port range variables need to be defined differently for each. For an iptables firewall, the following declaration works:

```
PRIVPORTS="0:1023"                   # Well-known, privileged port range
UNPRIVPORTS="1024:65535"             # Unprivileged port range
```

However, for nftables, the colon needs to be changed to a dash, as shown here:

```
PRIVPORTS="0-1023"                   # Well-known, privileged port range
UNPRIVPORTS="1024-65535"             # Unprivileged port range
```

Constants not listed here are defined in the context of the specific rules they are used with. One additional constant is needed for iptables or nftables. If you'll be using iptables, define the following:

```
IPT="/sbin/iptables"                 # Location of iptables on your system
```

If you'll be using nftables, define the following:

```
NFT="/usr/local/sbin/nft"              # Location of nft on your system
```

Enabling Kernel-Monitoring Support

Operating system support for various types of packet checking often overlaps with what the firewall can test for. When in doubt, aim for redundancy or defense in depth.

From the commands shown in the following lines, icmp_echo_ignore_broadcasts instructs the kernel to drop ICMP echo-request messages directed to broadcast or multicast addresses. (Another facility, icmp_echo_ignore_all, drops any incoming echo-request message. It should be noted that ISPs often rely on ping to help diagnose local network problems, and DHCP sometimes relies on echo-request to avoid address collision.)

```
# Enable broadcast echo Protection
echo "1" > /proc/sys/net/ipv4/icmp_echo_ignore_broadcasts
```

Source routing is rarely used legitimately today. Firewalls commonly drop all source-routed packets. This command disables source-routed packets:

```
# Disable Source Routed Packets
echo "0" > /proc/sys/net/ipv4/conf/all/accept_source_route
```

TCP SYN cookies are a mechanism to attempt speedier detection of and recovery from SYN floods. This command enables SYN cookies:

```
# Enable TCP SYN Cookie Protection
echo 1 > /proc/sys/net/ipv4/tcp_syncookies
```

ICMP redirect messages are sent to hosts by their adjacent routers. Their purpose is to inform the host that a shorter path is available. That is, the host and both routers are on the same network, and the new router is the router to which the original would send the packet as its next hop.

Routers generate redirect messages for hosts; hosts do not. Hosts are required to honor redirects and add the new gateway to their route cache, except in the cases indicated in RFC 1122, "Requirements for Internet Hosts—Communication Layers," Section 3.2.2.2: "A Redirect message SHOULD be silently discarded if the new gateway address it specifies is not on the same connected (sub-) net through which the Redirect arrived [INTRO:2, Appendix A], or if the source of the Redirect is not the current first-hop gateway for the specified destination (see Section 3.3.1)." These commands disable redirects:

```
# Disable ICMP Redirect Acceptance
echo "0" > /proc/sys/net/ipv4/conf/all/accept_redirects
# Don't send Redirect Messages
echo "0" > /proc/sys/net/ipv4/conf/all/send_redirects
```

rp_filter attempts to implement source address validation as described in RFC 1812, "Requirements for IP Version 4 Routers," Section 5.3.8. In short, packets are silently dropped if their source address is such that the host's forwarding table would not route a packet with that destination address out the same interface on which the packet was received. According to RFC 1812, if implemented, routers should enable this feature by default. This form of address validation is often not enabled on routers, so these commands disable it:

```
# Drop Spoofed Packets coming in on an interface, which, if replied to,
# would result in the reply going out a different interface.
for f in /proc/sys/net/ipv4/conf/*/rp_filter; do
    echo "1" > $f
done
```

log_martians logs packets received with impossible addresses, as defined in RFC 1812, Section 5.3.7. Impossible source addresses include multicast or broadcast addresses, addresses in the 0 and 127 networks, and the Class E reserved space. Impossible destination addresses include address 0.0.0.0, host 0 on any network, any host on the 127 network, and Class E addresses.

Currently, the Linux network code checks for the previously mentioned addresses. It does not check for private class addresses (nor could it do so without knowledge of the network a given interface was connected to). log_martians does not affect packet validity checking; it merely affects logging, which is set here:

```
# Log packets with impossible addresses.
echo "1" > /proc/sys/net/ipv4/conf/all/log_martians
```

Removing Any Preexisting Rules

The first thing to do when defining a set of filtering rules is to remove any existing rules from their chains. Otherwise, any new rules that you define will be added to the end of existing rules. Packets could easily match a preexisting rule before reaching the point in the chain that you are defining.

Removal is called *flushing* the chain.

For `iptables` the following command flushes all rules from all chains at once:

```
# Remove any existing rules from all chains
$IPT --flush
```

Specific tables can then be flushed using the `-t <table>` option:

```
$IPT -t nat --flush
$IPT -t mangle --flush
```

For `nftables`, the table name needs to be specified, and doing so will flush the rules from all chains within the table:

```
nft flush table <tablename>
```

If you're using the community-standard naming convention, you'll have a `filter` table and possibly a `nat` table which can be flushed with the following commands:

```
nft flush table filter
nft flush table nat
```

Other user-defined tables need to be flushed as needed by your specific firewall implementation. For `nftables`, this loop can be used to flush all chains in all tables:

```
for i in '$NFT list tables | awk '{print $2}''
do
        echo "Flushing ${i}"
        $NFT flush table ${i}
done
```

A better method is to delete not only the rules but also the chains and then the tables themselves. This is accomplished with two `for` loops through the `nftables` shell script:

```
for i in '$NFT list tables | awk '{print $2}''
do
        echo "Flushing ${i}"
        $NFT flush table ${i}
        for j in '$NFT list table ${i} | grep chain | awk '{print $2}''
        do
                echo "...Deleting chain ${j} from table ${i}"
                $NFT delete chain ${i} ${j}
        done
        echo "Deleting ${i}"
        $NFT delete table ${i}
done
```

Flushing the chains does not affect the default policy state currently in effect.

For `iptables`, the next step would be to delete any user-defined chains. They can be deleted with the following commands:

```
$IPT -X
$IPT -t nat -X
$IPT -t mangle -X
```

With `nftables`, all tables and chains are user defined, so the same syntax doesn't really apply. In either case, flushing the chains does not affect the default policy state currently in effect.

At this point, you have a basic script that defines some variables and clears out tables and chains, if any have been defined.

Resetting Default Policies and Stopping the Firewall

So far, the firewall has set some defaults that can be used regardless of the state of the Netfilter firewall. Before setting the default policies to DROP, I'll first reset the default policies to ACCEPT. This is useful for stopping the firewall completely, as you'll see shortly. These lines set the default policy:

```
# Reset the default policy
$IPT --policy INPUT    ACCEPT
$IPT --policy OUTPUT   ACCEPT
$IPT --policy FORWARD ACCEPT
$IPT -t nat --policy PREROUTING  ACCEPT
$IPT -t nat --policy OUTPUT ACCEPT
$IPT -t nat --policy POSTROUTING ACCEPT
$IPT -t mangle --policy PREROUTING ACCEPT
$IPT -t mangle --policy OUTPUT ACCEPT
```

With `nftables` there is no default policy for a chain in the same sense that there is for `iptables`, and the chains and tables have already been deleted. The effect of this is to set the policy to ACCEPT since there's no firewall running. Therefore, there's nothing to be done for `nftables` here.

Here's a final addition to what I deem to be the beginning of the firewall script, namely, the code to enable the firewall to be stopped easily. With this code placed below the previous code, when you call the script with an argument of `"stop"`, the script will flush, clear, and reset the default policies and the firewall will effectively stop:

```
if ["$1" = "stop" ]
then
echo "Firewall completely stopped!  WARNING: THIS HOST HAS NO FIREWALL RUNNING."
exit 0
fi
```

Prior to further configuration of `nftables`, the base tables need to be re-created. This can be accomplished using an `nftables` rules file which I'll call `setup-tables`. The contents of the `setup-tables` rules file are:

```
table filter {
        chain input {
                type filter hook input priority 0;
        }
```

```
        chain output {
                type filter hook output priority 0;
        }
}
```

This file is then loaded with the following command. This command should be added to the firewall script after the conditional to stop the firewall:

```
$NFT -f setup-tables
```

Enabling the Loopback Interface

You need to enable unrestricted loopback traffic. This enables you to run any local network-based services that you choose—or that the system depends on—without having to worry about getting all the firewall rules specified.

Local services rely on the loopback network interface. After the system boots, the system's default policy is to accept all packets. Flushing any preexisting chains has no effect. However, if the firewall is being reinitialized and had previously used a deny-by-default policy, the drop policy would still be in effect. Without any acceptance firewall rules, the loopback interface would still be inaccessible.

Because the loopback interface is a local, internal interface, the firewall can allow loopback traffic immediately. Here are the commands for the `iptables` script:

```
# Unlimited traffic on the loopback interface
$IPT -A INPUT  -i lo -j ACCEPT
$IPT -A OUTPUT -o lo -j ACCEPT
```

For `nftables`, the commands look like those shown after this text. The commands can be added to the main `rc.firewall` script that you're creating or can be added to a `localhost-policy` rules file. Adding the rules to a separate `localhost-policy` file looks like the following. The file assumes that the rules contained in the `setup-tables` file (shown earlier) have already been added to the firewall. If the `setup-tables` rules file hasn't been added, no processing will be done.

The `localhost-policy` file contains the following:

```
table filter {
        chain input {
                iifname lo accept
}
        chain output {
                oifname lo accept
}
```

This file is then loaded by adding the following command to `rc.firewall`:

```
$NFT -f localhost-policy
```

Alternatively, if you'll be adding it to the `rc.firewall` script, the following two lines will do the job:

```
$NFT add rule filter input iifname lo accept
$NFT add rule filter output oifname lo accept
```

Defining the Default Policy

By default, you want the firewall to drop everything. The two available options for the built-in chains in `iptables` are `ACCEPT` and `DROP`. `REJECT` is not a legal policy in `iptables` for a chain but can be used as a target, as you've seen before. User-defined chains and `nftables` chains cannot be assigned default policies.

Using a default policy of `DROP`, unless a rule is defined to either explicitly allow or reject a matching packet, packets are silently dropped. What you more likely want is to silently drop unwanted incoming packets, but to reject outgoing packets and return an ICMP error message to the local sender. The difference for the end user is that, for example, if someone at a remote site attempts to connect to your web server, that person's browser hangs until his or her system returns a TCP timeout condition. There is no indication whether your site or your web server exists. On the other hand, if you attempt to connect to a remote web server, your browser receives an immediate error condition indicating that the operation isn't allowed:

```
# Set the default policy to drop
$IPT --policy INPUT   DROP
$IPT --policy OUTPUT  DROP
$IPT --policy FORWARD DROP
```

As stated earlier, there are no default policies for a chain in `nftables`. A default can be set at the end of the given chain for `nftables`.

It's important to note that at this point, all network traffic other than local loopback traffic is blocked. If you're working on this firewall over the network, your connection will no longer be active and you may lock yourself out of the computer on which the firewall is being built.

Default Policy Rules and the First Matching Rule Wins

Within `iptables`, the default policies appear to be exceptions to the first-matching-rule-wins scenario. The default policy commands are not position dependent. They aren't rules, per se. A chain's default policy is applied after a packet has been compared to each rule on the chain without a match. This is notably different for `nftables` where the first matching rule always wins and there is no default policy.

For `iptables` the default policies are defined first in the script to define the default packet disposition before any rules to the contrary are defined. If the policy commands were executed at the end of the script, and if the firewall script contained a syntax error causing it to exit prematurely, the default accept-everything policy could be in effect. If a packet didn't match a rule (and rules are usually accept rules in a deny-everything-by-default firewall), the packet would fall off the end of the chain and be accepted by default. The firewall rules would not be accomplishing anything useful.

For `nftables` a drop rule for incoming traffic can be added to the end of the chain and a reject rule can be added to the end of the `OUTPUT` filter chain. This will have the same overall effect as the `iptables` default policies. But it's important to note that these rules should be added at the end of the firewall script and only after other rules to allow traffic have been created above them. Otherwise all traffic will be dropped or rejected from the computer where the firewall is running, including possibly your SSH session for configuring the firewall!

Using Connection State to Bypass Rule Checking

Specifying the state match for previously initiated and accepted exchanges enables you to bypass the firewall tests for the ongoing exchange. The initial client request remains controlled by the service's specific filters, however.

Notice that both the INPUT and the OUTPUT filters are necessary to bypass the rules in both directions. A connection isn't treated as a two-way exchange by the state module, and a symmetric dynamic rule is not generated.

Because the state module can require more RAM than older Linux firewall machines have, the iptables examples developed in this chapter typically provide the rules for both alternatives, with and without the state module. The nftables rules assume the use of the connection state module since nftables would typically run from newer computers.

Including Both Static and Dynamic `iptables` Rules

Resource limits in terms of scalability and state table timeouts can require that both the static and the dynamic rules be used. The top limit is a selling point with large commercial firewalls.

The scalability issue comes up in large firewalls designed to handle 50,000–100,000 simultaneous connections—that's a lot of state. System resources run out at some point, and connection tracking can't be done. Either the new connection has to be dropped or the software has to fall back to stateless mode.

There's also the issue of timeouts. Connection state isn't kept forever. Slow and quiescent connections can have their state information easily cleaned out to make room for other, more active connections. When a packet comes along later, the state information has to be rebuilt. In the meantime, the packet flow has to fall back to stateless mode while the transport stack looks up the connection information and informs the state module that the packet is indeed part of an established exchange:

```
$IPT -A INPUT  -m state --state ESTABLISHED,RELATED -j ACCEPT
    $IPT -A OUTPUT -m state --state ESTABLISHED,RELATED -j ACCEPT
    # Using the state module alone, INVALID will break protocols that use
    # bi-directional connections or multiple connections or exchanges,
    # unless an ALG is provided for the protocol.

    $IPT -A INPUT -m state --state INVALID -j LOG \
            --log-prefix "INVALID input: "
    $IPT -A INPUT -m state --state INVALID -j DROP

    $IPT -A OUTPUT -m state --state INVALID -j LOG \
            --log-prefix "INVALID output: "
    $IPT -A OUTPUT -m state --state INVALID -j DROP
```

For nftables, the following rules are added to the firewall script:

```
$NFT add rule filter input ct state established,related accept
$NFT add rule filter input ct state invalid log prefix \"INVALID input: \" limit
➥rate 3/second drop
$NFT add rule filter output ct state established,related accept
$NFT add rule filter output ct state invalid log prefix \"INVALID output: \"
➥limit rate 3/second drop
```

Source Address Spoofing and Other Bad Addresses

This section establishes some INPUT chain filters based on source and destination addresses. These addresses will never be seen in a legitimate incoming packet from the Internet.

At the packet-filtering level, one of the few cases of source address spoofing that you can identify with certainty as a forgery is your own IP address. This rule drops incoming packets claiming to be from you:

```
# Refuse spoofed packets pretending to be from
# the external interface's IP address
$IPT -A INPUT  -i $INTERNET -s $IPADDR -j DROP
```

The rule is similar for nftables because it takes advantage of the variables defined within the shell script rather than through native nftables rules:

```
$NFT add rule filter input iif $INTERNET ip saddr $IPADDR
```

There is no need to block outgoing packets destined to yourself. They won't return, claiming to be from you and appearing to be spoofed. Remember, if you send packets to your own external interface, those packets arrive on the loopback interface's input queue, not on the external interface's input queue. Packets containing your address as the source address never arrive on the external interface, even if you send packets to the external interface.

Firewall Logging

The -j LOG target enables logging for packets matching the rule. When a packet matches the rule, the event is logged in /var/log/messages, or wherever you've defined messages of the specified priority to be logged.

As explained in Chapter 1 and Chapter 2, private IP addresses are set aside in each of the Class A, B, and C address ranges for use in private LANs. They are not intended for use on the Internet. Routers are not supposed to route packets with private source addresses. Nevertheless, some routers do forward packets containing private source addresses in error.

Additionally, if someone on your ISP's subnet (that is, on your side of the router that you share) is leaking packets with private IP addresses, you'll see them even if the router doesn't forward them. Machines on your own LAN could also leak private addresses if your NAT or proxy configuration is set up incorrectly.

The next three sets of rules disallow incoming packets containing source addresses from any of the Class A, B, or C private network addresses. None of these packets should be seen on a public network:

```
# Refuse packets claiming to be from a Class A private network
$IPT -A INPUT  -i $INTERNET -s $CLASS_A -j DROP
```

```
# Refuse packets claiming to be from a Class B private network
$IPT -A INPUT  -i $INTERNET -s $CLASS_B -j DROP

# Refuse packets claiming to be from a Class C private network
$IPT -A INPUT  -i $INTERNET -s $CLASS_C -j DROP
```

The next rule disallows packets with a source address in the loopback network:

```
# Refuse packets claiming to be from the loopback interface
$IPT -A INPUT  -i $INTERNET -s $LOOPBACK -j DROP
```

The nft equivalent looks similar:

```
$NFT add rule filter input iif $INTERNET ip saddr $CLASS_A drop
$NFT add rule filter input iif $INTERNET ip saddr $CLASS_B drop
$NFT add rule filter input iif $INTERNET ip saddr $CLASS_C drop
$NFT add rule filter input iif $INTERNET ip saddr $LOOPBACK drop
```

Because loopback addresses are assigned to an internal, local software interface, any packet claiming to be from such an address is intentionally forged.

As with addresses set aside for use in private LANs, routers are not supposed to forward packets originating from the loopback address range. A router cannot forward a packet with a loopback destination address.

The next two rules primarily serve to log matching packets. The firewall's default policy is to deny everything. As such, broadcast addresses are dropped by default and must be explicitly enabled if they are wanted:

```
# Refuse malformed broadcast packets
$IPT -A INPUT  -i $INTERNET -s $BROADCAST_DEST -j LOG
$IPT -A INPUT  -i $INTERNET -s $BROADCAST_DEST -j DROP

$IPT -A INPUT  -i $INTERNET -d $BROADCAST_SRC  -j LOG
$IPT -A INPUT  -i $INTERNET -d $BROADCAST_SRC  -j DROP
```

The first pair of rules logs and denies any packet claiming to come from 255.255.255.255, the address reserved as the broadcast destination address. A packet will never legitimately originate from address 255.255.255.255.

The second pair of rules logs and denies any packet directed to destination address 0.0.0.0, the address reserved as a broadcast source address. Such a packet is not a mistake; it is a specific probe intended to identify a UNIX machine running network software derived from BSD. Because most UNIX operating system network code is derived from BSD, this probe is effectively intended to identify machines running UNIX.

The nftables equivalent looks similar; note how both the logging and drop statements appear in the same rule with nftables:

```
$NFT add rule filter input iif $INTERNET ip saddr $BROADCAST_DEST log limit
➥rate 3/second drop
$NFT add rule filter input iif $INTERNET ip saddr $BROADCAST_SRC log limit
➥rate 3/second drop
```

Clarification of the Meaning of IP Address 0.0.0.0

Address 0.0.0.0 is reserved for use as a broadcast source address. The Netfilter convention of specifying a match on any address, any /0, 0.0.0.0/0, or 0.0.0.0/0.0.0.0, doesn't match the broadcast source address. The reason is that a broadcast packet has a bit set in the Layer 2 frame header indicating that it's a broadcast packet destined for all interfaces on the network, rather than a point-to-point, unicast packet destined for a particular destination. Broadcast packets are handled differently from nonbroadcast packets. There is no legitimate nonbroadcast IP address 0.0.0.0.

The next two rules block two forms of directed broadcasts:

```
# Refuse directed broadcasts
# Used to map networks and in Denial of Service attacks
$IPT -A INPUT -i $INTERNET -d $SUBNET_BASE -j DROP
$IPT -A INPUT -i $INTERNET -d $SUBNET_BROADCAST -j DROP
```

The nftables rules look like this:

```
$NFT add rule filter input iif $INTERNET ip daddr $SUBNET_BASE drop
$NFT add rule filter input iif $INTERNET ip daddr $SUBNET_BROADCAST drop
```

With the deny-by-default policy and the firewall rules explicitly accepting packets based in part by matching on destination address, neither of these directed broadcast messages will be accepted by the firewall. These rules become more critical in larger setups in which the LAN uses real-world addresses.

With the use of variable-length network prefixes, a site's network and host fields may or may not fall on a byte boundary. For the sake of simplicity, the SUBNET_BASE is your network address, such as 192.168.1.0. The SUBNET_BROADCAST is your network's broadcast address, as in 192.168.1.255.

Just as with directed broadcast messages, limited broadcasts, confined to your local network segment, are likewise not accepted with the deny-by-default policy and the firewall rules explicitly accepting packets based in part by matching on destination address. Again, the following rule becomes more critical in larger setups in which the LAN uses real-world addresses:

```
# Refuse limited broadcasts
$IPT -A INPUT -i $INTERNET -d $BROADCAST_DEST -j DROP
```

The nftables rule looks like this:

```
$NFT add rule filter input iif $INTERNET ip daddr $BROADCAST_DEST drop
```

It should be noted that an exception must be made in later chapters for DHCP clients. Broadcast source and destination addresses are used between the DHCP client and server ports initially.

Multicast addresses are legal only as destination addresses. The next rule drops spoofed multicast network packets:

```
# Refuse Class D multicast addresses
# Illegal as a source address
$IPT -A INPUT -i $INTERNET -s $CLASS_D_MULTICAST -j DROP
```

Here's the `nftables` rule for the same:

```
$NFT add rule filter input iif $INTERNET ip saddr $CLASS_D_MULTICAST drop
```

Legitimate multicast packets are always UDP packets. As such, multicast messages are sent point-to-point, just as any other UDP message is. The difference between unicast and multicast packets is the class of destination address used (and the protocol flag carried in the Ethernet header). The next rule denies multicast packets carrying a non-UDP protocol:

```
$IPT -A INPUT -i $INTERNET ! -p udp -d $CLASS_D_MULTICAST -j DROP
```

The `nftables` version of this command looks like this:

```
$NFT add rule filter input iif $INTERNET ip daddr $CLASS_D_MULTICAST ip protocol
➡!= udp drop
```

Multicast functionality is a configurable option when you compile the kernel, and your network interface card can be initialized to recognize multicast addresses. The functionality is enabled by default in the default kernel from many newer distributions of Linux. You might want to enable these addresses if you subscribe to a network conferencing service that provides multicast audio and video broadcasts. (Multicast is also sometimes used on the local network for global resource discovery, such as with DHCP or routing.)

You won't generally see multicast destination addresses unless you've registered yourself as a recipient. Multicast packets are sent to multiple, but specific, targets by prior arrangement. I have seen multicast packets sent out from machines on my ISP's local subnet, however. The default policy drops multicast packets, even if you have registered as a recipient. You have to define a rule to accept the multicast address. The next rule allows incoming multicast packets for the sake of completeness:

```
$IPT -A INPUT  -i $INTERNET -p udp -d $CLASS_D_MULTICAST -j ACCEPT
```

And here's the `nftables` version:

```
$NFT add rule filter input iif $INTERNET ip daddr $CLASS_D_MULTICAST ip protocol
➡udp accept
```

Multicast registration and routing is a complicated process managed by its own IP layer control protocol, the Internet Group Management Protocol (IGMP, protocol 2). For more information on multicast communication, refer to the "Multicast over TCP/IP HOWTO" at http://www.tldp.org/HOWTO/Multicast-HOWTO.html. Additional resources include RFC 1458, "Requirements for Multicast Protocols"; RFC 1112, "Host Extensions for IP Multicasting" (updated by RFC 2236, "Internet Group Management Protocol Version 2"); and RFC 2588, "IP Multicast and Firewalls."

Class D IP addresses range from 224.0.0.0 to 239.255.255.255. The CLASS_D_ MULTICAST constant, 224.0.0.0/4, is defined to match on the first 4 bits of the address.

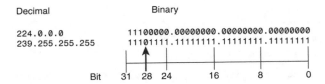

Figure 5.2   The matching first 4 bits in the masked Class D multicast
address range

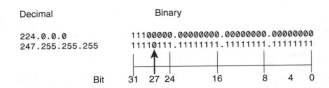

Figure 5.3   The matching first 5 bits in the masked Class E reserved
address range `240.0.0.0/5`

As shown in Figure 5.2, in binary, the decimal values 224 (`11100000B`) to
239 (`11101111B`) are identical through the first 4 bits (`1110B`).

The next rule in this section drops packets claiming to be from a Class E reserved
network:

```
# Refuse Class E reserved IP addresses
$IPT -A INPUT  -i $INTERNET -s $CLASS_E_RESERVED_NET -j DROP
```

The `nftables` equivalent is

```
$NFT add rule filter input iif $INTERNET ip saddr $CLASS_E_RESERVED_NET drop
```

Class E IP addresses range from `240.0.0.0` to `247.255.255.255`. The
`CLASS_E_RESERVED_NET` constant, `240.0.0.0/5`, is defined to match on the first 5 bits
of the address. As shown in Figure 5.3, in binary, the decimal values 240 (`11110000B`) to
247 (`11110111B`) are identical through the first 5 bits (`11110B`).

The IANA ultimately manages the allocation and registration of the world's IP address
space. For more information on IP address assignments, see http://www.iana.org/
assignments/ipv4-address-space/ipv4-address-space.xhtml. Some blocks of addresses are
defined as reserved by the IANA. These addresses should not appear on the public Internet.

Protecting Services on Assigned
Unprivileged Ports

Services intended for local or private use, in particular, often run on unprivileged
ports. For TCP-based services, a connection attempt to one of these services can be

distinguished from an ongoing connection with a client using one of these unprivileged ports through the state of the SYN and ACK bits. Blocking connection requests is sufficient. UDP-based services must simply be blocked unless the state module is used.

You should block incoming connection attempts to these ports for your own protection. You want to block outgoing connection attempts to protect yourself and others from mistakes on your end and to log potential internal security problems. It's safer to block these ports across the board and route related traffic on an exceptional, case-by-case basis.

Official Service Port Number Assignments

Port numbers are assigned and registered by the IANA. The information was originally maintained as RFC 1700, "Assigned Numbers." That RFC is now obsolete. The official information is dynamically maintained by the IANA at http://www.iana.org/assignments/port-numbers.

What kinds of mistakes might you need protection from? The worst mistake is offering dangerous services to the world, whether inadvertently or intentionally. A common mistake is running local network services that leak out to the Internet and bother other people. Another is allowing questionable outgoing traffic, such as port scans, whether this traffic is generated by accident or intentionally is sent out by someone on your machine. A deny-everything-by-default firewall policy protects you from many mistakes of these types.

The Problem with Port Scans

Port scans are not harmful in themselves. They're generated by network analysis tools. The problem with port scans today is that they are usually generated by people with less-than-honorable intentions. They are "analyzing" your network, not their own. Unfortunately, this leaves the merely curious looking guilty as well.

A deny-everything-by-default firewall policy enables you to run many private services behind the firewall without undue risk. These services must explicitly be allowed through the firewall to be accessible to remote hosts. This generalization is only an approximation of reality, however. Although TCP services on privileged ports are reasonably safe from all but a skilled and determined hacker, UDP services are inherently less secure, and some services are assigned to run on unprivileged ports. RPC services, usually run over UDP, are even more problematic. RPC-based services are bound to some port, often an unprivileged port. The portmap daemon maps between the RPC service number and the actual port number. A port scan can show where these RPC-based services are bound without going through the portmap daemon. Luckily, the use of portmap is becoming less and less common, so this isn't as much of a concern as it was a number of years ago.

Common Local TCP Services Assigned to Unprivileged Ports

Some services, usually LAN services, are offered through an officially registered, well-known unprivileged port. Additionally, some services, such as FTP and IRC, use more complex communication protocols that don't lend themselves well to packet filtering. The rules described in the following sections disallow local or remote client programs from initiating a connection to one of these ports.

FTP is a good example of how the deny-by-default policy isn't always enough to cover all the possible cases. The FTP protocol is covered later in this chapter. For now, the important idea is that FTP allows connections between two unprivileged ports. Because some services listen on registered unprivileged ports, and because the incoming connection request to these services is originating from an unprivileged client port, the rules allowing FTP can inadvertently allow incoming connections to these other local services as well. This situation is also an example of how firewall rules are logically hierarchical and order dependent. The rules explicitly protecting a private, local service running on an unprivileged port must precede the FTP rules allowing access to the entire unprivileged port range.

As a result, some of these rules appear to be redundant and will be redundant for some people. For other people running other services, the following rules are necessary to protect private services running on local unprivileged ports.

Disallowing Connections to Common TCP Unprivileged Server Ports

Connections to remote X Window servers should be made over SSH, which automatically supports X Window connections. By specifying the --syn flag, indicating the SYN bit, only connection establishment to the server port is blocked. Other connections initiated using the port as a client port are not affected.

X Window port assignment begins at port 6000 with the first running server. If additional servers are run, each is assigned to the next incremental port. As a small site, you'll probably run a single X server, so your server will listen only on port 6000. Port 6063 is typically the highest assigned port, allowing 64 separate X Window managers running on a single machine, although ranges up to 6255 and 6999 are also seen sometimes:

```
XWINDOW_PORTS="6000:6063"              # (TCP) X Window
```

The first rule ensures that no outgoing connection attempts to remote X Window managers are made from your machine:

```
# X Window connection establishment
$IPT -A OUTPUT -o $INTERNET -p tcp --syn \
      --destination-port $XWINDOW_PORTS -j REJECT
```

The syntax for port ranges is different for nftables, and therefore the XWINDOW_PORTS variable needs to be defined accordingly:

```
XWINDOW_PORTS="6000-6063"
$NFT add rule filter output oif $INTERNET ct state new tcp dport $XWINDOW_PORTS
➥reject
```

The next rule blocks incoming connection attempts to your X Window manager. Local connections are not affected because local connections are made over the loopback interface:

```
# X Window: incoming connection attempt
$IPT -A INPUT -i $INTERNET -p tcp --syn \
        --destination-port $XWINDOW_PORTS -j DROP
```

Here's the `nftables` entry:

```
$NFT add rule filter input iif $INTERNET ct state new tcp dport $XWINDOW_PORTS
↪drop
```

The remaining TCP-based services can be blocked with a single rule by use of the `multiport` match extension for `iptables`. Blocking incoming connections isn't necessary if the machine isn't running the service, but it's safer in the long run, in case you later decide to run the service locally.

Network File System (NFS) usually binds to UDP port 2049 but can use TCP. You shouldn't be running NFS on a firewall machine, but if you are, external access is denied.

Connections to Open Window managers should not be allowed. Linux is not distributed with the Open Window manager. Incoming connections to port 2000 don't need to be blocked. (This will not be the case later, when the firewall's FORWARD rules are protecting other local hosts.)

`squid` is a web cache and proxy server. `squid` uses port 3128 by default but can be configured to use a different port.

The following rule blocks local clients from initiating a connection request to a remote NFS server, Open Window manager, SOCKS proxy server, or `squid` web cache server:

```
NFS_PORT="2049"                          # (TCP) NFS
SOCKS_PORT="1080"                        # (TCP) socks
OPENWINDOWS_PORT="2000"                  # (TCP) OpenWindows
SQUID_PORT="3128"                        # (TCP) squid
# Establishing a connection over TCP to NFS, OpenWindows, SOCKS or squid

$IPT -A OUTPUT -o $INTERNET -p tcp \
        -m multiport --destination-port \
        $NFS_PORT,$OPENWINDOWS_PORT,$SOCKS_PORT,$SQUID_PORT \
        --syn -j REJECT

$IPT -A INPUT -i $INTERNET -p tcp \
        -m multiport --destination-port \
        $NFS_PORT,$OPENWINDOWS_PORT,$SOCKS_PORT,$SQUID_PORT \
        --syn -j DROP
```

For `nftables`, the same variables can be used and placed into rules that look like this:

```
$NFT add rule filter output oif $INTERNET \
tcp dport \
{$NFS_PORT,$SOCKS_PORT,$OPENWINDOWS_PORT,$SQUID_PORT} \
ct state new reject
$NFT add rule filter input iif $INTERNET \
tcp dport \
{$NFS_PORT,$SOCKS_PORT,$OPENWINDOWS_PORT,$SQUID_PORT} \
ct state new drop
```

Common Local UDP Services Assigned to Unprivileged Ports

TCP protocol rules can be handled more precisely than UDP protocol rules because of TCP's connection establishment protocol. As a datagram service, UDP doesn't have a connection state associated with it. Unless the state module is used, access to UDP services should simply be blocked. Explicit exceptions are made to accommodate DNS and any of the few other UDP-based Internet services you might use. Fortunately, the common UDP Internet services are often the type used between a client and a specific server. The filtering rules can often allow exchanges with one specific remote host.

NFS is the main UNIX UDP service to be concerned with and also is one of the most frequently exploited. NFS runs on unprivileged port 2049. Unlike the previous TCP-based services, NFS is primarily a UDP-based service. It can be configured to run as a TCP-based service, but usually it isn't.

Associated with NFS is the RPC lock daemon, lockd, for NFS. lockd runs on UDP port 4045:

```
NFS_PORT="2049"                          # NFS
LOCKD_PORT="4045"                        # RPC lockd for NFS

# NFS and lockd
$IPT -A OUTPUT -o $INTERNET -p udp \
          -m multiport --destination-port $NFS_PORT,$LOCKD_PORT \
          -j REJECT

   $IPT -A INPUT -i $INTERNET -p udp \
          -m multiport --destination-port $NFS_PORT,$LOCKD_PORT \
          -j DROP
```

The nftables rules look like this:

```
$NFT add rule filter output oif $INTERNET udp dport \
{$NFS_PORT,$LOCKD_PORT} reject
$NFT add rule filter input iif $INTERNET udp dport \
{$NFS_PORT,$LOCKD_PORT} drop
```

The TCP and UDP Service Protocol Tables

The remainder of this chapter is devoted to defining rules to allow access to specific services. Client/server communication, for both TCP- and UDP-based services, involves some kind of two-way communication using a protocol specific to the service. As such, access rules are always represented as an I/O pair. The client program makes a query, and the server sends a response. Rules for a given service are categorized as client rules or server rules. The client category represents the communication required for your local clients to access remote servers. The server category represents the communication required for remote clients to access the services hosted from your machines.

The application messages are encapsulated in either TCP or UDP transport protocol messages. Because each service uses an application protocol specific to itself, the particular characteristics of the TCP or UDP exchange are, to some extent, unique to the given service.

The exchange between client and server is explicitly described by the firewall rules. Part of the purpose of firewall rules is to ensure protocol integrity at the packet level. Firewall rules, expressed in `iptables` or `nftables` syntax, are not especially human readable, however. In each of the following sections, the service protocol at the packet-filtering level is presented as a table of state information, followed by the `iptables` and `nftables` rules expressing those states.

Each row in the table lists a packet type involved in the service exchange. A firewall rule is defined for each individual packet type. The table is divided into columns:

- Description contains a brief description of whether the packet is originating from the client or the server, and the packet's purpose.
- Protocol is the transport protocol in use, TCP or UDP, or the IP protocol's control messages, ICMP.
- Remote Address is the legal address, or range of addresses, that the packet can contain in the remote address field.
- Remote Port is the legal port, or range of ports, that the packet can contain in the remote port field.
- In/Out describes the packet's direction—that is, whether it is coming into the system from a remote location or whether it is going out from the system to a remote location.
- Local Address is the legal address, or range of addresses, that the packet can contain in the local address field.
- Local Port is the legal port, or range of ports, that the packet can contain in the local port field.
- TCP protocol packets contain a final column, TCP Flag, defining the legal `SYN-ACK` states that the packet may have.

Finally, in the few instances when the service protocol involves ICMP messages, notice that the IP Network-layer ICMP packets are not associated with the concept of a source or destination port, as is the case for Transport-layer TCP or UDP packets. Instead, ICMP packets use the concept of a control or status message type. ICMP messages are not sent to programs bound to particular service ports. Instead, ICMP messages are sent from one computer to another. (The ICMP packet contains a copy of at least some of the original packet that resulted in the error message. The receiving host identifies the process that the error refers to by examining the packet carried in the ICMP packet's data area.) Consequently, the few ICMP packet entries presented in the tables use the source port column to contain the message type. For incoming ICMP packets, the source port column is the Remote Port column. For outgoing ICMP packets, the source port column is the Local Port column.

Enabling Basic, Required Internet Services

Only one service is truly required: the Domain Name Service (DNS). DNS translates between hostnames and their associated IP addresses. You generally can't locate a remote host without DNS unless the host is defined locally.

Allowing DNS (UDP/TCP Port 53)

DNS uses a communication protocol that relies on both UDP and TCP. Connection modes include regular client-to-server connections, peer-to-peer traffic between forwarding servers and full servers, and primary and secondary name server connections.

Query lookup requests are normally done over UDP, both for client-to-server lookups and for peer-to-peer server lookups. The UDP communication can fail for a lookup if the information being returned is too large to fit in a single UDP DNS packet. The server sets a flag bit in the DNS message header indicating that the data is truncated. In this case, the protocol allows for a retry over TCP. Figure 5.4 shows the relationship between UDP and TCP during a DNS lookup. In practice, TCP isn't normally needed for queries. TCP is conventionally used for administrative zone transfers between primary and secondary name servers.

Zone transfers are the transfer of a name server's complete information about a network, or the piece (zone) of a network, that the server is authoritative for (that is, the official server). The authoritative name server is referred to as the primary name server. Secondary, or backup, name servers can periodically request zone transfers from their primary to keep their DNS caches up-to-date.

Figure 5.4   DNS client-to-server lookup

For example, one of your ISP's name servers is the primary, authoritative server for the ISP's address space. ISPs often have multiple DNS servers to balance the load, as well as for backup redundancy. The other name servers are secondary name servers, refreshing their information from the master copy on the primary server.

Zone transfers require careful access control between the primary and the secondary servers. A small system isn't likely to be an authoritative name server for a public domain's name space, nor is it likely to be a public backup server for that information. Larger sites could easily host both primary and secondary servers. Care must be taken that zone transfers are allowed only between these hosts. Numerous attacks have been successful because the attacker was able to grab a copy of an entire DNS zone and learn about the network topology in order to direct the attack at the most valuable assets.

Table 5.1 lists the complete DNS protocol the firewall rules account for.

Table 5.1 **DNS Protocol**

Description	Protocol	Remote Address	Remote Port	In/Out	Local Address	Local Port	TCP Flag
Local client query	UDP	NAMESERVER	53	Out	IPADDR	1024:65535	—
Remote server response	UDP	NAMESERVER	53	In	IPADDR	1024:65535	—
Local client query	TCP	NAMESERVER	53	Out	IPADDR	1024:65535	Any
Remote server response	TCP	NAMESERVER	53	In	IPADDR	1024:65535	ACK
Local server query	UDP	NAMESERVER	53	Out	IPADDR	53	—
Remote server response	UDP	NAMESERVER	53	In	IPADDR	53	—
Local zone transfer request	TCP	Primary	53	Out	IPADDR	1024:65535	Any
Remote zone transfer request	TCP	Primary	53	In	IPADDR	1024:65535	ACK
Remote client query	UDP	DNS client	1024:65535	In	IPADDR	53	—
Local server response	UDP	DNS client	1024:65535	Out	IPADDR	53	—
Remote client query	TCP	DNS client	1024:65535	In	IPADDR	53	Any
Local server response	UDP	DNS client	53	Out	IPADDR	53	—
Remote zone transfer request	TCP	Secondary	1024:65535	In	IPADDR	53	Any
Local zone transfer response	TCP	Secondary	1024:65535	Out	IPADDR	53	ACK

Allowing DNS Lookups as a Client

The DNS resolver client isn't a specific program. The client is incorporated into the network library code used by network programs. When a hostname requires a lookup, the resolver requests the lookup from a DNS server. Most computers are configured only as a DNS client. The server runs on a remote machine. For a home user, the name server is usually a machine owned by your ISP.

As a client, the assumption is that your machine is not running a local DNS server; if it is, you should ensure that you need to actually run the name server. There's no need to run extra services! Each client lookup goes through the resolver and is then sent to one of the remote name servers configured in /etc/resolv.conf. In general, it's better to install the client rules even if a local server is used. You'll avoid some confusing problems that could otherwise crop up at some point.

These rules must be installed in the firewall tables before any other rules can successfully specify a remote host by name, rather than by IP address, unless the remote host has an entry in the local /etc/hosts file.

DNS sends a lookup request as a UDP datagram:

```
NAMESERVER ="my.name.server"                # (TCP/UDP) DNS
if ["$CONNECTION_TRACKING" = "1" ]; then
    $IPT -A OUTPUT -o $INTERNET -p udp \
            -s $IPADDR --sport $UNPRIVPORTS \
            -d $NAMESERVER --dport 53 \
            -m state --state NEW -j ACCEPT
fi

$IPT -A OUTPUT -o $INTERNET -p udp \
        -s $IPADDR --sport $UNPRIVPORTS \
        -d $NAMESERVER --dport 53 -j ACCEPT

$IPT -A INPUT  -i $INTERNET -p udp \
        -s $NAMESERVER --sport 53 \
        -d $IPADDR --dport $UNPRIVPORTS -j ACCEPT
```

The nftables rules look like this:

```
$NFT add rule filter output oif $INTERNET ip saddr $IPADDR udp sport $UNPRIVPORTS
➥ip daddr $NAMESERVER udp dport 53 ct state new accept
$NFT add rule filter input iif $INTERNET ip daddr $IPADDR udp dport $UNPRIVPORTS
➥ip saddr $NAMESERVER udp sport 53 accept
```

If an error occurs because the returned data is too large to fit in a UDP datagram, the DNS client retries using a TCP connection.

The next two rules are included for the rare occasion when the lookup response won't fit in a DNS UDP datagram. They won't be used in normal, day-to-day operations. You could run your system without problems for months on end without the TCP rules. Unfortunately, every so often your DNS lookups hang without these rules. More typically, these rules are used by a secondary name server requesting a zone transfer from its primary name server:

```
if ["$CONNECTION_TRACKING" = "1" ]; then
    $IPT -A OUTPUT -o $INTERNET -p tcp \
            -s $IPADDR --sport $UNPRIVPORTS \
            -d $NAMESERVER --dport 53 \
            -m state --state NEW -j ACCEPT
fi

$IPT -A OUTPUT -o $INTERNET -p tcp \
        -s $IPADDR --sport $UNPRIVPORTS \
        -d $NAMESERVER --dport 53 -j ACCEPT

$IPT -A INPUT -i $INTERNET -p tcp ! --syn \
        -s $NAMESERVER --sport 53 \
        -d $IPADDR --dport $UNPRIVPORTS -j ACCEPT
```

The `nftables` rules look like this:

```
$NFT add rule filter output oif $INTERNET ip saddr $IPADDR tcp sport $UNPRIVPORTS
➥ip daddr $NAMESERVER tcp dport 53 ct state new accept
$NFT add rule filter input iif $INTERNET ip daddr $IPADDR tcp dport $UNPRIVPORTS
➥ip saddr $NAMESERVER tcp sport 53 tcp flags != syn accept
```

Allowing Your DNS Lookups as a Forwarding Server

Configuring a local forwarding name server can be a big performance gain. As shown in
Figure 5.5, when BIND is configured as a caching and forwarding name server, it functions both as a local server and as a client to a remote DNS server. The difference between
a direct client-to-server exchange and a forwarded server-to-server exchange is in the
source and destination ports used. Instead of initiating an exchange from an unprivileged
port, BIND initiates the exchange from its own DNS port 53. (The query source port is
now configurable. In newer versions of BIND, the local server makes its request from an
unprivileged port, by default.) A second difference is that forwarding server lookups of this
type are always done over UDP. (If the response is too large to fit in a UDP DNS packet,
the local server must revert to standard client/server behavior to initiate the TCP request.)

DNS BIND Port Usage

Historically, DNS servers used UDP port 53 as their source port when talking to other
servers. This distinguished client traffic from server-initiated traffic because the client
always uses a high, unprivileged port as its source. Later versions of BIND allow the server-
to-server source port to be configurable and use the unprivileged ports by default. All
examples in this book assume that BIND has been configured to use UDP port 53, rather
than an unprivileged port, for server-to-server queries.

Local client requests are sent to the local DNS server. The first time, BIND won't have
the lookup information, so it forwards the request to a remote name server. BIND caches
the returned information and passes it on to the client. The next time the same information is requested, BIND finds it in its local cache (according to the record's time to live
[TTL]) and doesn't do a remote request.

Figure 5.5   A DNS forwarding server lookup

If the lookup fails because of UDP packet size, the server will fall back to a TCP client-mode lookup. If the lookup fails because the remote server doesn't have the information, the local server will query the root cache server. Because of this, the client rules would need to allow DNS traffic to any server, rather than to the specific servers listed in the local configuration.

The alternative is to configure BIND not only as a forwarding server, but also as a slave to the remote servers specified in the BIND configuration file, named.conf. As a slave, the general client UDP rules aren't required.

Enabling Common TCP Services

It's likely that no one will want to enable all the services listed in this section, but most everyone will want to enable some subset of them. These are the services most often used over the Internet today. As such, this section is more of a reference section than anything else. This section provides rules for the following:

- Email
- SSH
- FTP
- Generic TCP service

Many other services are available that aren't covered here. Some of them are used on specialized servers, some are used by large businesses and organizations, and some are designed for use in local, private networks. Additional LAN and DMZ services are covered in Chapter 7.

Email (TCP SMTP Port 25, POP Port 110, IMAP Port 143)

Email is a service that almost everyone wants. How mail is set up depends on your ISP, your connection type, and your own choices. Email is sent across the network using the SMTP protocol assigned to TCP service port 25. Email is commonly received locally through one of three different protocols—SMTP, POP, or IMAP—depending on the services your ISP provides and on your local configuration.

SMTP is the general mail delivery protocol. Mail is delivered to the destination host machine, as defined most commonly by the MX record in the DNS for the given domain. The endpoint mail server determines whether the mail is deliverable (addressed to a valid user account on the machine) and then delivers it to the user's local mailbox.

POP and IMAP are mail retrieval services. POP runs on TCP port 110. IMAP runs on TCP port 143. Today's POP and IMAP protocols are typically run over a secure sockets layer (SSL) for encryption. POP/S and IMAP/S run on port 995 and 993 respectively. ISPs commonly make incoming mail available to their customers using one or both of these two services. Both services are usually authenticated by username and password. As far as mail retrieval is concerned, the difference between SMTP and POP or IMAP is that SMTP receives incoming mail and queues it in the user's local mailbox. POP and IMAP retrieve mail into the user's local mail program from the user's ISP, where the mail had been queued remotely in the user's SMTP mailbox at the ISP. Table 5.2 lists the complete client/server connection protocols for SMTP, POP, and IMAP. SMTP also uses specialized delivery mechanisms that your local network might use, such as ETRN, that effectively transfer all mail for a given domain for local processing.

Sending Mail over SMTP (TCP Port 25)

Mail is sent over SMTP. But whose SMTP server do you use to collect your mail and send it onward? ISPs offer SMTP mail service to their customers. The ISP's mail server acts as the mail gateway. It knows how to collect your mail, find the recipient host, and relay the mail. With UNIX, you can host your own local mail server, if you want. Your server will be responsible for routing the mail to its destination.

Table 5.2 **SMTP, POP, and IMAP Mail Protocols**

Description	Protocol	Remote Address	Remote Port	In/Out	Local Address	Local Port	TCP Flag
Send outgoing mail	TCP	ANYWHERE	25	Out	IPADDR	1024:65535	Any
Remote server response	TCP	ANYWHERE	25	In	IPADDR	1024:65535	ACK
Receive incoming mail	TCP	ANYWHERE	1024:65535	In	IPADDR	25	Any
Local server response	TCP	ANYWHERE	1024:65536	Out	IPADDR	25	ACK
Local client query	TCP	POP SERVER	110 or 995	Out	IPADDR	1024:65535	Any
Remote server response	TCP	POP SERVER	110 or 995	In	IPADDR	1024:65535	ACK
Remote client query	TCP	POP CLIENT	1024:65535	In	IPADDR	110 or 995	Any
Local server response	TCP	POP CLIENT	1024:65535	Out	IPADDR	110 or 995	ACK
Local client query	TCP	IMAP SERVER	143 or 993	Out	IPADDR	1024:65535	Any
Remote server response	TCP	IMAP SERVER	143 or 993	In	IPADDR	1024:65535	ACK
Remote client query	TCP	IMAP CLIENT	1024:65535	In	IPADDR	143 or 993	Any
Local server response	TCP	IMAP CLIENT	1024:65535	Out	IPADDR	143 or 993	ACK

Relaying Outgoing Mail through an External (ISP) Gateway SMTP Server

When you relay outgoing mail through an external mail gateway server, your client mail program sends all outgoing mail to your ISP's mail server. Your ISP acts as your mail gateway to the rest of the world. Your system doesn't need to know how to locate your mail destinations or the routes to them. The ISP mail gateway serves as your relay.

The following two rules enable you to relay mail through your ISP's SMTP gateway:

```
SMTP_GATEWAY="my.isp.server"              # External mail server or relay
if [ "$CONNECTION_TRACKING" = "1" ]; then
    $IPT -A OUTPUT -o $INTERNET -p tcp \
            -s $IPADDR --sport $UNPRIVPORTS \
            -d $SMTP_GATEWAY --dport 25 -m state --state NEW -j ACCEPT
fi
```

```
$IPT -A OUTPUT -o $INTERNET -p tcp \
        -s $IPADDR --sport $UNPRIVPORTS \
        -d $SMTP_GATEWAY --dport 25 -j ACCEPT

$IPT -A INPUT -i $INTERNET -p tcp ! --syn \
        -s $SMTP_GATEWAY --sport 25 \
        -d $IPADDR --dport $UNPRIVPORTS -j ACCEPT
```

The `nftables` commands look like this:

```
$NFT add rule filter output oif $INTERNET ip daddr $SMTP_GATEWAY tcp dport 25 ip
➥saddr $IPADDR tcp sport $UNPRIVPORTS accept
$NFT add rule filter input iif $INTERNET ip saddr $SMTP_GATEWAY tcp sport 25 ip
➥daddr $IPADDR tcp dport $UNPRIVPORTS tcp flags != syn accept
```

Sending Mail to Any External Mail Server

Alternatively, you can bypass your ISP's mail server and host your own. Your local server is responsible for collecting your outgoing mail, doing the DNS lookup on the destination hostname, and sending the mail to its destination. Your client mail program points to your local SMTP server rather than to the ISP's server.

The following two rules enable you to send mail directly to the remote destinations:

```
if [ "$CONNECTION_TRACKING" = "1" ]; then
    $IPT -A OUTPUT -o $INTERNET -p tcp \
            -s $IPADDR --sport $UNPRIVPORTS \
            --dport 25 -m state --state NEW -j ACCEPT
fi

$IPT -A OUTPUT -o $INTERNET -p tcp \
        -s $IPADDR --sport $UNPRIVPORTS \
        --dport 25 -j ACCEPT

$IPT -A INPUT -i $INTERNET -p tcp ! --syn \
        --sport 25 \
        -d $IPADDR --dport $UNPRIVPORTS -j ACCEPT
```

The `nftables` commands look like this:

```
$NFT add rule filter output oif $INTERNET ip saddr $IPADDR tcp sport $UNPRIVPORTS
➥tcp dport 25 accept
$NFT add rule filter input iif $INTERNET ip daddr $IPADDR tcp sport 25 tcp dport
➥$UNPRIVPORTS tcp flags != syn accept
```

Receiving Mail

How you receive mail depends on your situation. If you run your own local mail server, you can collect incoming mail directly on your Linux machine. If you retrieve your mail from your ISP account, you may or may not retrieve mail as a POP or IMAP client, depending on how you've configured your ISP email account, and depending on the mail delivery services the ISP offers.

Receiving Mail as a Local SMTP Server (TCP Port 25)

If you want to receive mail sent directly to your local machines from anywhere in the world, you need to run Sendmail, Gmail, or some other mail server program. These are the local server rules:

```
if [ "$CONNECTION_TRACKING" = "1" ]; then
    $IPT -A INPUT  -i $INTERNET -p tcp \
            --sport $UNPRIVPORTS \
            -d $IPADDR --dport 25 \
            -m state --state NEW -j ACCEPT
fi

$IPT -A INPUT  -i $INTERNET -p tcp \
        --sport $UNPRIVPORTS \
        -d $IPADDR --dport 25 -j ACCEPT

$IPT -A OUTPUT -o $INTERNET -p tcp ! --syn \
        -s $IPADDR --sport 25 \
        --dport $UNPRIVPORTS -j ACCEPT
```

The commands for the `nftables` script look like this:

```
$NFT add rule filter input iif $INTERNET tcp sport $UNPRIVPORTS ip daddr $IPADDR
➡tcp dport 25 accept
$NFT add rule filter output oif $INTERNET tcp sport 25 ip saddr $IPADDR tcp dport
➡$UNPRIVPORTS tcp flags != syn accept
```

Alternatively, if you'd rather keep your local email account relatively private and use your work or ISP email account as your public address, you can configure your work and ISP mail accounts to forward mail to your local server. In this case, you could replace the previous single rule pair, accepting connections from anywhere, with separate, specific rules for each mail forwarder.

Retrieving Mail as a POP Client (TCP Port 110 or 995)

Connecting to a POP server is a very common means of retrieving mail from a remote ISP or work account. If your ISP uses a POP server for customer mail retrieval, you need to allow outgoing client-to-server connections.

The server's address will be a specific hostname or address rather than the global, implied ANYWHERE specifier. POP accounts are user accounts associated with a specific user and password:

```
POP_SERVER="my.isp.pop.server"              # External pop server, if any
if [ "$CONNECTION_TRACKING" = "1" ]; then
    $IPT -A OUTPUT -o $INTERNET -p tcp \
            -s $IPADDR --sport $UNPRIVPORTS \
            -d $POP_SERVER --dport 110 -m state --state NEW -j ACCEPT
fi

$IPT -A OUTPUT -o $INTERNET -p tcp \
        -s $IPADDR --sport $UNPRIVPORTS \
        -d $POP_SERVER --dport 110 -j ACCEPT
```

```
$IPT -A INPUT -i $INTERNET -p tcp ! --syn \
        -s $POP_SERVER --sport 110 \
        -d $IPADDR --dport $UNPRIVPORTS -j ACCEPT
```

The commands for `nftables` look like the following; substitute 110 in place of 995 if your mail server uses regular POP without SSL:

```
$NFT add rule filter output oif $INTERNET ip saddr $IPADDR ip daddr $POP_SERVER
➥tcp sport $UNPRIVPORTS tcp dport 995 accept
$NFT add rule filter input iif $INTERNET ip saddr $POP_SERVER tcp sport 110 ip
➥daddr $IPADDR tcp dport $UNPRIVPORTS tcp flags != syn accept
```

Receiving Mail as an IMAP Client (TCP Port 143 or 993)

Connecting to an IMAP server is another common means of retrieving mail from a remote ISP or work account. If your ISP uses an IMAP server for customer mail retrieval, you need to allow outgoing client-to-server connections.

The server's address will be a specific hostname or address rather than the global, implied $ANYWHERE specifier. IMAP accounts are user accounts associated with a specific user and password:

```
IMAP_SERVER="my.isp.imap.server"        # External imap server, if any
if [ "$CONNECTION_TRACKING" = "1" ]; then
    $IPT -A OUTPUT -o $INTERNET -p tcp \
            -s $IPADDR --sport $UNPRIVPORTS \
            -d $IMAP_SERVER --dport 143 -m state --state NEW -j ACCEPT
fi

$IPT -A OUTPUT -o $INTERNET -p tcp \
        -s $IPADDR --sport $UNPRIVPORTS \
        -d $IMAP_SERVER --dport 143 -j ACCEPT

$IPT -A INPUT -i $INTERNET -p tcp ! --syn \
        -s $IMAP_SERVER --sport 143 \
        -d $IPADDR --dport $UNPRIVPORTS -j ACCEPT
```

The `nftables` rules look like the following; substitute 143 in place of 993 if your IMAP server doesn't use SSL:

```
$NFT add rule filter output oif $INTERNET ip saddr $IPADDR tcp sport $UNPRIVPORTS
➥ip daddr $IMAP_SERVER tcp dport 993 accept
$NFT add rule filter input iif $INTERNET ip saddr $IMAP_SERVER tcp sport 995 ip
➥daddr $IPADDR tcp dport $UNPRIVPORTS tcp flags != syn accept
```

Hosting a Mail Server for Remote Clients

Hosting public POP or IMAP services is unusual for a small system. You might do this if you offer remote mail services to a few friends, for example, or if their ISP mail service is temporarily unavailable. In any case, it's important to limit the clients your system will accept connections from, both on the packet-filtering level and on the server configuration level.

Hosting a POP Server for Remote Clients

POP servers are one of the most common and successful points of entry for hacking exploits. Firewall rules can offer some amount of protection, in many cases. Of course, you would limit access at the server configuration level as well. As always, and perhaps particularly so with mail server software, it is crucial to keep up-to-date with security updates for the software.

If you use a local system as a central mail server and run a local POP3 server to provide mail access to local machines on a LAN, you don't need the server rules in this example. Incoming connections from the Internet should be dropped. If you do need to host POP service for a limited number of remote individuals, the next two rules allow incoming connections to your POP server. Connections are limited to your specific clients' IP addresses:

```
if [ "$CONNECTION_TRACKING" = "1" ]; then
    $IPT -A INPUT  -i $INTERNET -p tcp \
            -s <my.pop.clients> --sport $UNPRIVPORTS \
            -d $IPADDR --dport 110 \
            -m state --state NEW -j ACCEPT
fi

$IPT -A INPUT  -i $INTERNET -p tcp \
        -s <my.pop.clients> --sport $UNPRIVPORTS \
        -d $IPADDR --dport 110 -j ACCEPT

$IPT -A OUTPUT -o $INTERNET -p tcp ! --syn \
        -s $IPADDR --sport 110 \
        -d <my.pop.clients> --dport $UNPRIVPORTS -j ACCEPT
```

The `nftables` rules look like this:

```
nft add rule filter input iif $INTERNET ip saddr <POP_CLIENTS> tcp sport
➥$UNPRIVPORTS ip daddr $IPADDR tcp dport 995 accept
$NFT add rule filter output oif $INTERNET ip saddr $IPADDR tcp sport 995 ip daddr
➥<POP_CLIENTS> tcp dport $UNPRIVPORTS tcp flags != syn accept
```

If your site were an ISP, you could use network address masking to limit which source addresses you would accept POP connection requests from:

```
POP_CLIENTS="192.168.24.0/24"
```

If yours is a residential site with a handful of remote POP clients, the client addresses would need to be stated explicitly, with a separate rule pair for each client address.

Hosting an IMAP Server for Remote Clients

IMAP servers are one of the most common and successful points of entry for hacking exploits. Firewall rules can offer some amount of protection, in many cases. Of course, you would limit access at the server configuration level as well. As always, and perhaps particularly so with mail server software, it is crucial to keep up-to-date with security updates for the software.

SSH (TCP Port 22)

With the expiration of the RSA patent in the year 2000, OpenSSH, secure shell, is included in Linux distributions. It is also freely available from software sites on the

Internet. SSH is considered far preferable to using telnet for remote login access because both ends of the connection use authentication keys for both hosts and users, and because data is encrypted. Additionally, SSH is more than a remote login service. It can automatically direct X Window connections between remote sites, and FTP and other TCP-based connections can be directed over the more secure SSH connection. Provided that the other end of the connection allows SSH connections, it's possible to route all TCP connections through the firewall using SSH. As such, SSH is something of a poor man's virtual private network (VPN).

The ports used by SSH are highly configurable. By default, connections are initiated between a client's unprivileged port and the server's assigned service port 22. The SSH client uses the unprivileged ports exclusively. The rules in this example apply to the default SSH port usage:

```
SSH_PORTS="1024:65535"          # RSA authentication
    or
SSH_PORTS="1020:65535"          # Rhost authentication
```

The client and server rules here allow access to and from anywhere. In practice, you would limit the external addresses to a select subset, particularly because both ends of the connection must be configured to recognize each individual user account for authentication. Table 5.3 lists the complete client/server connection protocol for the SSH service.

Table 5.3 **SSH Protocol**

Description	Protocol	Remote Address	Remote Port	In/Out	Local Address	Local Port	TCP Flag
Local client request	TCP	ANYWHERE	22	Out	IPADDR	1024:65535	Any
Remote server response	TCP	ANYWHERE	22	In	IPADDR	1024:65535	ACK
Local client request	TCP	ANYWHERE	22	Out	IPADDR	513:1023	Any
Remote server response	TCP	ANYWHERE	22	In	IPADDR	513:1023	ACK
Remote client request	TCP	SSH clients	1024:65535	In	IPADDR	22	Any
Local server response	TCP	SSH clients	1024:65535	Out	IPADDR	22	ACK
Remote client request	TCP	SSH clients	513:1023	In	IPADDR	22	Any
Local server response	TCP	SSH clients	513:1023	Out	IPADDR	22	ACK

Allowing Client Access to Remote SSH Servers

These rules allow you to connect to remote sites using SSH:

```
if [ "$CONNECTION_TRACKING" = "1" ]; then
    $IPT -A OUTPUT -o $INTERNET -p tcp \
            -s $IPADDR --sport $SSH_PORTS \
            --dport 22 -m state --state NEW -j ACCEPT
fi

$IPT -A OUTPUT -o $INTERNET -p tcp \
        -s $IPADDR --sport $SSH_PORTS \
        --dport 22 -j ACCEPT

$IPT -A INPUT -i $INTERNET -p tcp ! --syn \
        --sport 22 \
        -d $IPADDR --dport $SSH_PORTS -j ACCEPT
```

The `nftables` rules look like the following:

```
$NFT add rule filter output oif $INTERNET ip saddr $IPADDR tcp sport $SSH_PORTS
➥tcp dport 22 accept
$NFT add rule filter input iif $INTERNET tcp sport 22 ip daddr $IPADDR tcp dport
➥$SSH_PORTS tcp flags != syn accept
```

Allowing Remote Client Access to Your Local SSH Server

These rules allow incoming connections to your SSH server:

```
if [ "$CONNECTION_TRACKING" = "1" ]; then
    $IPT -A INPUT  -i $INTERNET -p tcp \
            --sport $SSH_PORTS \
            -d $IPADDR --dport 22 \
            -m state --state NEW -j ACCEPT
fi

$IPT -A INPUT  -i $INTERNET -p tcp \
        --sport $SSH_PORTS \
        -d $IPADDR --dport 22 -j ACCEPT

$IPT -A OUTPUT -o $INTERNET -p tcp ! --syn \
        -s $IPADDR --sport 22 \
        --dport $SSH_PORTS -j ACCEPT
```

The `nftables` rules look like the following:

```
$NFT add rule filter input iif $INTERNET tcp sport $SSH_PORTS ip daddr $IPADDR
➥tcp dport 22 accept
$NFT add rule filter output oif $INTERNET ip saddr $IPADDR tcp sport 22 tcp dport
➥$SSH_PORTS tcp flags != syn accept
```

FTP (TCP Ports 21, 20)

FTP remains one of the most common means of transferring files between two net-worked machines. Web-based browser interfaces to FTP have become common as well. Like telnet, FTP sends both authentication credentials and data communication in plain text over the network. Therefore, FTP is also considered to be an inherently insecure protocol. SFTP and SCP offer improvements to FTP in this regard.

FTP is used as the classic example of a protocol that isn't firewall or NAT friendly. Traditional client/server applications that communicate over TCP all work the same way. The client initiates the request to connect to the server.

Table 5.4 lists the complete client/server connection protocol for the FTP service.

Table 5.4 **FTP Protocol**

Description	Protocol	Remote Address	Remote Port	In/Out	Local Address	Local Port	TCP Flag
Local client query	TCP	ANYWHERE	21	Out	IPADDR	1024:65535	Any
Remote server response	TCP	ANYWHERE	21	In	IPADDR	1024:65535	ACK
Remote server port data channel request	TCP	ANYWHERE	20	In	IPADDR	1024:65535	Any
Local client port data channel response	TCP	ANYWHERE	20	Out	IPADDR	1024:65535	ACK
Local client passive data channel request	TCP	ANYWHERE	1024:65535	Out	IPADDR	1024:65535	Any
Remote server passive data channel response	TCP	ANYWHERE	1024:65535	In	IPADDR	1024:65535	ACK
Remote client request	TCP	ANYWHERE	1024:65535	In	IPADDR	21	Any
Local server response	TCP	ANYWHERE	1024:65535	Out	IPADDR	21	ACK
Local server port data channel response	TCP	ANYWHERE	1024:65535	Out	IPADDR	20	Any
Remote client port data channel response	TCP	ANYWHERE	1024:65535	In	IPADDR	20	ACK
Remote client passive data channel request	TCP	ANYWHERE	1024:65535	In	IPADDR	1024:65535	Any
Local server passive data channel response	TCP	ANYWHERE	1024:65535	Out	IPADDR	1024:65535	ACK

FTP deviates from this standard TCP, client/server communication model. FTP relies on two separate connections, one for the control or command stream, and one for passing the data files and other information, such as directory listings. The control stream is carried over a traditional TCP connection. The client binds to a high, unprivileged port and sends a connection request to the FTP server, which is bound to port 21. This connection is used to pass commands.

In terms of the second data stream connection, FTP has two alternative modes for exchanging data between a client and a server: port mode and passive mode. Port mode is the original, default mechanism. The client tells the server which secondary, unprivileged port it will listen on. The server initiates the data connection from port 20 to the unprivileged port the client specified.

This is the deviation from the standard client/server model. The server is initiating the secondary connection back to the client. This is why FTP is a protocol that requires ALG support for both the firewall and NAT. The firewall must account for an incoming connection from port 20 to a local unprivileged port. NAT must account for the destination address used for the secondary data stream connection. (The client has no knowledge that its network traffic is being NATed. The port and address it sent the server were its local, pre-NATed port and address.)

Passive mode is similar to the traditional client/server model in that the client initiates the secondary connection for the data stream. Again, the client initiates the connection from a high, unprivileged port. The server isn't bound to port 20 for the data connection, however. Instead, the server has told the client which high, unprivileged port the client should address the connection request to. The data stream is carried between unprivileged ports on both the client and the server.

In terms of traditional packet filtering, the firewall must allow TCP traffic between all unprivileged ports. Connection state tracking and ALG support allow the firewall to associate the secondary connection with a particular FTP control stream. NAT isn't an issue on the client side because the client is initiating both connections.

Allowing Outgoing Client Access to Remote FTP Servers

It's almost a given that most sites will want FTP client access to remote file repositories. Most people will want to enable outgoing client connections to a remote server.

Outgoing FTP Requests over the Control Channel

The next two rules allow an outgoing control connection to a remote FTP server:

```
if [ "$CONNECTION_TRACKING" = "1" ]; then
    $IPT -A OUTPUT -o $INTERNET -p tcp \
            -s $IPADDR --sport $UNPRIVPORTS \
            --dport 21 -m state --state NEW -j ACCEPT
fi

$IPT -A OUTPUT -o $INTERNET -p tcp \
        -s $IPADDR --sport $UNPRIVPORTS \
        --dport 21 -j ACCEPT
```

```
$IPT -A INPUT -i $INTERNET -p tcp ! --syn \
        --sport 21 \
        -d $IPADDR --dport $UNPRIVPORTS -j ACCEPT
```

The `nftables` rules look like this:

```
$NFT add rule filter output oif $INTERNET ip saddr $IPADDR tcp sport $UNPRIVPORTS
➥tcp dport 21 accept
$NFT add rule filter input iif $INTERNET ip daddr $IPADDR tcp sport 21 tcp dport
➥$UNPRIVPORTS accept
```

Port-Mode FTP Data Channels

The next two rules allow the standard data channel connection, in which the remote server calls back to establish the data connection from server port 20 to a client-specified unprivileged port:

```
if [ "$CONNECTION_TRACKING" = "1" ]; then
    $IPT -A INPUT  -i $INTERNET -p tcp \
            --sport 20 \
            -d $IPADDR --dport $UNPRIVPORTS \
            -m state --state NEW -j ACCEPT
fi

$IPT -A INPUT  -i $INTERNET -p tcp \
        --sport 20 \
        -d $IPADDR --dport $UNPRIVPORTS -j ACCEPT

$IPT -A OUTPUT -o $INTERNET -p tcp ! --syn \
        -s $IPADDR --sport $UNPRIVPORTS \
        --dport 20 -j ACCEPT
```

This unusual callback behavior, with the remote server establishing the secondary connection with your client, is part of what makes FTP difficult to secure at the packet-filtering level. Rules for `nftables` assume the use of the `ct state` module and therefore aren't needed.

Generic TCP Service

Most of the rules shown in this section are similar to each other. Rather than trying to provide rules for every type of TCP-based service, it's more useful to simply learn a general way to add a rule as needed for whatever service you need to provide.

The following generic rules apply to any TCP service to which you need to make a connection. Substitute the destination service port for <YOUR PORT HERE>:

```
if [ "$CONNECTION_TRACKING" = "1" ]; then
    $IPT -A OUTPUT -o $INTERNET -p tcp \
            -s $IPADDR --sport $UNPRIVPORTS \
            --dport <YOUR PORT HERE> -m state --state NEW -j ACCEPT
fi

$IPT -A OUTPUT -o $INTERNET -p tcp \
        -s $IPADDR --sport $UNPRIVPORTS \
        --dport <YOUR PORT HERE> -j ACCEPT
```

```
$IPT -A INPUT -i $INTERNET -p tcp ! --syn \
       --sport <YOUR PORT HERE> \
       -d $IPADDR --dport $UNPRIVPORTS -j ACCEPT
```

The nft rules look like this:

```
$NFT add rule filter output oif $INTERNET ip saddr $IPADDR tcp sport $UNPRIVPORTS
➥tcp dport <YOUR PORT HERE> accept
$NFT add rule filter input iif $INTERNET tcp sport <YOUR PORT HERE> ip daddr
➥$IPADDR tcp dport $UNPRIVPORTS accept
```

The following rules apply to enabling an incoming TCP connection on whatever port is necessary for the given service:

```
if [ "$CONNECTION_TRACKING" = "1" ]; then
    $IPT -A INPUT  -i $INTERNET -p tcp \
           --sport $UNPRIVPORTS \
           -d $IPADDR --dport <YOUR PORT HERE> \
           -m state --state NEW -j ACCEPT
fi

$IPT -A INPUT  -i $INTERNET -p tcp \
       --sport $UNPRIVPORTS \
       -d $IPADDR --dport <YOUR PORT HERE> -j ACCEPT

$IPT -A OUTPUT -o $INTERNET -p tcp ! --syn \
       -s $IPADDR \
       --dport $UNPRIVPORTS -j ACCEPT
```

The rules for `nftables` are as follows:

```
nft add rule filter input iif $INTERNET tcp sport $UNPRIVPORTS ip daddr $IPADDR
➥tcp dport <YOUR PORT HERE> accept
nft add rule filter output oif $INTERNET ip saddr $IPADDR tcp sport <YOUR PORT
➥HERE> tcp dport $UNPRIVPORTS accept
```

Enabling Common UDP Services

The stateless UDP protocol is inherently less secure than the connection-based TCP protocol. Because of this, many security-conscious sites completely disable, or else limit as much as possible, all access to UDP services. Obviously, UDP-based DNS exchanges are necessary, but the remote name servers can be explicitly specified in the firewall rules. As such, this section provides rules for only two services:

- Dynamic Host Configuration Protocol (DHCP)
- Network Time Protocol (NTP)

Accessing Your ISP's DHCP Server (UDP Ports 67, 68)

DHCP exchanges, if any, between your site and your ISP's server will necessarily be local client–to–remote server exchanges. Most often, DHCP clients receive temporary, or semi-permanent, dynamically allocated IP addresses from a central server that manages the ISP's customer IP address space. The server also typically provides your local host with other configuration information, such as the network subnet mask; the network MTU; the default, first-hop router addresses; the domain name; and the default TTL.

If you have a dynamically allocated IP address from your ISP, you need to run a DHCP client daemon on your machine.

Table 5.5 lists the DHCP message type descriptions, as quoted from RFC 2131, "Dynamic Host Configuration Protocol."

In essence, when the DHCP client initializes, it broadcasts a DHCPDISCOVER query to discover whether any DHCP servers are available. Any servers receiving the query may respond with a DHCPOFFER message indicating their willingness to function as server to this client; they include the configuration parameters that they have to offer. The client broadcasts a DHCPREQUEST message to accept one of the servers and to inform any remaining servers that it has chosen to decline their offers. The chosen server responds with a broadcast DHCPACK message, indicating confirmation of the parameters that it originally offered. Address assignment is complete at this point. Periodically, the client sends the server a DHCPREQUEST message requesting a renewal on the IP address lease. If the lease is renewed, the server responds with a unicast DHCPACK message. Otherwise, the client falls back to the initialization process. Table 5.6 lists the complete client/server exchange protocol for the DHCP service.

Table 5.5 **DHCP Message Types**

DHCP Message	Description
DHCPDISCOVER	Client broadcast to locate available servers
DHCPOFFER	Server to client in response to DHCPDISCOVER with offer of configuration parameters
DHCPREQUEST	Client message to servers either (a) requesting offered parameters from one server and implicitly declining offers from all others; (b) confirming correctness of previously allocated address after, for example, system reboot; or (c) extending the lease on a particular network address
DHCPACK	Server to client with configuration parameters, including committed network address
DHCPNAK	Server to client indicating that client's notion of network address is incorrect (for example, client has moved to new subnet) or client's lease has expired
DHCPDECLINE	Client to server indicating that network address is already in use
DHCPRELEASE	Client to server relinquishing network address and canceling remaining lease
DHCPINFORM	Client to server, asking only for local configuration parameters; client already has externally configured address

Table 5.6 **DHCP Protocol**

Description	Protocol	Remote Address	Remote Port	In/Out	Local Address	Local Port
DHCPDISCOVER; DHCPREQUEST	UDP	255.255.255.255	67	Out	0.0.0.0	68
DHCPOFFER	UDP	0.0.0.0	67	In	255.255.255.255	68
DHCPOFFER	UDP	DHCP SERVER	67	In	255.255.255.255	68
DHCPREQUEST; DHCPDECLINE	UDP	DHCP SERVER	67	Out	0.0.0.0	68
DHCPACK; DHCPNACK	UDP	DHCP SERVER	67	In	ISP/NETMASK	68
DHCPACK	UDP	DHCP SERVER	67	In	IPADDR	68
DHCPREQUEST; DHCPRELEASE	UDP	DHCP SERVER	67	Out	IPADDR	68

The DHCP protocol is far more complicated than this brief summary, but the summary describes the essentials of the typical client and server exchange.

The following firewall rules allow communication between your DHCP client and a remote server:

```
# Initialization or rebinding: No lease or Lease time expired.
$IPT -A OUTPUT -o $INTERNET -p udp \
        -s $BROADCAST_SRC --sport 67:68 \
        -d $BROADCAST_DEST --dport 67:68 -j ACCEPT

# Incoming DHCPOFFER from available DHCP servers

$IPT -A INPUT  -i $INTERNET -p udp \
        --sport 67:68 \
        --dport 67:68 -j ACCEPT
```

The `nftables` rules look like this:

```
$NFT add rule filter output oif $INTERNET ip saddr $BROADCAST_SRC udp sport 67-68
➥ip daddr $BROADCAST_DEST udp dport 67-68 accept
$NFT add rule filter input iif $INTERNET udp sport 67-68 udp dport 67-68 accept
```

Notice that DHCP traffic cannot be completely limited to your DHCP server. During initialization sequences, when your client doesn't yet have an assigned IP address or even the server's IP address, packets are broadcast rather than sent point-to-point. At the Layer 2 level, the packets may be addressed to your network card's hardware address.

Accessing Remote Network Time Servers (UDP Port 123)

Network time services such as NTP allow access to one or more public Internet time providers. This is useful to maintain an accurate system clock, particularly if your internal clock tends to drift, and to establish the correct time and date at bootup or after a power loss. A small-system user should use the service only as an Internet client. Few small sites have a satellite link to Greenwich, England; a radio link to an atomic clock; or an atomic clock of their own lying around.

ntpd is the server daemon. In addition to providing time service to clients, ntpd uses a peer-to-peer relationship among servers. Few small sites require the extra precision ntpd provides. ntpdate is the client program and uses a client-to-server relationship. The client program is all that a small site will need. Table 5.7 lists only the client/server exchange protocol for the NTP service. There is rarely, if ever, a reason to run ntpd itself because that's the server component. If you must run the NTP server (as opposed to the client), do so in a chroot environment.

The ntpd startup script that is run at boot time uses ntpdate to query a series of public time service providers. The ntpd daemon is started after the server's reply. These hosts would be individually specified in a series of firewall rules:

```
TIME_SERVER="my.time.server"           # External time server, if any

if [ "$CONNECTION_TRACKING" = "1" ]; then
    $IPT -A OUTPUT -o $INTERNET -p udp \
            -s $IPADDR --sport $UNPRIVPORTS \
            -d $TIME_SERVER --dport 123 \
            -m state --state NEW -j ACCEPT
fi

$IPT -A OUTPUT -o $INTERNET -p udp \
        -s $IPADDR --sport $UNPRIVPORTS \
        -d $TIME_SERVER --dport 123 -j ACCEPT

$IPT -A INPUT  -i $INTERNET -p udp \
        -s $TIME_SERVER --sport 123 \
        -d $IPADDR --dport $UNPRIVPORTS -j ACCEPT
```

The nftables script rules are:

```
$NFT add rule filter output oif $INTERNET ip saddr $IPADDR udp sport $UNPRIVPORTS
➥ip daddr $TIME_SERVER udp dport 123 accept
$NFT add rule filter input iif $INTERNET ip saddr $TIME_SERVER udp sport 123 ip
➥daddr $IPADDR udp dport $UNPRIVPORTS accept
```

Table 5.7 **NTP Protocol**

Description	Protocol	Remote Address	Remote Port	In/Out	Local Address	Local Port
Local client query	UDP	TIMESERVER	123	Out	IPADDR	1024:65535
Remote server response	UDP	TIMESERVER	123	In	IPADDR	1024:65535

Note that the previous rules are written for a standard client/server UDP communication. Depending on your particular client and server software, it's possible that one or both of them will use the NTP server-to-server communication model, with both the client and the server using UDP port 123.

Logging Dropped Incoming Packets

Any packet matching a rule can be logged by using the `-j LOG` target for `iptables` or log statement for `nftables`. Logging a packet has no effect on the packet's disposition, however. The packet must match an accept or drop rule. Some of the rules presented previously had logging enabled, before matching the packet a second time to drop it. Some of the IP address spoofing rules are examples.

Rules can be defined for the explicit purpose of logging certain kinds of packets. Most typically, packets of interest are suspicious packets indicating some sort of probe or scan. Because all packets are denied by default, if logging is desired for certain packet types, explicit rules must be defined before the packet falls off the end of the chain and the default policy takes effect. Essentially, out of all the denied packets, you might be interested in logging some of them, using rate-limited logging for some, and silently dropping others.

Which packets are logged is an individual matter. Some people want to log all dropped packets. For other people, logging all dropped packets could soon overflow their system logs. Some people, secure in the knowledge that the packets are dropped, don't care about them and don't want to know about them. Other people are interested in the obvious port scans or in some particular packet type.

Because of the first-matching-rule-wins behavior, you could log all dropped incoming packets with a single rule. The assumption here is that all packet-matching acceptance rules have been tested, and the packet is about to drop off the end of the chain and be thrown away:

```
$IPT -A INPUT -i $INTERNET -j LOG
```

Or for `nftables`:

```
$NFT add rule filter input iif $INTERNET log
```

Logging Dropped Outgoing Packets

Logging outgoing traffic blocked by the firewall rules is necessary for debugging the firewall rules and to be alerted to local software problems.

All traffic about to be dropped by the default policy could be logged:

```
$IPT -A OUTPUT -o $INTERNET -j LOG
```

For `nftables`:

```
$NFT add rule filter output oif $INTERNET log
```

Installing the Firewall

This section assumes that the firewall script is called `rc.firewall`. There's no reason that the script couldn't be called simply `fwscript` or something else either. In fact, on Debian systems the standard is closer to the single name, `fwscript`, rather than a name prefixed with an `rc.` as is the case on Red Hat. This section covers the commands as if the script was installed in either `/etc/rc.d/` for a Red Hat or SUSE system or `/etc/init.d/` for a Debian system.

As a shell script, initial installation is simple. The script should be owned by `root`. On Red Hat and SUSE:

```
chown root.root /etc/rc.d/rc.firewall
```

On Debian:

```
chown root.root /etc/init.d/rc.firewall
```

The script should be writable and executable by `root` alone. Ideally, the general user should not have read access. On Red Hat and SUSE:

```
chmod u=rwx /etc/rc.d/rc.firewall
```

On Debian:

```
chmod u=rwx /etc/init.d/rc.firewall
```

To initialize the firewall at any time, execute the script from the command line. There is no need to reboot:

```
/etc/rc.d/rc.firewall start
```

Technically, the `start` argument isn't required there, but it's a good habit anyway— again, I'd rather err on the side of completeness than have ambiguity with a firewall. The script includes a `stop` action that flushes the firewall entirely. Therefore, if you want to stop the firewall, call the same command with the `stop` argument:

```
/etc/rc.d/rc.firewall stop
```

Be forewarned: If you stop the firewall in this way, you are running with no protection. The attorneys tell me that I should tell you, "Always leave the firewall enabled!"

On Debian, change the path for the command to `/etc/init.d`. Start the firewall:

```
/etc/init.d/rc.firewall start
```

Stop the firewall on Debian:

```
/etc/init.d/rc.firewall stop
```

Tips for Debugging the Firewall Script

When you're debugging a new firewall script through an SSH or other remote connection, it's quite possible that you might lock yourself out of the system. Granted, this isn't a concern when you're installing the firewall from the console, but as someone who manages remote Linux servers, I find that access to the console is rarely possible. Therefore, a method is necessary for stopping the firewall automatically after it gets started, just in case the firewall locks out my connection. Cron to the rescue.

Using a cron entry, you can stop the firewall by running the script with a `stop` argument at some predefined interval. I find that every 2 minutes works well during initial debugging. If you'd like to use this method, set a cron entry with the following command as `root` (on Debian):

```
crontab -e
*/2 * * * * /etc/init.d/rc.firewall stop
```

On Red Hat and SUSE:

```
crontab -e
*/2 * * * * /etc/rc.d/rc.firewall stop
```

With this cron entry in place, you can start the firewall and have it stop every 2 minutes. Using such a mechanism is somewhat of a trade-off though, because you have to do your initial debugging before the clock hits a minute divisible by two! Additionally, it's up to you to remember to remove this cron entry when you've debugged the firewall. If you forget to remove this entry, the firewall will stop and you'll be running with no firewall again!

Starting the Firewall on Boot with Red Hat and SUSE

On Red Hat and SUSE, the simplest way to initialize the firewall is to edit `/etc/rc.d/rc.local` and add the following line to the end of the file:

```
/etc/rc.d/rc.firewall start
```

After the firewall rules are debugged and stable, Red Hat Linux provides a more standard way to start and stop the firewall. If you chose `iptables` while using one of the runlevel managers, the default runlevel directory contains a link to `/etc/rc.d/init.d/iptables`. As with the other startup scripts in this directory, the system will start and stop the firewall automatically when booting or changing runlevels.

One additional step is required to use the standard runlevel system, however. You must first manually install the firewall rules:

```
/etc/rc.d/rc.firewall
```

Then execute the command

```
/etc/init.d/iptables save
```

The rules will be saved in a file, `/etc/sysconfig/iptables`. After this, the startup script will find this file and load the saved rules automatically.

A word of caution is in order about saving and loading the firewall rules using this method. The `iptables save` and `load` features are not fully debugged at this point. If your particular firewall configuration results in a syntax error when saving or loading the rules, you must continue using some other startup mechanism, such as executing the firewall script from /etc/rc.d/rc.local.

Starting the Firewall on Boot with Debian

As with many other things, configuring the firewall script to start on boot is simpler on Debian than on other distributions. You can make the firewall start and stop on boot with the update-rc.d command. Run update-rc.d with the firewall script in /etc/init.d, and set your current directory to /etc/init.d/ as well:

```
cd /etc/init.d
update-rc.d rc.firewall defaults
```

See the man page for update-rc.d for more information on its usage beyond that shown here.

Other aspects of the firewall script depend on whether you have a registered, static IP address or a dynamic, DHCP-assigned IP address. The firewall script as presented in this chapter is set up for a site with a statically assigned, permanent IP address.

Installing a Firewall with a Dynamic IP Address

If you have a dynamically assigned IP address, the standard firewall installation method won't work without modification. The firewall rules would be installed before the network interfaces are brought up, before the system is assigned an IP address, and possibly before being assigned a default gateway router or name servers.

The firewall script itself needs the IPADDR and NAMESERVER values defined. Both the DHCP server and the local /etc/resolv.conf file can define up to three name servers. Also, any given site may or may not know the addresses of their name servers, default gateway router, or DHCP server ahead of time. Furthermore, it's not uncommon for your network mask, subnet, and broadcast addresses to change over time as the ISP renumbers its network. Some ISPs assign a different IP address on a frequent basis, with the result that your IP address can change numerous times during the course of an ongoing connection.

Your site must provide some means of dynamically updating the installed firewall rules as these changes occur. Appendix B, "Firewall Examples and Support Scripts," provides sample scripts designed to handle these changes automatically.

The firewall script could read these shell variables directly from the environment or could read them from a file. In any case, the variables would not be hard-coded into the firewall script, as they are in the example in this chapter.

Summary

This chapter led you through the processes involved in developing a standalone firewall using iptables and nftables. The deny-by-default policy was established. Some commonly used attack vectors were fixed at the beginning of the script, including source address spoofing, protecting services running on unprivileged ports, and DNS. Examples of rules for popular network services were shown. Finally, the issues involved in firewall installation were described, both for sites with a static IP address and for sites with a dynamically assigned IP address.

Chapter 6 uses the standalone firewall as the basis for building an optimized firewall. Chapter 7 uses it as the basis for a more complicated firewall architecture. A screened subnet architecture using two firewalls separating a DMZ perimeter network is described in Chapter 7. A small business could easily have the need and the resources for this more elaborate configuration. Chapter 8 uses the standalone firewall as the basis for its examples but does not build on this example directly.

II

Advanced Issues, Multiple Firewalls, and Perimeter Networks

Firewall Optimization

Chapter 5, "Building and Installing a Standalone Firewall," used both the `iptables` and `nftables` firewall administration programs to build a simple, single-system, custom-designed firewall. This chapter introduces firewall optimization. Optimization can be divided into three major categories: rule organization, use of the state module, and user-defined chains. The example in the preceding chapter was shown both with and without the use of the state module. This chapter focuses on rule organization and user-defined chains.

Rule Organization

Little optimization can be done using only the INPUT, OUTPUT, and FORWARD chains. Chain traversal is top to bottom, one rule at a time, until the packet matches a rule. The rules on a chain must be ordered hierarchically, from most general to most specific.

There is no hard-and-fast formula for rule organization. The two main underlying factors are which services are hosted on the machine and the machine's primary purpose, noting especially the services with the heaviest traffic on the machine. The requirements of a dedicated firewall and packet forwarder are very different from those of a bastion firewall protecting a dedicated web or mail server. Likewise, a site administrator is likely to place different performance priorities on a firewalled machine that serves primarily as a workstation than on a firewall that serves as both a residential gateway and a Linux server for a home.

The third underlying factor to consider when preparing to organize rules for firewall optimization is the available network bandwidth, the speed of the Internet connection. Optimization isn't likely to buy much, if anything, for a site with a residential-speed Internet connection. Even for a heavily accessed website, the machine's CPU isn't likely to break a sweat. The bottleneck is the Internet connection itself.

Begin with Rules That Block Traffic on High Ports

As the examples in Chapter 5 demonstrated, the bulk of the rules are antispoofing rules, or rules blocking traffic on specific high ports (such as NFS or X Windows). These types of rules must come before the rules allowing traffic to specific services. Obviously, the FTP data channel rules must come near the end of the rule list, even though you'd want the rules to be near the top of the list because FTP transfers tend to be large.

Use the State Module for ESTABLISHED and RELATED Matches

Using the state module's ESTABLISHED and RELATED matches essentially allows for moving all rules for ongoing exchanges to the head of the chains, as well as eliminating the need for specific rules for the server half of a connection. In fact, bypassing filter matching for ongoing, recognized, previously accepted exchanges is one of the two primary purposes of the state module.

The state module's second primary purpose is to serve a firewall-filtering function. Connection state tracking allows the firewall to associate packets with ongoing exchanges. This is particularly useful for connectionless, stateless UDP exchanges.

Consider the Transport Protocol

The transport protocol that the service runs over is another factor. In a static firewall, the overhead of testing every single incoming packet against all the spoofing rules is a big loss.

TCP Services: Bypass the Spoofing Rules

Even without the state module, for TCP-based services, the rule for the remote server half of a connection can bypass the spoofing rules. The TCP layer will drop incoming spoofed packets with the ACK bit set because the packet won't match any of the TCP layer's established connection states.

The remote client half of a rule pair must follow the spoofing rules, however, because the typical client rule covers both the initial connection request and the ongoing traffic from the client. If the SYN and ACK flags are tested for individually, the rules testing for the ACK flag in packets arriving from remote clients can bypass the spoofing tests. The spoofing tests must apply to only the initial SYN request.

Use of the state module also allows the rule for the remote client's incoming connection request, the initial SYN packet, to be logically separate from the rule for the client's subsequent ACK packets. Only the initial connection request, the initial NEW packet, needs to be tested against the spoofing rules.

UDP Services: Place Incoming Packet Rules after Spoofing Rules

Without the state module, for UDP-based services the rule for incoming packets must always follow the spoofing rules. The concept of client and server is maintained at the application level, assuming that it's maintained at all. At the firewall and UDP levels, without connection state, there is no indication of initiator and responder, other than the service port or unprivileged port used.

DNS is an example of a connectionless UDP service. Without connection state, there isn't a mapping between the destination address where the client sent a query and the source address in an incoming response packet. One of the reasons DNS cache poisoning is possible is that DNS server implementations do not check whether an incoming packet was a legitimate response from the server previously queried or whether the packet was sent from some other address. Furthermore, some implementations do not even ensure that a client made a request. An incoming, unrequested rogue packet could be used to update the local DNS cache even without an initial query having been made.

TCP versus UDP Services: Place UDP Rules after TCP Rules

Overall, UDP rules should be placed later in the firewall chains, after any TCP rules. This is because most Internet services run over TCP, and connectionless UDP services are typically simple, single-packet, query-and-response services. Testing the single or UDP packet or a handful of them against the preceding rules for ongoing TCP connections doesn't add noticeable drag to a UDP query and response. Multiconnection session protocols are not firewall friendly to begin with. Such services cannot pass through a firewall or NAT without specific ALG support.

ICMP Services: Place Their Rules Late in the Rule Chain

ICMP is another protocol whose firewall rules can be placed late in the rule chain. ICMP packets are small control and status messages. As such, they are sent relatively infrequently. Legitimate ICMP packets usually consist of a single, nonfragmented packet. With the exception of echo-request, ICMP packets are almost always sent as a control or status message in response to an exceptional outgoing packet of some kind.

Place Firewall Rules for Heavily Used Services as Early as Possible

Generally, there are no hard-and-fast rules for firewall rule placement in a list. Rules for heavily used services, such as the HTTP-related rules for a dedicated web server, should be placed as early as possible. Rules for applications that involve high, ongoing packet counts also should be placed as early as possible. However, as mentioned earlier, the data stream protocols for applications such as FTP require the rules to be placed near the end of the chain, after any other application rules, unless a specific helper is used for those protocols.

Use Traffic Flow to Determine Where to Place Rules for Multiple Network Interfaces

If the host has multiple network interfaces, rules specific to a given interface should be placed with regard to which interfaces will have the heaviest traffic flow. Rules for those interfaces should precede rules for other interfaces. Interface considerations are probably of little interest to a residential site, but they can have a major impact on throughput for a commercial site.

As a case in point, this issue came up several years ago with a small ISP that had built a firewall based on the ipfwadm and ipchains examples on the previous author Bob Ziegler's website. As shown in Figure 6.1 and Figure 6.2, the path that packets take through the operating system is very different between IPFW and Netfilter. Unlike Netfilter and iptables, with ipchains, packets passing between network interfaces are passed from the

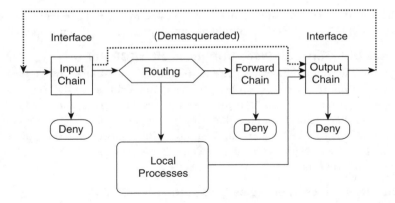

Figure 6.1   IPFW loopback and masqueraded packet traversal

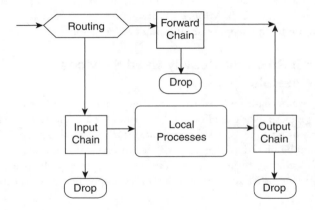

Figure 6.2   Netfilter packet traversal

INPUT chain to the FORWARD chain to the OUTPUT chain. The examples on the website were intended as examples for people at home. The input and output rules for the LAN were the last rules in the scripts. The rules specific to the local Linux host came first. The ISP's firewall was primarily functioning as a router or gateway. Through experimentation, the ISP found that moving the I/O rules for the LAN interface to the beginning of the INPUT and OUT-PUT chains resulted in more than a megabit-per-second increase in throughput.

User-Defined Chains

For iptables the filter table has three permanent, built-in chains: INPUT, OUTPUT, and FORWARD. iptables enables you to define chains of your own, called user-defined chains. In nftables all tables are user defined but in practical terms the filter table is still used.

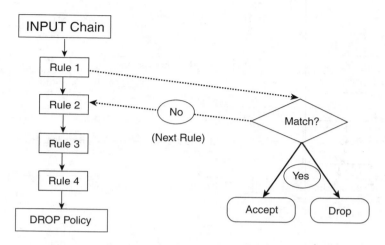

Figure 6.3   Standard chain traversal

    User-defined chains are treated as rule targets—that is, based on the set of matches specified in a rule, the target can branch off or jump to a user-defined chain. Rather than the packet being accepted or dropped, control is passed to the user-defined chain to perform more specific match tests relative to packets matching the branch rule. After the user-defined chain is traversed, control returns to the calling chain, and matching continues from the next rule in the calling chain unless the user-defined chain matched and took action on the packet.

    Figure 6.3 shows the standard, top-down rule traversal using the built-in chains.

    User-defined chains are useful in optimizing the rule set and therefore are often used. They allow the rules to be organized into categorical trees. Rather than relying on the straight-through, top-down checkoff list type of matching inherent in the standard chain traversal, packet match tests can be selectively narrowed down based on the characteristics of the packet. Figure 6.4 shows initial packet flow. After initial tests common to all incoming packets are performed, packet matching branches off based on the destination address in the packet.

    Branching is based on destination address in this example. Source address matching is done later in relation to specific applications, such as remote DNS or mail servers. In most cases, the remote address will be "anywhere." Matching on destination address at this point distinguishes among unicast packets targeted to this machine, broadcast packets, multicast packets, and (depending on whether it's the INPUT or FORWARD chain) packets targeted to internal hosts.

    Figure 6.5 details the user-defined chain for the protocol rules for packets specifically addressed to this host. As shown, user-defined chains can jump to other user-defined chains containing even more specific tests.

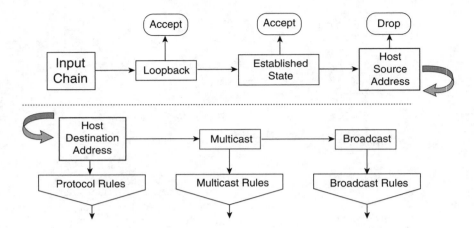

Figure 6.4   User-defined chains based on destination address

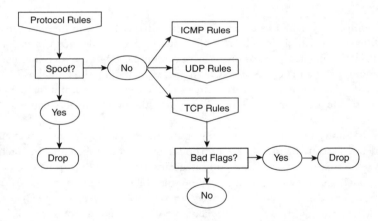

Figure 6.5   User-defined chains based on protocol

This list summarizes the characteristics of user-defined chains from Chapter 3, "`iptables`: The Legacy Linux Firewall Administration Program":

- User-defined chains are created with the -N or --new-chain operation.
- User-defined chain names can be up to 30 characters in length.
- User-defined chain names can contain hyphens (–) but not underscores (_).
- User-defined chains are accessed as rule targets.
- User-defined chains do not have default policies.

- User-defined chains can call other user-defined chains.
- If the packet doesn't match a rule on the user-defined chain, control returns to the next rule in the calling chain.
- The user-defined chain can be exited early, with control returning to the next rule in the calling chain, via use of the RETURN target.
- User-defined chains are deleted with the -X or --delete-chain operation.
- A chain must be empty before it can be deleted.
- A chain cannot have any references to it from other chains to be deleted.
- A chain is emptied specifically by name, or all existing chains are emptied if no chain is specified, with the -F or --flush operation.

The next section takes advantage of user-defined chains and the concepts presented in the section on rule organization to optimize the single-system firewall presented in Chapter 5.

Optimized Examples

The following shows optimized examples of the firewalls built in Chapter 5. The first example is for the iptables-based firewall. If you're using nftables, you can safely skip this section and go to the nftables script example instead.

The Optimized iptables Script

One new variable is declared, USER_CHAINS, which contains the names of all the user-defined chains used in the script. The chains are listed here:

- **tcp-state-flags**—Contains the rules to check for invalid TCP state flag combinations.
- **connection-tracking**—Contains the rules to check for state-related matches, INVALID, ESTABLISHED, and RELATED.
- **source-address-check**—Contains the rules to check for illegal source addresses.
- **destination-address-check**—Contains the rules to check for illegal destination addresses.
- **EXT-input**—Contains the interface-specific user-defined chains for the INPUT chain. In this example, the host has one interface connected to the Internet.
- **EXT-output**—Contains the interface-specific user-defined chains for the OUTPUT chain. In this example, the host has one interface connected to the Internet.
- **local-dns-server-query**—Contains the rules for outgoing queries from either the local DNS server or local clients.
- **remote-dns-server-response**—Contains the rules for incoming responses from a remote DNS server.

- **local-tcp-client-request**—Contains the rules for outgoing TCP connection requests and locally generated client traffic to remote servers.
- **remote-tcp-server-response**—Contains the rules for incoming responses from remote TCP servers.
- **remote-tcp-client-request**—Contains the rules for incoming TCP connection requests and remotely generated client traffic to local servers.
- **local-tcp-server-response**—Contains the rules for outgoing responses to remote clients.
- **local-udp-client-request**—Contains the rules for outgoing UDP client traffic to remote servers.
- **remote-udp-server-response**—Contains the rules for incoming responses from remote UDP servers.
- **EXT-icmp-out**—Contains the rules for outgoing ICMP packets.
- **EXT-icmp-in**—Contains the rules for incoming ICMP packets.
- **EXT-log-in**—Contains the logging rules for incoming packets before dropping them by the default INPUT policy.
- **EXT-log-out**—Contains the logging rules for outgoing packets before dropping them by the default OUTPUT policy.
- **log-tcp-state**—Contains the logging rules for TCP packets with illegal state flag combinations before dropping them.
- **remote-dhcp-server-response**—Contains the rules for incoming packets from this host's DHCP server.
- **local-dhcp-client-query**—Contains the rules for outgoing DHCP client packets.

Some interface-specific chains are prefaced with EXT to differentiate them from any user-defined chains containing rules for any LAN interfaces. This firewall example assumes that there is only one interface, the external interface. The point is to suggest that different rules and security policies could be defined on a per-interface basis.

The actual declaration in the firewall shell script would be as shown here:

```
USER_CHAINS="EXT-input                EXT-output \
            tcp-state-flags           connection-tracking  \
            source-address-check      destination-address-check \
            local-dns-server-query    remote-dns-server-response \
            local-tcp-client-request  remote-tcp-server-response \
            remote-tcp-client-request local-tcp-server-response \
            local-udp-client-request  remote-udp-server-response \
            local-dhcp-client-query   remote-dhcp-server-response \
            EXT-icmp-out              EXT-icmp-in \
            EXT-log-in               EXT-log-out \
            log-tcp-state"
```

Firewall Initialization

The firewall script starts out identically to the example in Chapter 5. Recall that a number of shell variables were set, including one called $IPT to define the location of the iptables firewall administration command:

```
#!/bin/sh

IPT="/sbin/iptables"                        # Location of iptables on your system
INTERNET="eth0"                             # Internet-connected interface
LOOPBACK_INTERFACE="lo"                     # However your system names it
IPADDR="my.ip.address"                      # Your IP address
MY_ISP="my.isp.address.range"              # ISP server & NOC address range
SUBNET_BASE="my.subnet.network"            # Your subnet's network address
SUBNET_BROADCAST="my.subnet.bcast"         # Your subnet's broadcast address
LOOPBACK="127.0.0.0/8"                      # Reserved loopback address range
CLASS_A="10.0.0.0/8"                        # Class A private networks
CLASS_B="172.16.0.0/12"                     # Class B private networks
CLASS_C="192.168.0.0/16"                    # Class C private networks
CLASS_D_MULTICAST="224.0.0.0/4"            # Class D multicast addresses
CLASS_E_RESERVED_NET="240.0.0.0/5"         # Class E reserved addresses
BROADCAST_SRC="0.0.0.0"                     # Broadcast source address
BROADCAST_DEST="255.255.255.255"           # Broadcast destination address
PRIVPORTS="0:1023"                          # Well-known, privileged port range
UNPRIVPORTS="1024:65535"                    # Unprivileged port range
```

A number of kernel parameters were also set; refer to Chapter 5 for an explanation of these parameters:

```
# Enable broadcast echo Protection
echo 1 > /proc/sys/net/ipv4/icmp_echo_ignore_broadcasts
# Disable Source Routed Packets
for f in /proc/sys/net/ipv4/conf/*/accept_source_route; do
    echo 0 > $f
done
# Enable TCP SYN Cookie Protection
echo 1 > /proc/sys/net/ipv4/tcp_syncookies
# Disable ICMP Redirect Acceptance
for f in /proc/sys/net/ipv4/conf/*/accept_redirects; do
    echo 0 > $f
done


# Don't send Redirect Messages
for f in /proc/sys/net/ipv4/conf/*/send_redirects; do
    echo 0 > $f
done
# Drop Spoofed Packets coming in on an interface, which, if replied to,
# would result in the reply going out a different interface.
for f in /proc/sys/net/ipv4/conf/*/rp_filter; do
    echo 1 > $f
done
# Log packets with impossible addresses.
for f in /proc/sys/net/ipv4/conf/*/log_martians; do
    echo 1 > $f
done
```

The built-in chains and any preexisting user-defined chains are emptied:

```
# Remove any existing rules from all chains
$IPT --flush
$IPT -t nat --flush
$IPT -t mangle --flush
```

The next step would be to delete the user-defined chains. They can be deleted with the following commands:

```
$IPT -X
$IPT -t nat -X
$IPT -t mangle -X
```

The default policy is first set to ACCEPT for all built-in chains:

```
# Reset the default policy
$IPT --policy INPUT    ACCEPT
$IPT --policy OUTPUT   ACCEPT
$IPT --policy FORWARD ACCEPT
$IPT -t nat --policy PREROUTING  ACCEPT
$IPT -t nat --policy OUTPUT ACCEPT
$IPT -t nat --policy POSTROUTING ACCEPT
$IPT -t mangle --policy PREROUTING ACCEPT
$IPT -t mangle --policy OUTPUT ACCEPT
```

Here is the final code for the beginning of the firewall script, namely, the code to enable the firewall to be stopped easily. With this code placed below the preceding code, when you call the script with an argument of stop the script will flush, clear, and reset the default policies, and the firewall will effectively stop.

```
if [ "$1" = "stop" ]
then
echo "Firewall completely stopped!  WARNING: THIS HOST HAS NO FIREWALL RUNNING."
exit 0
fi
```

Now reset the real default policy to DROP:

```
$IPT --policy INPUT    DROP
$IPT --policy OUTPUT   DROP
$IPT --policy FORWARD DROP
```

Traffic through the loopback interface is enabled:

```
# Unlimited traffic on the loopback interface
$IPT -A INPUT  -i lo -j ACCEPT
$IPT -A OUTPUT -o lo -j ACCEPT
```

Now the script starts differing from the example in Chapter 5.

The user-defined chains can now be created. Their names were included in the single shell variable, USER_CHAINS, for just this purpose:

```
# Create the user-defined chains
for i in $USER_CHAINS; do
    $IPT -N $i
done
```

Installing the Chains

Unfortunately, the function call–like nature of building and installing the chains doesn't lend itself to a serial, step-by-step explanation without the capability to show different places in the script simultaneously, side by side.

The idea is to place the rules on the user-defined chains and then to install those chains on the built-in INPUT, OUTPUT, and FORWARD chains. If the script contains an error and exits while building the user-defined chains, the built-in chains will contain no rules, the default DROP policy will be in effect, and, presumably, the loopback traffic will be enabled.

So, this first installation section is actually placed at the end of the firewall script. The first step is to check for illegal TCP state flag combinations:

```
# If TCP: Check for common stealth scan TCP state patterns
$IPT -A INPUT  -p tcp -j tcp-state-flags
$IPT -A OUTPUT -p tcp -j tcp-state-flags
```

Notice that the same chain can be referenced from more than one calling chain. The rules on the user-defined chains needn't be duplicated for the INPUT and OUTPUT chains. Now when the packet processing reaches this point, the processing will "jump" to the user-defined tcp-state-flags chain. When the processing is complete within that chain, the processing will be passed back here and continue on, unless a final disposition for the packet was found in the user-defined chain.

If the state module is being used, the next step is to bypass the firewall altogether if the packet is part of an ongoing, previously accepted exchange:

```
if [ "$CONNECTION_TRACKING" = "1" ]; then
    # Bypass the firewall filters for established exchanges
    $IPT -A INPUT  -j connection-tracking
    $IPT -A OUTPUT -j connection-tracking
fi
```

If the machine is a DHCP client, a provision must be made for the broadcast messages sent between the client and the server during initialization. A provision must also be made to accept the broadcast source address, 0.0.0.0. The source and destination address-checking tests would drop the initial DHCP traffic:

```
if [ "$DHCP_CLIENT" = "1" ]; then
    $IPT -A INPUT  -i $INTERNET -p udp \
            --sport 67 --dport 68 -j remote-dhcp-server-response
    $IPT -A OUTPUT -o $INTERNET -p udp \
            --sport 68 --dport 67 -j local-dhcp-client-query
fi
```

Now jump to the user-defined chain to drop incoming packets that are using this host's IP address as their source address. Then test for other illegal source and destination addresses:

```
# Test for illegal source and destination addresses in incoming packets
$IPT -A INPUT  ! -p tcp -j source-address-check
$IPT -A INPUT  -p tcp --syn -j source-address-check
$IPT -A INPUT  -j destination-address-check
```

```
# Test for illegal destination addresses in outgoing packets
$IPT -A OUTPUT -j destination-address-check
```

Locally generated outgoing packets don't need their source address checked because the firewall rules explicitly require this host's IP address in the source field. Destination address checking is performed on outgoing packets, however.

At this point, regular incoming packets addressed to this host's IP address can be handed off to the main section of the firewall. Any incoming packet that doesn't match a rule on the EXT-input chain will return here to be logged and dropped:

```
# Begin standard firewall tests for packets addressed to this host
$IPT -A INPUT -i $INTERNET -d $IPADDR -j EXT-input
```

A final set of tests on destination address is necessary. Broadcast and multicast packets are not addressed to this host's unicast IP address. They are addressed to a broadcast or multicast address.

As mentioned in Chapter 5, multicast packets won't be received unless you register to receive packets addressed to a particular multicast address. If you want to receive multicast packets, you must either accept all of them or add a rule specific to the particular address and port used for any given session. The following code enables you to choose whether to drop or accept the traffic:

```
# Multicast traffic
$IPT -A INPUT   -i $INTERNET -p udp -d $CLASS_D_MULTICAST -j [ DROP | ACCEPT ]
$IPT -A OUTPUT -o $INTERNET -p udp -s $IPADDR -d $CLASS_D_MULTICAST \
    -j [ DROP | ACCEPT ]
```

At this point, regular outgoing packets from this host can be handed off to the main section of the firewall. Any outgoing packet that doesn't match a rule on the EXT-output chain will return here to be logged and dropped:

```
# Begin standard firewall tests for packets sent from this host.
# Source address spoofing by this host is not allowed due to the
# test on source address in this rule.
$IPT -A OUTPUT -o $INTERNET -s $IPADDR -j EXT-output
```

Any broadcast messages are implicitly ignored by the last input and output rules. Depending on the nature of the public or external network that the machine is directly connected to, broadcasts could be very common on the local subnet. You probably don't want to log such messages, even with rate-limited logging.

Finally, any remaining packets are dropped by the default policy. Any logging would be done at this point:

```
# Log anything of interest that fell through,
# before the default policy drops the packet.
$IPT -A INPUT   -j EXT-log-in
$IPT -A OUTPUT -j EXT-log-out
```

This marks the end of the firewall and is the last reference to the INPUT and OUTPUT chains.

Building the User-Defined `EXT-input` and `EXT-output` Chains

This section describes the construction of the user-defined chains that were jumped to in the preceding section. At the top level, rules are built on the general `EXT-input` and `EXT-output` chains. These rules are jumps to more specific sets of matches contained in the dedicated user-defined chains you've created.

Note that the `EXT-input` and `EXT-output` layer is not necessary. The following rules and jumps could just as easily have been associated with the built-in `INPUT` and `OUTPUT` chains.

Using these chains has one advantage, however. Because the jumps to these chains are dependent on the source or destination address, you know at this point that the incoming packet is addressed to this host and has a source address believed to be legitimate. The outgoing packet is addressed from this host and has a destination address believed to be legitimate. Also, if the state module is in use, the packet is either the first packet in an exchange or a new, unrelated ICMP packet.

In summary, the `EXT-input` and `EXT-output` chains will be used to select traffic by protocol and by direction, in terms of client or server. Each rule will provide the branch point to the firewall rules specific to that protocol and packet characteristics. The matches performed by the `EXT-input` and `EXT-output` rules are the heart of the optimization available with user-defined chains.

DNS Traffic

The rules to identify DNS traffic come first. Until the DNS rules are installed, your network software won't be capable of locating services and hosts out on the Internet unless you use the IP address.

The first pair of rules match on queries from the local cache and forward name server, if you have one, and responses from the remote DNS server. The local server is configured as a slave to the remote, primary server, so the local server will fail if the lookup doesn't succeed. This configuration is less common for a small office/home office:

```
$IPT -A EXT-output -p udp --sport 53 --dport 53 \
        -j local-dns-server-query

$IPT -A EXT-input -p udp --sport 53 --dport 53 \
        -j remote-dns-server-response
```

The next pair of rules match on standard DNS client lookup requests over TCP, when the server's response is too large to fit in a UDP DNS packet. These rules would be used by both a forwarding name server and a standard client:

```
$IPT -A EXT-output -p tcp \
        --sport $UNPRIVPORTS --dport 53 \
        -j local-dns-server-query

$IPT A EXT-input -p tcp ! --syn \
        --sport 53 --dport $UNPRIVPORTS \
        -j remote-dns-server-response
```

What follows are the user-defined chains containing the actual `ACCEPT` and `DROP` rules.

local-dns-server-query and remote-dns-server-response

These two user-defined chains, `local-dns-server-query` and `remote-dns-server-response`, perform the final determination on the packet.

The `local-dns-server-query` chain selects the outgoing request packets based on the remote server's destination address. For this chain, you must define the name servers you'd like to use:

```
NAMESERVER_1="your.name.server"
NAMESERVER_2="your.secondary.nameserver"
NAMESERVER_3="your.tertiary.nameserver"

# DNS Forwarding Name Server or client requests
if [ "$CONNECTION_TRACKING" = "1" ]; then
    $IPT -A local-dns-server-query \
            -d $NAMESERVER_1 \
            -m state --state NEW -j ACCEPT

    $IPT -A local-dns-server-query \
            -d $NAMESERVER_2 \
            -m state --state NEW -j ACCEPT

    $IPT -A local-dns-server-query \
            -d $NAMESERVER_3 \
            -m state --state NEW -j ACCEPT
fi

$IPT -A local-dns-server-query \
        -d $NAMESERVER_1 -j ACCEPT

$IPT -A local-dns-server-query \
        -d $NAMESERVER_2 -j ACCEPT

$IPT -A local-dns-server-query \
        -d $NAMESERVER_3 -j ACCEPT
```

The `remote-dns-server-response` chain selects the incoming response packets based on the remote server's source address:

```
# DNS server responses to local requests
$IPT -A remote-dns-server-response \
        -s $NAMESERVER_1 -j ACCEPT

$IPT -A remote-dns-server-response \
        -s $NAMESERVER_2 -j ACCEPT

$IPT -A remote-dns-server-response \
        -s $NAMESERVER_3 -j ACCEPT
```

Notice that the final rules select on only the remote server's IP address. The calling rules on the `EXT-input` and `EXT-output` chains already have matched on the UDP or TCP header fields. Those match tests don't need to be performed again.

local-dns-client-request and *remote-dns-server-response*

These two user-defined chains, `local-dns-client-request` and `remote-dns-server-response`, perform the final determination on packets exchanged between local TCP clients and remote servers.

The `local-dns-client-request` chain selects the outgoing request packets based on the remote server's destination address and port. The `remote-dns-server-response` chain selects the incoming response packets based on the remote server's source address and port.

Local Client Traffic over TCP

The next pair of rules match on standard, local client traffic to remote servers over TCP:

```
$IPT -A EXT-output -p tcp \
        --sport $UNPRIVPORTS \
        -j local-tcp-client-request

$IPT -A EXT-input -p tcp ! --syn \
        --dport $UNPRIVPORTS \
        -j remote-tcp-server-response
```

Remember that these rules normally are not tested when the state module is used, with the exception of the first outgoing SYN request.

The specific reference to the TCP protocol is required in the following rules, even though the protocol field was matched on by the calling rule, because the source or destination port is specified. This is a syntactic requirement of `iptables`. Also note that you need to define the source and destination hosts within these rules, as indicated by the `<selected host>` and other such calls. In addition, if you use these rules, be sure to define variables for the ones you choose, such as POP_SERVER, MAIL_SERVER, NEWS_SERVER, and so on. The following code enables TCP traffic from local clients:

```
# Local TCP client output and remote server input chains

# SSH client
if [ "$CONNECTION_TRACKING" = "1" ]; then
    $IPT -A local-tcp-client-request -p tcp \
            -d <selected host> --dport 22 \
            -m state --state NEW \
            -j ACCEPT
fi

$IPT -A local-tcp-client-request -p tcp \
        -d <selected host> --dport 22 \
        -j ACCEPT

$IPT -A remote-tcp-server-response -p tcp ! --syn \
        -s <selected host> --sport 22  \
        -j ACCEPT
```

```
# Client rules for HTTP, HTTPS and FTP control requests
if [ "$CONNECTION_TRACKING" = "1" ]; then
    $IPT -A local-tcp-client-request -p tcp \
            -m multiport --destination-port 80,443,21 \
            --syn -m state --state NEW \
            -j ACCEPT
fi
$IPT -A local-tcp-client-request -p tcp \
        -m multiport --destination-port 80,443,21 \
        -j ACCEPT

$IPT -A remote-tcp-server-response -p tcp \
        -m multiport --source-port 80,443,21  ! --syn \
        -j ACCEPT

# POP client
if [ "$CONNECTION_TRACKING" = "1" ]; then
    $IPT -A local-tcp-client-request -p tcp \
            -d $POP_SERVER --dport 110 \
            -m state --state NEW \
            -j ACCEPT
fi

$IPT -A local-tcp-client-request -p tcp \
        -d $POP_SERVER --dport 110 \
        -j ACCEPT

$IPT -A remote-tcp-server-response -p tcp ! --syn \
        -s $POP_SERVER --sport 110  \
        -j ACCEPT

# SMTP mail client
if [ "$CONNECTION_TRACKING" = "1" ]; then
    $IPT -A local-tcp-client-request -p tcp \
            -d $MAIL_SERVER --dport 25 \
            -m state --state NEW \
            -j ACCEPT
fi

$IPT -A local-tcp-client-request -p tcp \
        -d $MAIL_SERVER --dport 25 \
        -j ACCEPT

$IPT -A remote-tcp-server-response -p tcp ! --syn \
        -s $MAIL_SERVER --sport 25  \
        -j ACCEPT

# Usenet news client
if [ "$CONNECTION_TRACKING" = "1" ]; then
    $IPT -A local-tcp-client-request -p tcp \
            -d $NEWS_SERVER --dport 119 \
            -m state --state NEW \
            -j ACCEPT
fi
$IPT -A local-tcp-client-request -p tcp \
        -d $NEWS_SERVER --dport 119 \
        -j ACCEPT
```

```
$IPT -A remote-tcp-server-response -p tcp ! --syn \
        -s $NEWS_SERVER --sport 119  \
        -j ACCEPT

# FTP client - passive mode data channel connection
if [ "$CONNECTION_TRACKING" = "1" ]; then
    $IPT -A local-tcp-client-request -p tcp \
            --dport $UNPRIVPORTS \
            -m state --state NEW \
            -j ACCEPT
fi

$IPT -A local-tcp-client-request -p tcp \
        --dport $UNPRIVPORTS -j ACCEPT

$IPT -A remote-tcp-server-response -p tcp  ! --syn \
        --sport $UNPRIVPORTS -j ACCEPT
```

Local Server Traffic over TCP

The next pair of rules match on standard, local server traffic to remote clients over TCP.
These would be applicable only if you're actually offering services to remote hosts:

```
$IPT -A EXT-input -p tcp \
        --sport $UNPRIVPORTS \
        -j remote-tcp-client-request

$IPT -A EXT-output -p tcp ! --syn \
        --dport $UNPRIVPORTS \
        -j local-tcp-server-response
```

The next pair of rules handle incoming data channel connections from remote FTP
servers when using port mode:

```
# Kludge for incoming FTP data channel connections
# from remote servers using port mode.
# The state modules treat this connection as RELATED
# if the ip_conntrack_ftp module is loaded.

$IPT -A EXT-input -p tcp \
        --sport 20 --dport $UNPRIVPORTS \
        -j ACCEPT

$IPT -A EXT-output -p tcp ! --syn \
        --sport $UNPRIVPORTS --dport 20 \
        -j ACCEPT
```

remote-tcp-client-request and *local-tcp-server-response*

These two user-defined chains, remote-tcp-client-request and local-tcp-
server-response, perform the final determination on packets exchanged between
remote TCP clients and local servers.

The remote-tcp-client-request chain selects the incoming request packets based
on the remote client's source address and port. The local-tcp-server-response chain

selects the outgoing response packets based on the remote client's destination address
and port:

```
# Remote TCP client input and local server output chains

# SSH server
if [ "$CONNECTION_TRACKING" = "1" ]; then
    $IPT -A remote-tcp-client-request -p tcp \
            -s <selected host> --destination-port 22 \
            -m state --state NEW \
            -j ACCEPT
fi

$IPT -A remote-tcp-client-request -p tcp \
        -s <selected host> --destination-port 22 \
        -j ACCEPT

$IPT -A local-tcp-server-response -p tcp  ! --syn \
        --source-port 22 -d <selected host> \
        -j ACCEPT

# AUTH identd server
$IPT -A remote-tcp-client-request -p tcp \
        --destination-port 113 \
        -j REJECT --reject-with tcp-reset
```

Local Client Traffic over UDP

The next pair of rules match on standard, local client traffic to remote servers over UDP:

```
# Local UDP client, remote server
$IPT -A EXT-output -p udp \
        --sport $UNPRIVPORTS \
        -j local-udp-client-request

$IPT -A EXT-input -p udp \
        --dport $UNPRIVPORTS \
        -j remote-udp-server-response
```

Bypassing Source Address Checking without Using the State Module

If you aren't using the state module, most TCP rules could still be placed before the source
address spoofing rules. TCP maintains connection state information itself. Only the first
incoming connection request, the first SYN packet, requires source address checking. You
can do this by reorganizing the rules and splitting the rule for incoming client traffic into two
tests, one for the initial SYN flag and one for all subsequent ACK flags.

Using the rules for a local web server as an example, the first rule would follow the
spoofing rules:

```
if [ "$CONNECTION_TRACKING" = "1" ]; then
    $IPT -A remote-tcp-client-request -p tcp \
            --destination-port 80 \
            -m state --state NEW \
            -j ACCEPT
```

```
    else
        $IPT -A remote-tcp-client-request -p tcp --syn \
                --destination-port 80 \
                -j ACCEPT
    fi
```

The next two rules would precede the spoofing rules:

```
$IPT -A INPUT -p tcp ! --syn \
        --source-port $UNPRIVPORTS \
        -d $IPADDR --destination-port 80 \
        -j ACCEPT

$IPT -A OUTPUT -p tcp  ! --syn \
        -s $IPADDR --source-port 80  \
        --destination-port $UNPRIVPORTS \
        -j ACCEPT
```

local-udp-client-request and *remote-udp-server-response*

These two user-defined chains, `local-udp-client-request` and `remote-udp-server-response`, perform the final determination on packets exchanged between local UDP clients and remote servers.

The `local-udp-client-request` chain selects the outgoing request packets based on the remote server's destination address and port. The `remote-udp-server-response` chain selects the incoming response packets based on the remote server's source address and port. Be sure to define the TIME_SERVER variable before implementing this rule:

```
# NTP time client
if [ "$CONNECTION_TRACKING" = "1" ]; then
    $IPT -A local-udp-client-request -p udp \
            -d $TIME_SERVER --dport 123 \
            -m state --state NEW \
            -j ACCEPT
fi

$IPT -A local-udp-client-request -p udp \
        -d $TIME_SERVER --dport 123 \
        -j ACCEPT

$IPT -A remote-udp-server-response -p udp \
        -s $TIME_SERVER --sport 123 \
        -j ACCEPT
```

ICMP Traffic

Finally, the last pair of rules match on incoming and outgoing ICMP traffic:

```
# ICMP traffic
$IPT -A EXT-input -p icmp -j EXT-icmp-in

$IPT -A EXT-output -p icmp -j EXT-icmp-out
```

EXT-icmp-in and EXT-icmp-out

These two user-defined chains, EXT-icmp-in and EXT-icmp-out, perform the final determination on ICMP packets exchanged between the local host and remote machines.

The EXT-icmp-in chain selects the incoming ICMP packets based on the message type. The EXT-icmp-out chain selects the outgoing ICMP packets based on the message type:

```
# Log and drop initial ICMP fragments
$IPT -A EXT-icmp-in --fragment -j LOG \
        --log-prefix "Fragmented incoming ICMP: "

$IPT -A EXT-icmp-in --fragment -j DROP

$IPT -A EXT-icmp-out --fragment -j LOG \
        --log-prefix "Fragmented outgoing ICMP: "

$IPT -A EXT-icmp-out --fragment -j DROP

# Outgoing ping
if [ "$CONNECTION_TRACKING" = "1" ]; then
    $IPT -A EXT-icmp-out -p icmp \
            --icmp-type echo-request \
            -m state --state NEW \
            -j ACCEPT
fi

$IPT -A EXT-icmp-out -p icmp \
        --icmp-type echo-request -j ACCEPT

$IPT -A EXT-icmp-in -p icmp \
        --icmp-type echo-reply -j ACCEPT

# Incoming ping

if [ "$CONNECTION_TRACKING" = "1" ]; then
    $IPT -A EXT-icmp-in -p icmp \
            -s $MY_ISP \
            --icmp-type echo-request \
            -m state --state NEW \
            -j ACCEPT
fi

$IPT -A EXT-icmp-in -p icmp \
        --icmp-type echo-request \
        -s $MY_ISP -j ACCEPT

$IPT -A EXT-icmp-out -p icmp \
        --icmp-type echo-reply \
        -d $MY_ISP -j ACCEPT

# Destination Unreachable Type 3
$IPT -A EXT-icmp-out -p icmp \
        --icmp-type fragmentation-needed -j ACCEPT
```

```
$IPT -A EXT-icmp-in -p icmp \
        --icmp-type destination-unreachable -j ACCEPT

# Parameter Problem
$IPT -A EXT-icmp-out -p icmp \
        --icmp-type parameter-problem -j ACCEPT

$IPT -A EXT-icmp-in -p icmp \
        --icmp-type parameter-problem -j ACCEPT

# Time Exceeded
$IPT -A EXT-icmp-in -p icmp \
        --icmp-type time-exceeded -j ACCEPT

# Source Quench
$IPT -A EXT-icmp-out -p icmp \
        --icmp-type source-quench -j ACCEPT

$IPT -A EXT-icmp-in -p icmp \
        --icmp-type source-quench -j ACCEPT
```

tcp-state-flags

The tcp-state-flags chain is the very first user-defined chain you will attach to both the built-in INPUT and OUTPUT chains. The tests match on TCP state flag combinations that are artificially crafted and often are used in stealth scans:

```
# All of the bits are cleared
$IPT -A tcp-state-flags -p tcp --tcp-flags ALL NONE -j log-tcp-state

# SYN and FIN are both set
$IPT -A tcp-state-flags -p tcp --tcp-flags SYN,FIN SYN,FIN -j log-tcp-state

# SYN and RST are both set
$IPT -A tcp-state-flags -p tcp --tcp-flags SYN,RST SYN,RST -j log-tcp-state

# FIN and RST are both set
$IPT -A tcp-state-flags -p tcp --tcp-flags FIN,RST FIN,RST -j log-tcp-state

# FIN is the only bit set, without the expected accompanying ACK
$IPT -A tcp-state-flags -p tcp --tcp-flags ACK,FIN FIN -j log-tcp-state

# PSH is the only bit set, without the expected accompanying ACK
$IPT -A tcp-state-flags -p tcp --tcp-flags ACK,PSH PSH -j log-tcp-state

# URG is the only bit set, without the expected accompanying ACK
$IPT -A tcp-state-flags -p tcp --tcp-flags ACK,URG URG -j log-tcp-state
```

log-tcp-state

The log-tcp-state chain is used for two reasons. First, the log message is prefixed with a specific explanatory message, and because this is a crafted packet, any IP or TCP options are reported. Second, the matching packet is dropped immediately. The two generalized logging chains that come up later are written under the assumption that the logged packets will be dropped by the default policy immediately upon return from the chains:

```
$IPT -A log-tcp-state -p tcp -j LOG \
        --log-prefix "Illegal TCP state: " \
        --log-ip-options --log-tcp-options

$IPT -A log-tcp-state -j DROP
```

connection-tracking

The connection-tracking chain is the second user-defined chain you will attach to both the built-in INPUT and OUTPUT chains. Matching packets bypass the firewall rules and are accepted immediately:

```
if [ "$CONNECTION_TRACKING" = "1" ]; then
    # Bypass the firewall filters for established exchanges
    $IPT -A connection-tracking -m state \
            --state ESTABLISHED,RELATED \
            -j ACCEPT

    $IPT -A connection-tracking -m state --state INVALID \
            -j LOG --log-prefix "INVALID packet: "
    $IPT -A connection-tracking -m state --state INVALID -j DROP
fi
```

local-dhcp-client-query and remote-dhcp-server-response

The local-dhcp-client-query and remote-dhcp-server-response chains contain the rules required of a DHCP client. Placement of these rules in the chain hierarchy is important in relation to any spoofing or generalized broadcast rules. Furthermore, the host will not configure its IP address until after receiving the DHCPACK commitment message from the server. The destination address that the server uses in the DHCPACK message depends on the particular server implementation. If you want to use this rule, you'll need to set DHCP_CLIENT to 1 and also define the DHCP_SERVER variable:

```
# Some broadcast packets are explicitly ignored by the firewall.
# Others are dropped by the default policy.
# DHCP tests must precede broadcast-related rules, as DHCP relies
# on broadcast traffic initially.

if [ "$DHCP_CLIENT" = "1" ]; then
    DHCP_SERVER="my.dhcp.server"

    # Initialization or rebinding: No lease or Lease time expired.

    $IPT -A local-dhcp-client-query \
            -s $BROADCAST_SRC \
            -d $BROADCAST_DEST -j ACCEPT

    # Incoming DHCPOFFER from available DHCP servers
```

```
$IPT -A remote-dhcp-server-response \
        -s $BROADCAST_SRC \
        -d $BROADCAST_DEST -j ACCEPT

# Fall back to initialization
# The client knows its server, but has either lost its lease,
# or else needs to reconfirm the IP address after rebooting.

$IPT -A local-dhcp-client-query \
        -s $BROADCAST_SRC \
        -d $DHCP_SERVER -j ACCEPT

$IPT -A remote-dhcp-server-response \
        -s $DHCP_SERVER \
        -d $BROADCAST_DEST -j ACCEPT

# As a result of the above, we're supposed to change our IP
# address with this message, which is addressed to our new
# address before the dhcp client has received the update.
# Depending on the server implementation, the destination address
# can be the new IP address, the subnet address, or the limited
# broadcast address.

# If the network subnet address is used as the destination,
# the next rule must allow incoming packets destined to the
# subnet address, and the rule must precede any general rules
# that block such incoming broadcast packets.

$IPT -A remote-dhcp-server-response \
        -s $DHCP_SERVER -j ACCEPT

# Lease renewal

$IPT -A local-dhcp-client-query \
        -s $IPADDR \
        -d $DHCP_SERVER -j ACCEPT

fi
```

source-address-check

The source-address-check chain tests for identifiably illegal source addresses. The chain is attached to the INPUT chain alone. The firewall rules guarantee that packets generated by this host contain your IP address as their source address. Notice that these rules would need some adjustment if the host has more than one network interface or if a private LAN is using private class IP addresses.

A DHCP client needs to handle DHCP-related broadcast traffic before performing these tests:

```
# Drop packets pretending to be originating from the receiving interface
$IPT -A source-address-check -s $IPADDR -j DROP

# Refuse packets claiming to be from private networks
```

```
$IPT -A source-address-check -s $CLASS_A -j DROP
$IPT -A source-address-check -s $CLASS_B -j DROP
$IPT -A source-address-check -s $CLASS_C -j DROP
$IPT -A source-address-check -s $CLASS_D_MULTICAST -j DROP
$IPT -A source-address-check -s $CLASS_E_RESERVED_NET -j DROP
$IPT -A source-address-check -s $LOOPBACK  -j DROP

$IPT -A source-address-check -s 0.0.0.0/8 -j DROP
$IPT -A source-address-check -s 169.254.0.0/16 -j DROP
$IPT -A source-address-check -s 192.0.2.0/24 -j DROP
```

destination-address-check

The `destination-address-check` chain tests for broadcast packets, misused multicast addresses, and well-known unprivileged service ports. The chain is attached to both the INPUT and OUTPUT chains. A DHCP client needs to handle DHCP-related broadcast traffic before performing these tests:

```
# Block directed broadcasts from the Internet

$IPT -A destination-address-check $BROADCAST_DEST -j DROP
$IPT -A destination-address-check -d $SUBNET_BASE -j DROP
$IPT -A destination-address-check -d $SUBNET_BROADCAST -j DROP
$IPT -A destination-address-check ! -p udp \
        -d $CLASS_D_MULTICAST -j DROP

# Avoid ports subject to protocol and system administration problems

# TCP unprivileged ports
# Deny connection requests to NFS, SOCKS, and X Window ports
$IPT -A destination-address-check -p tcp -m multiport \
        --destination-port
$NFS_PORT,$OPENWINDOWS_PORT,$SOCKS_PORT,$SQUID_PORT \
        --syn -j DROP

$IPT -A destination-address-check -p tcp --syn \
        --destination-port $XWINDOW_PORTS -j DROP

# UDP unprivileged ports
# Deny connection requests to NFS and lockd ports
$IPT -A destination-address-check -p udp -m multiport \
        --destination-port $NFS_PORT,$LOCKD_PORT -j DROP
```

Logging Dropped Packets with iptables

The EXT-log-in and EXT-log-out chains contain the rules that log packets immediately before the packets fall off the end of their respective chains and are dropped by the default policy. Almost all outgoing packets to be dropped are logged because they indicate either a problem in the firewall rules or an unknown (or unauthorized) service attempting to contact the outside world:

```
# ICMP rules

$IPT -A EXT-log-in -p icmp \
        ! --icmp-type echo-request -m limit -j LOG

# TCP rules

$IPT -A EXT-log-in -p tcp \
        --dport 0:19 -j LOG

# Skip ftp, telnet, ssh
$IPT -A EXT-log-in -p tcp \
        --dport 24 -j LOG

# Skip smtp
$IPT -A EXT-log-in -p tcp \
        --dport 26:78 -j LOG

# Skip finger, www
$IPT -A EXT-log-in -p tcp \
        --dport 81:109 -j LOG

# Skip pop-3, sunrpc
$IPT -A EXT-log-in -p tcp \
        --dport 112:136 -j LOG

# Skip NetBIOS
$IPT -A EXT-log-in -p tcp \
        --dport 140:142 -j LOG

# Skip imap
$IPT -A EXT-log-in -p tcp \
        --dport 144:442 -j LOG

# Skip secure_web/SSL
$IPT -A EXT-log-in -p tcp \
        --dport 444:65535 -j LOG

#UDP rules

$IPT -A EXT-log-in -p udp \
        --dport 0:110 -j LOG

# Skip sunrpc
$IPT -A EXT-log-in -p udp \
        --dport 112:160 -j LOG

# Skip snmp
$IPT -A EXT-log-in -p udp \
        --dport 163:634 -j LOG

# Skip NFS mountd
$IPT -A EXT-log-in -p udp \
        --dport 636:5631 -j LOG
```

```
# Skip pcAnywhere
$IPT -A EXT-log-in -p udp \
        --dport 5633:31336 -j LOG

# Skip traceroute's default ports
$IPT -A EXT-log-in -p udp \
        --sport $TRACEROUTE_SRC \
        --dport $TRACEROUTE_DEST -j LOG

# Skip the rest
$IPT -A EXT-log-in -p udp \
        --dport 33434:65535 -j LOG

# Outgoing Packets

# Don't log rejected outgoing ICMP destination-unreachable packets
$IPT -A EXT-log-out -p icmp \
        --icmp-type destination-unreachable -j DROP

$IPT -A EXT-log-out -j LOG
```

The Optimized `nftables` Script

The `nftables` script takes advantage of additional external rules files in `nftables` syntax:

- **nft-vars**—Contains variables related to the script, defined in `nftables` format rather than shell format
- **setup-tables**—Contains the main `filter` and `nat` table architecture, including `INPUT` and `OUTPUT` chains
- **localhost-policy**—Contains rules for localhost traffic
- **connectionstate-policy**—Sets the connection state policies
- **invalid-policy**—Sets policies related to invalid traffic
- **dns-policy**—Contains policies related to DNS lookups
- **tcp-client-policy**—Contains rules related to outbound client connections
- **tcp-server-policy**—Contains rules related inbound connections if the computer acts as a server
- **icmp-policy**—Contains rules related ICMP requests
- **log-policy**—Contains rules related to logging
- **default-policy**—Contains the final default policy rules for the firewall

Firewall Initialization

The firewall script starts out by defining the location of the `nftables` firewall administration command:

```
#!/bin/sh

NFT="/usr/local/sbin/nft"              # Location of nft on your system
```

A number of kernel parameters were also set; refer to Chapter 5 for an explanation of these parameters:

```
# Enable broadcast echo Protection
echo 1 > /proc/sys/net/ipv4/icmp_echo_ignore_broadcasts
# Disable Source Routed Packets
for f in /proc/sys/net/ipv4/conf/*/accept_source_route; do
    echo 0 > $f
done
# Enable TCP SYN Cookie Protection
echo 1 > /proc/sys/net/ipv4/tcp_syncookies
# Disable ICMP Redirect Acceptance
for f in /proc/sys/net/ipv4/conf/*/accept_redirects; do
    echo 0 > $f
done

# Don't send Redirect Messages
for f in /proc/sys/net/ipv4/conf/*/send_redirects; do
    echo 0 > $f
done
# Drop Spoofed Packets coming in on an interface, which, if replied to,
# would result in the reply going out a different interface.
for f in /proc/sys/net/ipv4/conf/*/rp_filter; do
    echo 1 > $f
done
# Log packets with impossible addresses.
for f in /proc/sys/net/ipv4/conf/*/log_martians; do
    echo 1 > $f
done
```

The first part of the script resets and deletes existing chains, as shown in Chapter 5:

```
for i in '$NFT list tables | awk '{print $2}''
do
    echo "Flushing ${i}"
    $NFT flush table ${i}
    for j in '$NFT list table ${i} | grep chain | awk '{print $2}''
    do
        echo "...Deleting chain ${j} from table ${i}"
        $NFT delete chain ${i} ${j}
    done
    echo "Deleting ${i}"
    $NFT delete table ${i}
done
```

Here is the final code for the beginning of the firewall script, namely, the code to enable the firewall to be stopped easily. With this code placed below the preceding code, when you call the script with an argument of "stop" the script will flush, clear, and reset the default policies, and the firewall will effectively stop.

```
if [ "$1" = "stop" ]
then
echo "Firewall completely stopped!  WARNING: THIS HOST HAS NO FIREWALL RUNNING."
exit 0
fi
```

Now the tables are re-created:

```
$NFT -f setup-tables
$NFT -f localhost-policy
$NFT -f connectionstate-policy
```

Building the Rules Files

The following sections show the files containing nftables rules for the various components of the firewall. The rules files use nftables-defined variables which are included within each rules file and housed in a file called nft-vars. The nft-vars file will grow as rules are added. To begin with, the nft-vars file contains the following:

```
define int_loopback = lo
define int_internet = eth0
define ip_external = <your external ip>
define subnet_external = <your external subnet>
define net_loopback = 127.0.0.0/8
define net_class_a = 10.0.0.0/8
define net_class_b = 172.16.0.0/16
define net_class_c = 192.168.0.0/16
define net_class_d = 224.0.0.0/4
define net_class_e = 240.0.0.0/5
define broadcast_src = 0.0.0.0
define broadcast_dest = 255.255.255.255
define ports_priv = 0-1023
define ports_unpriv = 1024-65535
```

Creating the Tables

The setup-tables rules create the filter and nat tables, create INPUT and OUTPUT chains for each, and hook those chains into their respective hooks within nftables so that the chains receive packets. The setup-tables rules are:

```
include "nft-vars"
table filter {
        chain input {
                type filter hook input priority 0;
        }
        chain output {
                type filter hook output priority 0;
        }
}
```

Enabling Localhost Traffic

Enabling localhost communication takes place in the localhost-policy rules file. Note the use of an nftables-defined variable ($int_loopback) in this example:

```
include "nft-vars"
table filter {
        chain input {
                iifname $int_loopback accept
        }
        chain output {
                oifname $int_loopback accept
        }
}
```

Enabling Connection State

Connection state tracking comes within the `connectionstate-policy` rules file:

```
include "nft-vars"
table filter {
        chain input {
                ct state established,related accept
                ct state invalid log prefix "INVALID input: " limit rate 3/second
                ➥drop
        }
        chain output {
                ct state established,related accept
                ct state invalid log prefix "INVALID output: " limit rate 3/
                ➥second drop
        }
}
```

Dropping Invalid Traffic

The rules to drop invalid traffic are contained in a rules file called `invalid-policy`:

```
include "nft-vars"
table filter {
        chain input {
                iif $int_internet ip saddr $ip_external drop
                iif $int_internet ip saddr $net_class_a drop
                iif $int_internet ip saddr $net_class_b drop
                iif $int_internet ip saddr $net_class_c drop
                iif $int_internet ip protocol udp ip daddr $net_class_d accept
                iif $int_internet ip saddr $net_class_e drop
                iif $int_internet ip saddr $net_loopback drop
                iif $int_internet ip daddr $subnet_external drop
        }
}
```

Enabling DNS Traffic

The rules to identify DNS traffic come first. Until the DNS rules are installed, your network software won't be capable of locating services and hosts out on the Internet unless you use the IP address.

For these rules, three new variables are added to the `nft-vars` file:

```
define nameserver_1 = <your nameserver ip>
define nameserver_2 = <second nameserver ip>
define nameserver_3 = <third nameserver ip, if necessary>
```

The file `dns-policy` is created to hold the following rules and then loaded in the main `rc.firewall` script with the command `nft -f dns-policy`:

```
include "nft-vars"
table filter {
        chain input {
                ip daddr { $nameserver_1,$nameserver_2,$nameserver_3 } udp sport
                ➥53 udp dport 53 accept
                ip daddr { $nameserver_1,$nameserver_2,$nameserver_3 } tcp sport
                ➥53 tcp dport $ports_unpriv accept
```

```
                        ip daddr { $nameserver_1,$nameserver_2,$nameserver_3 } udp sport
                        ➡53 udp dport $ports_unpriv accept
                }
                chain output {
                        ip daddr { $nameserver_1,$nameserver_2,$nameserver_3 } udp sport
                        ➡53 udp dport 53 accept
                        ip daddr { $nameserver_1,$nameserver_2,$nameserver_3 } tcp sport
                        ➡$ports_unpriv tcp dport 53 accept
                        ip daddr { $nameserver_1,$nameserver_2,$nameserver_3 } udp sport
                        ➡$ports_unpriv udp dport 53 accept
                }
        }
```

The first rule in the INPUT and OUTPUT chains matches on queries from the local
cache and forward name server, if you have one, and responses from the remote DNS
server. The local server is configured as a slave to the remote, primary server, so the local
server will fail if the lookup doesn't succeed. This configuration is less common for a small
office/home office.

The next rules in each of the INPUT and OUTPUT chains match on standard DNS client
lookup requests over TCP, when the server's response is too large to fit in a UDP DNS
packet. These rules would be used by both a forwarding name server and a standard client.

Local Client Traffic over TCP

Connecting from your computer to the Internet over TCP can be accomplished by adding specific output rules for the servers and services to which you want to connect. As
before, the rules shown for this purpose assume the use of the state tracking module. If
state tracking isn't enabled, a mirror rule needs to be added to the INPUT chain to enable
the traffic coming back in for a given connection.

The rules require the addition of a server_smtp variable to the nft-vars program:

```
define server_smtp = <your SMTP server>
```

The rules go into a file called tcp-client-policy which is then loaded into the
rc.firewall program with the command

```
nft -f tcp-client-policy
```

Here are the rules for tcp-client-policy:

```
include "nft-vars"
table filter {
        chain input {
        }
        chain output {
                tcp dport {21,22,80,110,143,993,995,443} tcp sport $ports_unpriv
                ➡accept
                ip daddr $server_smtp tcp dport 25 tcp sport $ports_unpriv accept
        }
}
```

Local Server Traffic over TCP

Enabling services from your local server to allow clients to connect to you is accomplished by adding specific rules to the INPUT chain. Ideally, you could limit the connections to known clients and then add a rule for the source address (ip saddr <your client ip>), but in the real world that's typically not possible.

The following file is loaded in the rc.firewall script with

```
nft -f tcp-server-policy
```

The rules file called tcp-server-policy contains the following to enable connections to port 22 (SSH) on the local server from any client:

```
include "nft-vars"
table filter {
    chain input {
        ip daddr $ip_external tcp sport $ports_unpriv tcp dport {22} accept
    }
    chain output {
    }
}
```

ICMP Traffic

Finally, the last pair of rules match on incoming and outgoing ICMP traffic. These rules are loaded into a file called icmp-policy:

```
include "nft-vars"
table filter {
    chain input {
        icmp type { echo-reply,destination-unreachable,parameter-
        ➥problem,source-quench,time-exceeded} accept
    }
    chain output {
        icmp type { echo-request,parameter-problem,source-quench} accept
    }
}
```

The file is then added to the main rc.firewall script with the command

```
nft -f icmp-policy
```

Logging Dropped Packets with `nftables`

The final rules for the firewall log packets that haven't been handled by other, previously loaded rules. Almost all outgoing packets to be dropped are logged because they indicate either a problem in the firewall rules or an unknown (or unauthorized) service attempting to contact the outside world.

The file is called log-policy and contains the following rules. Load the file just prior to the default policy with the command

```
nft -f log-policy
```

Here are the rules:

```
include "nft-vars"
table filter {
        chain input {
                log prefix "INPUT packet dropped: " limit rate 3/second
        }
        chain output {
                log prefix "OUTPUT packet dropped: " limit rate 3/second
        }
}
```

What Did Optimization Buy?

The goal of optimization is to get the packet through the filter processing as quickly as possible, with as few unnecessary tests as possible. Ideally, you want the packets flowing through at line speed.

In terms of the firewall itself, three factors affect performance: the number of rules installed in the kernel; the chain traversal length, or the number of rules that any given packet is tested against before it matches; and the total number of match tests performed on the packet. Also, when it comes to using the state module, remember that the trade-off is speed versus memory.

Note that some of the variations in the tables are artifacts of how the sample scripts in Chapter 5 and this chapter are organized, as well as some differences in the TCP state flag and source address checks between the two examples.

`iptables` Optimization

For `iptables`, the optimized versions have more rules than their straight-through counterparts! Even more surprising, the connection-tracking versions have more rules than the classic, stateless versions! Didn't we already conclude that use of the state match module reduces the number of rules by eliminating individual ACCEPT rules for server responses to client requests? Yes and no. . . . The absolute number of rules increases, because the static rules must remain present to account for any cases in which a state table entry has timed out or been replaced due to a resource shortage. The number of input rules *traversed* can drop dramatically.

Using user-defined chains results in a few more rules as well. The additional rules perform the intermediate packet selection and branching. There's a small amount of overhead in the top-level branching decisions. The overhead isn't significant, and even the small amount of apparent overhead is deceiving. The number of rules traversed isn't as critical a performance metric as the number of individual header field match tests performed.

Optimization with user-defined chains can significantly reduce the number of rules that a response packet must be tested against before reaching its final matching rule. What isn't obvious here is that the straight-through rule set includes a set amount of overhead because of the antispoofing rules. Because the example firewalls were client centered, the straight-through server traversal lengths are much longer than the client lengths as a result of the address checking done on the incoming packets.

Using the state module and thereby bypassing the firewall for established traffic dramatically reduces list traversal length for established connections. The increase in the number of rules traversed for new connections is the result of the duplicate rules, the connection-tracking rules, and their static counterparts.

Even with the state module, the initial packet always takes the static path. So the gain that the classic optimized version shows over the straight-through version still applies to the first packet.

Finally, the benefits of both optimization and connection state tracking are obvious! The categorization being performed by the user-defined chains dramatically reduces the actual number of tests that a packet is tested against in a classic packet-filtering firewall. Use of the state modules reduces the number of tests even further by skipping the rules altogether. Furthermore, the data channel connection is matched immediately as a RELATED connection.

What is perhaps least obvious, unless you've read the kernel firewall code, is that the real performance issue isn't the number of rules traversed, per se, but the number of comparison tests performed. Each unmatched traversed rule represents at least one comparison (for example, is the incoming packet an ICMP packet or a TCP packet, or is it arriving on the loopback interface or some other specific interface?). User-defined chains allow the comparisons to be partitioned by branching off into dedicated chains at critical comparison decision points.

nftables Optimization

For the nftables script, much of the processing was moved to native nftables rules files which were then loaded by the shell script. The benefit of this optimization is that it brings the rules closer to where they're processed without having to run a shell command for each and every individual rule.

The rules are also divided logically into multiple policy files, each containing rules for similar traffic. This enables easier maintenance and can be condensed or expanded as needed depending on your particular situation.

Summary

Chapter 5 introduced iptables and nftables by walking through the steps of building a simple firewall for a standalone system. This chapter discussed the ideas behind firewall optimization and then built user-defined chains to optimize the firewall example from Chapter 5. Finally, the effects of optimization were examined, as were the effects of using the state module.

Packet Forwarding

This chapter covers some of the basic issues underlying LAN security, the forwarding of gateway firewalls, and perimeter networks. Security policies are defined relative to the site's level of security needs, the importance or value of the data being protected, and the cost of lost data or privacy. This chapter opens by reviewing the firewalls presented in earlier chapters and then discusses issues that the site's policy maker must address when choosing server placement and determining security policies.

You may need Network Address Translation (NAT) to access the Internet from internal machines. NAT is not discussed until Chapter 8, "NAT—Network Address Translation." This chapter focuses on forwarding alone.

For readers familiar with `ipchains` or `ipfwadm`, forwarding and NAT were combined syntactically. Both functions were specified by a single forward rule. These logically distinct functions are clearly distinct in `iptables` and `nftables`. In fact, the two functions are handled by separate tables with separate chains. NAT is applied separately at a different point in the packet's traversal path through the system. This chapter focuses on the `iptables` services available in the `filter` table and in its extensions and the forward features of `nftables`. Chapter 8 looks at the services related to NAT.

The Limitations of a Standalone Firewall

The single-system firewall presented in Chapter 5, "Building and Installing a Standalone Firewall," is a basic bastion firewall, using only basic chains in the `filter` table. When the firewall is a packet-filtering router that has a network interface connected to the Internet and another connected to your LAN (referred to as a *dual-homed system*), the firewall applies rules to decide whether to forward or block packets crossing between the two interfaces. In this case, the packet-filtering firewall is a static router with traffic-screening rules enforcing local policies concerning which packets are allowed through the network interfaces.

As pointed out in Chapter 3, "`iptables`: The Legacy Linux Firewall Administration Program," Netfilter handles forwarded packets quite differently from the previous IPFW mechanism. Forwarded packets are inspected by the `FORWARD` chain alone. The `INPUT` and `OUTPUT` rules don't apply. Network traffic related to the local firewall host and network traffic related to the LAN have completely different sets of rules and rule chains.

Rules on the FORWARD chain can specify both the incoming and the outgoing interface. For a dual-homed host setup with a LAN, the firewall rules applied to the incoming and outgoing network interfaces represent an I/O pair—one rule for arriving packets and a reverse rule for departing packets. The rules are directional. The two interfaces are handled as a unit.

Traffic is not routed directly between the Internet and the LAN automatically. Packets to be forwarded won't flow without a rule pair to accept the traffic. The filtering rules applied to the two interfaces act as a firewall and static router between the two networks.

The firewall configuration presented in Chapter 5 is typically adequate for an individual home system with a single network interface.

As a standalone gateway firewall protecting a LAN, if the firewall machine is ever compromised, it's all over. Even if the firewall's local interfaces have completely different policies from those for forwarded traffic, if the system has been compromised, it won't be long before the interloper has gained root access. At that point, if not before, the internal systems are wide open as well. Chances are, a home LAN will never have to face this situation if the services offered to the Internet are chosen carefully and a stringent firewall policy is enforced. Still, a standalone gateway firewall represents a single point of failure. It's an all-or-nothing situation.

Many larger organizations and corporations rely on a single firewall setup, and many others use one of two other architectures: a screened-host architecture with no direct routing, or a screened-subnet architecture with proxy services, along with a perimeter DMZ network created either between or alongside the external firewall, separated from the private LAN. Public servers in the DMZ network have their own specialized, bastion firewalls as well. This means that these sites have a lot more computers at their disposal—and a staff to manage them.

DMZ: A Perimeter Network by Any Other Name

A perimeter network between two firewalls is called a *demilitarized zone* (DMZ). The purpose of a DMZ is to establish a protected space from which to run public servers (or services) and to isolate that space from the rest of the private LAN. If a server in the DMZ is compromised, that server remains isolated from the LAN; the gateway firewalls and bastion firewalls running on the other DMZ servers offer protection against the compromised server.

In addition to the single-system, standalone firewall, the firewall presented in Chapter 5 can be expanded to form the basis for a dual-homed gateway firewall protecting the host, which offers one or a few public services. A home LAN is often protected by a single-gateway firewall that both filters forwarded traffic and offers public services.

What options are available for a dual-homed system that can't afford the risk of a single-gateway firewall or the cost of many computers and a staff to manage them? Fortunately, a dual-homed firewall and LAN offer stronger security when the system is configured carefully. The question is this: Is the extra effort of maintaining the firewall worth the increased security in a trusted environment?

Basic Gateway Firewall Setups

Two basic gateway firewall setups are used here. As shown in Figure 7.1, the gateway has two network interfaces: one connected to the Internet and one connected to the DMZ. Public Internet services are offered from machines in the DMZ network. The gateway firewall offers no services. A second firewall, a choke firewall, is also connected to the DMZ network, separating the internal, private networks from the quasi-public server machines in the perimeter network. Private machines are protected behind the choke firewall on the internal LAN. Additionally, each of the server machines in the DMZ runs a specialized firewall of its own. If the gateway firewall or one of the servers fails, the public server machines in the DMZ continue to run their individual firewalls. The choke firewall protects the internal LAN from a compromised gateway or from any other compromised machine in the perimeter network. Traffic between the LAN and the Internet passes through both firewalls and crosses the perimeter network.

In the second setup, the gateway has three network interfaces: one connected to the Internet, one connected to the DMZ, and one connected to the private LAN. As shown in Figure 7.2, traffic between the LAN and the Internet, and traffic between the DMZ and the Internet, share nothing except the gateway's external network interface.

An advantage of this configuration over the first is that neither the LAN nor the DMZ shares the traffic load of both networks. Another advantage is that it's easier to define rules that refer to all LAN or DMZ traffic specifically, as opposed to traffic related to the other network. Another advantage is that a single-gateway host is less expensive than two separate firewall devices.

The disadvantage of this configuration over the first is that the gateway becomes a single point of failure for both networks. Also, the firewall rules in the single host include

Figure 7.1   A DMZ between a dual-homed gateway and a choke firewall

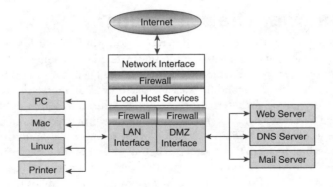

Figure 7.2   A tri-homed firewall separating a LAN and a DMZ

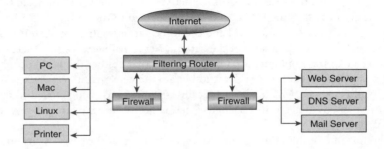

Figure 7.3   A filtering router in front of LAN and DMZ firewalls

all the complexity related to both the DMZ and the LAN. This complexity can become confusing when you're developing firewall rules by hand.

A common third alternative is to add a filtering router that separates LAN and DMZ traffic. DMZ servers run their own bastion firewalls. There may or may not be a generalized firewall between the router and the DMZ. As shown in Figure 7.3, the gateway firewall is separate from the router and protects the LAN. The filtering router performs some of the basic filtering for both the LAN and the DMZ. The gateway firewall doesn't need to provide this basic filtering, and it effectively functions similarly to the choke firewall in the first setup.

LAN Security Issues

Security issues are largely dependent on the size of the LAN, its architecture, and what it's used for. The services and architecture are also influenced by the public IP addressing available to the site. Perhaps even more basic than that is the type of Internet connection the site has: dial-up, DSL, wireless, cable, satellite, ISDN, leased line, or any of the other types of Internet connections. Following are some questions you should consider when creating a security policy for your site.

Is a public IP address dynamically and temporarily assigned via DHCP or IPCP? Does the site have a single permanently assigned public IP address or a block of them?

Are services offered to the Internet? Are these services hosted on the firewall machine, or are they hosted on internal machines? For example, you might offer email service from the gateway firewall machine but serve a website from an internal machine in the DMZ. When services are hosted from internal machines, you want to place those machines on a perimeter network and apply completely different packet-filtering and access policies to them. If services are offered from internal machines, is this fact visible to the outside, or are the services proxied or transparently forwarded via NAT so that they appear to be available from the firewall machine?

How much information do you want to make publicly available about the machines on your LAN? Do you intend to host local DNS services? Are local DNS database contents available to the Internet?

Can people log in to your machines from the Internet? How many and which local machines are accessible to them? Do all user accounts have the same access rights? Will incoming connections be proxied for additional access control?

Are all internal machines equally accessible to local users and from all local machines? Are external services equally accessible from all internal machines? For example, if you use a screened-host firewall architecture, users must log in to the firewall machine directly to have access to the Internet. No routing would be done at all.

Are private LAN services running behind the firewall? For example, is NFS used internally, or Samba, or a networked printer? Do you need to keep any of these services from leaking information or broadcast traffic to the Internet, such as SNMP, DHCP, or `ntpd`? Maintaining such services behind the secondary choke firewall ensures complete isolation of these services from the Internet.

Related to services designed for LAN use are questions about local versus external access to services designed for Internet use. Will you offer FTP internally but not externally, or will you possibly offer different kinds of FTP services to both? Will you run a private web server or configure different parts of the same site to be available to local users as opposed to remote users? Will you run a local mail server to send mail but use a different mechanism to retrieve incoming mail from the Internet (that is, will your mail be delivered directly to your machine's user accounts, or will you explicitly retrieve mail from an ISP)?

Configuration Options for a Trusted Home LAN

You must consider two kinds of internal network traffic. The first kind is local access to the gateway firewall, through the internal interface, as shown in Figure 7.4. The second is local access to the Internet, through the gateway machine's external interface.

Presumably, most small systems have no reason to filter packets between the firewall and the local network in general. However, because most home-based sites are assigned a

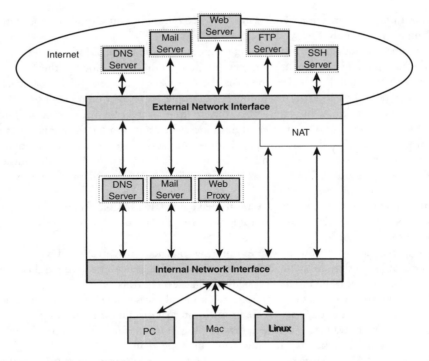

Figure 7.4   LAN traffic to the firewall machine and to the Internet

single IP address, one exception arises: NAT. Presumably, the only internal filtering-related action you must take will be to enable your own form of source address spoofing by applying NAT packets moving between your internal machines and the Internet. Most of the emphasis is on filtering packets between the firewall and the Internet.

> **How Trustworthy Are "Trusted Home LANs"?**
> Although small-business and residential sites often like to view their networks as "trusted," this is often not the case. The problem isn't the local users, but rather the high incidence rate of compromise among these systems.

LAN Access to the Gateway Firewall

In a home environment, chances are good that you'll want to enable unrestricted access between the LAN machines and the gateway firewall. (Some parents have reason to disagree.)

The assumption in this section is that any public services are hosted on the firewall. LAN hosts are purely client machines. The LAN is allowed to initiate connections to the firewall, but the firewall is not allowed to initiate connections to the LAN. There will be exceptions to this rule of thumb. You might want the firewall host to have access to a local, networked printer, for example. (A business site would never make this choice. The firewall would be as protected against problems originating in the LAN as it is from problems originating on the public Internet.)

Starting with the firewall developed in Chapter 5 as the basis, additional constants are needed in the firewall example to refer to the internal interface connecting to the LAN. This example defines the internal network interface as eth1; the LAN is defined as including Class C addresses ranging from 192.168.1.0 to 192.168.1.255; an external interface, the one facing the outside world, is defined as eth0:

```
LAN_INTERFACE="eth1"
EXTERNAL_INTERFACE="eth0"
LAN_ADDRESSES="192.168.1.0/24"
```

Allowing unrestricted access across the interfaces is a simple matter of allowing all protocols and all ports by default. Notice that the LAN can initiate new connections to remote servers, but new incoming connections from remote sites are not accepted. These are the iptables rules:

```
$IPT -A FORWARD  -i $LAN_INTERFACE -o $EXTERNAL_INTERFACE \
        -p tcp -s $LAN_ADDRESSES --sport $UNPRIVPORTS \
        -m state --state NEW,ESTABLISHED,RELATED -j ACCEPT

$IPT -A FORWARD -i $EXTERNAL_INTERFACE -o $LAN_INTERFACE \
        -m state --state ESTABLISHED,RELATED -j ACCEPT
```

Here are similar nftables rules:

```
$NFT add rule filter forward iif $LAN_INTERFACE oif $EXTERNAL_INTERFACE \
    ip protocol tcp ip saddr $LAN_ADDRESSES tcp sport $UNPRIVPORTS \
    ct state new,established,related accept
$NFT add rule filter forward iif $EXTERNAL_INTERFACE oif $LAN_INTERFACE ct state
➥established,related accept
```

Notice also that these two rules forward traffic. They do not affect local traffic between the LAN and the firewall itself. To access services on the firewall host, local INPUT and OUTPUT rules are needed as well:

```
$IPT -A INPUT  -i $LAN_INTERFACE \
        -p tcp -s $LAN_ADDRESSES --sport $UNPRIVPORTS \
        -m state --state NEW,ESTABLISHED,RELATED -j ACCEPT

$IPT -A OUTPUT -o $LAN_INTERFACE \
        -m state --state ESTABLISHED,RELATED -j ACCEPT
```

The nftables rules are:

```
$NFT add rule filter input iif $LAN_INTERFACE \
    ip protocol tcp ip saddr $LAN_ADDRESSES \
    tcp sport $UNPRIVPORTS ct state new,established,related accept
$NFT add rule filter output oif $LAN_INTERFACE ct state established,related
➥accept
```

Both the forwarding and the internal interface rules could be as service specific as the external interface rules in Chapter 5. In today's world, the internal interface and forwarding rules should be that specific. The rules in this section merely lay the groundwork, introducing the forwarding rules themselves.

LAN Access to Other LANs: Forwarding Local Traffic among Multiple LANs

If the machines on your LAN, or on multiple LANs, require routing among themselves, you need to allow access among the machines for the service ports that they require, unless they have alternative internal connection paths. In the former case, any local routing done between LANs would be done by the firewall.

The assumption in this section is that there is a gateway firewall with two network interfaces, a DMZ server network, an internal choke firewall with two network interfaces, and the LAN private network. This is the setup shown earlier in Figure 7.1. Traffic between the LAN and the Internet crosses through the DMZ network between the choke and gateway firewalls. This setup is common in smaller sites.

This example renames the internal network interface on the gateway as `DMZ_INTERFACE`. Another constant is needed for the firewall. The DMZ is defined as including Class C private addresses ranging from `192.168.3.0` to `192.168.3.255`:

```
DMZ_INTERFACE="eth1"
DMZ_ADDRESSES="192.168.3.0/24"
```

The following first two rules allow local access to the gateway firewall host from the LAN. In practice, the LAN would not be allowed access to all ports on the firewall. The second two rules allow the firewall itself to access specific services offered in the DMZ on a server-by-server basis. Again, a firewall in a larger setting would have little or no reason to access services hosted in the DMZ. In most cases, the firewall host wouldn't offer any services to the DMZ at all. In larger sites, it's probable that the firewall wouldn't offer any services to the LAN either:

```
$IPT -A INPUT  -i $DMZ_INTERFACE -s $LAN_ADDRESSES -d $GATEWAY \
        -m state --state NEW,ESTABLISHED,RELATED -j ACCEPT

$IPT -A OUTPUT -o $DMZ_INTERFACE -s $GATEWAY -d $LAN_ADDRESSES \
        -m state --state ESTABLISHED,RELATED -j ACCEPT

$IPT -A OUTPUT -o $DMZ_INTERFACE -s $GATEWAY -d $DMZ_ADDRESSES \
        -m state --state NEW,ESTABLISHED,RELATED -j ACCEPT

$IPT -A INPUT  -i $DMZ_INTERFACE -s $DMZ_ADDRESSES -d $GATEWAY \
        -m state --state ESTABLISHED,RELATED -j ACCEPT
```

The corresponding `nftables` rules are:

```
$NFT add rule filter input iif $DMZ_INTERFACE ip saddr $LAN_ADDRESSES ip daddr
�ាន$GATEWAY ct state new,established,related accept
$NFT add rule filter output oif $DMZ_INTERFACE ip saddr $GATEWAY ip daddr
➱$LAN_ADDRESSES ct state established,related accept
```

```
$NFT add rule filter output oif $DMZ_INTERFACE ip saddr $GATEWAY ip daddr
➥$DMZ_ADDRESSES ct state new,established,related accept
$NFT add rule filter input iif $DMZ_INTERFACE ip saddr $DMZ_ADDRESSES ip daddr
➥$GATEWAY ct state established,related accept
```

The next rules forward traffic between the internal networks and the Internet. The DMZ and LAN traffic is handled separately. The DMZ traffic represents incoming connection requests from the Internet. The LAN traffic represents outgoing connection requests to the Internet. Again, in practice the DMZ rules would be very specific by server address and service:

```
$IPT -A FORWARD  -i $EXTERNAL_INTERFACE -o $DMZ_INTERFACE \
        -d $DMZ_ADDRESSES \
        -m state --state NEW,ESTABLISHED,RELATED -j ACCEPT

$IPT -A FORWARD -i $DMZ_INTERFACE -o $EXTERNAL_INTERFACE \
        -s $DMZ_ADDRESSES \
        -m state --state ESTABLISHED,RELATED -j ACCEPT

$IPT -A FORWARD -i $DMZ_INTERFACE -o $EXTERNAL_INTERFACE \
        -s $LAN_ADDRESSES \
        -m state --state NEW,ESTABLISHED,RELATED -j ACCEPT

$IPT -A FORWARD  -i $EXTERNAL_INTERFACE -o $DMZ_INTERFACE \
        -d $LAN_ADDRESSES \
        -m state --state ESTABLISHED,RELATED -j ACCEPT
```

The nftables rules are:

```
$NFT add rule filter forward iif $EXTERNAL_INTERFACE oif $DMZ_INTERFACE ip daddr
➥$DMZ_ADDRESSES ct state new,established,related accept
$NFT add rule filter forward iif $DMZ_INTERFACE oif $EXTERNAL_INTERFACE ip saddr
➥$DMZ_ADDRESSES ct state established,related accept
$NFT add rule filter forward iif $DMZ_INTERFACE oif $EXTERNAL_INTERFACE ip saddr
➥$LAN_ADDRESSES ct state new,established,related accept
$NFT add rule filter forward iif $EXTERNAL_INTERFACE oif $DMZ_INTERFACE ip daddr
➥$LAN_ADDRESSES ct state established,related accept
```

Note that the preceding forwarding rules for the DMZ are not complete. Servers in the DMZ sometimes initiate outgoing connections as well, such as connection requests from a web proxy server or a mail gateway server.

On the choke firewall, the following rules forward traffic between the LAN and DMZ networks. Notice that the LAN can initiate new connections, but new incoming connections from either the DMZ or the Internet to the LAN are not accepted. Again, in practice, the LAN would be given more controlled access to the DMZ as well as to the gateway firewall, assuming that the gateway provided any services:

```
$IPT -A FORWARD  -i $LAN_INTERFACE -o $DMZ_INTERFACE \
        -s $LAN_ADDRESSES \
        -m state --state NEW,ESTABLISHED,RELATED -j ACCEPT

$IPT -A FORWARD -i $DMZ_INTERFACE -o $LAN_INTERFACE \
        -m state --state ESTABLISHED,RELATED -j ACCEPT
```

The `nftables` rules are:

```
$NFT add rule filter forward iif $LAN_INTERFACE oif $DMZ_INTERFACE ip saddr
➥$LAN_ADDRESSES ct state new,established,related accept
$NFT add rule filter forward iif $DMZ_INTERFACE oif $LAN_INTERFACE ct state
➥established,related accept
```

Configuration Options for a Larger or Less Trusted LAN

A business or an organization, and many home sites, would use more elaborate, specific mechanisms than the simple, generic forwarding firewall rules presented in the preceding two sections for a trusted home LAN. In less trusted environments, firewall machines are protected from internal users as strongly as from external users.

Port-specific firewall rules are defined for the internal interfaces as well as for the external interfaces. Internal rules might be a mirror image of the rules for the external interfaces, or the rules might be more inclusive. What is allowed through the choke firewall machine's internal network interface depends on the types of systems running on the LAN and the types of local services running in the DMZ, as well as which Internet services are accessible to the LAN according to local security policies.

For example, you might want to block local broadcast messages from reaching the gateway firewall. If not all your users are completely trusted, you might want to restrict what passes into the choke firewall from internal machines as strongly as what comes in from the Internet. Additionally, you should keep the number of user accounts to a bare minimum on the firewall machine. Ideally, a firewall has no user accounts, with the exception of a single unprivileged administrative account.

A home-based business might have a single IP address, requiring LAN Network Address Translation. However, businesses often lease several publicly registered IP addresses or an entire network address block. Public addresses are usually assigned to a business's public servers. With public IP addresses, outgoing connections are forwarded and incoming connections are routed normally. A local subnet can be defined to create a local, public DMZ.

Dividing Address Space to Create Multiple Networks

IP addresses are divided into two pieces: a network address and a host address within that network. As stated in Chapter 1, "Preliminary Concepts Underlying Packet-Filtering Firewalls," Class A, B, and C addresses are something of an artifact, but they remain the easiest addresses to use as examples because their network and host fields fall on byte boundaries. Class A, B, and C network addresses are defined by their first 8, 16, and 24 bits, respectively. Within each address class, the remaining bits define the host part of the IP address. This is shown visually in Table 7.1.

Subnetting is a local extension to the network address part of the local IP addresses. A local network mask is defined as one that treats some of the most significant host address

Table 7.1 **Network and Host Fields in an IP Address**

	Class A	Class B	Class C
Leading network bits	0	10	110
Network field	1 byte	2 bytes	3 bytes
Host field	3 bytes	2 bytes	1 byte
Network prefix	/8	/16	/24
Address range	1–126	128–191	192–223
Network mask	255.0.0.0	255.255.0.0	255.255.255.0

bits as if they were part of the network address. These additional network address bits serve to define multiple networks locally. Remote sites are not aware of local subnets. They see the address range as normal Class A, B, or C addresses.

For example, let's take the Class C private address block 192.168.1.0. The base address, known as the network address, is 192.168.1.0 for this example. The network mask for this example is 255.255.255.0, exactly matching the first 24 bits, the network address, of the 192.168.1.0/24 network.

This network can be divided into two local networks by defining the first 25 bits, rather than the first 24 bits, as the network portion of the address. In current parlance, we say that the local network has a prefix length of 25 rather than 24. The most significant bit of the host address field is now treated as part of the network address field. The host field now contains 7 bits rather than 8. The network mask becomes 255.255.255.128, or /25 in CIDR notation. Two subnetworks are defined: 192.168.1.0, addressing hosts from 1 to 126, and 192.168.1.128, addressing hosts from 129 to 254. Each subnet loses two host addresses because each subnet uses the lowest host address, 0 or 128, as the network address and uses the highest host address, 127 or 255, as the broadcast address. Table 7.2 shows this in tabular form.

Subnetworks 192.168.1.0 and 192.168.1.128 can be assigned to two separate internal network interface cards. Each subnet consists of two independent networks, each containing up to 126 hosts.

Table 7.2 **Class C Network 192.168.1.0 Subnetted into Two Subnets**

Subnet Number	None	0	1
Network address	192.168.1.0	192.168.1.0	192.168.1.128
Network mask	255.255.255.0	255.255.255.128	255.255.255.128
First host address	192.168.1.1	192.168.1.1	192.168.1.129
Last host address	192.168.1.254	192.168.1.126	192.168.1.254
Broadcast address	192.168.1.255	192.168.1.127	192.168.1.255
Total hosts	254	126	126

Table 7.3 **Class C Network `192.168.1.0` Subnetted into Four Subnets**

Subnet Number	0	1	2	3
Network address	192.168.1.0	192.168.1.64	192.168.1.128	192.18.1.192
Network mask	255.255.255.192	255.255.255.192	255.255.255.192	255.255.255.192
First host address	192.168.1.1	192.168.1.65	192.168.1.129	192.168.1.193
Last host address	192.168.1.62	192.168.1.126	192.168.1.190	192.168.1.254
Broadcast address	192.168.1.63	192.168.1.127	192.168.1.191	192.168.1.255
Total hosts	62	62	62	62

Subnetting allows for the creation of multiple internal networks, each containing different classes of client or server machines and each with its own independent routing. Different firewall policies can then be applied to the networks.

Of course, this example showed the network being divided into two portions. The network can in fact be divided into many parts in order to create a number of smaller networks. It's quite common to see a network with a subnet mask of 255.255.255.252 or /30 used between routers at two locations. Table 7.3 takes the process one step further and shows the same network divided into four subnets.

Selective Internal Access by Host, Address Range, or Port

Traffic through a firewall machine's internal interface can be selectively limited, just as traffic through the external interface is. For example, on a firewall for a small, residential site, rather than letting everything through on the internal interface, traffic could be limited to DNS, SMTP, POP, and HTTP. In this case, let's say that a firewall machine provides these services for the LAN. Local machines are not allowed any other access to outside services. In this case, forwarding isn't done.

Point of Interest

In this example, local hosts are limited to specific services: DNS, SMTP, POP, and HTTP. Because POP is a local mail retrieval service in this case, and because DNS, SMTP, and HTTP are proxied services, no direct Internet access is being made by LAN clients. In each case, the local clients are connecting to local servers. POP is a local LAN service. The three other servers establish remote connections on the client's behalf.

This example would be used only by a small, likely residential, site. Placing the mail gateway and POP services on the firewall host can require the host to have user accounts. It is not necessary that these accounts be login accounts, however.

Configuration Options for an Internal LAN

The following example considers a firewall machine with an internal interface connected to a LAN. Constants for the internal interface are as shown here:

```
LAN_INTERFACE="eth1"              # Internal interface to the LAN
LAN_GATEWAY="192.168.1.1"         # Firewall machine's internal
                                  # Interface address
LAN_ADDRESSES="192.168.1.0/24"    # Range of addresses used on the LAN
```

LAN machines point to the firewall machine's internal interface as their name server:

```
# Generic gateway response rule
$IPT -A OUTPUT  -o $LAN_INTERFACE \
       -s $LAN_GATEWAY \
       -d $LAN_ADDRESSES --dport $UNPRIVPORTS \
       -m state --state ESTABLISHED,RELATED -j ACCEPT

# Service-specific LAN request rules

$IPT -A INPUT -i $LAN_INTERFACE -p udp \
       -s $LAN_ADDRESSES --sport $UNPRIVPORTS \
       -d $LAN_GATEWAY --dport 53 \
       -m state --state NEW,ESTABLISHED,RELATED -j ACCEPT

$IPT -A INPUT -i $LAN_INTERFACE -p tcp \
       -s $LAN_ADDRESSES --sport $UNPRIVPORTS \
       -d $LAN_GATEWAY --dport 53 \
       -state --state NEW,ESTABLISHED,RELATED -j ACCEPT
```

The matching nftables rules are:

```
$NFT add rule filter output oif $LAN_INTERFACE \
     ip saddr $LAN_GATEWAY ip daddr $LAN_ADDRESSES \
     tcp dport $UNPRIVPORTS ct state established,related accept

$NFT add rule filter input iif $LAN_INTERFACE \
     ip protocol udp ip saddr $LAN_ADDRESSES \
     udp sport $UNPRIVPORTS ip daddr $LAN_GATEWAY \
     udp dport 53 ct state new,established,related accept

$NFT add rule filter input iif $LAN_INTERFACE \
     ip protocol tcp ip saddr $LAN_ADDRESSES \
     tcp sport $UNPRIVPORTS ip daddr $LAN_GATEWAY \
     tcp dport 53 ct state new,established,related accept
```

LAN machines also point to the firewall as their SMTP and POP server:

```
# Sending mail - SMTP

$IPT -A INPUT  -i $LAN_INTERFACE -p tcp \
       -s $LAN_ADDRESSES --sport $UNPRIVPORTS \
       -d $GATEWAY --dport 25 \
       -state --state NEW,ESTABLISHED,RELATED -j ACCEPT

# Receiving Mail - POP

$IPT -A INPUT  -i $LAN_INTERFACE -p tcp \
       -s $LAN_ADDRESSES --sport $UNPRIVPORTS \
       -d $GATEWAY --dport 110 \
       -state --state NEW,ESTABLISHED,RELATED -j ACCEPT
```

Finally, a local web caching proxy server is running on the firewall machine on port 8080. Internal machines point to the web server on the firewall as their proxy, and the web server forwards any outgoing requests on their behalf, along with caching any pages retrieved from the Internet. All connections to the proxy are via port 8080. Secure web and FTP access to remote sites is initiated by the proxy server:

```
$IPT -A INPUT   -i $LAN_INTERFACE -p tcp \
        -s $LAN_ADDRESSES --sport $UNPRIVPORTS \
        -d $GATEWAY --dport 8080 \
        -state --state NEW,ESTABLISHED,RELATED -j ACCEPT
```

Here's the `nftables` rule; notice how all of the destination ports (for SMTP, POP, and proxy) are handled in one rule:

```
$NFT add rule filter input iif $LAN_INTERFACE \
   tcp dport { 25,995,8080 } ip saddr $LAN_ADDRESSES \
   tcp sport $UNPRIVPORTS ip daddr $GATEWAY \
   ct state new,established,related accept
```

Remember that the web server will use the FTP passive-mode protocol to retrieve data from remote FTP sites. The firewall's external interface will need input and output rules to access remote FTP, HTTP, and HTTPS service ports. The gateway host must also have rules for the external interface to account for email and local DNS queries to remote hosts.

Configuration Options for Multiple LANs

Adding a second internal LAN allows this example to be developed further. The next example can be better secured than the preceding example. As shown in Figure 7.5, the DNS, SMTP, POP, and HTTP services are offered from server machines in a second LAN rather than from the firewall machine. The second LAN may or may not serve as a public DMZ. It's equally possible that the second LAN represents an internal service LAN, and its services are not offered to the Internet (although, in that case, the firewall could be required to at least be a mail gateway, depending on the local firewall configuration). In either case, firewall hosts do not typically host services. In this example, traffic is routed between the two LANs by the internal interfaces on the firewall machine.

The following variables are used to define the LAN, network interfaces, and server machines in this example:

```
CLIENT_LAN_INTERFACE="eth1"          # Internal interface to the LAN
SERVER_LAN_INTERFACE="eth2"          # Internal interface to the LAN
CLIENT_ADDRESSES="192.168.1.0/24"    # Range of addresses used on the client LAN
SERVER_ADDRESSES="192.168.3.0/24"    # Range of addresses used on the server LAN
DNS_SERVER="192.168.3.2"             # LAN DNS server
```

The first rule covers all server responses back to clients in the client LAN:

```
$IPT -A FORWARD   -i $SERVER_LAN_INTERFACE -o $CLIENT_LAN_INTERFACE \
        -s $SERVER_ADDRESSES -d $CLIENT_ADDRESSES \
        -m state --state ESTABLISHED,RELATED -j ACCEPT
```

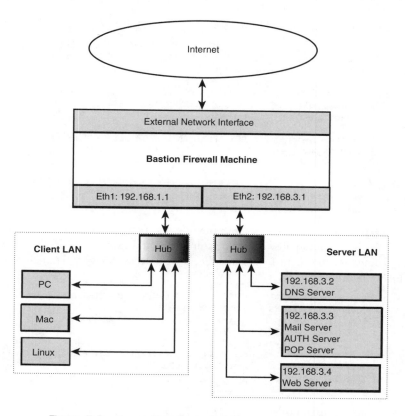

Figure 7.5   Separating clients and servers in multiple LANs

The second rule covers all ongoing connection traffic from the LAN clients to the local servers in the server LAN:

```
$IPT -A FORWARD  -i $CLIENT_LAN_INTERFACE -o $SERVER_LAN_INTERFACE \
        -s $CLIENT_ADDRESSES -d $SERVER_ADDRESSES \
        -m state --state ESTABLISHED,RELATED -j ACCEPT
```

The third rule covers all remote server responses back to client requests from the local servers in the server LAN:

```
$IPT -A FORWARD  -i $EXTERNAL_INTERFACE -o $SERVER_LAN_INTERFACE \
        -d $SERVER_ADDRESSES \
        -m state --state ESTABLISHED,RELATED -j ACCEPT
```

The fourth rule covers all local server responses back to client requests from the remote hosts on the Internet:

```
$IPT -A FORWARD  -i $SERVER_LAN_INTERFACE -o $EXTERNAL_INTERFACE \
        -s $SERVER_ADDRESSES \
        -m state --state ESTABLISHED,RELATED -j ACCEPT
```

These four rules are expressed in `nftables` syntax as follows:

```
$NFT add rule filter forward iif $SERVER_LAN_INTERFACE oif $CLIENT_LAN_INTERFACE \
    ip saddr $SERVER_ADDRESSES ip daddr $CLIENT_ADDRESSES \
    ct state established,related accept

$NFT add rule filter forward iif $CLIENT_LAN_INTERFACE oif $SERVER_LAN_INTERFACE \
    ip saddr $CLIENT_ADDRESSES ip daddr $SERVER_ADDRESSES \
    ct state established,related accept

$NFT add rule filter forward iif $EXTERNAL_INTERFACE oif $SERVER_LAN_INTERFACE \
    ip daddr $SERVER_ADDRESSES \
    ct state established,related accept

$NFT add rule filter forward iif $SERVER_LAN_INTERFACE oif $EXTERNAL_INTERFACE \
    ip saddr $SERVER_ADDRESSES \
    ct state established,related accept
```

Local machines use the DNS server in the SERVER_LAN as their name server. Just as with the rules between the firewall's internal interface and external interface, server access rules are defined for the client LAN's interface. Client access rules are defined for the server LAN's interface:

```
$IPT -A FORWARD -i $CLIENT_LAN_INTERFACE -o $SERVER_LAN_INTERFACE -p udp \
        -s $CLIENT_ADDRESSES --sport $UNPRIVPORTS \
        -d $DNS_SERVER --dport 53 \
        -m state --state NEW -j ACCEPT

$IPT -A FORWARD -i $CLIENT_LAN_INTERFACE -o $SERVER_LAN_INTERFACE -p tcp \
        -s $CLIENT_ADDRESSES --sport $UNPRIVPORTS \
        -d $DNS_SERVER --dport 53 \
        -m state --state NEW -j ACCEPT
```

Here are the `nftables` rules:

```
$NFT add rule filter forward iif $CLIENT_LAN_INTERFACE oif $SERVER_LAN_INTERFACE \
    ip saddr $CLIENT_ADDRESSES ip daddr $DNS_SERVER \
    udp dport 53 udp sport $UNPRIVPORTS \
    ct state new accept

$NFT add rule filter forward iif $CLIENT_LAN_INTERFACE oif $SERVER_LAN_INTERFACE \
    ip saddr $CLIENT_ADDRESSES ip daddr $DNS_SERVER \
    tcp dport 53 tcp sport $UNPRIVPORTS \
    ct state new accept
```

The DNS server on the second LAN needs to get its information from an external source. If the local server were a cache-and-forward server to an external server, forwarding unresolved lookups to the external server, the firewall's forwarding rules for its internal server LAN interface and external Internet interface would be these:

```
$IPT -A FORWARD -i $SERVER_LAN_INTERFACE -o $EXTERNAL_INTERFACE -p udp \
        -s $DNS_SERVER --sport 53 \
        -d $NAME_SERVER_1 --dport 53 \
        -m state --state NEW -j ACCEPT
```

```
$IPT -A FORWARD -i $SERVER_LAN_INTERFACE -o $EXTERNAL_INTERFACE -p udp \
       -s $DNS_SERVER --sport $UNPRIVPORTS \
       -d $NAME_SERVER_1 --dport 53 \
       -m state --state NEW -j ACCEPT

$IPT -A FORWARD -i $SERVER_LAN_INTERFACE -o $EXTERNAL_INTERFACE -p tcp \
       -s $DNS_SERVER --sport $UNPRIVPORTS \
       -d $NAME_SERVER_1 --dport 53 \
       -m state --state NEW -j ACCEPT
```

These are the `nftables` rules, condensing the UDP rules into a single rule:

```
$NFT add rule filter forward iif $SERVER_LAN_INTERFACE oif $EXTERNAL_INTERFACE \
     udp sport { 53,$UNPRIVPORTS } udp dport 53 \
     ip saddr $DNS_SERVER ip daddr $NAME_SERVER \
     ct state new accept

$NFT add rule filter forward iif $SERVER_LAN_INTERFACE oif $EXTERNAL_INTERFACE \
     tcp sport $UNPRIVPORTS tcp dport 53 \
     ip daddr $NAME_SERVER ip saddr $DNS_SERVER \
     ct state new accept
```

Summary

This chapter covered some of the firewall options available when you're protecting a LAN. Security policies are defined relative to the site's level of security needs, the importance of the data being protected, and the cost of lost data or privacy. Starting with the bastion firewall developed in Chapter 5 as the basis, LAN and firewall setup options were discussed in increasingly complex configurations.

8

NAT—Network Address Translation

Network Address Translation is a technology to substitute one source or destination address in the IP header with another address. Traditionally, it's an IP address translation technology to map packets between two different addressing realms. NAT's most common use is to map outgoing connections between a privately addressed local network and the publicly addressable Internet. In fact, that was what it was originally proposed to do, primarily in conjunction with the then newly defined private class address spaces; both were attempts to alleviate the IPv4 address space shortage.

This chapter introduces the concept of NAT and tells what the various types of NAT are typically used for.

The Conceptual Background of NAT

NAT was first presented in 1994 in RFC 1631, "The IP Network Address Translator (NAT)," which was later replaced by RFC 3022, "Traditional IP Network Address Translator (Traditional NAT)." NAT was proposed as a possible short-term, temporary solution (to be used until IPv6 was deployed) to the growing shortage of public IP addresses. NAT also was seen as a possible solution to the growing demands on routers that handled non-contiguous address blocks. It was thought that NAT might possibly reduce or eliminate the need for CIDR, which, in turn, was prompting address reallocations and changes to router software and network configurations. NAT was also seen as a means to avoid the cost and overhead of local network renumbering when the address spaces were reallocated, or when a site changed service providers and was assigned a new public address block.

NAT was seen not only as a short-term solution, but also as a solution that conceivably could cause more problems than it solved. With the exception of FTP, most problematic application protocols were thought to be legacy protocols that would gradually fall into disuse. It was assumed that, in the face of NAT, network application developers would naturally become more mindful of end-to-end considerations, would be careful not to embed address information in new applications' data, and would avoid diverging from the standard client/server model.

Just the opposite turned out to be the case. IPv6 has yet to be deployed, giving NAT permanent, long-term status. Use of NAT became almost universal as Internet access became more available to the general public and available IPv4 addresses became ever more scarce. The standard application protocols of the time and the common standard protocols still in use today—including DNS, HTTP, SMTP, POP, and NNTP—work just fine with NAT, and all NAT implementations provide special support for FTP.

NAT's success at transparent translation is a result of the standard client/server connection characteristics of these common protocols. The exceptions didn't turn out to be a few legacy and oddball applications, however. Internet applications have become increasingly interactive. Newer applications sometimes don't have a clear client/server relationship. Sometimes a single server coordinates communication among multiple users, who may also initiate communication among themselves, independent of the server. Multiple servers can operate in conjunction with distributed services running across multiple NAT address domains, or with services that are provided by different kinds of servers operating cooperatively. Certain legacy multimedia and other multistreaming and two-way, multiconnection sessions can initiate connections in both directions, may have many simultaneous connections per session, and may rely on both TCP and UDP simultaneously. The client isn't always a stationary, permanently addressable entity, as with dynamic client location in terms of mobile devices and telecommuting employees. Some services rely on end-to-end packet and data integrity, as do the IPsec encryption and authentication protocols.

These network applications do not work with NAT transparently. Specific Application-layer gateway (ALG) support for each application must be provided for NAT to be capable of translating these packets correctly. In the case of encryption, end-to-end Transport-layer security protocols using encryption and authentication methods don't work, period.

Regardless of the difficulties associated with NAT, its usefulness ensures that it's here to stay for the duration of IPv4. In the meantime, firewall folks are looking at alternative ways of firewalling to solve the problems that the newer protocols introduce, both in terms of NAT and in terms of packet filtering itself.

We need alternative firewalling methods because firewalling itself has problems when implemented with current technology. NAT isn't the only problem. Multimedia and the cost and overhead of Application-level gateways are gradually forcing the issue. Some of these protocols simply cannot be filtered with current firewall (and NAT) approaches.

Three general categories of NAT exist, as described in RFC 2663, "IP Network Address Translator (NAT) Terminology and Considerations":

- Traditional, outbound, unidirectional NAT is used for networks with private address space. Outgoing sessions can be initiated from the private LAN to remote Internet hosts. Incoming sessions cannot be initiated from remote hosts to local hosts in the privately addressed LAN.

  Traditional NAT is divided into two general subtypes, although the two subtypes can overlap in practice:

- Basic NAT performs address translation only. It is usually used to map local private source addresses to one from a pool of public addresses. For the duration of all sessions initiated by a particular local host, there is a one-to-one mapping between a particular public and private address pair.

- Network Address and Port Translation (NAPT) performs address translation but also replaces the local LAN host's source port with a source port on the NAT device. It is usually used to map local private source addresses to a single public address (as in Linux masquerading). Because the NAT device has a single IP address to map all outgoing private LAN connections to, the private and public source port pair is used to associate a particular connection with a particular private host address and a particular connection from that host.

- Bidirectional NAT performs two-way address translation, allowing both outbound and inbound connections. There is a one-to-one mapping between a public address and a private address. Effectively, the public address is a public alias for the local host's private address. This allows remote hosts to address the private host by the public address associated with it. The NAT device translates the public destination address in the incoming packet to the private address that the local host is actually assigned.

  One use of this is bidirectional address mapping between IPv4 and IPv6 address spaces. Although both addresses are routable within their own address spaces, IPv6 addresses are not routable within the IPv4 address space. A host in the IPv4 address space cannot directly reference a host in the IPv6 address space. Likewise, a host in the IPv6 space cannot directly reference a host in the IPv4 space. It is the IPv6 host's address that is being translated back and forth between the two addressing realms.

  Another use for bidirectional NAT that is more relevant to Linux users is to forward connections between the Internet and privately addressed local servers when the site offers public services from a LAN but has a single public IP address.

- Twice NAT performs two-way source and destination address translation, but both the source and destination addresses are translated in both directions. Twice NAT is used when the source and destination networks' address spaces collide. This could be because one site mistakenly used public addresses assigned to someone else. Twice NAT can be used as a convenience when a site is renumbered or assigned to a new public address block but the owner doesn't want to administer the new address assignments immediately.

The advantages of NAT include these:

- Packets containing standard application protocol data are transparently translated between networks.

- Standard client/server services "just work" with NAT.

- NAT alleviates the problems caused by the growing shortage of available IP addresses by sharing one public address or a small block of public addresses among an entire local network.
- NAT reduces the need for both local and public IP address renumbering.
- NAT reduces the need to deploy and administer more complicated routing schemes within larger local networks.
- In NAT's most common form in conjunction with private IP addresses, unwanted incoming traffic isn't passed along because the local machines aren't addressable.
- In one of NAT's other forms, it's used to allow virtual servers, in which a server farm appears to be a single, addressable server for load balancing.

The disadvantages of NAT include these:

- NAT introduces single points of failure within the network by maintaining critical state within the network itself.
- Maintaining critical state on the NAT device breaks the Internet paradigm in that packets can no longer be automatically rerouted around failed NAT routers.
- NAT breaks the Internet paradigm of end-to-end transparency by modifying packet contents en route.
- As a result of modifying addressing information, application-specific NAT support is required for any application that embeds local addresses or ports in the application payload.
- As a result of modifying addressing information for applications that embed local addresses or ports in the application payload, incoming packets destined to a NAT host must be defragmented before forwarding.
- NAT increases resource and performance requirements for NAT devices, which otherwise would be dedicated to fast datagram forwarding. NAT represents not only the overhead of defragmentation, packet inspection, and packet modification, but also the overhead of state maintenance, state timeouts, and state garbage collection.
- Because of state maintenance within the network and the associated resource requirements, NAT devices are not infinitely scalable. Additionally, without complicated sharing techniques, hosts cannot use multiple peer NAT devices, an aspect of the single point of failure.
- Bidirectional, multistream protocols require application-specific NAT support to forward incoming secondary streams to the proper local host. (Note that these protocols generally require ALG support for firewalling as well.)
- NAT can break the capability to run multiple instances of the same local network client application in connection with the same remote server. This problem tends to occur with network games and IRC, where the session has associated incoming streams.

- NAT cannot be used with transport-mode IPsec for end-to-end security for a few reasons:
  - End-to-end Transport-layer security techniques are not possible because the techniques rely on end-to-end integrity of the packet header contents for authentication.
  - End-to-end Transport-layer security techniques are not possible because the techniques rely on end-to-end integrity of the packet's data payload, which also relies on packet header integrity.
  - End-to-end Transport-layer security techniques are not possible because data encryption renders the packet's contents unavailable for inspection. NAT modifications are not possible to change embedded address and port information.
  - Security trust relationships must be extended into the network from the endpoint hosts, possibly to a point outside the local site altogether. IPsec and most VPN technologies must be extended to the NAT device (in other words, IPsec tunnel mode). Again, the NAT device becomes a single point of failure because the NAT device must terminate the VPN and establish a new link as a proxy to the destination.

NAT Semantics with `iptables` and `nftables`

Both `iptables` and `nftables` provide full NAT functionality, including both source (SNAT) and destination (DNAT) address mapping. The term *full NAT* isn't a formal term; I'm referring to the capability to perform both source and destination NAT, to specify one or a range of translation addresses, to perform port translation, and to perform port remapping.

A partial implementation of NAPT, known as "masquerading" among Linux users, was provided in earlier Linux releases. It was used to map all local, private addresses to the single public IP address of the site's single public network interface.

NAT and forwarding were often spoken of as two components of the same thing because masquerading was specified as part of the FORWARD rule's semantics. Blurring the concepts was irrelevant functionally. Now it's very important to keep the distinction in mind. Forwarding and NAT are two distinct functions and technologies.

Forwarding is routing traffic between networks. Forwarding routes traffic between network interfaces *as is*. Connections can be forwarded in either direction.

Masquerading sits on top of forwarding as a separate kernel service. Traffic is masqueraded in both directions, but not symmetrically. Masquerading is unidirectional. Only outgoing connections can be initiated. As traffic from local machines passes through the firewall to a remote location, the internal machine's IP address and source port are replaced with the address of the firewall machine's external network interface and a free source port on the interface. The process is reversed for incoming responses. Before the packet is forwarded to the internal machine, the firewall's destination IP address and port are replaced with the real IP address and port of the internal machine participating in the connection. The firewall machine's port determines whether incoming traffic, all of which is addressed to the firewall machine, is destined to the firewall machine itself or to a particular local host.

The semantics of forwarding and NAT are separated in `iptables`. The function of forwarding the packet is done in the `filter` table using the FORWARD chain. The function of applying NAT to the packet is done in the `nat` table, using one of the `nat` table's POSTROUTING, PREROUTING, or OUTPUT chains:

- Forwarding is a routing function. The FORWARD chain is part of the `filter` table.

- NAT is a translation function that is specified in the `nat` table. NAT takes place either before or after the routing function. The `nat` table's POSTROUTING, PREROUTING, and OUTPUT chains are part of the `nat` table. Source NAT is applied on the POSTROUTING chain after a packet has passed through the routing function. Source NAT is also applied on the OUTPUT chain for locally generated, outgoing packets. (The `filter` table OUTPUT chain and the `nat` table OUTPUT chain are two separate, unrelated chains.) Destination NAT is applied on the PREROUTING chain before passing the packet to the routing function.

Which Destination Address Is Seen Where?

Destination NAT is applied on the `nat` table's PREROUTING chain, before the routing decision is made. Rules on the PREROUTING chain must match on the original destination address in the packet's IP header. Rules on the `filter` table's INPUT or FORWARD chain must match on the modified, NATed address in the same packet header. Likewise, if that same packet were to also have source NAT applied after the routing decision is made, and if the destination address were important to match on, the rule on the `nat` table's POSTROUTING chain would match on the modified destination address.

Source NAT is applied on the `nat` table's POSTROUTING chain, after the routing decision is made. Rules on any chain match on the original source address. The source address is modified immediately before sending the packet on to the next hop or destination host. The modified source address isn't seen on the host applying the source NAT.

None of these distinctions between forwarding and NAT was an apparent issue with `ipfwadm` and `ipchains`. The forwarding rule pair wasn't necessary when masquerading. Two-way forwarding and NAT were implied by a single rule. The incoming local interface was implied by the source address. The translated source address was taken from the outgoing public interface specification. Reverse translation for response packets was implied without an explicit rule.

> **Don't Go Overboard Using NAT Syntax**
>
> The rest of this chapter presents the `nat` table syntax. Another word of caution is called for when looking at the complete NAT syntax. The following sections describe the simpler, more general syntax used with NAT, which is what will be used most commonly. The average site won't have a use for the specialized features available in the `nat` table.
>
> Both SNAT and DNAT rules can specify the protocol, source and destination addresses, source and destination ports, and state flags, in addition to the translated address and ports. When this is done, the `nat` table rules look very much like `filter` table rules. It's very easy to confuse NAT rules with firewall rules, especially for people who are used to `ipchains` syntax. Actual filtering is done in the FORWARD chain.
>
> You could mirror the match fields between the FORWARD rules and the NAT rules; the two sets of rules could look nearly identical. For large rule sets, it would quickly become an error-prone, administrative nightmare and would accomplish very little.
>
> Remember that `iptables` forwarding and NAT are two completely separate functions. The actual firewall filtering is done by the rules in the `filter` table. For most people, it's best to keep the `nat` table rules simple.

Source NAT

Two forms of source NAT exist in the `iptables` `nat` table, specified as two distinct targets, SNAT and MASQUERADE. SNAT is standard source address translation. MASQUERADE is a specialized form of source NAT for use in environments in which an arbitrary, dynamically assigned IP address is assigned on a temporary, connection-by-connection basis. As of this writing, there is masquerading support in `nftables`.

Both targets are used on the `iptables` `nat` table's POSTROUTING chain. Source address modifications are applied after the routing decision has been made to choose the proper outgoing interface. Thus, SNAT rules are associated with an outgoing interface, not with an incoming interface.

Because `nftables` doesn't include any default tables, the `nat` table must be configured before any of the examples in this chapter will work. To do so, you can add a nat table to the `setup-tables` rules file that was developed in previous chapters. The end result looks like this:

```
table filter {
        chain input {
                type filter hook input priority 0;
        }
        chain output {
                type filter hook output priority 0;
        }
        chain forward {
                type filter hook forward priority 0;
        }
}
```

```
table nat {
      chain prerouting {
            type nat hook prerouting priority 0;
      }
      chain postrouting {
            type nat hook postrouting priority 0;
      }
      chain output {
            type nat hook output priority 0;
      }
}
```

This file, saved as `setup-tables`, can be loaded with the command

```
nft -f setup-tables
```

Standard SNAT

This is the general syntax for SNAT:

```
iptables -t nat -A POSTROUTING -o <outgoing interface> ... \
      -j SNAT --to-source <address>[-<address>][:port-port]
```

For `nftables` the general syntax is

```
add rule nat postrouting oif <outgoing interface> \
   snat <address>[:port-port]
```

The address is the source address to substitute for the original source address in the packet, presumably the address of the outgoing interface. Source NAT is what NAT is traditionally used for, to allow outgoing connections. Specifying a single translation address performs NAPT, allowing all local, privately addressed hosts to share your site's single, public IP address.

Optionally, a range of source addresses can be specified. Sites that have a block of public addresses would use this range. Outgoing connections from local hosts would be assigned one of the available addresses, with the public address being associated with a particular local host's IP address.

MASQUERADE Source NAT

The general syntax for MASQUERADE for `iptables` is as follows:

```
iptables -t nat -A POSTROUTING -o <outgoing interface> ... \
      -j MASQUERADE [--to-ports <port>[-port]]
```

MASQUERADE doesn't have an option to specify a particular source address to use on the NAT device. The source address used is the address of the outgoing interface.

The optional port specification is one source port or a range of source ports to choose from on the NAT device's outgoing interface.

As with SNAT, the ellipsis represents any other packet selectors that are specified. For example, MASQUERADE could be applied to only a select local host.

Destination NAT

Two forms of destination NAT exist in the `iptables nat` table, specified as two distinct targets: DNAT and REDIRECT. DNAT is standard destination address translation. REDIRECT is a specialized form of destination NAT that redirects packets to the NAT device's input or loopback interface. There is no redirect target for `nftables`.

The two `iptables` targets can be used on either of the `iptables nat` table's PREROUTING or OUTPUT chains. Destination address modifications are applied before the routing decision is made to choose the proper interface. Thus, on the PREROUTING chain, DNAT and REDIRECT rules are associated with an incoming interface for packets that are to be forwarded through the device or that are addressed to this host's incoming interface. On the OUTPUT chain, DNAT and REDIRECT rules refer to locally generated, outgoing packets from the NAT host itself.

Standard DNAT

The general syntax for DNAT is as shown here:

```
iptables -t nat -A PREROUTING -i <incoming interface> ... \
        -j DNAT --to-destination <address>[-<address>][:port-port]
```

and

```
iptables -t nat -A OUTPUT -o <outgoing interface> ... \
        -j DNAT --to-destination <address>[-<address>][:port-port]
```

The nftables syntax is

```
nft add rule nat prerouting iif <incoming interface> \
    dnat <destination address>[:port-port]
```

and

```
nft add rule nat output oif <outgoing interface> \
    dnat <destination address>[:port-port]
```

The address is the destination address to substitute for the original destination address in the packet, presumably the address of a local server.

Optionally, a range of destination addresses can be specified. Sites that have a pool of public, peer servers would use this range. Incoming connections from remote sites would be assigned to one of the servers. These addresses could be public addresses assigned to the internal machines. For example, a pool of peer servers appears to be a single server to remote hosts. Alternatively, the addresses could be private addresses, and the servers wouldn't be directly visible or addressable from the Internet. In the latter case, the site probably doesn't have public addresses to assign to the servers. Remote hosts attempt to connect to the service on the NAT host. The NAT host forwards the connections transparently to the privately addressed internal server.

The final port specification is another option. The port specifies the destination port, or port range, on the target host's incoming interface that the packet should be sent to.

The ellipsis represents any other packet selectors that are specified. For example, DNAT could be applied to redirect incoming connections from a specific remote host to an internal host. Another use might be to redirect incoming connections to a particular service port to the actual server running in the local network.

REDIRECT Destination NAT

The general syntax for REDIRECT is shown here:

```
iptables -t nat -A PREROUTING -i <incoming interface> ... \
        -j REDIRECT [--to-ports <port[-port]>
```

and

```
iptables -t nat -A OUTPUT -o <outgoing interface> ... \
        -j REDIRECT [--to-ports <port[-port]>
```

Remember, REDIRECT redirects the packet to this host, which is the host performing the redirect.

Packets arriving on the incoming interface are presumably addressed to some other local host. Another alternative could be that the packet is targeted to a particular local service port, and the packet is redirected to a different port on the host transparently.

Locally generated packets, destined for somewhere else, are redirected back to the loopback interface on this host. Again, a packet targeted to a specific remote service might be redirected back to the local machine, perhaps to a caching proxy, for example.

Optionally, a different destination port or port range can be specified. If no port is specified, the packet is delivered to the destination port that the sender defined in the packet.

The ellipsis represents any other packet selectors that are specified. For example, REDIRECT could be applied to redirect incoming connections to a specific service to a server, logger, authenticator, or some kind of inspection software on the local host. The packet could be sent on from this host after some kind of inspection function was performed. Another use might be to redirect outgoing connections to a particular service back to a server or an intermediate service on this host.

Examples of SNAT and Private LANs

Source NAT is by far the most common form of NAT. Using NAT to give outgoing Internet access to local, privately addressed hosts was the original purpose of NAT. The following sections provide some simple, real-world examples of using the nat table's MASQUERADE and SNAT targets.

Masquerading LAN Traffic to the Internet

The MASQUERADE version of source NAT is intended for people with dial-up accounts who get a different IP address assigned at each connection. It also is used by people with *always on* connections but whose ISP assigns them a different IP address on a regular basis. This version applies only to iptables.

The simplest example is a PPP connection. These sites often use a single rule to masquerade all outgoing connections from the LAN:

```
iptables -t nat -A POSTROUTING -o ppp0 -j MASQUERADE
```

Masquerading—and NAT in general—is set up with the first packet. With masquerading, a single nat rule can be sufficient. The NAT and connection state tracking take care of the incoming packets. The FORWARD rule pair is necessary, though, as in this example:

```
iptables -A FORWARD -o ppp0 \
        -m state --state NEW,ESTABLISHED,RELATED -j ACCEPT

iptables -A FORWARD -o <LAN interface> \
        -m state --state ESTABLISHED,RELATED -j ACCEPT
```

In this simple type of setup, the incoming interface doesn't need to be specified. FORWARD rules refer to traffic crossing between interfaces. If the host has a single network interface and a single ppp interface, anything forwarded out one interface must necessarily originate from the other interface. Anything accepted by the FORWARD rules in the filter table during routing will be masqueraded by the POSTROUTING rule in the nat table.

Even with short-term phone connections, the single FORWARD rule allowing outgoing NEW connections should be broken out into rules for specific services. Depending on the networked devices in the LAN and how they operate, you most likely want to limit what LAN traffic gets forwarded.

Here's an example of a single FORWARD rule pair:

```
iptables -A FORWARD -i <LAN interface> -o ppp0 \
        -m state --state NEW,ESTABLISHED,RELATED -j ACCEPT

iptables -A FORWARD -i -ppp0 -o <LAN interface> \
        -m state --state ESTABLISHED,RELATED -j ACCEPT
```

In this example, the single FORWARD rule pair is broken out into several more specific rules allowing only DNS queries and standard web access. Other LAN traffic isn't forwarded, as shown by these commands:

```
iptables -A FORWARD -i -ppp0 -o <LAN interface> \
        -m state --state ESTABLISHED,RELATED -j ACCEPT
iptables -A FORWARD -o ppp0 \
        -m state --state RELATED,ESTABLISHED -j ACCEPT

iptables -A FORWARD -o ppp0 -p udp \
        --sport 1024:65535 -d <name server> --dport 53 \
        -m state --state NEW -j ACCEPT

iptables -A FORWARD -o ppp0 -p tcp \
        --sport 1024:65535 -d <name server> --dport 53 \
        -m state --state NEW -j ACCEPT

iptables -A FORWARD -o ppp0 -p tcp \
        -s <local host> --sport 1024:65535 --dport 80 \
        -m state --state NEW -j ACCEPT
```

The single MASQUERADE rule on the nat table's POSTROUTING chain remains unchanged. All forwarded traffic is masqueraded. (Locally generated traffic going out the ppp0 interface is not masqueraded because the traffic is identified with the interface's IP address, by definition.) The FORWARD rules in the filter table are limiting what traffic is forwarded and, therefore, what traffic is seen at the POSTROUTING chain.

Applying Standard NAT to LAN Traffic to the Internet

Assuming that that same site had a dynamically assigned but semipermanent IP address or that it has a permanently assigned IP address, the more general SNAT version of source NAT would be used. Just as in the masquerading example, small residential sites often forward and NAT all outgoing LAN traffic:

```
iptables -t nat -A POSTROUTING -o <external interface> \
 -j SNAT \
           --to-source <external address>
```

For nftables, a single rule is all that's necessary:

```
nft add rule nat postrouting ip saddr <source addresses> \
    oif <external interface> snat <external address>
```

As with masquerading, a single SNAT rule can be sufficient. The NAT and connection state tracking take care of the incoming packets. For iptables, the FORWARD rule pair is necessary, however, as in the following example:

```
iptables -A FORWARD -o <external interface>\
         -m state --state NEW,ESTABLISHED,RELATED -j ACCEPT

iptables -A FORWARD -o <LAN interface> \
         -m state --state ESTABLISHED,RELATED -j ACCEPT
```

In the case of small sites with 24x7 connections, it's especially important to be selective about what traffic gets forwarded. The single FORWARD rule allowing outgoing *new* connections isn't sufficient. Trojans and viruses are common. The newer networked devices can tend to be somewhat promiscuous about what they do over the network. There's a good chance that Microsoft Windows machines and devices such as networked printers are generating far more traffic than you realize. Also, much of that local traffic is broadcast. It's a good idea to avoid the risk of forwarding broadcast traffic. Routers are no longer supposed to forward directed broadcast traffic by default, but many still do. (Limited broadcasts don't cross network boundaries without a relay agent to duplicate the packet and pass it on. Most devices use limited broadcasts.) A final reason is the case of attaching work laptops to the home network. Many employers don't want offsite laptops to have Internet access without VPN or the protection of their corporate firewalls and antivirus software.

Examples of DNAT, LANs, and Proxies

For the residential and small-business site, destination NAT was probably the most welcome addition to Linux NAT when it was added to `iptables`.

Host Forwarding

DNAT provides the host-forwarding capability that, until now, was available only through third-party solutions. For small sites with a single public IP address, DNAT allows incoming connections to local services to be transparently forwarded to a server running in a DMZ. Public services aren't required to run on the firewall machine.

With a single IP address, remote sites send client requests to the firewall machine. The firewall is the only local host that's visible to the Internet. The service (for example, a web or mail server) itself is hosted internally in a private network. For packets arriving on that service's port, the firewall changes the destination address to that of the local server's network interface and forwards the packet to the private machine. The reverse is done for server responses. For packets from the server, the firewall changes the source address to that of its own external interface and forwards the packet on to the remote client.

The most common example is forwarding incoming HTTP connections to a local web server:

```
iptables -t nat -A PREROUTING -i <public interface> -p tcp \
        --sport 1024:65535 -d <public address> --dport 80 \
        -j DNAT --to-destination <local web server>
```

The `nftables` rule looks like this:

```
nft add rule nat prerouting iif <public interface> \
    tcp sport 1024-65535 ip daddr <public address> \
    tcp dport 80 dnat <local web server>
```

The tricky part is the question of what address is seen on each chain. Destination NAT was applied before the packet reached the FORWARD chain. So the rule on the FORWARD chain must refer to the internal server's private IP address rather than to the firewall's public address:

```
iptables -A FORWARD -i <public interface> -o <DMZ interface> -p tcp \
        --sport 1024:65535 -d <local web server> --dport 80 \
        -m state --state NEW -j ACCEPT
```

For `iptables` the rule looks like this:

```
nft add rule filter forward iif <public interface> \
    oif <DMZ interface> tcp sport 1024-65535 \
    tcp dport 80 ip daddr <local web server> \
    ct state new accept
```

Connection tracking and NAT automatically reverse the translation for packets returning from the server. Because the initial connection request was accepted, a generic FORWARD rule suffices to forward the return traffic from the local server to the Internet:

```
iptables -A FORWARD -i <DMZ interface> -o <public interface> \
        -m state --state ESTABLISHED,RELATED -j ACCEPT
```

The nftables version looks like this:

```
nft add rule filter forward iif <DMZ interface> \
    oif <public interface> \
    ct state established,related accept
```

Of course, don't forget that ongoing traffic from the client must be forwarded as well because the convention used in this book has been to separate individual service rules specifying the NEW state from a single rule for all ESTABLISHED or RELATED traffic:

```
iptables -A FORWARD -i <public interface> -o <DMZ interface> \
        -m state --state ESTABLISHED,RELATED -j ACCEPT
```

For nftables:

```
nft add rule filter forward iif <public interface> \
    oif <DMZ interface> \
    ct state established,related accept
```

Summary

This chapter covered Network Address Translation. Initially, three basic types of NAT were described. NAT's original purpose, what it is used for today, and its advantages and disadvantages were discussed as well.

In iptables, NAT features are accessed through the nat table and that table's chains rather than through the filter table and the FORWARD chain. The implications of packet flow through the operating system, and the differences between what address rules match against on the FORWARD chain versus on the nat chains, were discussed.

iptables implements both source NAT and destination NAT. Source NAT is divided into two subcategories, SNAT and MASQUERADE. SNAT is regular source address translation. MASQUERADE is a specialized implementation of source NAT. It removes any NAT table state as soon as a connection is dropped.

Destination NAT is also divided into two subcategories, DNAT and REDIRECT. DNAT is regular destination address translation. REDIRECT is special case of destination address translation. It is an alias for redirecting packets to the local host, regardless of the packet's original destination.

Finally, a series of real-world, practical examples of NAT were presented.

Debugging the Firewall Rules

So now the firewall is set up, installed, and activated. But nothing works! You're locked out. Who knows what's going on? Now what? Where do you even begin?

Firewall rules are notoriously difficult to get right. If you're developing by hand, bugs will invariably crop up. Even if you produce a firewall script with an automatic firewall-generation tool, your script undoubtedly will require customized tweaking eventually.

This chapter introduces additional reporting features of the `iptables` and `nftables` tools and other system tools. The information is invaluable when debugging your firewall rules. This chapter explains what the information can tell you about your firewall.

General Firewall Development Tips

Tracking down a problem in the firewall is detailed and painstaking. There are no short-cuts to debugging the rules when something goes wrong. In general, the following tips can make the process a bit easier:

- Always execute the rules from a complete test script, like the one I've shown how to build throughout this book. Be sure that the script flushes all existing rules, removes any existing user-defined chains, and resets the default policies first. Otherwise, you can't be sure which rules are in effect or in which order.

- Don't execute new rules from the command line. Especially don't execute the default policy rules from the command line. You'll be cut off immediately if you're logged in using X Windows or remotely from another system, including a system on the LAN.

- Execute the test script from the console if you can. Working in X Windows at the console might be more convenient, but the danger remains of losing access to X Windows locally. Be prepared for the possibility of needing to switch over to a virtual console to regain control. If you must use a remote machine to test the firewall script, use cron to automatically stop the firewall in case you get locked out. Be sure to remove the cron job before going live with the firewall, though.

- Remember that flushing the rule chains does not affect the default policy currently in effect.

- With a deny-by-default policy, always enable the loopback interface immediately.

- When feasible, work on one service at a time. Add rules one at a time, or as input and output rule pairs if you aren't using the state module. Test as you go. This makes it much easier to isolate problem areas in the rules right away. Liberal use of the `echo` command within the firewall script can help to narrow down the location of rules that are problematic within the script.

- The first matching rule wins. Order is important. Use the list commands as you go to get a feel for how the rules are ordered. Trace an imaginary packet through the list.

- If the script appears to hang, chances are good that a rule is referencing a symbolic hostname rather than an IP address before the DNS rules have been enabled. Any rule using a hostname instead of an address must come after the DNS rules, unless the host has an entry in the `/etc/hosts` file.

- The `filter` table is implied by default for `iptables` but not for `nftables`.

- Most match modules require you to reference the module by name with the `-m` option before specifying the module's feature syntax, as in `-m state --state NEW`.

- When a service doesn't work, log all dropped packets going in both directions, as well as all relevant accepted packets. Do the log entries in `/var/log/messages` or `/var/log/kern.log` show anything being dropped when you try the service? If they do, you can adjust your firewall rules to allow the packets. If not, the problem must be elsewhere.

- If you have Internet access from the firewall machine but not from the LAN, double-check that IP forwarding is enabled by running `cat /proc/sys/net/ipv4/ip_forward`. The value `1` should be reported. IP forwarding can be permanently configured by hand in `/etc/sysctl.conf` or in the firewall script itself. The first configuration method takes effect when the network is restarted. If IP forwarding wasn't enabled, you can enable it immediately by typing the following line as `root` or by including it in the firewall script and reexecuting the script:
  ```
  echo "1" > /proc/sys/net/ipv4/ip_forward
  ```

- If a service works on the LAN but not externally, turn on logging for accepted packets on the internal interface. Use the service *very* briefly to see which ports, addresses, flags, and so forth are in use in both directions. You won't want to log accepted packets for any length of time, or you'll have hundreds or thousands of log entries in `/var/log/messages`.

- If a service doesn't work at all, temporarily insert input and output rules at the beginning of the firewall script to accept everything in both directions and log all traffic. Is the service available now? If so, check the log entries in `/var/log/messages` to see which ports are in use.

Listing the Firewall Rules

It's a good idea to list the rules you've defined, to double-check that they are installed and are in the order you expect. The -L command lists the actual rules for a given chain as they exist in the internal kernel table. Rules are listed in the order in which they are matched against a packet.

The basic format of the `iptables` list command is as follows (run as `root`):

```
iptables [-v -n] -L [chain]
```

or

```
iptables [-t <table>] [-v -n] -L [chain]
```

The first format refers to the default `filter` table. If a specific chain isn't specified, the command lists all rules on the three built-in `filter` table chains, plus any user-defined chains.

The second format is needed to list the rules on the `nat` or `mangle` table.

Adding the -v option is useful to see the interface to which the rule applies. Adding the -n option is useful if the firewall rules refer to remote or illegal addresses, to avoid the lengthy name resolution time for those addresses. Remember that if a chain is specified, it must follow the -L command. Also note that -L is a command and -v and -n are options. They cannot be combined as in -Lvn.

Unlike using `iptables` to define actual rules, using `iptables` to list existing rules can be done from the command line. The output goes to your terminal or can be redirected into a file.

The syntax for `nftables` looks like this:

```
nft list [chain|table] <tablename> [chain] <name> [-a -n -n]
```

The name of the table is always required with any list command, but when requesting a chain list you don't need to use the table keyword. The astute reader will recognize that there are no default table names for `nftables`. The `list tables` command shows all tables:

```
nft list tables
```

The -a option adds the handle number to the listing, which can be helpful for inserting or deleting individual rules. The first -n option prevents the IP-to-DNS name translation. Adding a second -n prevents the port-to-service name lookup as well.

`iptables` Table Listing Example

The basic format of the `iptables` table list command to list all rules on all `filter` table chains is this:

```
iptables -vn -L INPUT
iptables -vn -L OUTPUT
iptables -vn -L FORWARD
```

or

```
iptables -vn -L
```

Notice that the preceding list commands show only the rules in the `filter` table chains.

The next three sections use seven sample rules on the `INPUT` chain to illustrate the differences among the various listing format options available to you with the `filter` table and to explain what the output fields mean. Using the different listing format options, the same seven sample rules are listed with varying degrees of detail and readability. The listing format options and fields are the same for the `INPUT`, `OUTPUT`, and `FORWARD` chains.

iptables -L INPUT

Here is an abbreviated list of seven rules from an `INPUT` chain using the default listing options:

```
> iptables -L INPUT

1    INPUT (policy DROP)
2    target      prot opt source                  destination
3    ACCEPT      all  --  anywhere               anywhere
4    LOG         icmp -f anywhere               anywhere          \
     LOG level warning prefix 'Fragmented ICMP: '
5    DROP        tcp  --  anywhere               anywhere          \
     tcp flags:FIN,SYN,RST,PSH,ACK,URG/NONE
6    ACCEPT      all  --  anywhere               anywhere          \
     state RELATED,ESTABLISHED
7    ACCEPT      udp  --  192.168.1.0/25         my.host.domain   \
     udp spts:1024:65535 dpt:domain state NEW
8    REJECT      tcp  --  anywhere               my.host.domain2  \
     tcp dpt:auth reject-with icmp-port-unreachable
9    ACCEPT      tcp  --  192.168.1.0/25         my.host.domain   \
     multiport dports http,https tcp spts:1024:65535 \
     flags:SYN,RST,ACK/SYN state NEW
```

Line Numbers in Listings

The line numbers in the listings throughout this chapter are not part of the output; they are simply reference markers. Numbers can be generated by adding the `--line-numbers` option to the command. The "line numbers" generated are the rules' positions within the chain.

Line 1 identifies the listing as being for the `INPUT` chain. The `INPUT` chain's default policy is `DROP`.

Line 2 contains these column headings:

- `target` refers to the target disposition of a packet matching the rule `ACCEPT`, `DROP`, `LOG`, or `REJECT`.

- `prot` is an abbreviation for *protocol*, which can be `all`, `tcp`, `udp`, or `icmp`, as well as a value from `/etc/protocols`.

- `opt` stands for *fragmentation options*, which would have been set with either the `-f` or the `! -f` option. A `!` in the first space indicates the `! -f` option, which means to match either unfragmented packets or the first fragment in a series. An f in the second space indicates the -f option, which means to match the second and subsequent fragments.

- source is the source address in the IP packet header.
- destination is the destination address in the IP packet header.

Line 3 illustrates how the simple -L list command, without qualifying arguments, lacks some important detail. The rule appears to accept all incoming packets—tcp, udp, and icmp—from anywhere. The missing detail, in this case, is the interface, lo. This is the rule accepting all input on the loopback interface.

Line 4 is a rule to log any (second and subsequent) fragmented ICMP packets. The default logging level for syslog is warn. The LOG rule has an associated --log-prefix string defined for it.

Line 5 is a rule that drops TCP packets without any state flags set.

Line 6 is a rule that accepts any incoming packet that is part of an ESTABLISHED connection, or a packet RELATED to such a connection (that is, an associated ICMP error or FTP data connection).

Line 7 is a rule that accepts incoming UDP DNS requests from hosts in the local network, 192.168.1.0/25. Notice that the network is divided into two subnets, so the hosts could range from 192.168.1.1 to 192.168.1.126.

Line 8 is a rule that rejects incoming TCP auth requests or queries to the local identd server. The ICMP Type 3 error message returned contains the default port-unreachable code. It isn't evident in the listing that the machine has two network interfaces. Requests are rejected from the "external" network, domain2.

Line 9 accepts incoming TCP connection requests from the local LAN for standard HTTP web connections and HTTPS web connections. A destination port list was defined with the multiport match option.

iptables -n -L INPUT

The -n option reports all fields as numeric values rather than symbolic names. This option can save time if your rules use a lot of specific IP addresses that otherwise would require DNS lookups before being listed. Additionally, a port range is more informative if it is listed as 23:79 rather than as telnet:finger.

Using the same seven sample rules from the INPUT chain, the following shows what the listing output looks like using the -n numeric option:

```
> iptables -n -L INPUT

1    INPUT (policy DROP)
2    target     prot opt source               destination
3    ACCEPT     all  --  0.0.0.0/0            0.0.0.0/0
4    LOG        icmp -f  0.0.0.0/0            0.0.0.0/0          \
     LOG flags 0 level 4 prefix 'Fragmented ICMP: '
5    DROP       tcp  --  0.0.0.0/0            0.0.0.0/0          \
     tcp flags:0x023F/0x020
```

```
6    ACCEPT     all  --  0.0.0.0/0            0.0.0.0/0        \
     state RELATED,ESTABLISHED
7    ACCEPT     udp  --  192.168.1.0/25       192.168.1.2      \
     udp spts:1024:65535 dpt:53 state NEW
8    REJECT     tcp  --  0.0.0.0/0            192.168.1.254    \
     tcp dpt:113 reject-with icmp-port-unreachable
9    ACCEPT     tcp  --  192.168.1.0/25       192.168.1.2      \
     multiport dports 80,443 tcp spts:1024:65535 flags:0x0216/0x022 state NEW
```

iptables -v -L INPUT

The -v option produces more verbose output, including the interface name. Reporting the interface name is especially helpful when the machine has more than one network interface.

Using the same seven sample rules from the INPUT chain, the following shows what the listing output looks like using the –v verbose option:

```
> iptables -v -L INPUT

1    INPUT (policy DROP 0 packets, 0 bytes)
2    pkts bytes target     prot opt in      out      source             \
        destination
3    32   3416 ACCEPT      all  --  lo       any      anywhere           \
        anywhere
4    0       0 LOG         icmp -f  any      any      anywhere           \
        anywhere             LOG level warning prefix 'Fragmented ICMP: '
5    0       0 DROP        tcp  --  any      any      anywhere           \
        anywhere             tcp flags:FIN,SYN,RST,PSH,ACK,URG/NONE
6    94   6586 ACCEPT      all  --  any      any      anywhere           \
        anywhere             state RELATED,ESTABLISHED
7    1      65 ACCEPT      udp  --  eth0     any      192.168.1.0/25     \
        my.host.domain      udp spts:1024:65535 dpt:domain state NEW
8    0       0 REJECT      tcp  --  eth1     any      anywhere           \
        my.host.domain2     tcp dpt:auth reject-with icmp-port-unreachable
9    1      48 ACCEPT      tcp  --  eth0     any      192.168.1.0/25     \
        my.host.domain      multiport dports http,https tcp spts:1024:65535 \
        flags:SYN,RST,ACK/SYN state NEW
```

nftables Table Listing Example

The basic format that I typically use when listing nftables rules for the filter table is

```
nft list table filter -a
```

This assumes that the filter table has been defined. You can use the list tables command to find all tables if the filter table isn't the name of the table for which you need the listing. Here's an abbreviated list of rules for the INPUT chain of the filter table, as an example:

```
1 table ip filter {
2      chain input {
3              type filter hook input priority 0;
4              iifname "lo" accept # handle 5
5              ct state established,related accept # handle 8
```

```
6              ct state invalid log prefix "INVALID input: " limit rate 3/second
               ➥drop # handle 11
7              iif eth0 ip saddr 255.255.255.255 drop # handle 18
8              log # handle 19
9              drop # handle 20
10      }
11   }
```

Line 1 shows the name of the table.

Line 2 shows the name of the chain.

Line 3 shows the type of table, the hook, and its priority.

Line 4 shows a rule using the localhost interface (lo) with a verdict or disposition of accept. The parts following the # indicate the handle number (5 in this case) for accessing this rule directly.

Line 5 shows a connection state rule matching established or related packets with a disposition of accept and its handle, 8.

Line 6 shows a rule for connection state of invalid which will be logged with a prefix of "INVALID input:". The logging will be rate limited to 3 per second and the packet will ultimately be dropped. This rule's handle is 11.

Line 7 expresses a rule for packets arriving on eth0 with a source address of 255.255.255.255 which will be dropped. The handle is 18.

Line 8 shows a rule to log all packets that haven't yet been filtered or processed by a preceding rule. This rule's handle is 19.

Line 9 shows the final disposition of any packets that make it this far without encountering a matching rule. Their fate is to be dropped. The rule handle is 20.

Lines 10 and 11 show the closing braces from the rule definition.

As you can see by the rule output, you could copy this output or redirect the output to a file and immediately re-create the existing rules.

Interpreting the System Logs

syslogd and its sibling rsyslogd are the service daemons that log system events. On a typical system, the main system log file is /var/log/messages. Many programs use syslog's standard logging services. Other programs, such as the Apache web server, maintain their own separate log files.

syslog Configuration

Not all log messages are equally important—or even interesting. This is where /etc/syslog.conf comes in. The configuration file /etc/syslog.conf enables you to tailor the log output to meet your own needs.

Messages are categorized by the subsystem that produces them. In the man pages, these categories are called *facilities* (see Table 9.1).

Table 9.1 **syslog Log Facility Categories**

Facility	Message Category
auth or security	Security/authorization
authpriv	Private security/authorization
cron	cron daemon messages
daemon	System daemon-generated messages
ftp	FTP server messages
kern	Kernel messages
lpr	Printer subsystem
mail	Mail subsystem
news	Network news subsystem
syslog	syslogd-generated messages
user	User program–generated messages
uucp	UUCP subsystem

Within any given facility category, log messages are divided into *priority* types. The priorities, in increasing order of importance, are listed in Table 9.2.

An entry in syslog.conf specifies a logging facility, its priority, and where to write the messages. Not obvious is that the priority is inclusive. It's taken to mean all messages at that priority and higher. If you specify messages at the error priority, for example, all messages at priority error and higher are included—crit, alert, and emerg.

Logs can be written to devices, such as the console, as well as to files and remote machines.

Tips about Log Files in **/var/log**

syslogd doesn't create files. It only writes to existing files. If a log file doesn't exist, you can create it with the touch command and then make sure that it is owned by root. For security purposes, log files are often not readable by general users. The security log file, /var/log/secure, in particular, is readable by root alone.

Table 9.2 **syslog Log Message Priorities**

Priority	Message Type
debug	Debug messages
info	Informational status messages
notice	Normal but important conditions
warning or warn	Warning messages
err or error	Error messages
crit	Critical conditions
alert	Immediate attention required
emerg or panic	System is unusable

These two entries write all kernel messages to both the console and
/var/log/messages. Messages can be duplicated to multiple destinations:

```
kern.*                                  /dev/console
kern.*                                  /var/log/messages
```

This entry writes panic messages to all default locations, including
/var/log/messages, the console, and all user terminal sessions:

```
*.emerg                                      *
```

The next two entries write authentication information related to root privilege
and connections to /var/log/secure, and user authorization information to
/var/log/auth. With the priority defined at the info level, debug messages won't
be written:

```
authpriv.info                           /var/log/secure
auth.info                               /var/log/auth
```

The next two entries write general daemon information to /var/log/daemon, and
mail traffic information to /var/log/maillog:

```
daemon.notice                           /var/log/daemon
mail.info                               /var/log/maillog
```

Daemon messages at the debug and info priorities and mail messages at the debug
priority are not logged (author's preference). named, crond, and systematic mail checking
produce uninteresting informational messages on a regular basis.

The final entry logs all message categories of priority info or higher to
/var/log/messages, with the exception of auth, authpriv, daemon, and mail. In this
case, the latter four message facilities are set to none because their messages are directed to
their own dedicated log files:

```
*.info;auth,authpriv,daemon,mail.none      /var/log/messages
```

More Information about `syslog` Configuration

For a more complete description of syslog configuration options and sample
configurations, see the man pages for syslog.conf(5) and sysklogd(8).

---

syslogd can be configured to write the system logs to a remote machine. A site that
uses a networked server configuration similar to the example in Chapter 7, "Packet Forwarding," with services offered from internal machines in the DMZ, might want to keep
a remote copy of the system logs. Maintaining a remote copy offers two advantages: First,
log files are consolidated on a single machine, making it easier for a system administrator
to monitor the logs. Second, the information is protected if one of the server machines is
ever compromised.

Chapter 11, "Intrusion Detection and Response," discusses the importance of system
logs during recovery if a system is ever compromised. One of the first things an attacker
does after successfully gaining root access to a compromised machine is to either erase

the system logs or install trojan programs that won't log his or her activities. The system log files are either gone or untrustworthy at exactly the time you need them most. Maintaining a remote copy of the logs helps protect this information, at least until the hacker replaces the daemons writing the log file information.

To log system information remotely, both the local logging configuration and the remote logging configuration require slight modifications.

On the remote machine collecting the system logs, add the `-r` option to the `syslogd` invocation. The `-r` option tells `syslogd` to listen on the UDP port 514 for incoming log information from remote systems.

On the local machine producing the system logs, edit `syslogd`'s configuration file, `/etc/syslog.conf`, and add lines specifying what log facilities and priorities you want written to a remote host. For example, the following copies all log information to hostname:

```
*.*                     @hostname
```

`syslogd` output is sent over UDP. Both the source and the destination ports are 514. The client firewall rule would be as follows:

```
iptables -A OUTPUT -o <out-interface> -p udp \
        -s <this host> --sport 514 \
        -d <log host> --dport 514 -j ACCEPT
```

Firewall Log Messages: What Do They Mean?

To generate firewall logs, the kernel must be compiled with firewall logging enabled. By default, individually matched packets are logged as `kern.warn` (priority 4) messages. Most of the IP packet header fields are reported when a packet matches a rule with the LOG target. Firewall log messages are written to `/var/log/messages` by default. The following analysis applies to both `nftables` and `iptables`.

You could duplicate the firewall log messages to a different file by creating a new log file and adding a line to `/etc/syslog.conf`:

```
kern.warn                               /var/log/fwlog
```

As a TCP example, this rule denying access to the `portmap/sunrpc` TCP port 111 would produce the following message in `/var/log/messages`:

```
iptables -A INPUT -i $EXTERNAL_INTERFACE -p tcp \
        --dport 111 -j LOG --log-prefix "DROP portmap: "

iptables -A INPUT -i $EXTERNAL_INTERFACE -p tcp \
        --dport 111 -j DROP

nft add rule filter input iif $EXTERNAL_INTERFACE tcp dport 111 log prefix "DROP
➥portmap: " drop

  (1)     (2)     (3)     (4)        (5)          (6)     (7)
Jun 19 15:24:16 firewall kernel: DROP portmap: IN=eth0 OUT=
```

```
                       (8)
MAC=00:a0:cc:40:9b:a8:00:a0:cc:d4:a7:81:08:00

      (9)                (10)         (11)
SRC=192.168.1.4 DST=192.168.1.2 LEN=60

   (12)        (13)       (14)       (15)      (16)
TOS=0x00 PREC=0x00 TTL=64 ID=57743    DF

    (17)        (18)        (19)        (20)
PROTO=TCP SPT=33926 DPT=111 WINDOW=5840

    (21)   (22)  (23)
RES=0x00 SYN URGP=0
```

The log message fields are numbered for the purposes of discussion:

- Field 1 is the date, `Jun 19`.
- Field 2 is the time the log was written, `15:24:16`.
- Field 3 is the computer's hostname, `firewall`.
- Field 4 is the log facility generating the message, `kernel`.
- Field 5 is the `log-prefix` string defined in the `LOG` rule.
- Field 6 is the incoming network interface that the input rule is attached to, `eth0`.
- Field 7 is the outgoing interface, which has no value in a rule on the `INPUT` chain.
- Field 8 is the MAC address of the interface that the packet is arriving on, followed by eight pairs of garbage hexadecimal digits.
- Field 9 is the packet's source address, `192.168.1.4`.
- Field 10 is the packet's destination address, `192.168.1.2`.
- Field 11 is the IP packet's total length in bytes, `LEN=60`, including both the packet header and its data.
- Field 12 is the type of service (`TOS`) field's 3 service bits, plus a reserved trailing bit, `TOS=0x00`.
- Field 13 is the `TOS` field's top 3 precedence bits, `PREC=0x00`.
- Field 14 is the packet's time to live (`TTL`) field, `TTL=64`. Time to live is the maximum number of hops (that is, routers visited) remaining before the packet expires.
- Field 15 is the packet's datagram ID, `ID=57743`. The datagram ID is either the packet ID or the segment to which this TCP fragment belongs.
- Field 16 is the fragment flags field, indicating that the Don't Fragment (`DF`) bit is set.
- Field 17 is the message protocol type contained in the packet, `PROTO=TCP`. Field values include 6 (TCP), 17 (UDP), 1 (`ICMP/<code>`), and `PROTO=<number>` for other protocol types.
- Field 18 is the packet's source port, `33926`.

- Field 19 is the packet's destination port, `111`.
- Field 20 is the sender's window size, `WINDOW=5840`, which indicates the amount of data that it is willing to accept and buffer from this host at this time.
- Field 21 reports the reserved field in the TCP header. All 4 bits must be `0`.
- Field 22 is the TCP state field. In this case, the `SYN` flag is set.
- Field 23 is the urgent pointer, which indicates the amount of data considered to be urgent. The field is `0` because the `URG` flag isn't set.

When interpreting the log message, the most interesting fields are these:

```
Jun 19 15:24:16 DROP portmap: IN=eth0 SRC=192.168.1.4 DST=192.168.1.2
PROTO=TCP SPT=33926 DPT=111 SYN
```

This says that the dropped packet is a TCP packet coming in on the `eth0` interface from an unprivileged port at `192.168.1.4`. It was a TCP connection request targeted to this machine's (`192.168.1.2`) port `111`, the `sunrpc/portmap` port. (This can be a common message because `portmap` historically is one of the most commonly targeted services.)

As a UDP example, this rule denying access to the `portmap/sunrpc` UDP port `111` would produce the following message in `/var/log/messages`:

```
iptables -A INPUT -i $EXTERNAL_INTERFACE -p udp \
        --dport 111 -j LOG --log-prefix "DROP portmap: "

iptables -A INPUT -i $EXTERNAL_INTERFACE -p udp \
        --dport 111 -j DROP

nft add rule filter input iif $EXTERNAL_INTERFACE udp dport 111 log prefix "DROP
➥portmap: " drop

  (1)      (2)      (3)      (4)        (5)          (6)      (7)
Jun 19 15:24:16 firewall kernel: DROP portmap: IN=eth0 OUT=

                          (8)
         MAC=00:a0:cc:40:9b:a8:00:a0:cc:d4:a7:81:08:00

             (9)              (10)          (11)
         SRC=192.168.1.4 DST=192.168.1.2 LEN=28

         (12)        (13)      (14)      (15)
         TOS=0x00  PREC=0x00  TTL=40  ID=50655

          (16)        (17)       (18)      (19)
         PROTO=UDP  SPT=33926  DPT=111  LEN=8
```

The log message fields are numbered for the purposes of discussion:

- Field 1 is the date, `Jun 19`.
- Field 2 is the time the log was written, `15:24:16`.
- Field 3 is the computer's hostname, `firewall`.

- Field 4 is the log facility generating the message, `kernel`.
- Field 5 is the `log-prefix` string defined in the `LOG` rule.
- Field 6 is the incoming network interface to which the input rule is attached, `eth0`.
- Field 7 is the outgoing interface, which has no value in a rule on the `INPUT` chain.
- Field 8 is the MAC address of the interface that the packet is arriving on, followed by eight pairs of garbage hexadecimal digits.
- Field 9 is the packet's source address, `192.168.1.4`.
- Field 10 is the packet's destination address, `192.168.1.2`.
- Field 11 is the IP packet's total length in bytes, `LEN=28`, including both the packet header and its data.
- Field 12 is the `TOS` field's 3 service bits, plus a reserved trailing bit, `TOS=0x00`.
- Field 13 is the `TOS` field's top 3 precedence bits, `PREC=0x00`.
- Field 14 is the packet's `TTL` field, `TTL=40`. Time to live is the maximum number of hops (that is, routers visited) remaining before the packet expires.
- Field 15 is the packet's datagram ID, `ID=50655`.
- Field 16 is the message protocol type contained in the packet, `PROTO=UDP`. Field values include 6 (TCP), 17 (UDP), 1 (`ICMP/<code>`), and `PROTO=<number>` for other protocol types.
- Field 17 is the packet's source port, `33926`.
- Field 18 is the packet's destination port, `111`.
- Field 19 is length of the UDP packet, including both the header and data, `LEN=8`.

When interpreting the log message, the most interesting fields are these:

```
Jun 19 15:24:16 DROP portmap: IN=eth0 SRC=192.168.1.4 DST=192.168.1.2
PROTO=UDP SPT=33926 DPT=111
```

This says that the dropped packet is a UDP packet coming in on the `eth0` interface from an unprivileged port at `192.168.1.4`. It was a UDP exchange targeted to this machine's (`192.168.1.2`) port `111`, the `sunrpc/portmap` port. (This can be a common message because `portmap` historically is one of the most commonly targeted services.)

Checking for Open Ports

Listing your firewall rules with `iptables -L` is the main tool available for checking for open ports. Open ports are defined to be open by your `ACCEPT` rules. Beyond the `iptables -L` command, other tools such as `netstat` are helpful for finding out what ports are listening on the firewall.

`netstat` has several uses. In the next section, we'll use it to check for active ports so that we can double-check that the TCP and UDP ports in use are the ports that the firewall rules are accounting for.

Just because `netstat` reports the port as listening or open doesn't mean that it's accessible through the firewall rules. Following this, a third-party port-scanning tool, Nmap, is introduced. These tools should be used from an external location to test exactly which ports are listening on the firewall. `netstat` is a good indicator of services that are running on the machine. Remember, if the service isn't absolutely necessary, you should disable it and consider removing it entirely, especially from a firewall. Let firewalls be firewalls—they shouldn't run extra services.

netstat -a [-n -p -A inet]

`netstat` reports various network status information. Quite a few command-line options are documented to select what information `netstat` reports. The following options are useful for identifying open ports, reporting whether they are in active use and by whom, and reporting which programs and which specific processes are listening on the ports:

- `-a` lists all ports that either are in active use or are being listened to by local servers.

- `-n` displays the hostnames and port identifiers in numeric format. Without the `-n` option, the hostnames and port identifiers are displayed as symbolic names, as much as will fit in 80 columns. Using `-n` avoids a potentially long wait while remote hostnames are looked up. Not using `-n` produces a more readable listing.

- `-p` lists the name of the program listening on the socket. You must be logged in as `root` to use the `-p` option.

- `-A inet` specifies the address family reported. The listing includes the ports in use as they are associated with your network interface cards. Local address family socket connections aren't reported, including local network-based connections in use by programs (such as any X Window program you might have running).

> **Types of Sockets—TCP/IP and Linux**
>
> Sockets were introduced in BSD 4.3 UNIX in 1986, and the concepts have largely been adopted by Linux. Two main socket types were the Internet domain, `AF_INET`, and the UNIX domain, `AF_UNIX`, sockets. `AF_INET` is the TCP/IP socket used across a network. `AF_UNIX` is a socket type local to the kernel. The UNIX domain socket type is used for interprocess communication on the same computer; it is more efficient than using TCP/IP for local sockets. Nothing goes out on the network.

The following `netstat` output is limited to the `INET` domain sockets. The listing reports all ports being listened to by network services, including the program name and the specific process ID of the listening program:

```
> netstat -a -p -A inet

1  Active Internet connections (servers and established)
2  Proto Recv-Q Send-Q Local Address     Foreign Address State    PID/
   Program name
```

```
3  tcp    0   143 internal:ssh     netserver:62360 ESTABLISHED
   15392/sshd
4  tcp    0    0 *:smtp           *:*              LISTEN
   3674/sendmail: acce
5  tcp    0    0 my.host.domain:www *:*            LISTEN  638/httpd
6  tcp    0    0 internal:domain  *:*              LISTEN  588/named
7  tcp    0    0 localhost:domain *:*              LISTEN  588/named
8  tcp    0    0 *:pop-3          *:*              LISTEN  574/xinetd
9  udp    0    0 *:domain         *:*                      588/named
10 udp    0    0 internal:domain  *:*                      588/named
11 udp    0    0 localhost:domain *:*                      588/named
```

Line 1 identifies the listing as including local servers and active Internet connections. This selection was indicated with the -A inet option to netstat.

Line 2 contains these column headings:

- Proto refers to the transport protocol the service runs over, TCP or UDP.
- Recv-Q is the number of bytes received from the remote host but not yet delivered to the local program.
- Send-Q is the number of bytes sent from the local program that haven't been acknowledged by the remote host yet.
- Local Address is the local socket, network interface, and service port pair.
- Foreign Address is the remote socket, remote network interface, and service port pair.
- State is the local socket's connection state for sockets using the TCP protocol, either ESTABLISHED connection or LISTENing for a connection request, as well as a number of intermediate connection establishment and shutdown states.
- PID/Program name is the process ID (PID) and program name that owns the local socket.

Line 3 shows that an SSH connection is established over the internal LAN network interface from a machine known as netserver. The netstat command was typed from this connection.

Line 4 is a sendmail listening for incoming mail on the SMTP port associated with all network interfaces, including the external interface connected to the Internet, the internal LAN interface, and the loopback, localhost interface.

Line 5 shows that a local web server is listening for connections on the external interface to the Internet.

Line 6 shows that the name server is listening on the internal LAN interface for DNS lookup connection requests from local machines over TCP.

Line 7 shows that the name server is listening on the loopback interface for DNS lookup connection requests from clients on this machine over TCP.

Line 8 shows that xinetd is listening for connections on the POP port associated with all interfaces on behalf of popd. (xinetd is listening on all interfaces for incoming POP connections. If a connection request arrives, xinetd starts a popd server to service the request.) The firewall and higher-level security mechanisms at the `tcp_wrappers` level and the `popd` configuration level limit incoming connections to the LAN machines.

Line 9 shows that the name server is listening on all interfaces for DNS server-to-server communications and is accepting local lookup requests over UDP.

Line 10 shows that the name server is listening on the internal LAN network interface for DNS server-to-server communications and lookup requests over UDP.

Line 11 shows that the name server is listening on the loopback interface for DNS lookup requests from local clients on this machine over UDP.

`netstat` Output Reporting Conventions

In `netstat` output, the local and foreign (that is, remote) addresses are listed as `<address:port>`. Under the `Local Address` column, the address is the name or IP address of one of your network interface cards. When the address is listed as *, it means that the server is listening on all network interfaces rather than on just a single interface. The port is either the symbolic or the numeric service port identifier that the server is using. Under the `Foreign Address` column, the address is the name or IP address of the remote client currently participating in a connection. The * . * is printed when the port is idle or for the default daemon. The port is the remote client's port on its end.

Idle servers listening over the TCP protocol are reported as listening for a connection request. Idle servers listening over the UDP protocol are reported as blank. UDP has no state—the `netstat` output is simply making a distinction between stateful TCP and stateless UDP.

Checking a Process Bound to a Particular Port with `fuser`

The `fuser` command identifies which processes are using a particular file, filesystem, or network port. `netstat -a -A inet` will report a port number rather than a service name if the port doesn't have an entry in `/etc/services`. `fuser` can be useful to determine which program is bound to that port.

The general `fuser` command format to identify which program is bound to a given port is as follows:

```
fuser -n tcp|udp -v <port number>[,<remote address>[,<remote port>]
```

For example,

```
> fuser -n tcp -v 515
```

produces the following output:

```
                    USER        PID ACCESS COMMAND
515/tcp             root        718 f....  lpd
```

The `-v` option produces the USER, ACCESS, and COMMAND fields. Without the `-v` option, the port/protocol and PID would be reported. You would need to use `ps` to identify the program assigned that process ID.

The access field codes refer to the type of access that the file or filesystem is being accessed by the process as. The f indicates that the object is open.

The next section describes Nmap.

Nmap

Nmap is a much more powerful network security auditing tool that includes many of the newer stealth scanning techniques in use today. You should check your system security with Nmap; it's a given that other people will. Nmap is available at http://www.insecure .org/nmap/. You should use Nmap from a host outside of your firewall to check that the firewall isn't listening on unexpected ports.

The following sample Nmap output reports the state of all TCP and UDP ports. Because the verbose option isn't used, Nmap reports only the ports that are open and that have servers listening on them. Nmap output includes the scanned hostname, IP address, port, open or closed state, transport protocol in use on that port, and symbolic service port name from /etc/services. Because choke is an internal host, additional ssh and ftp ports are open for internal LAN access:

```
> nmap -sT router

Starting nmap V. 2.54BETA7 ( www.insecure.org/nmap/ )
Interesting ports on choke.private.lan (192.168.1.2):
(The 3100 ports scanned but not shown below are in state: filtered)
Port      State       Service
21/tcp    open        ftp
22/tcp    open        ssh
53/tcp    open        domain
80/tcp    open        http
443/tcp   open        https

Nmap run completed -- 1 IP address (1 host up) scanned in 236 seconds
```

Summary

This chapter introduced the iptables rule-listing mechanism, Linux port and network daemon information available via netstat, and a third-party tool available for verifying that the firewall rules are installed and working as you expect.

This chapter emphasized the firewall rules and the ports they protect. Chapter 10, "Virtual Private Networks," shifts the focus away from firewalls and into the broader topic of network and system security.

Virtual Private Networks

Contributed by Carl B. Constantine

The use of virtual private networks, or VPNs, is fast becoming the preferred method for accessing remote and private networks by home users and business users alike. This chapter discusses VPNs, providing both some background on VPNs themselves and insight on how you might implement a VPN using Linux.

Overview of Virtual Private Networks

VPN systems are designed to connect two or more devices or networks securely over a public network such as the Internet. A VPN is so named because it is virtual, using an already existing infrastructure; it is private, having the data encapsulated through a secure protocol; and it is a network, because it connects two or more devices or networks together. VPNs are popular today because they provide a better value proposition than setting up individual leased connections between locations, especially for road warriors or other short-lived connections. VPNs can also provide seamless operation. After initial configuration is done, the networks connected with a VPN can operate as if they were one network.

VPN Protocols

Most VPN systems use one of three main protocols: Point-to-Point Tunneling Protocol (PPTP), Layer 2 Tunneling Protocol (L2TP), or IP Security (IPsec). This section looks at all three.

PPTP and L2TP

Point-to-Point Tunneling Protocol was originally designed and developed by a consortium of companies to encapsulate non-TCP/IP protocols such as IPX over the Internet using Generic Routing Encapsulation (GRE). Security in the protocol was added later. Layer 2 Tunneling Protocol (L2TP) is widely considered to be the successor to PPTP for most environments.

Generic Routing Encapsulation

Many protocols are currently available that are designed to encapsulate or hide one protocol in another, normally IP. GRE is designed to be more generic (hence the name) than these other protocols. As such, however, it may not fit the need of specifically encapsulating protocol X over protocol Y; instead, it is designed to be a simple, general-purpose encapsulation protocol that reduces the overhead of providing encapsulation. RFC 2784, "Generic Routing Encapsulation (GRE)," describes GRE in detail.

PPTP and L2TP are very popular in many corporate environments, particularly those that are Windows-centric. There are both PPTP and L2TP clients for Windows, Linux, OS X, and major mobile platforms as well.

IPsec

IPsec was designed with security in mind and is considered the de facto standard for secure private communication across public networks such as the Internet. As mentioned previously, IPsec has been included in IPv6 and can also be used in the current IPv4 standard.

IPsec provides data integrity, authentication, and confidentiality. All IPsec services are at the IP layer and provide protection for IP and upper-layer protocols. These services are provided by two traffic security protocols, the Authentication Header (AH) and the Encapsulating Security Payload (ESP). IPsec uses a cryptographic key-management system through the Internet Key Exchange (IKE) protocol and a managed Security Association (SA) connection system.

IPsec offers many advantages compared to other secure network access methods. One of the biggest advantages is that IPsec can work in the background without the user even knowing what's happening.

Authentication Header

Normal IP packets consist of a header and a payload. The header contains both source and destination IP addresses that are required for routing. The payload consists of information that may be confidential. Headers can be spoofed or altered using a man-in-the-middle type of attack. The AH actually signs the outbound packet digitally, verifying the identity of source and destination addresses and the integrity of the payload data.

AH provides only authentication, not encryption, and can be configured in one of two ways: in transport mode or in tunnel mode. Transport mode really applies only to the host implementation and provides protection for the upper-level protocols as well as selected IP header fields. Using transport mode, the AH is inserted after the IP header and before the upper-layer protocol (TCP, UDP, ICMP, and so forth), or before other IPsec headers that may already have been inserted.

The AH in tunnel mode protects the entire IP packet, including the entire inner IP header. As in transport mode, the AH is inserted after the outer IP header of the packet.

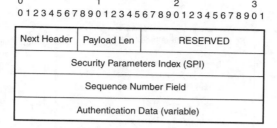

Figure 10.1   The AH header format

The AH is inserted after the IP header. In IPv4 implementations, the IP header contains the protocol number 51 (AH). The AH is shown in Figure 10.1.

All fields in AH format must always be present and are included in the Integrity Check Value (ICV) computation.

Encapsulating Security Payload

Using ESP guarantees the integrity and confidentiality of the data in the original message by means of a secure encryption of either the original payload by itself or the combination of the headers and payload of the original packet.

ESP can be used in transport mode or tunnel mode, like AH, to provide encryption and authentication. Transport mode is applicable only to host implementations. It provides protection for the upper-layer protocols, but not for the IP header. For tunnel mode, the ESP is inserted after the IP header and before any upper-layer protocol such as TCP and UDP, or before any other IPsec headers that may already be inserted. In the current IPv4 implementation of TCP/IP, the ESP is placed after the IP header but before the upper-layer protocol. This makes ESP compatible with non-IPsec-aware hardware.

ESP's tunnel mode may be used in either hosts or security gateways. You must use ESP in tunnel mode if you deploy a security gateway. In tunnel mode, the inner IP header carries the proper source and destination addresses, whereas the outer IP header may contain distinct IP addresses such as addresses of security gateways. ESP protects the entire packet in tunnel mode, including the inner IP header. The position of the ESP packet is similar to that of transport mode.

ESP can use a wide variety of encryption algorithms for security services.

Transport and Tunnel Modes

In transport mode, the IPsec gateway is the destination of the protected packets—a machine acts as its own gateway. In tunnel mode, an IPsec gateway provides protection for packets to and from other systems.

The ESP is inserted after the IP header. In IPv4 implementations, the IP header contains the protocol number 50 (ESP). Figure 10.2 shows an example of an ESP.

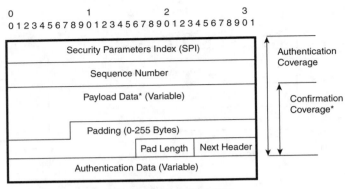

Figure 10.2   The ESP format

Internet Key Exchange

The Internet Key Exchange, or IKE, is an important part of an IPsec VPN. IKE itself is a hybrid protocol and allows for negotiation and authentication of keyed material for security associations in a protected manner.

Security Associations

To have secure traffic, there must be two security associations—one for each direction. The security association is essentially a one-way channel negotiated by the higher-level IPsec system and used by the lower level.

A security association is defined by three things:

- The destination IP address
- The protocol (AH or ESP)
- The security parameter index (SPI)

An SA can be used in transport mode or tunnel mode. A transport-mode SA is a security association between two hosts. A tunnel-mode SA is a security association applied to an IP tunnel. If either end of an SA is a security gateway, the SA is a tunnel-mode security association. Security association between two security gateways is always the tunnel-mode SA, just like an SA between a host and a security gateway.

Linux and VPN Products

Linux has a number of robust VPN solutions, with IPsec support being available from the Linux 2.6 kernel series and onward. This section looks at some of the Linux VPN software.

Openswan/Libreswan

Openswan and its fork Libreswan are open-source implementations of VPN software that work very well with Linux. Openswan and/or Libreswan are included with many Linux distributions, including Fedora, Debian, Ubuntu, and Red Hat. Openswan/Libreswan are among the easier Linux implementations of VPN software to set up. More information can be found at http://www.openswan.org/ and https://libreswan.org.

OpenVPN

OpenVPN is a popular VPN implementation for Linux, with software also available for Windows and OS X. OpenVPN uses static key and TLS authentication and has a variety of options for running a server and client-to-client VPN scenarios as well.

PPTP

PPTP support is typically provided by the PPTP daemon, `pptpd`. Configuring `pptpd` is fairly straightforward but suffers from a lack of overall power by itself when compared to other Linux VPN server solutions such as OpenVPN.

VPN and Firewalls

A VPN can be placed in front of a firewall, be placed behind a firewall, or be part of a firewall implementation. Placing the VPN in front of a firewall is not very common. It is more common to use a firewall/VPN combo or to put the VPN behind the firewall itself.

Combining a VPN system and a firewall is one of the more flexible solutions. It requires less hardware but also creates a single point of failure. A more robust solution is to have a VPN behind the firewall or as part of a DMZ configuration.

If your firewall also performs NAT, you may run into some troubles with some VPN configurations. In particular, your firewall must be set up to route packets based on the protocol (GRE, AH, ESP) instead of on the port alone.

A NAT/firewall is typically incompatible with the AH protocol regardless of the mode (transport or tunnel). IPsec VPNs using AH digitally sign the outbound packet, both data payload and headers, with a hash value appended to the packet. AH doesn't encrypt the packet contents (data payload). If a NAT/firewall is between the IPsec endpoints, it rewrites either the source address or the destination address with one of its own (depending on the NAT setup). The VPN at the receiving end tries to verify the integrity of the inbound packet by computing its own hash value and complains that the hash value appended to the packet doesn't match. The VPN, unaware of the NAT/firewall in the middle, thinks that the packet has been altered.

You can use IPsec with ESP in tunnel mode with authentication. ESP in tunnel mode encapsulates the entire original packet (including headers) in a new IP packet. The new packet's source address is the outbound address of the sending VPN gateway, and its destination address is the inbound address of the VPN at the receiving end. When using ESP in tunnel mode with authentication, the packet contents are encrypted. The encrypted contents (the original packet), not the new headers, are signed with a hash value appended to the packet.

Integrity checks are performed over the combination of the original header plus the original payload. If you're using ESP in tunnel mode with authentication, these are not changed by the NAT/firewall.

A NAT/firewall may interfere with IPsec (both AH and ESP) if it prevents the two VPN gateways from successfully negotiating security associations using ISAKMP/IKE with X.509 certificates. If the two VPN gateways exchange signed certificates that bind each gateway's identity to its IP address, NAT address rewriting will cause the IKE negotiation to fail.

It is for this reason that combination VPN and firewall configurations are becoming so popular. Rules to manage this situation can be set up and maintained easily.

Summary

Virtual private networks are popular because they leverage existing infrastructure to provide a seamless network experience to end users. Numerous implementations of VPNs are available, taking advantage of the different protocols available for creating VPNs. As you would expect, Linux has several options available, Openswan and OpenVPN among others.

Some problems exist when connecting VPNs through NAT-enabled firewalls. This is because IPsec creates a digital signature based on the IP header, which is altered during the NAT process.

III

Beyond **iptables** and **nftables**

11

Intrusion Detection and Response

You've now built a firewall with Linux using `iptables` or `nftables`. The layered security approach includes both network- and host-based security. Where the firewall provides security for both the network and the hosts, there are also steps that must be taken on the firewall machine itself, as well as on the hosts within the network. Whether it takes the form of filesystem integrity checking, virus/rootkit scanning, or monitoring the network for suspicious activity, these processes help ensure that your data remains safe.

This chapter is about host and network security and intrusion detection. The goal of the chapter is to provide a high-level overview of some of the concepts so that you can do further research into the specific areas of interest. The chapter widens the scope beyond that of the firewall machine to include the security of the network, as well as suggestions for individual computers within the network.

Detecting Intrusions

How do you know when you've been attacked successfully? Administrators and intrusion analysts have posed that question for a long time. The methods used for detecting successful attacks used to be more art than science. Luckily, various tools are now available to make intrusion detection much more science than art.

With that said, the primary tool for intrusion detection still remains a human who can gather data from a number of sources and make an intelligent, educated decision about the meaning of the data. The current tools are sophisticated and can perform some of this correlation themselves, but the true worth of an intrusion analyst is proven in the ability to assess the situation and present likely causes and effects.

Many times, an attack is detected when a service outage is reported. In this way, it's important to actively monitor your services using a package such as Nagios. By actively monitoring as many services as possible, you can quickly spot an anomaly that warrants further investigation.

If you run a web server, rather than monitoring merely whether the server is listening (usually on TCP port 80) you should monitor specific text on one or more web pages. If you monitor only the state of the server and whether it's listening, you won't catch a defacement of the website. In essence, you should monitor the behavior of the specific services to ensure that they are running as expected rather than making sure that they are merely running.

It's also important to monitor resources such as disk space, memory usage, and load average. Monitoring these resources can indicate if a process has run away and is consuming too many resources (as might be the case with a poorly written exploit). Additionally, monitoring disk space is another useful task. If you normally consume 25% of the disk and suddenly the disk usage jumps to 85%, you'll want to investigate to see whether an attacker is using the server as a drop point for files.

Basic service monitoring, performed as much as you can, as often as you can, will help provide an early warning of anomalies. Monitoring services will also help improve the reliability of the services, all security considerations aside. Monitoring should not, however, replace intrusion detection tools such as Snort or Suricata, nor should it replace a good security policy implemented through an in-depth strategy.

After an anomaly has been noted, whether through normal service monitoring or through another means, it's up to you to investigate the anomaly. Your investigation should conform to the security policy you have in place. One of the first responses would likely be to determine whether an intrusion has actually taken place. There could be many reasons why the load average just spiked or why the disk usage has increased, so you shouldn't assume that an attack has happened merely because of an outage alert.

Determining the root cause of a service outage is a difficult task that usually ends in a service being restarted or some similar routine procedure being performed to clear up the outage. However, it's important to look for underlying causes of such outages to ensure that an attack isn't under way or that an attack hasn't already occurred. It is in this area, event correlation, where a human is most necessary. For example, did the disk partition just run out of space because an attacker is using the space or because the log files filled up the partition?

Symptoms Suggesting That the System Might Be Compromised

Often, successful attackers will try to hide their tracks, and therefore simple service monitoring won't be of assistance. The attackers might be far more skillful at hiding their tracks than you are at tracking down anomalous system states.

Linux systems are too diverse, customizable, and complicated to define an ironclad, fully comprehensive list of definitive symptoms proving that the system is compromised. As with any kind of detective or diagnostic work, you must look for clues where you can—as systematically as you can. RFC 2196, "Site Security Handbook," provides a list of signs to check for. Though unmaintained, the "Steps for Recovering from a UNIX or NT System Compromise," available from CERT at http://www.cert.org/historical/tech_tips/win-unix-system_compromise.cfm?, provides another list of anomalies to check for.

The following sections incorporate and extend the ideas found in both lists, including all or most of their points in one form or another. The anomalies have been roughly categorized into the following: indications related to the system logs; changes to the system configuration; changes related to the filesystem, file contents, file access permissions, and file size; changes to user accounts, passwords, and user access; problems indicated in the security audit reports; and unexpected performance degradation. The anomalous indications often cross category boundaries.

System Log Indications

System log indications include unusual error and status messages in the logs, truncated log files, deleted log files, and emailed status reports:

- **System log files**—Unexplained entries in the system log files, shrinking log files, and missing log files all suggest that something is wrong. For example, `/var/log/messages` contains the majority of the system log information on most Linux systems. If that log file is zero-sized or is missing large portions, additional investigation is warranted.

- **System daemon status reports**—Instead of (or in addition to) writing to the log files, some daemons such as `crond` send status reports in email. Having unusual or missing reports suggests that something is not right.

- **Anomalous console and terminal messages**—Unexplained messages, possibly meant to announce the hacker's presence, during a login session are obviously suspicious.

- **Repeated access attempts**—Ongoing login attempts or illegal file access attempts through FTP or a web server, particularly attempts to subvert a web application, are suspicious when the attempts are persistent, even if the attempts appear to end in repeated failure.

System Configuration Indications

System configuration indications include modified configuration files and system scripts, unintended processes running inexplicably, unexpected service port usage and assignments, and changes in network device operational status:

- **cron jobs**—Check the cron configuration scripts and executables for modification.

- **Altered system configuration files**—A filesystem integrity check, manual or using a tool as described in Chapter 14, "Filesystem Integrity," would indicate changed configuration files in `/etc`. These files are critical to proper system functioning. Any change to a file (such as in `/etc/`, like `/etc/passwd`, `/etc/group`, and similar files) is important to check.

- **Unexplained services and processes, as shown by ps**—Unexpectedly running programs are a bad sign. Be aware that as part of the attack, the ps command itself may have been replaced. More on this later.

- **Unexpected connection and unexpected port usage, as shown by netstat or tcpdump**—Unexpected network traffic is a bad sign.

- **System crashes and missing processes**—System crashes, as well as unexpected server crashes, might be suspect. A system crash can also suggest an attacker-initiated system reboot, which could be necessary to restart certain critical system processes after replacement with a trojan version.

- **Changes in device configuration**—Reconfiguring a network interface to be in promiscuous or debug mode is a sign that a packet sniffer is installed.

Filesystem Indications

Filesystem indications include new files and directories, missing files and directories, altered file contents, md5sum or sha1sum mismatches, new setuid programs, and rapidly growing or overflowing filesystems:

- **New files and directories**—Besides files with suddenly bad digital signatures, you might discover new files and directories. Especially suspicious are filenames starting with one or more dots and legitimate-sounding filenames appearing in unlikely places.

- **setuid and setgid programs**—New setuid files, and newly set setgid files, are a good place to start looking under the hood for problems.

- **Missing files**—Missing files, particularly log files, indicate a problem of some kind.

- **Rapidly changing filesystem sizes, as shown by df**—If the machine is compromised, rapidly growing filesystems might be a sign of a hacker's monitoring program producing large log files.

- **Modified public file archives**—Check the contents of your web and FTP areas for new or modified files.

User Account Indications

User account indications include new user accounts, changes to the passwd file, unusual activity in the user process accounting reports or missing process accounting reports, changes to user files—especially environmental files—and loss of account access:

- **New and modified user accounts**—New accounts in /etc/passwd and processes running under new or unexpected user IDs as shown by ps are indications of new accounts. Accounts with suddenly missing passwords indicate an open account.

- **User accounting records**—Unusual user accounting reports, inexplicable logins, missing or edited log files (such as /var/log/lastlog, /var/log/pacct, or /var/log/usracct), and irregular user activity are signs of trouble.

- **Changes to root or user accounts**—A serious sign is a user's login environment that has been modified or damaged to the point that the account is inaccessible. Of particular concern are changes to users' `PATH` environment variable or `ssh`
  `authorized_keys`.
- **Loss of account access**—Similar to changes to a user's login environment is
  intentional access denial, whether by changing the account password, by removing
  the account, or, for regular users, by changing the runlevel to single-user mode.

Security Audit Tool Indications

Security audit tool indications include filesystem integrity mismatches, file size changes,
changes to file permission mode bits, new `setuid` and `setgid` programs, alerts from
intrusion detection tools such as Snort, and service-monitoring data.

Files with mismatched hash signatures can be files that are new, files whose lengths or
creation or modification dates have changed, and files whose access modes are altered.
Of particular concern are newly installed trojan horse programs. Frequent targets for
replacement are programs managed by `inetd` or `xinetd`, `inetd` or `xinetd` itself, `ls`,
`ps`, `netstat`, `ifconfig`, `telnet`, `login`, `su`, `ftp`, `syslogd`, `du`, `df`, `sync`, and the `libc`
library.

System Performance Indications

System performance indications include unusually high load averages and heavy disk
access.

Unexplained, poor system performance could be caused by unusual process activity,
unusually high load averages, excessive network traffic, or heavy filesystem access.

If your system shows signs of a successful compromise, don't panic. Don't reboot the
system—important information could be lost. Simply physically disconnect the system
from the Internet.

What to Do If Your System Is Compromised

Regardless of how an anomaly is investigated, the intrusion analyst must take care when
performing the investigation. If attackers notice that there's an investigator currently looking around on the same system, it's much more likely that they will slash and burn their
way out of the system. If an attacker thinks he or she is being followed or monitored, the
attacker might begin deleting anything and everything in the way, causing real damage
to the systems in question. An attack that might have resulted in only a defacement of a
website might suddenly turn into deletion of entire partitions if the attacker notices the
investigation.

After it has been determined that there has been a successful attack or that an attack
is currently under way, a number of responses frequently occur. These will, of course, be
dependent on your security policy.

If storage space is available, take a snapshot of the entire system in its current state for later analysis. If that isn't an option for you, at least snapshot the system logs under /var/log and the system configuration files under the /etc directory.

Keep a log. Write down everything. Documenting what you do and what you find not only is good for reporting the incident to a response team, your ISP, or a lawyer but also helps you keep track of what you've examined and what remains to be done.

If an attack has occurred or is currently under way, one of the first priorities is usually to stop the attack and prevent further damage from occurring. Keeping in mind that an attacker who notices an investigator on the same system is more likely to cause collateral damage, unplugging the system from the network is a common recommendation. With the network cable unplugged, the attacker simply can't cause additional damage. There is, of course, the possibility that the attacker will be using a tool to monitor the network interface and automatically cover his or her tracks should that interface's status change.

Looking for subtle changes to the system is part of this phase. Attackers may have set up a cron job to restart their daemons if they are stopped. In addition, it's quite typical for attackers to replace common Linux utilities such as ls and ps with their own versions in order to hide their processes and files. In this regard, a program such as Chkrootkit can be helpful for detecting host-based intrusions.

The tools you use to mitigate damage will be determined by the type of attack. For example, a denial-of-service attack against a router will necessarily require different steps to mitigate the attack. The steps you might take to determine whether the system is compromised are the same steps to take in analyzing the compromised system:

1. Check the system logs and use netstat and lsof to see which processes are running and which ports are bound. Check the contents of the system configuration files. Verify the contents and access modes of all your files and directories by checking their digital signatures. Check for new setuid programs. Compare configuration and user files against clean backup copies. It's very likely that the attacker installed trojan horse programs in place of the very system tools you're using to analyze the system.

2. Take stock of any volatile information, such as which processes are running and which ports are in use.

3. Boot off an external drive or a backup copy of the system. Examine the system using the clean tools from the unaffected system. As an alternative, install the disk drives as secondary drives in a noncompromised system, and examine the disks as data.

4. Determine how the attacker succeeded in gaining entry, and determine what was done to your system.

5. If possible, completely reinstall the system from the original Linux distribution media.

6. Correct the security vulnerability, whether by making a more careful selection of services to run, by reconfiguring servers more securely, by defining access lists at the

`xinetd` or `tcp_wrappers` level and at the individual server level, by installing a packet-filtering firewall, or by installing application proxy servers.

7. Install and configure any system integrity packages.

8. Enable all logging.

9. Restore user and special configuration files known to be untainted.

10. Create MD5 or SHA checksums for the system binaries and static configuration files.

11. Reconnect the system to the network and install any new security upgrades from your Linux vendor.

12. Create MD5 or SHA checksums for the newly installed binaries, and store the checksum database on a USB drive, CD/DVD, or some other system.

13. Monitor the system for recurring illegal access attempts.

Incident Reporting

An *incident* can be a number of things; you need to define it for yourself. For example, an incident might be defined as an anomalous attempt to gain or escalate privilege or compromise the confidentiality, integrity, or availability of one or more systems.

It is good practice to monitor your system log files, system integrity reports, and system accounting reports as a matter of habit. Even with minimal logging enabled, sooner or later you'll see something that your security policy dictates is important enough to report. With full logging enabled, you'll have plenty of log entries to ponder 24 hours a day.

Some access attempts are more serious than others. Some will annoy you personally more than others. The following sections start by discussing reasons why you might want to report an incident and cover considerations concerning which types of incidents you might report. These are individual decisions. The remaining sections focus on the various reporting groups available and the kind of information you need to supply if you choose to report something.

Why Report an Incident?

You might want to report an incident even if the attack attempt was unsuccessful. These are some of the reasons:

- **To end the probes**—Your firewall ensures that most probes remain harmless. But even harmless probes are annoying if they occur repeatedly. Persistent, repeated, ongoing scans fill your log files. Depending on how you've defined the notification triggers in any log-monitoring software that you run, repeated probes can pester you with continual email notifications. However, in today's age of seemingly endless probes from bots owned by unaware broadband users, especially those in the United States, it would simply be too time-consuming for most people to report every probe.

- **To help protect other sites**—Automated probes and scans are generally building a database of all vulnerable hosts in a large IP address block. When identified as potentially vulnerable to specific exploits, these hosts are targeted for selective attacks. Today's sophisticated analysis and cracking tools can compromise a vulnerable system and hide their tracks in seconds. Reporting an incident might put a stop to the scans before someone somewhere else gets hurt.

- **To inform the system or network administrator**—Attacking sites quite often are compromised systems, host a compromised user account, have misconfigured software, are being spoofed, or have an individual troublemaker. System administrators are usually responsive to an incident report. ISPs tend to stop their troublemaking customers before other customers start complaining that remote sites have blocked access from their address block and that they can't exchange email with a friend or family at a remote site.

- **To receive confirmation of the attack**—Sometimes you might simply want confirmation that what you're seeing in the logs is a problem. Sometimes you might want confirmation that a remote site was indeed leaking packets unintentionally because of a faulty configuration. The remote site also is often glad for the heads-up that its network isn't behaving as it had intended.

- **To increase awareness and monitoring by all involved parties**—If you report the incident to the attacking site, the site ideally will monitor its configurations and user activities more carefully. If you report the incident to an abuse center, the abuse staff can contact the remote site with more clout than an individual carries, keep an eye out for continued activity, and better help customers who have been compromised. If you report the incident to a security newsgroup, other people can get a better idea of what to watch out for.

What Kinds of Incidents Might You Report?

Which incidents you report depends completely on your tolerance, how serious you consider different probes to be, and how much time you care to devote against what is a global, exponentially growing infestation. It comes down to how you define the term *incident*. In different people's minds, incidents can range anywhere from simple port scans to attempts to access your private files or system resources, to denial-of-service attacks, to crashing your servers or your entire system, to gaining `root` login access to your system:

- **Denial-of-service attacks**—Any kind of denial-of-service attack is blatantly hostile. It's difficult not to take such an attack personally. These attacks are the electronic form of vandalism, obstruction, harassment, and theft of service. Because some forms of denial-of-service attacks are possible because of the inherent nature of networked devices, you can do little or nothing about some forms of attack other than to report the incidents and block the attacker's entire address block.

- **Attempts to reconfigure your system**—An attacker can't reconfigure your servers without a `root` login account on your machine, but he or she could conceivably modify your system's in-memory, network-related tables—or try, at least. Exploits to consider include these:

  - Unauthorized DNS zone transfers to or from your machine over TCP

  - Changes to your in-memory routing tables

  - Attempts to reconfigure your network interfaces or routing tables via probes to UDP port 161 for `snmpd`

- **Attempts to gain login account access**—Probes to `ssh` TCP port 22 are obvious. Less obvious are probes to ports associated with servers known to be exploitable, either historically or currently. Buffer overflow exploits are generally intended ultimately to execute commands and gain shell access. The `mountd` exploit is an example of this.

- **Attempts to access nonpublic files**—Attempts to access private files, such as the `/etc/passwd` file, configuration files, or proprietary files, show up in your FTP log (`/var/log/xferlog` or `/var/log/messages`) and in your web server access log (`/var/log/httpd/error_log`).

- **Attempts to use private services**—By definition, any service you haven't made available to the Internet is private. These are the private services potentially available through your public servers, such as attempts to relay mail through your mail server. Chances are, people are up to no good if they're trying to use your machine instead of their own or their ISP's. Relay attempts show up in your mail log file (`/var/log/maillog`).

- **Attempts to store files on your disk**—If you host an improperly configured anonymous FTP site, it's possible for someone to set up a repository of stolen software or media on your machine. Attempts to upload files are recorded in your FTP log (`/var/log/xferlog`) if `ftpd` is configured to log file uploads.

- **Attempts to crash your system or individual servers**—Buffer overflow attempts against programs available through your website are possibly the easiest to identify by error messages written in the web server log files. Other reports of erroneous data will appear in your general syslog file (`/var/log/messages`), your general daemon log (`/var/log/daemon`), your mail log (`/var/log/maillog`), your FTP log (`/var/log/xferlog`), or your secure access log (`/var/log/secure`).

- **Attempts to exploit specific, known, currently exploitable vulnerabilities**—Attackers find new vulnerabilities with each new software release (and old ones too).

To Whom Do You Report an Incident?

You have a number of options in terms of whom you report an incident to:

- **`root`, `postmaster`, or `abuse` at the offending site**—The obvious place to lodge a complaint is with the administrator of the offending site. Informing the system administrator is often all that's required to take care of a problem. This isn't always possible, though, because many probes originate from spoofed, nonexistent IP addresses.

- **Network coordinator**—If the IP address doesn't have a DNS entry, contacting the coordinator for the network address block is often helpful. The coordinator can contact the administrator at the offending site or put you in direct contact. If the IP address doesn't resolve through the `host` or `dig` commands, you can almost always find the network coordinator by supplying the address to the `whois` databases. The `whois` command is hard-wired into the ARIN database. Three major databases are available through the web:

  - **ARIN**—The American Registry for Internet Numbers maintains the IP address database for the Western Hemisphere, the Americas. ARIN is located at http://whois.arin.net/ui.

  - **APNIC**—The Asia Pacific Network Information Centre maintains the IP address database for Asia. APNIC is located at http://www.apnic.net/apnic-bin/whois.pl.

  - **RIPE**—The Réseaux IP Européens maintains the IP address database for Europe. RIPE is located at https://apps.db.ripe.net/search/query.html.

- **Your ISP abuse center**—If scans are originating from within your ISP's address space, your abuse center is the place to contact. Your ISP can be helpful with scans originating elsewhere, too, by contacting the offending site on your behalf. Chances are good that your machine isn't the only machine being probed on the ISP's network.

- **Your Linux vendor**—If your system is compromised because of a software vulnerability in its distribution, your vendor will want to know so that a security upgrade can be developed and released.

What Information Do You Supply?

An incident report must contain enough information to help the incident response team track down the problem. When contacting the site from which the attack originated, remember that your contact person might be the individual who intentionally launched the attack. What you include out of the following list depends on whom you are contacting and how comfortable you are including the information, as well as whatever privacy and other policies may be in effect:

- Your email address
- Your phone number, if appropriate

- Your IP address, hostname, and domain name
- The IP addresses and hostnames, if available, involved in the attack
- The date and time of the incident (including your time zone relative to GMT)
- A description of the attack
  - How you detected the attack
  - Representative log file entries showing the incident
  - A description of the log file format
  - References to advisories and security notices describing the nature and significance of the attack, if relevant
  - What you want the person to do (fix it, confirm it, explain it, monitor it, or be informed of it)

Summary

This chapter focused on monitoring system integrity and intrusion detection. If you suspect that a system might be compromised, you can refer to this chapter's list of potential problem indications. If you see some of these indications and conclude that the system is compromised, you can make use of the list of recovery steps discussed. Finally, incident-reporting considerations were discussed, and pointers were given on whom you might report an incident to.

Chapter 12, "Intrusion Detection Tools," looks at the implementation of some of the things you learned in this chapter by looking at the specific tools involved in intrusion detection and system testing.

Intrusion Detection Tools

In the preceding chapter you learned the concepts of intrusion detection and intrusion response. Rarely are two attacks exactly the same, though the techniques used frequently rely on a common set of methods and result in many of the same symptoms, as described in the preceding chapter. It is through these common methods and symptoms that intrusion detection tools are able to assist the intrusion analyst with his or her job.

The intrusion analyst has much to choose from when looking for software tools to assist in problem correlation, diagnosis, and resolution. This chapter focuses on the software tools used in intrusion detection and tools that can help in any administrator's toolkit. The chapter begins with a look at network sniffers and continues through tools to check for rootkits and into filesystem checkers and log file monitoring.

Intrusion Detection Toolkit: Network Tools

Some of the primary tools of security and network administrators alike are network analysis tools. These include network sniffers, intrusion detection software, and network analyzers.

A network sniffer is software that passively listens to traffic received and sent by a network interface. TCPDump is simple enough that beginners can learn it quickly yet powerful enough to provide the necessary functionality for multiple protocols in multiple situations. Using TCPDump, it's possible to view traffic in numerous formats including ASCII and use expressions to fine-tune the exact traffic to be viewed through the tool.

TCPDump is manual and primitive intrusion detection software. If you know what you're looking for, TCPDump can help you spot the anomalous traffic as it passes through the network. TCPDump in and of itself won't know that an attack just passed under its nose; that's the job of the intrusion analyst (as well as other software). However, TCPDump almost always becomes an integral tool for investigating active attacks because it allows the analyst to watch the attack in real time.

TCPDump is covered in depth in Chapter 13, "Network Monitoring and Attack Detection." There you'll find coverage of normal protocol activity, as well as a look at some exploits through the eyes, or nose as it were, of TCPDump.

When it comes to tools that listen to the network and perform some level of analysis on the traffic, Snort is an excellent choice. Snort is provider- and enterprise-class intrusion detection software that's both widely deployed and mature. Snort works using the concept of intrusion signatures. The theory is that many attacks follow the same pattern or look the same or very similar at the network level.

Consider this example: Assume that a packet is received on a certain port with its header flags set a certain way. When this occurs, it is always a precursor to an attack or an attempt to exploit a certain vulnerability. It can be said that this particular attack has, therefore, a signature that identifies it as malicious traffic. This signature, unique to the exploit of this vulnerability, can then be used by software such as Snort to detect that there was an attempt to exploit the vulnerability. Snort can then perform an action based on this detection (or can take no action).

ntop is network analysis software, as opposed to the sniffer that produces reports of usage based on protocol, flow, host, and other parameters. Using ntop is recommended at strategic points in the network to establish a baseline of the normal traffic flows on the network.

I chose to feature ntop here because it's simple to get working quickly. However, I also recommend other analysis software for network traffic. Among other analysis software, MRTG is another excellent choice for traffic analysis, as are RRDtool and Scrutinizer.

Creating baseline traffic reports and keeping them up-to-date helps not only to spot anomalies, including both unexpected increases and decreases in the traffic, but also to track when new bandwidth might be necessary. It is this dual use—security anomalies and bandwidth usage monitoring—that makes traffic analysis invaluable.

To establish traffic baselines and effectively monitor the network for intrusions using Snort and TCPDump on large networks, it's important to place the tools at strategic locations within the network. Most large networks (even medium and small ones) use switches to pass traffic. Understanding the difference between switches and hubs is important when considering where to place network tools.

Switches and Hubs and Why You Care

On a switched network, any given network interface would receive only traffic destined for it as well as broadcast traffic. In a hub network environment the network interface receives all traffic, whether that traffic is destined for it or for another device. This is why switched networks are faster than hubbed networks—the unnecessary traffic isn't sent to all ports of the switch.

There are situations in which a network interface might receive all traffic or a greater subset than merely its own in a switched network, such as those when a switch is configured to mirror the traffic to a specific port. In practice this can be done, but it may result in performance problems for the switch because it now has to copy all traffic to two ports instead of one. Refer to your switch's documentation for more information.

Regardless of where the traffic originates, if it comes into the interface where the sniffer is running, the traffic can be captured. The key, at a network level, is to place sniffers and the related intrusion detection software in the right locations. For host-based traffic sniffing, the placement of the sniffer is obvious, on the host itself.

ARPWatch

Another item to be discussed in Chapter 13 is ARPWatch. ARPWatch is software that watches for new devices on the network. ARPWatch can be helpful for auditing the devices on the network, especially wireless networks.

Rootkit Checkers

A *rootkit* is a piece of software or a grouping of software that attempts to exploit one or more vulnerabilities with the goal of enabling an attacker to gain elevated privileges or perform any other type of attack against the target. Frequently, rootkits are used by less skilled attackers who use the software built by another attacker but don't really understand the underlying exploit; they're just interested in the results.

Many rootkits not only run the initial exploit to give the attacker `root` privileges but also attempt to mask or hide the fact that an attack has been launched. They do this by deleting log files or certain entries from log files, planting trojan horse versions of programs, and employing other means. There is also nothing stopping an attacker from chaining rootkits together for multiple levels of deception and possible exploit.

Like network-centric attacks, rootkits frequently have signatures or leave other traces that identify them. These traces and signatures might be the aforementioned removal of log files, the presence of one or more processes, or other changes to the system that are specific to the rootkit software or the exploit.

Also as with network-centric attacks, there is software to search for the signatures and traces of rootkits as well. One such application is Chkrootkit.

Running Chkrootkit

Before you can run Chkrootkit, you need to get it. Chkrootkit can be downloaded from http://www.chkrootkit.org/ and is also included as a package with many flavors of Linux. After it's downloaded, Chkrootkit needs to be unarchived and compiled:

```
tar -zxvf chkrootkit.tar.gz
cd chkrootkit-<NNNN>
make sense
```

Yes, that does say `make sense` in the code example. Although Chkrootkit is a shell script, some additional functionality is gained by compiling the code. Compiling is not required, but because it's quick and adds some additional levels of checking, I recommend doing so. Specifically, compiling Chkrootkit will enable these additional checks, though the standard packages from a given operating system may also have them:

- `ifpromisc`
- `chklastlog`
- `chkwtmp`
- `check_wtmpx`

- chkproc
- chkdirs
- strings

Of all the tools used in this book, Chkrootkit is probably the easiest to use. To run Chkrootkit, from within the `chkrootkit` source directory you simply type this:

```
./chkrootkit | less
```

You aren't required to pipe the output to `less`, but there is a copious amount of output. So if you actually want to read the output, you'll probably need to pipe it somewhere—unless, of course, you have a huge scrollback buffer.

Because running Chkrootkit produces a lot of output, it is wise to pipe the output to `more` or `less`, depending on your preference. Alternatively, you could redirect the output to a file:

```
./chkrootkit > output.txt
```

Chkrootkit will output a number of lines informing you what it is currently checking for along with the ultimate status of the check. The output will look similar to this:

```
Checking 'amd'... not found
Checking 'basename'... not infected
Checking 'biff'... not infected
Checking 'chfn'... not infected
Checking 'chsh'... not infected
Searching for ShitC Worm... nothing found
Searching for Omega Worm... nothing found
Searching for Sadmind/IIS Worm... nothing found
Searching for MonKit... nothing found
Searching for Showtee... nothing found
```

As you can see from the output sample, it doesn't appear that any trojaned files or rootkits were detected. An infected file or detection of a rootkit will look similar to the following:

```
Checking 'bindshell'... INFECTED (PORTS:  1524 31337)
```

Even though the output from Chkrootkit seems to indicate that the computer is infected with bindshell, Chkrootkit does sometimes produce false positives. However, if you see the INFECTED output from Chkrootkit, it's in your best interest to assume that Chkrootkit reported correctly and take steps to mitigate the damage.

A false positive occurs when a tool detects and reports a problem when in fact there is no problem. The underlying cause for false positives varies depending on the nature of the software reporting the occurrence. False positives are not as bad as false negatives. A false negative occurs when there really is a problem but the problem is not reported by tools that should find it.

False positives and negatives are not limited to computing. Imagine the case in which a person goes to a doctor and gets an ultrasound scan. Based on the scan results, the doctor reports that the person has cancer. However, on further examination it appears that the initial report was incorrect. This is an example of a false positive. Although additional tests were unnecessarily performed based on the false positive, it is still much better than having a false negative, with the cancer going unnoticed and untreated.

Because Chkrootkit reports using tools on the computer, it may report a false negative. There are ways around this problem as described later in this section.

What If Chkrootkit Says the Computer Is Infected?

If Chkrootkit says your computer is infected, the first thing you should do is tell yourself to remain calm. Although you should not assume so, there is a chance that Chkrootkit is reporting a false positive. If Chkrootkit reports an infection, you should immediately take steps to mitigate any further damage.

The preceding chapter of the book looked at incident response. Therefore, it would be redundant to cover that same material in this chapter. However, as with all tools of this nature, false positives come with the territory. It's in your best interest to take the notice seriously, but it might also be wise to try to determine whether Chkrootkit has reported a false positive.

Chkrootkit uses various means to find rootkits. Many times Chkrootkit looks for a certain signature in a file based on a known trojaned version of the file. Other times Chkrootkit looks for ports that are open that have been known to be the result of a rootkit or other attack. This was the case for the report of infection highlighted earlier in this section. Chkrootkit reported that it believed that the computer was infected with the bindshell rootkit. It based this finding on two ports that it found open, 1524 and 31337. In reality, these ports were open because of another security tool, PortSentry, that listens on those ports in hopes of catching other infected hosts. I used the program lsof with the -i option to determine the exact program that was listening on those ports.

With dozens of rootkits reported by Chkrootkit, you probably won't know the exact ramifications of being infected by a given rootkit. Further, there's a good chance that if one rootkit has been run, multiple rootkits have been run, making cleanup all that much more difficult. To begin the process of damage control, you can search the web for each individual rootkit to determine what actions it takes when it's run. However, realize that, by definition, after a rootkit has been run successfully, the attacker has root privileges on the computer and therefore may have done much greater damage to the system or may be in the process of doing so now!

Whenever Chkrootkit reports an infection, you should take it seriously and always assume the worst. Prudence suggests that you should immediately unplug the computer from the network and take steps to clean up from the rootkit. In reality, it's rarely that easy or cut-and-dried.

Limitations of Chkrootkit and Similar Tools

Chkrootkit is a powerful and incredibly helpful tool but it is not without limitations. These limitations aren't really specific to Chkrootkit but rather are a limitation of any tool that attempts to perform complex checks such as this. One such limitation, false positives, has already been discussed. Another limitation of Chkrootkit and other tools like it is that they rely, by default, on programs included with the Linux computer itself, programs that may have been compromised or altered to avoid detection by prying eyes such as those of Chkrootkit and related utilities.

Here's a partial list of programs that Chkrootkit uses; keep in mind that these programs may themselves in turn rely on libraries or other things on the Linux computer that also may be compromised:

- `awk`
- `cut`
- `echo`
- `egrep`
- `find`
- `head`
- `id`
- `ls`
- `netstat`
- `ps`
- `sed`
- `strings`
- `uname`

Another limitation of tools such as Chkrootkit that is shared by similar tools is that it can detect only rootkits that have been reported and for which it has been configured. Some unlucky soul has to be the first to have the rootkit run on his or her computer. If you happen to be that person, Chkrootkit won't help. Realize, though, that there is a fair chance that multiple rootkits will be run on the computer, which will make detection easier. I realize that this is small consolation.

Using Chkrootkit Securely

It's a good idea to use known-good sets of system binaries when using a tool such as Chkrootkit. Many rootkits replace vital system binaries such as /bin/ps with versions of their own. Therefore, if you try to use ps to find unknown processes, you may not be able to see them because the trojaned version of ps hides them.

Chkrootkit gives two methods for working around this problem. The first method involves using a known-good set of binaries, probably mounted from a CD-ROM. The second method involves physically mounting the possibly compromised hard drive into a different computer and then running the check from there. This second method is more appropriate for forensics after a successful attack than for investigating a possible attack.

Mounting a CD-ROM with known-good versions of binaries is a safe and easy method for performing a thorough examination using Chkrootkit. This method assumes that you have a CD-ROM with the correct binaries already on the disc. To run Chkrootkit with a CD-ROM copy of the binaries, first mount the CD. This is usually accomplished using the `mount` command, although sometimes it's mounted automatically. A common method for mounting the CD-ROM drive in most modern Linux distributions is shown here:

```
mount -t iso9660 /dev/cdrom /mnt/cdrom
```

Chkrootkit uses the `-p` option to define the location of the binaries it should use. Therefore, if the CD-ROM is mounted at `/mnt/cdrom`, you'd run Chkrootkit like so:

```
./chkrootkit -p /mnt/cdrom
```

The other method for running Chkrootkit is to physically mount the possibly compromised hard drive into another computer and run Chkrootkit against the contents of that drive. This is accomplished by specifying an alternate "root" directory for Chkrootkit. Assume that the second drive is mounted at `/mnt/drive2`:

```
./chkrootkit -r /mnt/drive2
```

When Should Chkrootkit Be Run?

Chkrootkit should be run whenever you like. There is no recommended schedule for Chkrootkit. I personally run it at irregular intervals for fun, but then again I'm just that type of guy. You should most definitely run Chkrootkit anytime you observe any suspicious activity on the computer or on other computers that may interact with or reside on the same network block as the computer in question. Whenever you run Chkrootkit, you should always hop out to the website, http://www.chkrootkit.org/, to check for a new version of the tool. A new signature for a rootkit or additional functionality might have been added since the version you're using.

You can also run Chkrootkit nightly from cron. However, I wouldn't rely on such a report being entirely accurate, but it could provide an early warning of an anomaly that needs your attention. Running Chkrootkit from cron might look like this:

```
0 4 * * * /path/to/chkrootkit
```

The cron entry shown will run Chkrootkit every morning at 4:00 a.m. and `root` (the recipient of cron job output) will receive a report every morning detailing the run of Chkrootkit.

Filesystem Integrity

Hand in hand with a rootkit checker such as Chkrootkit goes filesystem integrity software. Filesystem integrity software monitors important files on the computer and generates reports based on changes to those files. The administrator can then watch for unexpected changes to the files in question. For example, if files such as `/etc/resolv.conf` or even `/etc/shadow` change for no apparent reason, the administrator can take action.

Some popular filesystem integrity tools are OSSEC, Samhain, and AIDE. AIDE is covered in detail, and a more complete description of how filesystem integrity works is given, in Chapter 14, "Filesystem Integrity."

Log Monitoring

Log files are monitored to watch for anomalies that might indicate an attack. Although this method is used successfully, it can result in huge amounts of data and become cumbersome on large networks.

When combined with other tools, log monitoring can be made to work. For example, using log monitoring on a few key systems can reduce the amount of data being received. However, this and other such measures are really stopgap measures because they do little to ensure the security of the systems that aren't monitored.

Numerous packages are available to monitor log files. One such package is Swatch. I'll briefly cover Swatch here just to give you a taste of some of the capabilities of these types of tools.

Swatch

Swatch is available with many Linux distributions as an add-on package or can be downloaded from http://swatch.sourceforge.net/. Swatch is highly configurable and can perform a number of actions based on a match.

Swatch works in several modes, including a mode called single-pass, which has the program parse a log file once, searching for matches and taking action based on those matches. Another mode sees Swatch perform a running tail (`tail -f`) of a log file looking for matches. By default, Swatch monitors `/var/log/messages`, but it can be configured to monitor any file or even a socket.

Because Swatch is so powerful, I don't feel as though I can do it justice in a book on Linux firewalls. I invite you to read more about Swatch. For now, I'll give a recipe for monitoring a log file with Swatch. Another such recipe shows up in Chapter 13, in the section on Snort titled "Automated Intrusion Monitoring with Snort."

Using Swatch to Monitor SSH Login Failures

There are constant brute-force login attempts against SSH. These usually don't result in much of anything except annoyance. However, it's generally useful to monitor log files for these and other attempts to brute-force attack a server. Swatch can be configured to send an email (or do any number of other actions) when such an attempt is logged. This section shows how to send an email alert when an authentication failure is logged.

The system logs a line similar to the following when a login is attempted and fails:

```
Jun  7 17:09:10 ord sshd[3434]: error: \
     PAM: Authentication failure for root from 192.168.1.10
```

There are a number of unique items on this line, but I'll choose to look for the words "Authentication failure" because that is the type of thing I want to be alerted on. The Swatch syntax is painfully easy yet can be incredibly powerful. This is because Swatch uses regular expression syntax for matching. The match in this case is rather trivial. Simply telling Swatch what to watch for with the aptly titled `watchfor` configuration directive and then giving it one or more actions to perform when a match is noted is all that's required for Swatch configuration. For example, to look for the words "Authentication failure" and have an email sent, the Swatch configuration consists of the following:

```
watchfor /Authentication failure/
    mail
```

These two lines are saved in `~/.swatchrc`. In this case, I'm doing so as `root` because Swatch will need read access to the log file in question.

Next, start Swatch and tell it what file to monitor. Again, the default is `/var/log/messages`. However, I'm creating this example on a Debian system and so the authentication failures are logged to `/var/log/auth.log` by default. Therefore, I point Swatch at the correct configuration file and start it:

```
swatch —tail-file=/var/log/auth.log
```

Swatch will now monitor the log file for the words "Authentication failure" and will send an email to `root` if and when the words are found.

As previously stated, there are several options for alerts, including executing other programs. These programs could be shell scripts or really anything, so the possibilities are virtually limitless.

How to Not Become Compromised

Virtually nothing can be done to stop an attacker with unlimited resources and unlimited time. From DoS attacks to rootkits to physical attacks, if someone wants at your data badly enough, chances are that he or she can get to it, given no other constraints. That said, there are many things you can do to limit your exposure to most risks.

Neither this chapter nor this book deals with physical attacks on any level. If an attacker is onsite and can simply walk off with the computer or hard drive containing the data, there's no amount of firewalling that will help. If the attacker has physical access to the computer or device holding the data, the attacker can steal the data itself or possibly plant his or her own malicious trojan software.

This section gives some general suggestions that are field tested to keep systems secure. These suggestions are by no means all-encompassing; rather they are merely things I suggest to help ensure system integrity.

Secure Often

Securing the computing environment is a continual process rather than an endpoint. As you work to secure systems and networks, new vulnerabilities are being discovered and new software is being developed. There is simply no magic bullet that enables you to be done and complete when it comes to securing a computer environment. This book has been devoted to securing a network and its systems through the use of a firewall built on Linux. This chapter has introduced some of the other aspects of a security-in-depth process.

Using the tools available to you, such as those already introduced in this chapter, you can secure a computer and the network on which it resides. There are, of course, additional steps you can take to further enhance the security of the environment.

Bastille Linux

Bastille Linux is a program that helps automate the process of system security as well as report on the security of the system. Bastille Linux implements many of the security best practices that you could find by reading volumes of material and countless websites. All of those best practices are implemented through a wizardlike interface (command line or GUI) that contains a lot of information on not only what you're being asked but why it's important.

Bastille Linux goes so far as to give recommendations for certain features. Unlike many tools that try to give recommendations, Bastille gets it right by explaining the reasoning behind the proposed change, as well as the implications that it might have if you choose to use the step.

Finally, Bastille also includes an undo process so that you can quickly undo any changes that might be causing problems. Bastille is welcomed by experienced Linux administrators and those new to Linux alike. Some Linux distributions include Bastille as a package. More information on Bastille Linux can be found at http://bastille-linux.sourceforge.net.

Update Often

Although by far the most effortless of any task in this book, keeping a computer system up-to-date is an often-overlooked aspect of system security. The best way to ensure that a computer will be broken into is to leave it running without updating it.

One of the greatest strengths of Linux and open-source software is security. Some people attempt to argue that this security is achieved because open-source software is less popular. Of course, this completely ignores market-share statistics such as Netcraft's web server survey showing that Apache holds nearly 40% of the web server market and even more if one excludes the placeholder sites running Microsoft IIS.

Part of this security strength comes from the open-source community's ability to provide fixes within hours of the vulnerability disclosure. It's quite common for fixes to be available the same day as the disclosure, even for security issues that weren't previously publicly disclosed. For events in which a fix might take a little time, the community has historically been excellent at providing workarounds to mitigate and sometimes eliminate the vulnerabilities entirely.

Both of these characteristics, quick fixes and quick workarounds, work to your advantage in maintaining system security. However, for either one to be of use, you need to keep track of their availability by monitoring mailing lists and security websites. Most major Linux vendors offer announce-only security mailing lists in which subscribers receive an email whenever a vulnerability is disclosed.

Keeping software up-to-date is an important aspect of system security. I recommend updating as often as possible while obviously paying attention to the software that's being updated to ensure that none of the updates breaks live systems.

Test Often

It's not enough to secure often and update often, though those two items certainly go a long way toward ensuring a secure environment. Another basic point of security in depth is to test often. Testing ensures that the security policies are being enforced and the implementation of those security policies is successful.

Penetration testing is another important aspect of system security. Penetration testing, or pen-testing, is a process by which the security of a system is tested by trying a number of attack vectors to get the system to behave in an unexpected way. The definition of penetration testing is purposely vague so that it is not limited to attacks of only a certain class or type.

Penetration testing can be both informal and formal. The informal pen-tests are typically run by security administrators or even developers using anything from manual attempts to break into an application to automated attacks using a number of tools. A formal pen-test would be done by a third party who would likely use a combination of both manual and automated attacks to test the system. The type and frequency of pen-testing is a matter for your security policy.

Of course, when you do test, it's important to test both as if you were a normal attacker and as if you were an insider. Testing as a normal attacker means testing the application or system without any knowledge other than that which can be gleaned from outside of the system. In other words, if you're testing a web application, view the source of the web page to see what parameters are being used. Many times, testing as a normal attacker also means that you'll have to test from a location external to the local network. This is especially important when testing a firewall rule set.

This section examines some of the tools you can use to test a network and computer system. As with other lists presented in this chapter, it is not meant to be all-encompassing or comprehensive. Rather, the tools examined here provide a good starting point on which you can build your knowledge of security and penetration-testing concepts and facilities.

Nmap

Nmap, the Network Mapper, is a program used to identify open ports and available devices on a network. Nmap is frequently used by the intrusion analyst to determine what ports are open and listening on a given host. In the context of a firewall, Nmap can be used from an external location to test the firewall rules to ensure that no unexpected ports are open and available.

Nmap is available as a package on many popular Linux distributions. If Nmap isn't available on your distribution, it can be downloaded from http://www.nmap.org/.

Nmap includes many options for probing hosts and entire networks. These options are too numerous to cover in depth here. In practice, I've found the following syntax to be most useful for performing the aforementioned port scan, this one looking for TCP ports:

```
nmap -sS -v <host>
```

For example, to scan the host 192.168.1.10 for open TCP ports, the following syntax would be used:

```
nmap -sS -v 192.168.1.10
```

Note that the use of the -v option enables extra verbosity. Although this option is not required, it is recommended, and you can even add additional instances of -v to increase the verbosity.

Various types of TCP scans are available with Nmap. I chose a SYN scan because I've found it to generally be the most reliable for this type of test.

When Nmap begins a scan, it sends an initial ping or ICMP echo request to the target host. Sometimes the target doesn't respond to the ICMP echo request. In these cases, you can disable the initial ICMP echo request sent by Nmap by using the -P0 option.

As previously stated, several options are available with Nmap. Typing simply nmap at the command line will print a relatively verbose set of usage instructions containing many of these options.

hping3

hping3 is another network utility that can be used to test for open ports and also to test the behavior of network applications and devices. hping3 enables the user to set numerous attributes of a network packet, or craft the packet as it's sometimes called. When packets are crafted, the behavior of the network application or device can be observed.

hping3 is used in Chapter 13 to show how some attacks might look when viewed with TCPDump.

Nikto

Nikto is a program to test a web server for known vulnerabilities and also to provide information on that web server. Nikto can be downloaded from http://www.cirt.net/Nikto2.

Because Nikto is web server specific, its coverage will be limited here. However, if you are running a web server, I highly recommend Nikto to test the server for a number of vulnerabilities.

Summary

This chapter provided a look at intrusion detection tools and some basic security principles. From things like TCPDump, to sniffer placement, to filesystem integrity, the chapter showed you around the world of intrusion detection.

These intrusion detection tools are best when coupled with security practices such as regular updating, enhanced security measures, and penetration testing to ensure that the security of the system is as you expect.

The next chapter of the book looks more in depth at network security by examining TCPDump, a key tool in any administrator's toolbox.

Network Monitoring
and Attack Detection

This chapter uses the knowledge you've gained throughout the book and in the preceding couple of chapters specifically to show how you might use some of the tools for everyday monitoring and also for investigation.

The chapter begins with an overview of network monitoring, or sniffing. The information in the beginning of this chapter builds on what you've already seen in the first two chapters of the book. This chapter then continues with a look at TCPDump, a key tool in the network security analyst's toolkit. Finally, the chapter also looks at two helpful security software packages: Snort and ARPWatch.

Listening to the Ether

Armed with the basic knowledge of some of the core protocols from the first two chapters, you're ready to begin listening to the network. Exactly what you may see when you begin monitoring your network will depend on several factors, not the least of which is the network topology itself.

A modern Ethernet network is a collection of endpoint devices such as computers with network interfaces, interconnected using a hub or switch. The difference between a hub and a switch is important to both network performance and security. In a hub environment, every Ethernet frame is copied to every port on the hub, and therefore every device is connected to the hub. Contrast a hub environment with a switched environment. In a switched environment, the switch sends frames to the specific port to which a given device is connected. In other words, with a switch, traffic goes only to the devices that should receive it. If an intruder can monitor the network in a hub environment, the intruder will see all frames destined for all devices connected to that hub. In a switch environment, the intruder will see only traffic destined for that host or broadcast traffic that is copied to all ports.

Most managed switches enable the administrator to configure a certain port to receive all traffic. Cisco calls this a "span" port, whereas others call it a "mirror" port. In effect, by copying all traffic to the one port on the switch, the administrator can monitor all the traffic for that switch to look for possible intrusions or other anomalies. Of course, this can also be dangerous. If an attacker gains control over the device at the end of that port, the attacker too can listen to everything! Also, in heavy traffic environments performance degradation will likely occur if you attempt to monitor all ports. Therefore, choosing where to monitor your network is important.

If you don't have a managed switch or a switch that enables you to copy all traffic to one port, you'll need to find another means to listen to the traffic. I don't recommend removing the switch in favor of a hub. However, one method would be to connect a hub to the firewall and then connect your intrusion detection or monitoring computer to that hub as well, and finally connect the hub into the main switch. In this way you can monitor internal firewall traffic without (much) performance degradation and without compromising much of the safety that a switch provides.

As I wrote the sentence about the safety of a switch, I was reminded of some types of attacks that enable an attacker to listen to other traffic on a switch, even if it wasn't destined for the port where the attacker resides. These attacks, primarily ARP spoofing, involve interfering with the normal operation of ARP. A good primer on ARP spoofing can be found in the paper "An Introduction to Arp Spoofing," available online at http://packetstormsecurity.org/papers/protocols/intro_to_arp_spoofing.pdf.

Choosing monitoring points within a network is more art than science and is inevitably debatable. There are those who say that only the interior of the network is important to monitor because the firewall will prevent the outside traffic from being important anyway. There are others who maintain that external points should be monitored so that you can see what is being attempted on the network. And there are those, like myself, who believe that both internal and external points should be monitored. Monitoring the internal network is important for (I hope) obvious reasons. You can look for anomalous traffic and also monitor for unexpected conditions and performance. However, I believe that monitoring the external network is important as well. I cut my computer security teeth at an Internet provider where everything important was on the external network by nature. Therefore, I was able to see just how valuable it was to know what's happening on the outside as a means to prevent attacks from being successful.

You have to make decisions that work in your environment. It may not make sense to deploy a computer outside of your firewall just for intrusion detection. All security is a trade-off between the assets you are trying to protect and the limited resources available to protect them.

Three Valuable Tools

An ever-growing number of tools and software exist to monitor network traffic. Some of these tools are free (as in price and speech), and some cost quite a bit of money. I've used both the expensive tools and the free ones, and I'm confident in saying that the free ones are better. The expensive tools are weak on functionality but strong on the pretty. The interfaces for many of the products provide a nice "look and feel" (though many of them seem to be somewhat unstable). In general, the open-source tools are a bit more involved to set up and use, but they provide better functionality and with a little work can produce some of the nicest-looking graphs and other pictures that the expensive tools provide. For my money, I'd rather have intrusion detection tools that I can use quickly and easily when investigating a potential attack. Dealing with cumbersome, nonintuitive GUIs only gets in the way of the business of intrusion detection.

This section looks at a few monitoring tools with special emphasis on the tools that are covered later in the book.

TCPDump

One of the primary tools in an intrusion detection analyst's toolkit should be TCPDump. TCPDump places a network interface into promiscuous mode so that it captures every packet that arrives. Of course, this means that TCPDump needs to be run from the computer experiencing the possible intrusion or needs to be run from a computer that is the recipient of a "spanned" port in a switch environment. TCPDump is examined in greater detail in the next section.

Snort

Snort is one of the best intrusion detection systems available, free or otherwise. Snort captures network traffic in much the same way that TCPDump does. However, Snort uses a database of well-known attack signatures to provide a level of detection as well. Whereas TCPDump is more of a manual monitor, Snort is more automated insofar as the analyst doesn't need to manually examine each packet. You can get more information on Snort at http://www.snort.org/.

ARPWatch

ARPWatch is a tool used to monitor ARP traffic on a network. The goal would be for an administrator to spot possible ARP spoofing attempts as well as unknown devices that have entered the network. ARPWatch can be downloaded from http://ee.lbl.gov/. Like other tools, ARPWatch needs to be compiled before use if your system doesn't have it available as a package. ARPWatch is examined later in this chapter, in the section "Monitoring with ARPWatch."

TCPDump: A Simple Overview

Recall what you've read in earlier chapters. You learned about IP addressing, subnetting, and the headers of some of those core protocols. In this chapter the TCPDump tool will be examined, and you will see some of those protocols up close and personal. Armed with an understanding of how to monitor your network at this level, you can be confident that you'll be able to troubleshoot a wide range of problems, not just those related to computer security.

An important tool in the intrusion analyst's toolkit is TCPDump. At a basic level, TCPDump is real-time packet capture and analysis software. This means that TCPDump can be used to eavesdrop on network communication as it travels through the network.

As has already been mentioned, however, the amount of traffic that one can eavesdrop on is dictated by the network topology. If the computer from which TCPDump is running is connected to a switched network, TCPDump will see only traffic destined for that host or broadcast/multicast traffic. A good approach in a switched network would be to use a "span" port to which all network traffic will be copied by the switch itself. Of course, none of this is of concern in a hub-based network because all traffic is copied to all ports on the hub.

TCPDump places the network interface into promiscuous mode. Before you get too excited, consider that on busy interfaces this means that a huge amount of traffic will be flying past the screen, which has the potential to slow down the traffic ever so slightly. In any event, a large amount of traffic will be too much for a human to comprehend, so you'll want to capture the output to a file, pipe the output to a pager, or filter the traffic to look for something specific. Filtering through a TCPDump expression is by far the best option, but the choices are by no means mutually exclusive. I usually use a filter and a pager such as `less`, just in case something interesting flies past my screen too quickly.

TCPDump can filter traffic by virtually any criteria you can imagine. Most commonly for the intrusion analyst, you'll look at traffic by protocol, host, port number, or a combination thereof. Before I go further, I would be remiss if I didn't recommend reading or at least referring to the TCPDump(1) manual page (type `man tcpdump` to read it). The man page is a comprehensive document providing not only syntax but samples of use, as well as some protocol diagrams. If you get stuck trying to use TCPDump and you don't have a copy of this book handy, maybe you should buy two copies of the book. Alternatively, use the TCPDump man page for reference too.

Obtaining and Installing TCPDump

TCPDump can be downloaded from http://www.tcpdump.org/. TCPDump requires the PCap library libpcap, so while you're downloading TCPDump, you should download libpcap as well. Most popular Linux distributions also include TCPDump as an available package. For example, if you're using Debian, you can simply type this:

```
apt-get install tcpdump
```

The package maintenance system will install TCPDump and any prerequisites too. For everyone else, you can probably search your distribution's repository for a package or just download the source and compile it, which I recommend. Should you attempt to compile TCPDump without having libpcap installed, you'll see an error similar to the following while running the configure script for TCPDump:

```
checking for main in -lpcap... no
configure: error: see the INSTALL doc for more info
```

Installation of both libpcap and TCPDump is fairly straightforward as far as compiling software goes. Unarchive each piece of source code, run the configure script, compile, and install.

In essence:

```
tar -zxvf libpcap-<version>.tar.gz
cd libpcap-<version>
./configure
make
make install
```

Do the same for TCPDump:

```
tar -zxvf tcpdump-<version>.tar.gz
cd tcpdump-<version>
./configure
make
make install
```

TCPDump Options

TCPDump accepts a wide range of command-line options that alter its behavior, the amount of data captured, and the way in which the data is captured. Such a wide range of options means that you have the power to significantly change how the program operates. For TCPDump, you'll find that you frequently use a common set of options for most data capture activities, and you may not use others at all.

Some of the more commonly used options include those listed in Table 13.1.

Examining each of these options in turn reveals the steps necessary for performing basic packet capture and analysis. Not all of these options are necessarily required to capture traffic with TCPDump (in fact, none of them is required). It's perfectly valid to simply type the tcpdump command on the command line to start capturing traffic. However, in practice many of these options are necessary to gain the level of detail needed in order to properly analyze the traffic.

Table 13.1 **Some Common Options for TCPDump**

Option	Description
-i <interface>	Specifies the interface to use
-v	Produces output in verbose mode
-vv	Produces output in really verbose mode
-x	Causes TCPDump to print the packet itself in hexadecimal format
-X	Causes TCPDump to also print the output in ASCII
-n	Tells TCPDump not to perform DNS lookups for the IP addresses seen during the capture
-F <file>	Reads the expression from <file>
-D	Prints available interfaces
-s <length>	Sets the length for each packet of the capture to <length>

The `-i <interface>` option changes the default interface on which TCPDump will listen for packets to capture. By default, TCPDump will listen on the first interface, `eth0`. However, for multihomed machines it may be necessary to use this option so that the correct traffic is captured. For example, on a firewall the `eth0` interface might be connected to the internal network while the `eth1` interface is connected to the Internet. You may be interested in seeing the traffic that's hitting your external interface (`eth1`); thus, you would use the `-i <interface>` option in TCPDump.

The verbose mode options, `-v`, `-vv`, and `-vvv` (not included in Table 13.1), cause TCPDump to print more (and more, and more) information about each packet received. With `-v` this information includes such important things as the TTL, packet ID, length, and options. Experimentation is usually necessary during a packet capture to determine which of these options will suit your needs. Different protocols may not have much (or any) additional information to print, so adding verbosity with these switches won't do any good.

The `-x` option causes TCPDump to also print hex dumps of each packet. For my eyes, this option isn't particularly helpful because I don't read hex so well. However, using the lowercase `-x` is required to take advantage of the ASCII dump of the packets that can be had by using the uppercase `-X`. Therefore, I'll rarely if ever use just `-x` and instead use both `-x` and `-X`. Although some parts of the packet may be printed by using just `-X`, using both can be helpful.

A sometimes-helpful option out of the most common options is the `-s <length>` option. Using this option is helpful to print the contents of packets themselves rather than the default 68 bytes only. If you're interested only in the headers of packets, this option won't be of much, if any, use. However, if you'd like to peek inside the packet itself, this option will help to ensure that the packet capture isn't truncated.

An option that becomes more useful the more you use TCPDump is the `-F <file>` option. This option tells TCPDump to read the contents of `<file>` for the filter expression rather than reading the command line. This option is very handy for longer expressions or expressions that are used frequently (or even infrequently). After using TCPDump for a while, you may get tired of typing the same old filter expression to capture the same packets week after week. Storing that expression in a file and then reading the expression from the file when using TCPDump is a great way to save time.

When just starting out with TCPDump, an option that you may find useful is the `-D` option. The `-D` option informs TCPDump to print a list of interfaces on which you can perform the packet capture. Because packet captures are interface dependent, knowing which interface to use is the most important thing you will have to choose. In Linux, it's somewhat easier to choose the right interface because interface names are usually simple, like `eth0` for the first Ethernet card. However, in Windows, `-D` is much more important because interface names can be quite difficult to remember.

A final option worth noting is the `-n` option. Using `-n` tells TCPDump not to perform reverse DNS lookups on the hosts as it sees them during the capture. Doing reverse lookups frequently slows down packet capture and naturally also increases the amount of traffic. Therefore, adding `-n` is helpful for speeding up the capture as well as reducing the signal-to-noise ratio. When I forget to set the -n option, I sometimes find myself asking, "Why is this machine performing DNS lookups?" only to realize that the lookups are the result of my packet capture activity.

TCPDump Expressions

Now the fun begins. By default, TCPDump will capture and output every packet that hits the interface. Sometimes this is useful for quickly listening to some traffic on a quiet interface. However, most captures will make use of expressions in TCPDump. A TCPDump expression is a collection of criteria for network traffic that you'd like to view with TCPDump. Expressions consist of one or more qualifiers and possibly a primitive, both of which are discussed in the following subsections. An expression might be used to capture only traffic that originates from a certain host or that is destined for a certain host. The possibilities with expressions and combinations of expressions give you the ability to home in on exactly the packets you need to see to assess a given network situation.

One of the more powerful features of expressions is the capability to negate. For instance, if you want to listen to all traffic except network traffic on port 80 (usually HTTP traffic), you could have TCPDump capture all traffic except that which is transmitted or received on port 80. TCPDump can use other logical terms as well, such as AND, OR, and the already-mentioned negation keyword NOT.

TCPDump expressions are enclosed within single quotes (') and can be grouped together by enclosing the various parts of a given expression within parentheses. This means that you can combine multiple expressions to capture only that traffic that is of interest. The key to grouping expressions together is the use of the logical terms AND, OR, and NOT. TCPDump has three qualifiers, each of which is introduced in turn in the discussion that follows. The first kind of qualifier is the type qualifier.

TCPDump's Type Qualifier

Just as TCPDump has three kinds of qualifiers, the type qualifier itself contains some variations, including host, port, portrange, and net. The host qualifier is used to specify the host or destination of interesting traffic. The port type qualifier is not surprisingly used to specify the port on which to capture packets, and portrange specifies a series of ports, such as 5060-5080. The net type is used to specify the subnet for interesting traffic. You could use the net qualifier in an expression to listen for traffic on an entire range of addresses. Of course, there are times when you don't want to listen to an entire range of addresses. TCPDump also accepts the modifier mask with the net qualifier to specify the subnet mask. You can also use CIDR notation to specify the mask bits.

Before I go further, here's an example of a TCPDump expression to capture traffic on port 80:

```
tcpdump 'port 80'
```

Because this expression uses only a single criterion (port 80), there's no need to enclose it within parentheses. If, however, the goal was to capture traffic on port 80 with a source or destination of one or more specific hosts, say `192.168.1.10` and `192.168.1.11`, then parentheses would be required, as in this example:

```
tcpdump 'port 80 and (host 192.168.1.10 or host 192.168.1.11)'
```

Parentheses are required only for logical grouping. In practice, you'll suffer no penalty for using them, and truthfully I normally use them just out of habit. When writing the preceding simple port `80` example, I included the parentheses at first, only to go back and remove them after I thought about what I was doing. Old habits die hard. Speaking of unnecessary terms, the term `host` in the example isn't required either—more on that later.

Here are some examples using the net type qualifier to listen for traffic in both directions for the network listed:

```
tcpdump 'net 192.168.1'
```

Here's that same example using CIDR notation:

```
tcpdump 'net 192.168.1.0/24'
```

And finally, here's that same example using the `mask` modifier:

```
tcpdump 'net 192.168.1.0 mask 255.255.255.0'
```

If you fail to specify a type qualifier (host, net, port, portrange) within a TCPDump expression, the host type is assumed. Therefore, don't be surprised when you receive a "parse error" when attempting something like this:

```
tcpdump '80'
```

Really, you probably wanted to have TCPDump listen for traffic on port `80`:

```
tcpdump 'port 80'
```

TCPDump's Direction Qualifier

Another kind of qualifier within a TCPDump expression is the direction qualifier. The previous examples will look for traffic flowing in either direction, coming or going, on port `80`, for instance. For example, this might mean that traffic destined for a web server running at `192.168.1.10` will be captured, but so will traffic leaving the computer at `192.168.1.10` and destined for another server on port `80`. You can also specify the direction with which to capture traffic by using a direction qualifier. The terms `src` for the source and `dst` for the destination are the two direction qualifiers used by TCPDump. Adding the destination term to one of the previous examples yields an expression that will look for port `80` traffic going to `192.168.1.10` or `192.168.1.11`:

```
tcpdump 'port 80 and (src 192.168.1.10 or src 192.168.1.11)'
```

The direction qualifier isn't limited to looking for traffic on certain addresses. It's perfectly valid to look for traffic with a source or destination of a specific port, as in this example that looks for traffic with a destination of port 25 (usually SMTP):

```
tcpdump 'dst port 25'
```

There are direction qualifiers that are specific to 802.11 wireless link-layer traffic. These include ra, ta, addr1, addr2, addr3, and addr4. Additionally, some protocols use the terms inbound and outbound to specify the direction. See the TCPDump man page for more details on these qualifiers.

TCPDump's Protocol Qualifier

A final kind of qualifier for use in a TCPDump expression is the protocol qualifier. Not surprisingly, protocol qualifiers enable you to choose which protocols should be captured with TCPDump. The protocols that can be captured with TCPDump include, among others, Ethernet (abbreviated ether for TCPDump syntax), WLAN, TCP, UDP, ICMP, IP, IPv6 (abbreviated ip6 for TCPDump syntax), ARP, reverse ARP (abbreviated to rarp), and more.

Primitives

Aside from the main three qualifiers (type, direction, and protocol), there are also what are known as primitives for use in TCPDump expressions. Primitives are keywords that help to specify additional parameters for the packet capture. Some highlights of commonly used primitives include

- Arithmetic operators
- broadcast
- gateway
- greater
- less

The arithmetic operators include +, -, *, /, >, <, >=, <=, =, !=, and a few others. TCPDump can use quite complex arithmetic operators and packet offsets to look into packets. I prefer to leave it as an exercise for the reader to dive into these areas should you find it necessary to do so.

The broadcast primitive, when prepended with either ip or ether, will look for packets that are IP or Ethernet broadcasts respectively, though ether is the default type to look for. For example, a TCPDump expression looking for ip broadcast will search for broadcasts on an IP network. However, if the interface card on which TCPDump is listening has no subnet mask or if the any interface is being used, this broadcast primitive will not work.

The primitives greater and less are used to search for packets with a length greater than or equal to or less than or equal to the given length. These primitives are functionally equivalent to using the arithmetic operators for the same. So, for example, the syntax

```
len >= 1500
```

is equivalent to this:

```
greater 1500
```

Beyond the Basics with TCPDump

You should now have a feel for the basic syntax of TCPDump, including some of the options, the syntax, and TCPDump expressions. The amount of troubleshooting and diagnosis that can be accomplished with even a basic grasp of TCPDump syntax makes it an essential tool for anyone managing networked computers. However, to examine more difficult problems, you may find that you need to go beyond the basics of TCPDump.

Going beyond the basics of TCPDump requires deeper understanding of the protocols themselves. Knowing the flags of TCP or the types of ICMP can help to narrow the focus to only the packets of interest. Although this information and knowing how to use it with TCPDump is not mandatory, having the ability to call on the information at any time is valuable to say the least. Take the time to familiarize yourself with TCPDump's more involved syntax. It costs nothing but time to test a packet-filtering expression to see how it works under various network conditions.

Using TCPDump to Capture Specific Protocols

In this section, I'll give some examples that show you how to capture various forms of network traffic for monitoring purposes. Included among the examples, you'll see what a DNS query looks like through TCPDump, some ICMP (`ping`) examples, and various TCP- and UDP-based protocols. After you see how normal traffic looks, I'll then show you some of the fun stuff. Specifically, I'll show what some types of attacks look like through TCPDump so that you might be able to quickly detect these when they come into (or out of) your network.

Throughout this section, I'll be using a few different programs to generate traffic for TCPDump to capture. My primary tool for TCP-related captures will be telnet. I'll use telnet to generate traffic and mirror what the real protocol (or close to it) does in the real world. Generation of DNS queries will be accomplished using both the `dig` command and the `host` command. The ping and `traceroute` commands will be used. Finally, the `hping3` command will be used to generate ICMP traffic as well as other interesting packets, especially in the attack section. With the exception of `hping3`, all of these programs are installed on most major Linux distributions.

Using TCPDump in the Real World

So far in this chapter, you've seen a number of examples of using TCPDump to capture various types of traffic. These examples were given to show the usage of TCPDump in relation to expressions and other options. Now it's time to give you real-life examples of using TCPDump to capture specific types of traffic. The situations in which you might use these examples will vary, but I'll try to give some clue as to why you might use a given example, where I can. It might be helpful to see how a filter expression is built when trying to capture in the real world. I briefly touched on this topic earlier. However, before giving recipe-type solutions, I'll show you how to build a filter with the specific goal of capturing an HTTP conversation.

Building a Filter to Capture an HTTP Conversation

HTTP is the language of the Web. Usually HTTP rides over TCP, which in turn rides on IP. I'm choosing HTTP as the first real-world capture only because people are generally familiar with browsing a web page, even though they may not be familiar with the underlying protocol.

Recall that IP is a connectionless protocol whereas TCP is a connection-oriented protocol. TCP uses a three-way handshake to begin a conversation. HTTP takes advantage of the connection-oriented nature of TCP and in fact knows nothing of lower-layered (remember the OSI model) protocols. As far as HTTP is concerned, it hands its data down to the next lower layer and is done. To that end, when an HTTP conversation is initiated, the first thing you should see through TCPDump is the three-way handshake of TCP followed by protocol-specific data.

For the most part, HTTP traffic flows to a destination of port 80.

> **Note**
>
> The ports on which various services normally operate can be found by examining the file /etc/services. With that in mind, the true source for port number assignments is IANA. You can view the most current and complete list of official port number assignments at the URL http://www.iana.org/assignments/port-numbers. However, remember that there's nothing preventing someone from running a service on a port other than the official port number!

Because HTTP is usually found on port 80, it would be a good idea to start with a basic TCPDump expression that looks only for port 80 traffic, such as this one:

```
tcpdump 'port 80'
```

Running that command and then generating some traffic by surfing to a web page yields these results:

```
tcpdump: verbose output suppressed, use -v or -vv for full protocol decode
listening on eth0, link-type EN10MB (Ethernet), capture size 96 bytes

17:15:38.934337 IP client.braingia.org.4485 > test.example.com.www: \
        S 523004834:523004834(0) win 5840 \
                <mss 1460,sackOK,timestamp 249916003 0,nop,wscale 0>

17:15:38.984650 IP test.example.com.www > client.braingia.org.4485: S \
        2810959978:2810959978(0) ack 523004835 win 5792 \
                <mss 1460,sackOK,timestamp 1320060704 249916003,nop,wscale 0>

17:15:38.984684 IP client.braingia.org.4485 > test.example.com.www: \
        . ack 1 win 5840 <nop,nop,timestamp 249916008 1320060704>

17:15:38.985326 IP client.braingia.org.4485 > test.example.com.www: \
        P 1:462(461) ack 1 win 5840 <nop,nop,timestamp 249916008 1320060704>

17:15:39.038067 IP test.example.com.www > client.braingia.org.4485: . \
        ack 462 win 6432 <nop,nop,timestamp 1320060710 249916008>
```

```
17:15:39.065141 IP test.example.com.www > client.braingia.org.4485: . \
        1:1449(1448) ack 462 win 6432 <nop,nop,timestamp 1320060712 249916008>

17:15:39.065183 IP client.braingia.org.4485 > test.example.com.www: . \
        ack 1449 win 8688 <nop,nop,timestamp 249916016 1320060712>
```

> **Note**
> I've separated the results for greater readability, and I'll continue to do so throughout the rest of this chapter.

Notice the first two lines from the TCPDump output. In this case, the first line tells me that I really should have more verbose output enabled in order to see anything interesting within the packet, and the second line gives a status of the interface on which TCPDump is listening, as well as the size of the capture.

The next line is the first line of the capture and is also coincidentally the first packet (SYN) sent in the TCP three-way handshake. The first thing you'll notice on the line is a timestamp, followed by the protocol (IP). Next is the hostname of the computer that initiated the packet (client.braingia.org) together with the source port for the traffic (4485). This combination, source computer and source port, are known as the Source. The greater-than sign (>) shows the direction of the flow in relation to the Destination for this traffic, which, as you can see from that line, is test.example.com.www. The www signifies the destination port that the traffic is headed for on the destination computer.

The next item of interest on the TCPDump output line is the Flags section, in this case indicated by an uppercase S. Recall from Chapter 1, "Preliminary Concepts Underlying Packet-Filtering Firewalls," that the TCP header can contain various flags to indicate certain conditions for the packet. If you guessed that S indicates a packet with the SYN flag set, you may have just won a valuable prize. Following the Flags section is the Sequence Number space for the packet, indicating the sequence numbers that will be covered within this packet. In the case of the example, the Sequence Number space (523004834:523004834(0)) is zero length. The next item on this line is the Window size, as indicated by the win 5840 in the output. Finally, enclosed within brackets are options contained in the packet. Although these options can be of interest at certain times, you'll rarely need to care much about them in the real world.

You've now seen one single packet of a TCP three-way handshake through TCPDump. Don't worry, it does get more exciting than this, really it does. The next line in the capture contains the response packet coming back from test.example.com. Notice that the timestamp has increased and the protocol is still IP. However, now the source computer is test.example.com on port 80 and the destination is client.braingia.org.4485. Notice also that the SYN flag is set as evidenced by the S following the source > destination area. The sequence number space is different now, though, 2810959978:2810959978(0). This is because test.example.com chose its own sequence number as part of the process. The first difference of real interest because we haven't seen it before is the ack 523004835. This is the second part of the TCP three-way handshake, namely, what's commonly referred to as the SYN-ACK packet. In this packet, the original destination computer is answering or acknowledging the call to initiate a TCP connection on the specified port. Notice that the number following the `ack` is equal to the original sequence number (523004834) plus one. This is the protocol itself in action.

The third packet in the capture, depicted again here for reference, is the final packet in the connection setup for TCP:

```
17:15:38.984684 IP client.braingia.org.4485 > test.example.com.www: . \
        ack 1 win 5840 <nop,nop,timestamp 249916008 1320060704>
```

In this packet, the original source acknowledges the connection setup. Notice that there is a single dot (.) where the flags would normally show up. This usually means that there are no flags set; however, some flags like ACK show up in a different place on the output line. The source side sets the ACK flag and also sets an initial sequence number for this connection. At this point, the TCP connection is said to be established. That sure seems like a lot of work, but didn't I promise that this section was about HTTP? Sure enough. The next packets with capture output indicate that an HTTP connection is progressing:

```
17:15:38.985326 IP client.braingia.org.4485 > test.example.com.www: \
        P 1:462(461) ack 1 win 5840 <nop,nop,timestamp 249916008 1320060704>

17:15:39.038067 IP test.example.com.www > client.braingia.org.4485: . ack \
        462 win 6432 <nop,nop,timestamp 1320060710 249916008>

17:15:39.065141 IP test.example.com.www > client.braingia.org.4485: . \
        1:1449(1448) ack 462 win 6432 <nop,nop,timestamp 1320060712 249916008>

17:15:39.065183 IP client.braingia.org.4485 > test.example.com.www: . \
        ack 1449 win 8688 <nop,nop,timestamp 249916016 1320060712>
```

The source sends the beginning of the data for this communication. Notice that the PUSH flag was set in the initial packet and that the sequence numbers increment. The two sides acknowledge sequence numbers and data is transferred. But with the TCPDump command that I ran (`tcpdump 'port 80'`), there isn't much else to see. Therefore, I'll improve that command to include the options I normally include to peek inside the packets. I'll leave it up to the reader to see what each of the options actually does, as explained earlier in the chapter. Here's the improved command for TCPDump:

```
tcpdump -vv -x -X -s 1500 'port 80'
```

With this command running, I can generate additional web traffic. Here are two and a half packets from the result, picking up from just after the three-way handshake:

```
18:18:51.986230 IP (tos 0x0, ttl 64, id 10907, offset 0, flags [DF], \
        length: 513) client.braingia.org.4564 > test.example.com.www: \
                P [tcp sum ok] 1:462(461) ack 1 win 5840 <nop,nop,timestamp
                        250295308 1320440053>
        0x0000:  0090 2741 78f0 00e0 1833 2ee8 0800 4500  .. 'Ax....3....E.
        0x0010:  0201 2a9b 4000 4006 044b c0a8 010a 455d  ..*.@.@..K....E]
        0x0020:  0302 11d4 0050 0c9b 1ea0 9627 33f8 8018  .....P.....'3...
        0x0030:  16d0 4915 0000 0101 080a 0eeb 340c 4eb4  ..I.........4.N.
        0x0040:  50f5 4745 5420 2f20 4854 5450 2f31 2e30  P.GET./.HTTP/1.0
        0x0050:  0d0a 486f 7374 3a20 7777 772e 6272 6169  ..Host:.text.exam
```

```
0x0060: 6e67 6961 2e6f 7267 0d0a 4163 6365 7074  ple.com..Accept
0x0070: 3a20 7465 7874 2f68 746d 6c2c 2074 6578  :.text/html,.tex
0x0080: 742f 706c 6169 6e2c 2061 7070 6c69 6361  t/plain,.applica
0x0090: 7469 6f6e 2f6d 7377 6f72 642c 2061 7070  tion/msword,.app
0x00a0: 6c69 6361 7469 6f6e 2f70 6466 2c20 6170  lication/pdf,.ap
0x00b0: 706c 6963 6174 696f 6e2f 6f63 7465 742d  plication/octet-
0x00c0: 7374 7265 616d 2c20 6170 7006 6963 6174  stream,.applicat
0x00d0: 696f 6e2f 782d 7472 6f66 662d 6d61 6e2c  ion/x-troff-man,
0x00e0: 2061 7070 6c69 6361 7469 6f6e 2f78 2d74  .application/x-t
0x00f0: 6172 2c20 6170 706c 6963 6174 696f 6e2f  ar,.application/
0x0100: 782d 6774 6172 2c20 6170 706c 6963 6174  x-gtar,.applicat
0x0110: 696f 6e2f 7274 662c 2061 7070 6c69 6361  ion/rtf,.applica
0x0120: 7469 6f6e 2f70 6f73 7473 6372 6970 742c  tion/postscript,
0x0130: 2061 7070 6c69 6361 7469 6f6e 2f67 686f  .application/gho
0x0140: 7374 7669 6577 2c20 7465 7874 2f2a 0d0a  stview,.text/*..
0x0150: 4163 6365 7074 3a20 6170 706c 6963 6174  Accept:.applicat
0x0160: 696f 6e2f 782d 6465 6269 616e 2d70  61630  ion/x-debian-pac
0x0170: 6b61 6765 2c20 6175 6469 6f2f 7369  kage,.audio/basi
0x0180: 632c 202a 2f2a 3b71 3d30 2e30 310d 0a41  c,.*/*;q=0.01..A
0x0190: 6363 6570 742d 456e 636f 6469 6e67 3a20  ccept-Encoding:.
0x01a0: 677a 6970 2c20 636f 6d70 7265 7373 0d0a  gzip,.compress..
0x01b0: 4163 6365 7074 2d4c 616e 6775 6167 653a  Accept-Language:
0x01c0: 2065 6e0d 0a55 7365 722d 4167 656e 743a  .en..User-Agent:
0x01d0: 204c 796e 782f 322e 382e 3472 656c 2e31  .Lynx/2.8.4rel.1
0x01e0: 206c 6962 7777 772d 464d 2f32 2e31 3420  .libwww-FM/2.14.
0x01f0: 5353 4c2d 4d4d 2f31 2e34 2e31 204f 7065  SSL-MM/1.4.1.Ope
0x0200: 6e53 534c 2f30 2e39 2e36 630d 0a0d 0a    nSSL/0.9.6c....
18:18:52.039595 IP (tos 0x0, ttl 48, id 25346, offset 0, flags [DF], \
        length: 52) test.example.com.www > client.braingia.org.4564: .
                [tcp sum ok] 1:1(0) ack 462 win 6432 <nop,nop,timestamp
                        1320440059 250295308>
0x0000: 00e0 1833 2ee8 0090 2741 78f0 0800 4500  ...3....'Ax...E.
0x0010: 0034 6302 4000 3006 ddb0 455d 0302 c0a8  .4c.@.0...E]....
0x0020: 010a 0050 11d4 9627 33f8 0c9b 206d 8010  ...P...'3....m..
0x0030: 1920 6799 0000 0101 080a 4eb4 50fb 0eeb  ..g.......N.P...
0x0040: 340c                                      4.
18:18:52.047021 IP (tos 0x0, ttl 48, id 25347, offset 0, flags [DF], \
        length: 1500) test.example.com.www > client.braingia.org.4564:\
                . 1:1449(1448) ack 462 win 6432 <nop,nop,timestamp \
                        1320440059 250295308>
0x0000: 00e0 1833 2ee8 0090 2741 78f0 0800 4500  ...3....'Ax...E.
0x0010: 05dc 6303 4000 3006 d807 455d 0302 c0a8  ..c.@.0...E]....
0x0020: 010a 0050 11d4 9627 33f8 0c9b 206d 8010  ...P...'3....m..
0x0030: 1920 b9f7 0000 0101 080a 4eb4 50fb 0eeb  ..........N.P...
0x0040: 340c 4854 5450 2f31 2e31 2032 3030 204f  4.HTTP/1.1.200.O
0x0050: 4b0d 0a44 6174 653a 2054 7565 2c20 3237  K..Date:.Tue,.27
0x0060: 204a 756c 2032 3030 3420 3233 3a31 393a  .Jul.2004.23:19:
0x0070: 3030 2047 4d54 0d0a 5365 7276 6572 3a20  00.GMT..Server:.
0x0080: 4170 6163 6865 2f31 2e33 2e32 3620 2855  Apache/1.3.26.(U
0x0090: 6e69 7829 2044 6562 6961 6e20 474e 552f  nix).Debian.GNU/
0x00a0: 4c69 6e75 7820 6d6f 645f 6d6f 6e6f 2f30  Linux.mod_mono/0
0x00b0: 2e31 3120 6d6f 645f 7065 726c 2f31 2e32  .11.mod_perl/1.2
0x00c0: 360d 0a43 6f6e 6e65 6374 696f 6e3a 2063  6..Connection:.c
0x00d0: 6c6f 7365 0d0a 436f 6e74 656e 742d 5479  lose..Content-Ty
0x00e0: 7065 3a20 7465 7874 2f68 746d 6c3b 2063  pe:.text/html;.c
0x00f0: 6861 7273 6574 3d69 736f 2d38 3835 392d  harset=iso-8859-
```

Notice that this output contains an actual request (see the first packet, near GET./.HTTP/1.0) and also contains a portion of the response from the web server. All of this traffic is in plain text because HTTP is not encrypted. This output contains both hex and ASCII. To obtain output with just ASCII, remove the -x and -X from the command and replace them with a single -A. I personally find the dual hex and ASCII output to be helpful at times.

That's all there is to capturing HTTP traffic with TCPDump. Obvious improvements for the command would be to expand the expression to look for a specific source or destination. It's important to understand that only traffic on port 80 will be found with the command as given. If you're running HTTP traffic on another port, substitute that port instead of (or in addition to) the port found in the sample command.

Capturing an SMTP Conversation

Capturing an SMTP conversation is not unlike capturing an HTTP session. Begin with the basic TCPDump options that you'd like to use and then build an expression to grab the appropriate type of data, including protocol, port, and source or destination hosts. For example, here's a simple capture of port 25 traffic along with my normal TCPDump choice of options:

```
tcpdump -vv -x -X -s 1500 'port 25'
```

The TCP three-way handshake is again present, as you might expect:

```
20:40:08.638690 murphy.debian.org.45772 > test.example.com.smtp: \
       S [tcp sum ok] 1485971964:1485971964(0) win 5840 <mss 1460,
            sackOK,timestamp 795074473 0,nop,ws cale 0> (DF) \
                (ttl 57, id 65109, len 60)
0x0000   4500 003c fe55 4000 3906 deae 9252 8a06    E..<.U@.9....R..
0x0010   455d 0302 b2cc 0019 5892 21fc 0000 0000    E].....X.!.....
0x0020   a002 16d0 8ffe 0000 0204 05b4 0402 080a    ..............
0x0030   2f63 dfa9 0000 0000 0103 0300             /c.........
20:40:08.638769 test.example.com.smtp > murphy.debian.org.45772: S \
       [tcp sum ok] 2853594323:2853594323(0) ack 1485971965 win 5792 \
            <mss 1460,sackOK,timestamp 132 1286843 795074473,nop,wscale 0> \
                (DF) (ttl 64, id 0, len 60)
0x0000   4500 003c 0000 4000 4006 d604 455d 0302    E..<..@.@...E]..
0x0010   9252 8a06 0019 b2cc aa16 64d3 5892 21fd    .R.......d.X.!.
0x0020   a012 16a0 f5b6 0000 0204 05b4 0402 080a    ..............
0x0030   4ec1 3cbb 2f63 dfa9 0103 0300             N.<./c......
20:40:08.640600 murphy.debian.org.45772 > test.example.com.smtp: . \
       [tcp sum ok] 1:1(0) ack 1 win 5840 <nop,nop,timestamp \
            795074473 1321286843> (DF) (ttl 57, id 65110, len 52)
0x0000   4500 0034 fe56 4000 3906 deb5 9252 8a06    E..4.V@.9....R..
0x0010   455d 0302 b2cc 0019 5892 21fd aa16 64d4    E].....X.!...d.
0x0020   8010 16d0 244c 0000 0101 080a 2f63 dfa9    ....$L......./c..
0x0030   4ec1 3cbb                                  N.<.
```

There's nothing really new of interest during the three-way handshake process. Notice, though, that the ASCII output isn't of much use during the three-way handshake.

As with HTTP, after the initial TCP handshake is done, the SMTP conversation gets under way:

```
20:40:08.683352 test.example.com.smtp > murphy.debian.org.45772: P \
        [tcp sum ok] 1:51(50) ack 1 win 5792 <nop,nop,timestamp \
            1321286848 795074473> (DF) (ttl 64,id 22639, len 102)
0x0000   4500 0066 586f 4000 4006 7d6b 455d 0302    E..fXo@.@.}kE]..
0x0010   9252 8a06 0019 b2cc aa16 64d4 5892 21fd    .R........d.X.!.
0x0020   8018 16a0 bd07 0000 0101 080a 4ec1 3cc0    ............N.<.
0x0030   2f63 dfa9 3232 3020 6466 7730 2e69 6367    /c..220.test.exa
0x0040   6d65 6469 612e 636f 6d20 4553 4d54 5020    mple.com.ESMTP.
0x0050   506f 7374 6669 7820 2844 6562 6961 6e2f    Postfix.(Debian/
0x0060   474e 5529 0d0a                             GNU)..
20:40:08.684581 murphy.debian.org.45772 > test.example.com.smtp: . [tcp sum ok]
 1:1(0) ack 51 win 5840 <nop,nop,timestamp 795074478 1321286848> (DF) (ttl 57, i
d 65111, len 52)
0x0000   4500 0034 fe57 4000 3906 deb4 9252 8a06    E..4.W@.9....R..
0x0010   455d 0302 b2cc 0019 5892 21fd aa16 6506    E]......X.!...e.
0x0020   8010 16d0 2410 0000 0101 080a 2f63 dfae    ....$......./c..
0x0030   4ec1 3cc0                                   N.<.
20:40:08.685428 murphy.debian.org.45772 > test.example.com.smtp: P [tcp sum ok]
 1:25(24) ack 51 win 5840 <nop,nop,timestamp 795074478 1321286848> (DF) (ttl 57,
 id 65112, len 76)
0x0000   4500 004c fe58 4000 3906 de9b 9252 8a06    E..L.X@.9....R..
0x0010   455d 0302 b2cc 0019 5892 21fd aa16 6506    E]......X.!...e.
0x0020   8018 16d0 3cc4 0000 0101 080a 2f63 dfae    ....<......./c..
0x0030   4ec1 3cc0 4548 4c4f 206d 7572 7068 792e    N.<.EHLO.murphy.
0x0040   6465 6269 616e 2e6f 7267 0d0a              debian.org..
```

Capturing an SSH Conversation

Although it's not possible to actually capture an SSH conversation, you can look at some of the connection setup portions of the protocol. Because SSH is encrypted, though, none of the credentials or other data during the actual session is available for you to view. It should be noted, however, that if you can gain access to the private key of the server, you could theoretically decrypt the contents of the SSH connection. Doing this is well beyond the scope of this text.

I'll leave it as an exercise for the reader to capture an SSH connection, including setup, should you want to view what a normal connection looks like for SSH.

Capturing Other TCP-Based Protocols

Capturing other TCP-based protocols follows much the same process as that in the examples shown. For example, capturing POP3 connections can be accomplished and the entire stream can be captured because POP3, like SMTP, is not encrypted during transit. One protocol is of particular interest because it has confounded network administrators for a long time. That protocol is FTP.

FTP utilizes two TCP ports, 20 and 21. Port 21 is normally used for commands and is sometimes referred to as the *control channel*. Port 20 in FTP is used for data and is sometimes aptly titled the *data channel*. Therefore, if you want to capture FTP traffic with TCPDump, you need to grab both ports 20 and 21 to see everything.

A trend over the past few years has been protocols that use nonstandard ports to circumvent firewalls and packet capturing and filtering. Such programs, including much of the peer-to-peer software, can be somewhat difficult to find during packet captures because most of the data during the conversation is binary and is thus not human readable.

Capturing a DNS Query

TCPDump handles DNS queries a little differently from a packet that's simply TCP. More information can be gleaned from just the initial packet result line as opposed to making it necessary to increase the snaplen with the -s option. For example, consider the following trace of a simple DNS query that was looking for the IP address of a host named www.braingia.org:

```
21:18:39.289121 192.168.1.10.1514 > 192.168.1.1.53: 60792+ A? www.braingia.org.
➥(34) (DF)
```

```
21:18:39.289568 192.168.1.1.53 > 192.168.1.10.1514: 60792*- 1/2/2 A 192.168.1.50
➥(118) (DF)
```

In the packet trace we see host 192.168.1.10 on an ephemeral port communicating with a destination of 192.168.1.1 on port 53. A query ID number is given; in this case it's 60792. You see that the query ID number is followed by a +. This symbol indicates that the querier asked for recursion on this query. The A? on the trace line indicates that this was an address query. The query was for www.braingia.org, as is shown, and the size of the query is 34 bytes, which does not include IP or UDP overhead.

The answer comes quickly, as we see in the next line of the trace, which shows that the source is now 192.168.1.1 talking to the destination of 192.168.1.10. As you can see, the answer was contained in the same query ID, 60792; however, this time there are two extra characters, the * and the -. The * in a response indicates that this is an authoritative answer, and the - indicates that recursion is available and not set. The next portion of the response, 1/2/2, indicates the number of answer records (1), the number of name server records (2), and the number of additional records (2). The first answer given in this case is of type A and is 192.168.1.50. Finally, the size of the response is given to be 118 bytes.

Capturing pings

Although it may seem innocent enough, ICMP (the protocol behind ping) has been used fairly often as a means by which to attack hosts and otherwise wreak havoc. Therefore, as a security analyst, an administrator, or a curious bystander, you should know that it's in your best interest to see some of the normal activity for ICMP through TCPDump so that you might be able to spot an anomaly later.

I'll go out onto a limb and say that ICMP is most frequently used for the simple echo request and echo reply provided by ping. However, ICMP can be and is used for much more than that, including informing a fast sender when to slow down (Source Quench), redirecting to other hosts (Redirect), and many other areas. Refer to Chapter 1 for more information on ICMP, or, as always, refer to the original RFC on ICMP for the authoritative information on the protocol.

Attacks through the Eyes of TCPDump

You've seen what normal TCP and UDP packet traces look like through TCPDump, but how will you know whether someone or something is acting abnormally? Unfortunately, finding nefarious activity is not that easy. Buried in normal packet traces may be signs that someone is attempting an attack on your server. An attacker will obviously attempt to disguise his or her activity, making detection even more difficult. Not only do you have to wade through all the normal traffic within a packet trace, but you then have to search for the proverbial needle in a haystack to find what may be an attack attempt or even one in progress.

Recall from Chapter 11, "Intrusion Detection and Response," that not everything that falls outside of normal activity can be termed an attack. Some of it is the result of malfunctioning or misconfigured equipment. More often than not, abnormal activity spotted in a packet trace is due to reconnaissance of one form or another. And the large majority of reconnaissance work is done through automation. Rather than spending many fruitless hours searching for a vulnerable host, attackers will automate the process and have the program alert them when it finds an interesting host.

There are naturally exceptions to the rule of automation. Attacks may be the result of directed activity against your server or network. Before the attack there is usually some manual reconnaissance that takes place. This may include the would-be attacker manually crafting or creating packets to attempt to exploit possible holes in your server or network. More often than not, however, the attacker will have had some automated reconnaissance data that directed his or her efforts in your direction. If an automated scan alerted the attacker that one of your servers may be vulnerable to a particular type of attack, you may find the hosts or your entire subnet within the sights of the attacker.

Leaving a host vulnerable or making a host appear vulnerable and then observing the attacks is the premise behind a honeypot. A *honeypot* is a host or device that shows up as vulnerable to an attacker and thus looks like a target for attack. The idea is that by watching the methods that attackers use to exploit a hole or watching what they do when they compromise the host, the observer can learn from it and defend against such activity.

As if all the possible reasons already given for seeing abnormal activity aren't enough, here's one more: you'll also encounter accidental connections that may appear to be attacks. In other words, at times someone simply mistypes an IP address when attempting to connect to his or her server. Anyone who has ever answered the telephone only to find out that the caller dialed incorrectly can relate to this situation.

In summary, there are some basic categories within which abnormal activity might fall:

- Automated or semiautomated reconnaissance scan
- Directed attack
- Misconfigured equipment

- Wrong number
- Malfunctioning equipment

With those categories in mind, this section examines some abnormal packet traces or traces that you shouldn't see under normal conditions. By no means does this section include all the possible crafted and abnormal packets. The hope is to give you an understanding of some of the types of things to look for when performing an investigation.

Normal Scan (Nmap)

Sometimes an attacker will scan your subnet or individual IP address for open ports. This scan can be anything from an innocent attempt to look for a service to reconnaissance for an attack. Many times, these scans are completely automated, with an attacker setting up one or more robots (bots) to automatically scan for vulnerable versions of software to exploit.

This simulation was created with the Nmap program with the following command line:

```
nmap -sT 192.168.1.2
```

The TCPDump capture of the port scan is shown in the following text; note that I've truncated the output because Nmap scanned for more than 1650 ports. I've divided the capture to make explaining it easier as well.

Nmap scans begin with an ICMP echo request to the target host, as shown here. Note, however, that this ICMP exchange can be disabled by the person running the Nmap scan, so it might not always show up:

```
12:31:21.834284 IP 192.168.1.10 > 192.168.1.2: icmp 8: echo request seq 27074
12:31:21.834508 IP 192.168.1.2 > 192.168.1.10: icmp 8: echo reply seq 27074
```

Next, Nmap looks for port 80, the default HTTP port. Notice that the scan comes from an ephemeral port on the scanner's side aimed for port 80 on the recipient. In this case, the recipient host 192.168.1.2 is listening on port 80, and a TCP response is sent back to the scanning host with the TCP RST flag set and the sequence number set:

```
12:31:21.834318 IP 192.168.1.10.60034 > 192.168.1.2.80: . ack 2624625246 win 4096
12:31:21.834363 IP 192.168.1.2.80 > 192.168.1.10.60034: R \
        2624625246:2624625246(0) win 0
```

Next, Nmap looks for the telnet port (tcp/23). Notice the difference between this and the preceding scan. Aside from the ports being different, the response packet is also different. In this case, the recipient host is not listening on TCP port 23, so it responds with a packet with the TCP RST flag set but with the TCP sequence number set to 0:

```
12:31:21.935005 IP 192.168.1.10.3171 > 192.168.1.2.23: S 752173650:752173650(0) \
        win 5840 <mss 1460,sackOK,timestamp 1421906912 0,nop,wscale 0>
12:31:21.935046 IP 192.168.1.2.23 > 192.168.1.10.3171: R 0:0(0) ack 752173651
↪win 0
```

The following packets are essentially the same as the preceding telnet port scan insofar as the recipient host is not listening on the ports being scanned:

```
12:31:21.935129 IP 192.168.1.10.3172 > 192.168.1.2.554: S 758180552:758180552(0)
➡\
        win 5840 <mss 1460,sackOK,timestamp 1421906912 0,nop,wscale 0>
12:31:21.935186 IP 192.168.1.2.554 > 192.168.1.10.3172: R 0:0(0) ack 758180553
➡win 0
12:31:21.935149 IP 192.168.1.10.3174 > 192.168.1.2.21: S 751983738:751983738(0) \
        win 5840 <mss 1460,sackOK,timestamp 1421906912 0,nop,wscale 0>
12:31:21.935289 IP 192.168.1.2.21 > 192.168.1.10.3174: R 0:0(0) ack 751983739 win
➡0
12:31:21.935255 IP 192.168.1.10.3175 > 192.168.1.2.1723: S 757954867:757954867(0)
➡\
        win 5840 <mss 1460,sackOK,timestamp 1421906912 0,nop,wscale 0>
12:31:21.935320 IP 192.168.1.2.1723 > 192.168.1.10.3175: R 0:0(0) \
        ack 757954868 win 0
```

Finally, another open port is found. This time the open port is `tcp/25`, the well-known SMTP port:

```
12:31:21.935381 IP 192.168.1.10.3176 > 192.168.1.2.25: S 762467904:762467904(0) \
        win 5840 <mss 1460,sackOK,timestamp 1421906912 0,nop,wscale 0>
12:31:21.935448 IP 192.168.1.2.25 > 192.168.1.10.3176: S 2645882457:2645882457(0)
➡\
        ack 762467905 win 5792 <mss 1460,sackOK,timestamp \
            921140115 1421906912,nop,wscale 7>
```

As stated previously, the Nmap scan continues for another 1650 or so ports. I chose to save a tree by not showing the remainder of the port scans here. Rest assured that they look largely the same as the ones already shown.

The response you take when port scanned depends on your security policy. If I notice a wide port scan, one in which a large number of ports are scanned, I'll usually take steps to block the host. However, because I'm not at the computer 24 hours a day (close, but not quite), I use a tool called PortSentry to monitor for this type of activity. However, other anti–port scan software exists, including a plug-in for Snort.

Smurf Attack

A Smurf attack is a DoS attack whereby the attacker sends ICMP echo requests with a forged source address to one or more broadcast addresses. The forged source address is the recipient of the attack, and it will be inundated with echo replies from the broadcast addresses of other networks. Imagine echo replies coming from 254 hosts directed at a machine with a small or slow Internet connection. Now imagine those replies coming from 100 networks of 254 hosts each. It doesn't take long for an entire network to become bogged down receiving ICMP replies.

The following trace was created with the `hping3` command:

```
hping3 -1 -a 192.168.1.2 192.168.1.255
```

On the network under attack, only one host responded to the broadcasted `ping`; however, there's no way to guarantee that other networks wouldn't have a large number of hosts that respond:

```
12:57:06.871156 IP 192.168.1.2 > 192.168.1.255: icmp 8: echo request seq 0
12:57:06.871637 IP 192.168.1.8 > 192.168.1.2: icmp 8: echo reply seq 0
12:57:07.870259 IP 192.168.1.2 > 192.168.1.255: icmp 8: echo request seq 256
12:57:07.871008 IP 192.168.1.8 > 192.168.1.2: icmp 8: echo reply seq 256
12:57:08.870132 IP 192.168.1.2 > 192.168.1.255: icmp 8: echo request seq 512
12:57:08.870880 IP 192.168.1.8 > 192.168.1.2: icmp 8: echo reply seq 512
```

There is no good host-based defense for a Smurf attack. Even if ICMP replies are disabled on the individual host, the bandwidth is still being consumed by all the replies coming into the network.

To effectively counter a Smurf attack, ICMP echo requests directed to broadcast addresses mustn't cross router boundaries. This means that you're relying on others to be good netizens. In addition, ICMP echo replies must be filtered as far upstream from your location as possible. However, I'm not an advocate of filtering ICMP echo replies. A better solution is to rate-limit the echo replies as far upstream as possible while still allowing the replies for all the good that they do in problem diagnosis.

Xmas Tree and TCP Header Flags

The Xmas Tree attack is so named because all the bit flags are set to on within the TCP header. The idea is to cause the recipient host to respond, thus causing a DoS. Recall the TCP flag bits SYN, RST, ACK, URG, and others from Chapter 1. These bits should never all appear at the same time, and when they do it's an indication of a crafted packet.

Xmas Tree attacks are quite uncommon. However, it's important to consider the TCP flags when examining packets. Setting these flags with invalid combinations is almost always an indication of a crafted packet (though it also in a few instances could indicate broken or misconfigured software). The goal of the crafted packet might be anything from reconnaissance to an active attack such as one to get through a firewall.

The following capture sets the TCP flags SYN, FIN, RST, and PUSH, which should never show up in a real packet. It was created with the hping3 command:

```
hping3 -SFRP 192.168.1.2
```

There are three packets in this capture. Notice that the source port increments and that the destination port is 0. The TCP flags are also shown, SFRP in this case. Seeing this in the wild should cause the intrusion analyst to immediately begin investigating the packets according to the security policy.

```
13:20:03.989780 IP (tos 0x0, ttl 64, id 2270, offset 0, flags [none], length: \
        40) 192.168.1.10.2687 > 192.168.1.2.0: SFRP [tcp sum ok] \
            925164686:925164686(0) win 512
13:20:04.989734 IP (tos 0x0, ttl 64, id 9285, offset 0, flags [none], \
        length: 40) 192.168.1.10.2688 > 192.168.1.2.0: SFRP [tcp sum ok] \
            1113258177:1113258177(0) win 512
13:20:05.989731 IP (tos 0x0, ttl 64, id 26951, offset 0, flags [none], \
        length: 40) 192.168.1.10.2689 > 192.168.1.2.0: SFRP [tcp sum ok] \
            2097818687:2097818687(0) win 512
```

LAND Attack

The LAND attack is a DoS attack against computers running Microsoft Windows. The attack was originally reported to affect Windows 95 and Windows NT back in 1997. Microsoft eventually patched the vulnerability for the operating systems. However, the vulnerability resurfaced in Microsoft's newer operating systems, including Windows XP Service Pack 2 and even Windows Server 2003.

The LAND attack is quite trivial and occurs when the source and destination addresses and ports are set to the recipient host and the SYN flag is set.

hping3 again provides an easy way to re-create this for testing:

```
hping3 -k -S -s 25 -p 25 -a 192.168.1.2 192.168.1.2
```

The capture through TCPDump is shown next. Notice that the source and destination addresses and ports are the same and that the source port is not incrementing and that it's also below the ephemeral ports:

```
13:42:28.079339 IP 192.168.1.2.25 > 192.168.1.2.25: S 764505725:764505725(0) win
➥512
13:42:29.079462 IP 192.168.1.2.25 > 192.168.1.2.25: S 2081780101:2081780101(0) \
      win 512
13:42:30.079461 IP 192.168.1.2.25 > 192.168.1.2.25: S 390202112:390202112(0) win
➥512
```

Recording Traffic with TCPDump

While consulting for a small Internet provider, I noticed that there was a routine and significant spike in network traffic at about 3:00 a.m. every morning, lasting anywhere from 15 minutes to an hour. My goal was to determine the cause of this traffic spike. Because the traffic was routine and at an odd hour, my initial thought was that it was the result of an automatic update process for the servers on the network.

Most of the servers in the network were running Debian Linux and using apt-proxy. This meant that only one local server would contact the off-site Debian update servers and obtain any updates necessary. All the other servers in the local network would then contact that local master server. This setup cut the Internet utilization immensely.

Although the master server could certainly be a contributing factor, I didn't feel that there would be enough update traffic on a nightly basis to warrant such a significant spike in traffic. My assumption was confirmed when I looked at the update schedule on the master server and found that it was actually looking for updates at a different time anyway, and thus it wasn't contributing to the 3:00 a.m. spike at all.

With that cause eliminated, I needed to look at the traffic itself at 3:00 a.m. However, I wasn't really looking forward to staying awake until that hour, and if I was awake, I might not be in shape to read a packet trace. Enter cron. By using cron to fire TCPDump, I could capture the packet trace to a file for later analysis. No great surprise here and I wasn't breaking any new ground, but it seemed like a fair solution to the problem. I configured the switch to copy packets to the port on which the monitoring machine was connected and got to work on the TCPDump portion.

TCPDump offers a couple of features that come in handy for this type of trace. The first feature is the capability to write the output to a file (record, if you will) and then read that file in later (playback). The second helpful feature is the capability to exit after capturing a certain number of packets. Granted, I could have used another means to stop the packet trace, such as another cron job to kill the TCPDump capture, but I thought that using TCPDump's native capability was the quickest and easiest solution.

All the TCPDump commands I've shown so far in this chapter have used expressions such as `port 80` or `host <n>.<n>.<n>.<n>`. Expressions are helpful when you're looking for specific and known traffic. However, expressions aren't of much help when you're unsure of what exactly you're searching for, as was the case here. The best option was to capture everything and then work on a filter during playback.

The two TCPDump options of interest that haven't been covered yet in the chapter are `-w` and `-c`. The `-w` option causes TCPDump to place the raw output into the specified file so that it can later be fed back through TCPDump. The resulting file is in TCPDump's native format and is thus not readable by a plain-text pager such as `cat`, `less`, or `more`. The `-c` option informs TCPDump that it should exit after it captures `<N>` packets. Getting `<N>` correct seemed to be the most difficult part of the capture.

The capture results needed to show me only basic information about the packet, including source and destination, as well as a few bits of the packet. To that end, the TCPDump command was rather easy to craft:

```
/usr/sbin/tcpdump -c 25000 -w dumpfile -n
```

In this command I have TCPDump exiting after capturing 25,000 packets, writing the capture to a file called `dumpfile`, and not performing DNS queries for the source and destination. Getting to this command did require some level of testing to see just how long it took to capture 25,000 packets and what information was included in the capture. After it was tested, I entered the command into cron with this schedule:

```
5 3 * * * /usr/sbin/tcpdump -c 25000 -w dumpfile -n
```

That is, every morning at 3:05 a.m. the capture would take place. Then at a better hour, like 11:00 a.m. when I get out of bed, I'd look to see whether indeed there was traffic the prior evening that required me to look at the `dumpfile`. If there was traffic, I'd log in to the server and run a command to read the `dumpfile`:

```
tcpdump -r dumpfile -X -vv
```

Running this command gave me an idea of what traffic was out there. Intermingled with the normal traffic was an FTP conversation between one of the ISP's larger customers and another host on the Internet. The FTP traffic was easily the most frequent packet I was seeing within the trace. Another night's packet trace confirmed it. I had the ISP contact its customer to find out whether this was known activity and, if so, to let the customer know that it might be going over its bandwidth allocation for the month.

This example is somewhat typical of a security analyst's job. Spot an anomaly, investigate the anomaly while ruling out possibilities, and take action based on the investigation.

Although the ultimate cause of this particular anomaly turned out not to be any type of unauthorized attack, the result of the investigation was a happier customer because that customer could take corrective action before exceeding its bandwidth for the month.

Automated Intrusion Monitoring with Snort

Snort is an excellent intrusion detection software package combining best-in-class technology with open-source configurability. Snort actually has a few different modes of operation, including a sniffer mode, a packet logger mode, an intrusion detection mode, and what is called inline mode. It is the intrusion detection mode that is of interest in this section. However, inline mode is also notable because it provides a way to configure Snort and `iptables` to work together to dynamically accept or drop packets based on Snort rules. For the purposes of this chapter, when referring to Snort I'm referring specifically to the intrusion detection mode.

When in intrusion detection mode, Snort works by using a number of rules that define anomalous traffic. Many of these rules come predefined for you by Sourcefire, the makers of Snort. Many other rules are available from the community, and of course you can also write your own rules as necessary.

In addition to rules, Snort has a number of preprocessors that enable modules to view and alter packets before they are handled by the intrusion detection engine of the software. Preprocessors can be developed to suit your needs, though the preprocessors already available are helpful. The preexisting preprocessors include two types of port scan detectors to help detect and take action when a port scan is detected. There are also preprocessors to reassemble TCP streams to provide stateful analysis and preprocessors to decode RPC traffic and inspect HTTP traffic. Other preprocessors are described in detail in the Snort documentation available with Snort or online at https://www.snort.org/documents.

Snort works by detecting and reporting on events. The actual process of reporting on events can be configured through event handling within Snort. Event handling calls for configuration based on thresholds. This highly configurable aspect of Snort helps to prevent being inundated with log entries and alerts.

Normally you'd want to be notified in some way when certain Snort rules are triggered. Snort uses output modules that can be configured to send the output to various locations. A commonly used output module is the alert_syslog module, which sends alerts to the local syslog facility. Other output modules exist, including alert_fast and alert_full. The former puts a fast entry into the file specified, and the latter sends the entire packet header along with the event message. Other output modules exist, and more information on them can be found within the Snort documentation.

One interesting output module is the database output module. The database module enables Snort alerts to be sent to an SQL database. Using this output module enables you to leverage software which can generate reports on the alerts and events in Snort.

Snort has numerous additional features and nuances that help make it one of the best, if not the best, intrusion detection software available.

Obtaining and Installing Snort

Snort is available with many Linux distributions as an additional package, and most distributions also include the Snort rules, either included with the Snort package or as an add-on package. You can also download Snort from http://www.snort.org/.

Installation of Snort and the default rules should nearly always be done by installing the package available with your distribution. If this isn't possible or if the available package doesn't include the options you'd like, you'll need to compile from source.

The Snort package comes in a gzip archive and therefore needs to be unzipped and unarchived prior to being compiled:

```
tar -zxvf snort-<version>.tar.gz
```

After it's unzipped and unarchived, you can cd into the Snort source directory and run the configure script:

```
cd snort-<version>
./configure
```

It is at the point of running the configure script where many compile-time options can be set. To obtain a list of some of these options, notably options to enable support for certain databases or enable certain other features, type the following:

```
./configure --help
```

In addition, the INSTALL document and other documentation within the <snort-source>/doc directory explain these and other options available when compiling Snort from source.

Running the configure script, along with any options, will result in Snort looking for various prerequisites. For example, when compiling Snort from source, you might receive an error indicating that one or more prerequisites can't be found, such as this error:

```
checking for pcre.h... no
  ERROR! Libpcre header not found, go get it from
  http://www.pcre.org
```

With that error in mind, I was able to install the pcre development files, rerun the configure script, and continue.

After the configure script has run successfully, compile the software by typing this:

```
make
```

The software will now compile. Should you get any errors during this phase, consult the Snort documentation and mailing list archives to see whether you've received a known error for your architecture.

Finally, after the software is compiled, install it by typing the following:

```
make install
```

The software will now be installed and should be ready to use. By default, the software is installed into /usr/local/bin. You can test the basic Snort command by typing this:

```
/usr/local/bin/snort -?
```

You should see output with help options, similar to this:

```
  ,,_    -*> Snort! <*-
 o" )~  Version 2.3.3 (Build 14)
  ''''   By Martin Roesch & The Snort Team: http://www.snort.org/team.html
       (C) Copyright 1998-2004 Sourcefire Inc., et al.

USAGE: ./snort [-options] <filter options>
Options:
    -A     Set alert mode: fast, full, console, or none (alert file alerts only)
          "unsock" enables UNIX socket logging (experimental).
...
<output truncated>
```

Configuring Snort

The source code for Snort includes a sample configuration file. If you've installed from your distribution's package, that too should include a sample Snort configuration file. Usually this file is called snort.conf. On most popular distributions, including Debian, this file (along with a number of Snort rules) is placed in /etc/snort/.

If you're working with a source installation, the sample snort.conf configuration file is located in <snort-source>/etc/ and sample rules are located in <snort-source>/rules/. For those working with a source code version, I recommend creating a directory in either /etc/ or /usr/local/etc/ called snort and placing the snort.conf configuration file and the Snort rules in that directory. In addition, the default Snort configuration file calls various map and extra configuration files as well. These files can also be found in the <snort-source>/etc/ directory. Creating the directory and copying all the files into it would look like this (again, this is applicable only to those who have compiled Snort from source):

```
mkdir /etc/snort
cp <snort-source>/etc/snort.conf /etc/snort/
cp <snort-source>/etc/*.map /etc/snort/
cp <snort-source>/etc/*.config /etc/snort/
cp <snort-source>/rules/*.rules /etc/snort/
```

One additional and important change is done to the snort.conf configuration file. After you've copied it to the /etc/snort directory, edit the file and change the RULE_PATH variable from its default of ../rules to /etc/snort. The line should look like this when you're done:

```
var RULE_PATH /etc/snort
```

Finally, create the Snort log directory with the following command:

```
mkdir /var/log/snort
```

With all the groundwork done, it's time to officially start Snort for the first time. If you've installed from your distribution's package, it's likely that you can start Snort through the normal run control mechanism, such as `/etc/init.d/snort start`. If you've compiled from source, you'll need to start Snort manually and point to the location of its configuration file:

```
/usr/local/bin/snort -c /etc/snort/snort.conf
```

If you receive any errors, chances are that there are missing files. Check the Snort source directory structure for the missing files and copy them to the appropriate location, based on the configuration file.

If all goes well, you should see a message such as this, near the end of the output:

```
--== Initialization Complete ==--
```

As you can see, the shell prompt didn't return. This is because Snort was not told to fork into daemon mode. Press Ctrl+C to kill Snort and add a `-D` to the command line. It should now look like this:

```
/usr/local/bin/snort -c /etc/snort/snort.conf -D
```

Snort will start again and this time fork off into the background, returning you to the shell prompt.

There is, of course, much more to Snort configuration than merely getting it running with the default options and rule sets. For more information on specific Snort configurations, refer to the Snort documentation.

Testing Snort

With Snort now running in the background, you could assume that it's running perfectly fine and that log entries will be placed into `/var/log/snort` for you. However, I'm not one to assume things, especially about computer security. Therefore, to test the Snort installation I'll use the handy `hping3` tool to craft a packet or two and fire them toward the host running Snort.

In this case, I'm just looking for verification that Snort is running and monitoring something. The default rules look for bad packets, so crafting one of those should be trivial with `hping3`. From another host on the network (`192.168.1.10`), I ran the following `hping3` command toward the host running Snort (`192.168.1.2`):

```
hping3 -X 192.168.1.2
```

The `-X` option causes an Xmas scan to be run. Looking in `/var/log/snort` on the host running Snort reveals that the alert file has received some information, and there is also a new directory called `192.168.1.10`, which was the source of the test packets. Inside that directory are files corresponding to the packets I sent, the contents of which are shown here:

```
[**] BAD-TRAFFIC tcp port 0 traffic [**]
06/07-16:19:00.712543 192.168.1.10:1984 -> 192.168.1.2:0
TCP TTL:64 TOS:0x0 ID:48557 IpLen:20 DgmLen:40
*2****** Seq: 0xED1609B Ack: 0x13E893C5 Win: 0x200 TcpLen: 20
=+=+=+=+=+=+=+=+=+=+=+=+=+=+=+=+=+=+=+=+=+=+=+=+=+=+=+=+=+=+=+=+=+
```

```
[**] BAD-TRAFFIC tcp port 0 traffic [**]
06/07-16:19:00.712610 192.168.1.2:0 -> 192.168.1.10:1984
TCP TTL:64 TOS:0x0 ID:10034 IpLen:20 DgmLen:40 DF
***A*R** Seq: 0x0 Ack: 0xED1609B Win: 0x0 TcpLen: 20
=+=+=+=+=+=+=+=+=+=+=+=+=+=+=+=+=+=+=+=+=+=+=+=+=+=+=+=+=+=+=+=+
```

As you can see from the output, Snort has captured what it believes to be (correctly so) bad TCP packets. The alert log file `/var/log/snort/alert` also contains information that is especially useful for sorting the alerts. Here are the log entries from the alert log file that correspond to the previously shown entries from the specific host file:

```
[**] [1:524:8] BAD-TRAFFIC tcp port 0 traffic [**]
[Classification: Misc activity] [Priority: 3]
06/07-16:19:00.712543 192.168.1.10:1984 -> 192.168.1.2:0
TCP TTL:64 TOS:0x0 ID:48557 IpLen:20 DgmLen:40
*2****** Seq: 0xED1609B Ack: 0x13E893C5 Win: 0x200 TcpLen: 20

[**] [1:524:8] BAD-TRAFFIC tcp port 0 traffic [**]
[Classification: Misc activity] [Priority: 3]
06/07-16:19:00.712610 192.168.1.2:0 -> 192.168.1.10:1984
TCP TTL:64 TOS:0x0 ID:10034 IpLen:20 DgmLen:40 DF
***A*R** Seq: 0x0 Ack: 0xED1609B Win: 0x0 TcpLen: 20
```

As you can see from these entries, there are some additional items such as `Classification` and `Priority` that can help to, well, classify and prioritize the alert. Both the classification and the priority can be configured within the alert log file.

Receiving Alerts

I recommend working with Snort to gain experience with rules and configuration options before configuring it to send alerts in email or via another means. You might easily find yourself overwhelmed by alerts with the default Snort rules, depending on your network layout.

Recall from Chapter 11 that log file–monitoring software was introduced and a recipe was given for using Swatch to monitor log files for certain events, at which time it would send an email based on the alert. If you see where I'm going with this, congratulations!

Using Swatch to Monitor for Snort Alerts

With its default configuration, Snort logs to `/var/log/snort/alert`. Therefore, creating a Swatch configuration to monitor this file is quite easy. Again, it would be easy to overwhelm yourself or the system with alerts and emails from Swatch, so you should use caution when configuring any actions based on Snort alerts until you've had a chance to configure Snort further.

Recall that Snort logs some prioritization data within `/var/log/snort/alert`. Therefore, you could set up a Swatch rule to watch for anything with a certain priority, say 3, for example, and send an email when that's seen. This would be placed within your Swatch configuration file which, by default, is `~/.swatchrc`. Here's the configuration entry:

```
watchfor /Priority: 3/
  mail
```

Starting Swatch and pointing it toward the Snort alert file, `/var/log/snort/alert`, looks like this:

```
swatch --tail-file=/var/log/snort/alert
```

Now when an alert with `Priority: 3` is logged, an email will be sent by Swatch.

Final Thoughts on Snort

Snort comes highly recommended as a means to automate the task of intrusion detection. I've only been able to touch on the very basics of Snort here in hopes of giving you a starting point for working with it. From here, you can combine Snort with MySQL and ACID to create an enterprise-class intrusion detection system. Snort can be configured just as you need and extended to fit any size of organization.

Monitoring with ARPWatch

ARPWatch is a daemon that watches for new Ethernet interfaces on a network. If a new ARP entry is seen, it could be indicative of a rogue computer somewhere within the network.

ARPWatch uses the PCap library, which may not (yet) be on your system. If it's not, you'll find out during the configuration process for ARPWatch. The PCap library, commonly known as libpcap, can be downloaded from http://www.tcpdump.org/. The PCap library is used for other network- and security-related programs such as TCPDump. Because TCPDump was already covered, I'll forgo repeating the instructions for installing libpcap in this chapter and instead refer you to the section "TCPDump: A Simple Overview" for those instructions.

Installation of ARPWatch involves untarring the ARPWatch archive that you download, usually something like `tar -zxvf arpwatch.tar.Z`. From there, change the directory into the ARPWatch directory and run the configure script:

```
./configure
```

You'll see a (I hope somewhat) familiar series of output statements, something like this:

```
creating cache ./config.cache
checking host system type... i686-pc-linux-gnu
checking target system type... i686-pc-linux-gnu
checking build system type... i686-pc-linux-gnu
checking for gcc... gcc
checking whether the C compiler (gcc ) works... yes
... (output truncated) ...
```

If you see an error to the effect of the following, you'll need to install libpcap:

```
checking for main in -lpcap... no
configure: error: see the INSTALL doc for more info
```

Refer to the section on TCPDump earlier in this chapter for information on installing the PCap library.

For the rest of you, and if you're joining us again after installing PCap, the next step to compile ARPWatch is to make it. From the command line within the ARPWatch source code directory, type this:

```
make
```

ARPWatch will now compile and you'll see messages indicating the progress, as well as possibly a warning or two:

```
report.o(.text+0x409): the use of 'mktemp' is dangerous, better use 'mkstemp'
gcc -O2 -DDEBUG -DHAVE_FCNTL_H=1 -DHAVE_MEMORY_H=1 -DTIME_WITH_SYS_TIME=1 \
        -DHAVE_BCOPY=1 -DHAVE_STRERROR=1 -DRETSIGTYPE=void -DRETSIGVAL= \
              -DHAVE_SIGSET=1 -DDECLWAITSTATUS=int -DSTDC_HEADERS=1 \
                    -DARPDIR=\"/usr/local/arpwatch\" -DPATH \
                          _SENDMAIL=\"/usr/sbin/sendmail\" -I.\
                                -Ilinux-include -c ./arpsnmp.c
gcc -O2 -DDEBUG -DHAVE_FCNTL_H=1 -DHAVE_MEMORY_H=1 -DTIME_WITH_SYS_TIME=1 \
        -DHAVE_BCOPY=1 -DHAVE_STRERROR=1 -DRETSIGTYPE=void -DRETSIGVAL= \
              -DHAVE_SIGSET=1 -DDECLWAITSTATUS=int -DSTDC_HEADERS=1 \
                  -DARPDIR=\"/usr/local/arpwatch\" \
                          -DPATH_SENDMAIL=\"/usr/sbin/sendmail\" \
                              -I. -Ilinux-include -o arpsnmp \
                                    arpsnmp.o db.o dns.o \
                                          ec.o file.o intoa.o \
        machdep.o util.o report.o setsignal.o version.o
report.o: In function 'report':
report.o(.text+0x409): the use of 'mktemp' is dangerous, better use 'mkstemp'
```

After it's compiled, install ARPWatch with the following command:

```
make install
```

ARPWatch will be installed (by default) into `/usr/local/sbin`. This directory is usually in `root`'s path, but if you type `arpwatch` and receive a `command not found` error, you probably need to preface the command with its directory, like this:

```
/usr/local/bin/arpwatch
```

As ARPWatch runs, it will report to the SYSLOG daemon about new MAC addresses found on the network. This means that ARPWatch will usually output to `/var/log/messages`, so you can run a `grep` command to find out about the new hosts as ARPWatch finds them:

```
grep arpwatch /var/log/messages
```

ARPWatch will also send email to the `root` account on a system detailing the new hosts. The email contains details such as the date, the IP address, and the MAC address:

```
    hostname: client.example.com
  ip address: 192.168.1.10
ethernet address: 0:e1:18:34:2f:e8
ethernet vendor: <unknown>
    timestamp: Saturday, May 22, 2004 11:25:59 -0500
```

In both of these ways, it's possible to know virtually instantly when a new host appears on the network. Such information would be helpful to the security administrator when monitoring for possible unauthorized use of a network.

ARPWatch will run in the background as a daemon, silently (or ideally silently) going about its business and reporting back to you as needed. If, for some reason, ARPWatch shuts off, maybe because the machine rebooted, the existing entries will be written to a file called `arp.dat` (the location of this file varies greatly; if you need to find it, run `find / -name "arp.dat"`). If you need to reset ARPWatch's monitoring database so that it will "pick up" all the hosts on the network again, run these commands from within the directory in which you locate ARPWatch:

```
rm arp.dat
touch arp.dat
```

A tip about using ARPWatch: Make sure that the ARPWatch data file, `arp.dat`, is monitored for unauthorized changes. If an attacker can alter this file and add his or her own entry manually, ARPWatch won't alert you to the presence of the new host. Make sure that the `arp.dat` file is monitored by AIDE (covered in Chapter 14, "Filesystem Integrity") or through other similar means.

Summary

This chapter showed you some of the tools used in intrusion detection. The goal was to provide you with some hands-on experience based on the concepts introduced in previous chapters. You learned about network sniffers in this chapter and focused specifically on TCPDump. Some packets and attack types were viewed through the eyes of TCPDump as well.

Other tools introduced and discussed in this chapter included Snort, which provides an excellent intrusion detection system. Finally, using ARPWatch to monitor for new and unexpected ARP entries on the network was also discussed.

The next chapter looks at filesystem integrity through the eyes of AIDE, a filesystem integrity checker.

14

Filesystem Integrity

Integrity is one of three commonly used principles of computer security; confidentiality and availability are the other two. In the purest sense of the three principles, integrity simply refers to the means by which you ensure that data is authentic and has not been altered or tampered with in any way. One aspect of ensuring data integrity is ensuring the integrity of the system on which the data is housed.

This chapter looks at some very specific means you have at your disposal when running Linux to ensure data integrity. These include examining the files on a Linux system to make sure that they haven't been altered without your knowledge and looking for anomalies that may indicate the presence of an intruder on the system.

Filesystem Integrity Defined

Maintaining system integrity is yet another layer of security meant to give you, the security administrator, a warm, fuzzy feeling. For the purposes of this chapter, the term *filesystem integrity* refers to the verifiable knowledge that the computer system and the objects contained therein are in a known-good state. Although that's a wide definition, filesystem integrity in this chapter will simply entail verification that the files located on the computer have not been tampered with or altered. As such, this chapter concentrates on tools to assist you in checking the files.

Practical Filesystem Integrity

Various tools are available to check the integrity of files on the system. In this chapter, I'll show AIDE, the Advanced Intrusion Detection Environment. AIDE is an open-source filesystem integrity-checking tool.

A basic integrity check of a file usually involves obtaining checksum values of the files on the computer and comparing those checksums against known-good values. Checksums are sometimes also referred to as hash values or signatures. More complex checking is done by tools such as AIDE, as you'll see later in the chapter.

Checksums are frequently used to verify the integrity of a downloaded file. For example, many Linux FTP repositories contain a file called sha1sums. Inside of that sha1sums file are the checksums of the files as they reside on the FTP server. When you download the file, you can then verify the checksum against the downloaded file. If your checksum value matches the checksum on the server, you know you have a good file. If the values don't match, something went wrong with the download and you can save some time rather than trying to work with a corrupt file or wasting a CD-R.

A hands-on example would be helpful. Jump into a console and type the following:

```
sha1sum /etc/passwd
```

You'll see a value such as this:

```
dbf758aecfc31b789336d019f650d404fc280d64 /etc/passwd
```

Note that your value will be substantially different from mine, unless you're running the command against my password file, in which case I have other problems that need attention.

If you add a user, delete a user, or make any change that affects the password file, that `sha1sum` value will change. For example, if you make a change to someone's name within the `passwd` file, the `sha1sum` of the `passwd` file will change because the file's contents are now different. Continuing with the preceding example, you can change the name of the root user by running this (as `root`):

```
chfn root
```

You'll be presented with various options for changing the account information for the user, beginning with the Full Name. Change the Full Name value to whatever you'd like, and continue with changes to other values if you'd like. Now running a `sha1sum` against `/etc/passwd` will show a different checksum for the file:

```
sha1sum /etc/passwd
a22e91a7bb7a21ca6c2b9d4f32e03f4ed3eeec37 /etc/passwd
```

Installing AIDE

AIDE is a filesystem integrity-checking tool offering many of the features you'd expect from such a program. More information on AIDE, including links to download, is available at http://aide.sourceforge.net.

As with other tools featured in the book, AIDE is available as a package for most popular Linux distributions, or it can be downloaded and compiled. However, you will probably also need some prerequisites before attempting to compile AIDE. If this is the case, the configure script for AIDE will inform you of these prerequisites, which you will then need to download and compile (or install from operating system packages) before continuing with AIDE's compilation. Compiling AIDE follows the same pattern as other software compilation, such as this in Linux:

```
tar -zxvf aide-<NNNN>.tar.gz
cd aide-<NNNN>
./configure
make
make install
```

The remainder of this chapter shows usage of compiled AIDE rather than a prepackaged version; specific paths and commands may be slightly different if you run a packaged version. The underlying concepts remain the same.

Configuring AIDE

AIDE, like many other Linux applications, operates using a configuration file. The configuration file is text based and contains information that the program uses to determine the characteristics it will use when it runs. The first time you run AIDE you'll create and initialize the database that will be used for future checks of the filesystem's integrity. That database is then manually checked over for sanity, and you'll run an update process that will be used from then on to look for changes that occur on the filesystem.

Creating an AIDE Configuration File

After AIDE has been installed, the first thing you'll want to do is create a configuration file. The AIDE configuration file is normally called `aide.conf` and is located in `/etc/` or `/etc/aide/` for a packaged version of AIDE. Comments within the AIDE configuration file begin with a pound sign (#). There are three categories of lines within the AIDE configuration file: configuration lines, macro lines, and selection lines. In Debian, the AIDE configuration is located in `/etc/aide` and is split among several directories, including a generic `aide.conf` file as well as a directory containing specific rules and another directory containing settings.

The heart of the AIDE configuration file is the selection lines that you use to determine what objects on the filesystem will be monitored. Configuration lines are also important in determining how AIDE will operate, and macro lines are important for creating advanced configurations. AIDE uses a series of `parameter=value` directives to indicate the type of checking to perform on a given object. Table 14.1 lists some of those directives.

AIDE also enables the administrator to create custom groups containing the default groups. Doing so can save you time and improve the readability of the configuration file. You might use a custom group to combine other groups of commonly used checks. For example, creating a group called `MyGroup` with commonly used types of checks is as simple as this:

```
MyGroup p+i+n+m+md5
```

These groupings, whether default or custom, are used to determine the type of check that will be performed on a given selection. You also configure the files and directories to be checked using a selection line in the configuration file. Selection lines consist of the object to be checked together with the type of check to be performed. The object can be a file, a directory, a regular expression, or more commonly a combination of a file along with some regular expression syntax. I'll take a glance at regular expressions in a later section, but for now I'll show simple examples of the selection process.

Table 14.1 **AIDE Configuration Directives**

Directive	Description
p	Permissions
i	inode
n	Number of links
u	User
g	Group
s	Size
b	Block count
m	mtime
a	atime
c	ctime
ftype	File type
S	Check for growing size
sha1	sha1 checksum
sha256	sha256 checksum
sha512	sha512 checksum
rmd160	rmd160 checksum
tiger	tiger checksum
R	p+i+n+u+g+s+m+c+md5
L	p+i+n+u+g
E	Empty group
>	Growing logfile p+u+g+i+n+S
haval	haval checksum
gost	gost checksum
crc32	crc32 checksum

The following selection line would examine everything in the /etc directory, specifically looking at the number of links, the user who owns a given file, the group who owns
a given file, and the size of the file:

```
/etc n+u+g+s
```

A change to one of those attributes that occurs unexpectedly might indicate tamper-
ing. The next example uses a custom group called MyGroup as the check for the files
within the /bin directory:

```
/bin MyGroup
```

Objects can be ignored or skipped by using an exclamation point (!), as in the following example, which causes AIDE to ignore everything in /var/log:

```
!/var/log/.*
```

Ignoring objects that change frequently can drastically reduce the number of irrelevant lines that appear in the AIDE report. However, you should be careful not to ignore too much; otherwise, you might miss important filesystem changes.

Rule lines in the configuration file use regular expressions to enable powerful matching capabilities. Don't worry if you're not familiar with the black magic involved in regular expressions; I'll go easy on you here.

A primary concern with matching files in AIDE is that you don't leave room for an attacker to circumvent the file integrity checker. This could occur if you specified a file-name without fully qualifying the file. For example, if you wanted to skip checking a file in the `/var/log/` directory because it changes, you might use this (seemingly correct) syntax:

```
!/var/log/maillog
```

However, due to the regular expression matching that occurs, an attacker could create a file called this:

```
/var/log/maillog.crack
```

Because you've excluded `/var/log/maillog` already, AIDE will not check anything that begins with `/var/log/maillog`. To solve this problem you add a dollar sign ($) to the end of the file. In regular expression syntax, a $ indicates the end-of-line. Therefore, by changing the syntax for the file you want to exclude and adding a $, you use the most specific match for that filesystem check:

```
!/var/log/maillog$
```

By default, AIDE will create a file-based database called `aide.db.new`. This file is then moved (manually) for future checks. Therefore, there's not really a need to alter this behavior within the context of the configuration file; however, you certainly can change the path and name of this file using the configuration options:

```
database=file:<filename>
database_out=file:<filename>
```

AIDE can also use an SQL database server such as PostgreSQL to store database contents, although that configuration is beyond the scope of this book.

A Sample AIDE Configuration File

At the very least you need to tell AIDE what parts of the filesystem to check and what rules to use for those checks. You can also add numerous other bits to the configuration to alter how AIDE performs. For the purposes of this section, I'll show a very basic configuration file with the caveat that you should add to it as you see necessary for your Linux installation.

If you've compiled AIDE, open the file `/usr/local/etc/aide.conf`. If the file doesn't exist, create it. Place the following lines within the file:

```
/bin R
/sbin R
/etc R+a
/lib R
/usr/lib R
```

If you're using a packaged version from a distribution such as Debian, the configuration file and several wrapper scripts are already provided, so you can safely skip this step.

Initializing the AIDE Database

With a quick and basic configuration file in hand, it's time to initialize the AIDE database. This process can take a varying length of time depending on how many files you're checking and the amount of resources the computer has available. Initializing the AIDE database is as simple as running the following for the compiled version:

```
/usr/local/bin/aide --init
```

Alternatively, on Debian with a packaged version, you should run

```
aideinit
```

AIDE will now initialize the database based on the criteria you chose in the configuration file. When it's complete, you'll see a message similar to this:

```
AIDE, version 0.15.1

### AIDE database initialized.
```

The next step is to rename (move) the newly created database to `aide.db` so that it becomes the default or master database:

```
mv /usr/local/etc/aide.db.new /usr/local/etc/aide.db
```

Now you should be able to run a check of the database to verify that everything is working okay:

```
/usr/local/bin/aide --check
```

If everything goes well, you'll see output similar to the following:

```
AIDE, version 0.15.1

### All files match AIDE database. Looks okay!
```

With the AIDE database initialized, you should immediately copy the database to a disk, preferably a read-only media such as a CD-R, or you should securely copy it to another computer. If you leave the AIDE database on the computer, attackers may be able to simply alter the AIDE database to cover their tracks after replacing system files with their own! Each time you update the AIDE database from this point forward, you should always copy the resulting database file to secure media.

Scheduling AIDE to Run Automatically

AIDE is best run using a cron job (scheduled task). Therefore, you should schedule AIDE to run automatically without your intervention. AIDE is commonly run once per day, but you should schedule it to run according to your security policy. The easiest and quickest method to have AIDE run daily is to create a `crontab` entry.

Creating a `crontab` entry is a matter of running this (as `root`):

```
crontab -e
```

To run AIDE nightly at 2:00 a.m., enter the following line into `crontab`:

```
0 2 * * * /usr/local/bin/aide --check
```

For more information on the format of `crontab` entries, see your distribution's documentation.

Monitoring AIDE for Bad Things

Okay, so you have this shiny new filesystem integrity-checking tool all set up and running. But now what? Now you sit and wait for something to happen. Usually nothing does, and even when it appears that something bad might have happened, many times it hasn't.

AIDE will continue to monitor the filesystem according to the rules you configured. Thanks to the cron job, you'll receive reports nightly containing the files and the attributes for those files that have changed since the database was initialized or last updated. Many times these changes will be completely benign. Recall the example from the beginning of the chapter. If you add a user, files such as `/etc/passwd` and `/etc/shadow` will change. AIDE will notice and report accordingly, assuming that you're checking `/etc`. However, if you didn't add a user or make other changes to `/etc/passwd` or `/etc/shadow`, you might examine more closely to make sure that an attacker hasn't altered either one of those important files.

Of course, there are other files that AIDE will be reporting on. You should closely monitor the AIDE report for files that were altered unexpectedly. For example, the files `/bin/su` or `/usr/bin/passwd` should rarely be altered and then only by certain known software updates. Therefore, if a file such as `/bin/su` shows up in an AIDE report, you need to look into it immediately to see when and why that file changed. Taking this example one step further, assume for a moment that AIDE ran overnight through its normal process. In the morning you awake to find an email containing some of the following lines:

```
AIDE 0.15.1 found differences between database and filesystem!!
Start timestamp: 2014-07-31 23:50:17

Summary:
  Total number of files:    16112
  Added files:              0
  Removed files:            0
  Changed files:            1
```

```
---------------------------------------------------
Changed files:
---------------------------------------------------

changed: /etc/adjtime


---------------------------------------------------
Detailed information about changes:
---------------------------------------------------

File: /etc/adjtime
 Atime    : 2014-07-11 05:43:38               , 2014-07-31 23:36:06
```

The AIDE check that you scheduled found something. You can quickly tell from the summary lines what has been found:

```
Summary:
  Total number of files:      16112
  Added files:                0
  Removed files:              0
  Changed files:              1
```

Next you'll see a slightly more detailed summary of the files that have been added, changed, or removed since the database was initialized or last updated. In this case, there's only one file that's been changed:

```
File: /etc/adjtime
 Atime    : 2014-07-11 05:43:38                 , 2014-07-31 23:36:06
```

Based on this report, it's easy to see that something changed with /etc/adjtime.

Cleaning Up the AIDE Database

Over time, you'll notice that AIDE check reports become longer and longer. This is usually the result of normal activity on the server, such as adding and deleting users, updating software, and changing settings in configuration files. You should regularly update the AIDE database not only to shorten reports but also to better track when unexpected changes occur. If you don't regularly update the AIDE database, you might miss a change that resulted from an attack.

You may be asking, "How often should I update the AIDE database?" The answer depends largely on your needs and your security policy. When you first start to use AIDE, I expect that you should be updating the database at least for the first few runs (again, depending on your security policy) and, more important, refining the configuration file. You'll find that certain files change so often that you need to either exclude them entirely or change the types of checks that occur on those files.

It is much better to change the types of checks than to simply skip the files altogether. Some file attributes that AIDE can check will not change often or at all for the same file. Attributes such as inode and ctime shouldn't change. Therefore, if you notice that certain files keep showing up in the AIDE report and you've ruled out nefarious activity, you should change the type of check that occurs on that file within the AIDE configuration file.

A file that regularly changes on some systems is the Samba password file, /etc/samba/ smbpasswd. On such systems, the file regularly shows up in the report where everything in the /etc/ directory is examined using the R check (refer to Table 14.2). A more appropriate check type for this file might include things that don't change often such as inode and ctime. Such a check would appear like this in the AIDE configuration file:

```
/etc/samba/smbpasswd$ c+i
```

Note the use of the $ at the end of the filename in the example to indicate the end-of-line.

As the AIDE report runs, you'll be able to use more granularity to refine the files that are checked and the checks themselves. After you update the AIDE configuration file, you'll need to update the database so that the changes take effect. This process is accomplished by running this command:

```
/usr/local/bin/aide --update
```

After the update is complete, you'll have a new database file, /usr/local/etc/aide .db.new, by default. This file should be moved to overwrite the existing database:

```
mv /usr/local/etc/aide.db.new /usr/local/etc/aide.db
```

Now running aide --check will give a clean result:

```
AIDE, version 0.15.1

### All files match AIDE database. Looks okay!
```

After you update the database, you should copy the file to secure media or to another computer to ensure the integrity of the database.

With the AIDE configuration file and database updated and AIDE scheduled to run nightly, you now have an infrastructure in place to verify the integrity of your filesystem. From here you can read on to find out about more advanced configurations for AIDE, or you can go to Chapter 12 to find out about the rootkit-checking tool called Chkrootkit.

Changing the Output of the AIDE Report

You might want a little more flexibility in the location of the AIDE report. For example, you may not want to receive emails if everything is okay with the AIDE report, or you may want to have AIDE report into a file instead of providing standard output. AIDE has four basic options for configuring output that can be configured through the AIDE configuration file.

Linux Output Streams

Linux has three generic streams of output that are created when a program runs. These streams are referred to as `STDIN`, `STDOUT`, and `STDERR`, which are abbreviations for Standard Input, Standard Output, and Standard Error, respectively. When you see a referral to `STDOUT`, it refers to the normal method of output to the screen, and `STDERR` indicates output as a result of an error condition. As you might expect, `STDIN` refers to the method of input when read from the input file descriptor.

The general AIDE configuration option called `report_url` configures how output is displayed. By default, output is displayed to `STDOUT`. Output can be displayed to any or all of the following:

- `STDOUT` (default)
- `STDERR`
- Text file
- File descriptor

Of these four possibilities, `STDOUT`, `STDERR`, and text file are of interest. Future versions of AIDE may include output configurations for automated email and automated output to the syslog facility.

Of particular interest is the text file type of output for AIDE. This output type is specified using this configuration line:

```
report_url=file:/<path>/<filename>
```

For example, to configure AIDE reports to go to a file called `aidereport.txt` in the `/var/log/aide` directory that you create, you would use this configuration option in the AIDE configuration file:

```
report_url=file:/var/log/aide/aidereport.txt
```

However, the `report_url` configuration option is only one means for getting output into a file. Because you're running the AIDE report from cron, you could also simply redirect the output to a file. For example, recall the `crontab` entry shown earlier in the chapter:

```
0 2 * * * /usr/local/bin/aide --check
```

You could alter that cron entry to redirect the output to a file. Doing so would cause all output to go to that file and would also enable additional features such as date-based naming. This can be done with a little shell trick using runquotes (sometimes called a backtick, usually found with the tilde [~] on the keyboard). Here's the new cron entry:

```
0 2 * * * /usr/local/bin/aide --check >/var/log/aide/aidereport-'date +%m%d%Y'
➥.txt
```

Now the AIDE report will run and redirect STDOUT to a file called

`/var/log/aide/aidereport-<date>.txt`

For example, for a report run on March 12, 2014, the file would be called

`/var/log/aide/aidereport-03122014.txt`

With a redirected configuration such as the one shown, you will no longer receive emails when AIDE runs through its normal cron job. Rather, you will receive emails only when an error occurs with the AIDE cron job. Because you'll no longer be receiving the emails, you may be tempted to ignore your monitoring duties and just let all the AIDE reports pile up. However, you should still monitor the AIDE reports by looking at them for anomalies and cleaning them up as appropriate.

Obtaining More Verbose Output

AIDE reports can be configured with additional verbosity. Adding verbosity to AIDE is valuable when you're troubleshooting rule matching. For example, when you set the verbose configuration option, you'll be able to see how AIDE builds the list of files to check. If you're seeing unexpected results or if files are being included or excluded for mysterious reasons, adding this option to the configuration or adding it as a command-line option will help.

The configuration option to add verbosity is as follows:

`verbose=<N>`

In this case, `<N>` is a positive integer with a maximum value of 255. In practice, only numbers above 200 give additional debugging output for most of the checks. Therefore, to add the maximum verbosity level, you would use this configuration setting:

`verbose=255`

With this configuration set, you'll see much additional output during an AIDE run:

```
Handling / with s "/bin" with node "/"
Handling / with s "/sbin" with node "/"
Handling / with s "/etc" with node "/"
Handling / with s "/lib" with node "/"
Handling /usr with s "/usr/lib" with node "/usr"
tree: "/"
2        ^/bin
3        ^/sbin
4        ^/etc
5        ^/lib
tree: "/usr"
6        ^/usr/lib

AIDE, version 0.15.1

### All files match AIDE database. Looks okay!
```

The output is much more verbose (as you would expect) and includes the functions being called within the AIDE program itself, as well as details on the files that AIDE is checking as it is checking them. Using this output can be invaluable when you're trying to troubleshoot a problem with your AIDE configuration.

Defining Macros in AIDE

Macros are used in AIDE to define commonly used objects and objects to be used as variables throughout an AIDE configuration file. You might use an AIDE macro to define the top-level directory to be used within the configuration. You would then use this macro within selection lines, and it would be substituted like a variable in that selection line. You also might use a macro to set a variable based on certain criteria. Macros can then be used within the AIDE configuration within control structures (decisional blocks of code) to alter the configuration of AIDE based on the outcome of the control structure.

Macros are defined using the following syntax:

```
@@define <macro> <definition>
```

Macros can also be undefined with this syntax:

```
@@undef <macro>
```

Macros are used within the configuration with the following syntax:

```
@@{<macro>}
```

An example of using a macro in a simple way is to create a macro for a complex directory hierarchy so that you don't have to type it into the configuration file multiple times. Assume that you have a certain structure of directories on the computer that you want to define using a macro:

```
@@define BASEDIR /usr/src/linux
```

This macro could then be used later within the configuration of selections for AIDE:

```
@@{BASEDIR}/.config R
!@@{BASEDIR}/doc
```

A more powerful use of macros involves changing the configuration based on some criteria. For example, macros can be used within two types of control structures, one based on whether the macro has been defined and the other based on the host from which the AIDE program is being run.

These control structures are basically `if/then/else` statements, and they have associated negations as well. The syntax for determining whether a macro has been defined is this:

```
@@ifdef <macro>
```

The negation for the `@@ifdef` evaluation is as shown here:

```
@@ifndef <macro>
```

For determining the current host, this is the syntax:

```
@@ifhost <hostname>
```

The negation for the `@@ifhost` evaluation is, as you might guess, the following:

```
@@ifnhost <hostname>
```

Regardless of which control structure is used, it must be closed using this statement:

```
@@endif
```

Multiple control structures can be grouped using an `else` type of structure that you would expect for an associated `if` statement. The syntax is simply as follows:

```
@@else
```

Here's an example of how each of these might be used. The first example checks to see whether the macro called SOURCE has been defined and, if not, defines it:

```
@@ifndef SOURCE
@@define SOURCE /usr/src
@@endif
```

The second example looks at the hostname of the computer from which AIDE is being run and sets a macro based on the results of that check. This might be helpful if you have directory structures that differ among various hosts and you'd like to use only one common AIDE configuration file among them. Here's the second example:

```
@@ifhost cwa
@@define LOCALBINDIR /usr/local/sbin
@@endif
```

Finally, here is an example using an `else` statement:

```
@@ifhost cwa
@@define LOCALBINDIR /usr/local/sbin
@@else@@define LOCALBINDIR /usr/local/bin
@@endif
```

For all the examples, recall that you'd use these macros later within the configuration using the following syntax:

```
@@{<macro>}
```

The Types of AIDE Checks

You may be wondering about the different types of checks AIDE can perform. Some of the checks are described again in Table 14.2. Note that this isn't an exhaustive list and new options will likely be added over time.

It's probably helpful to break down the types of AIDE checks into categories. There are three basic categories of AIDE checks: what I will term standard checks, grouped checks, and checksums. The standard type of AIDE check looks for information that can be gathered from the file or the file's descriptor. These checks are listed in Table 14.3.

Table 14.2 **AIDE Check Types**

Directive	Description
p	Permissions
ftype	File type
i	inode
n	Number of links
l	Link name
u	User
g	Group
s	Size
b	Block count
m	mtime
a	atime
c	ctime
S	Check for growing size
md5	md5 checksum
sha1	sha1 checksum
sha256	sha256 checksum
sha512	sha512 checksum
rmd160	rmd160 checksum
tiger	tiger checksum
R	p+i+n+u+g+s+m+c+md5
L	p+i+n+u+g
E	Empty group
>	Growing logfile p+u+g+i+n+S
haval	haval checksum
gost	gost checksum
crc32	crc32 checksum

These standard checks all utilize filesystem functions that are built in or native in Linux and can be found from the inode entry for the file. As such, running a given standard check is less resource intensive than a checksum check. Some of these checks lend themselves to certain files, whereas others will cause the file to show up in a report nearly every time the check is run. For example, the ctime of a given file should not change unless the file is deleted or replaced with another.

It may not be readily apparent what some of the standard checks actually do. Table 14.4 describes what may be the more obscure checks within this group.

On the other hand, grouped checks combine some of the more commonly used standard checks, as described in Table 14.5.

Table 14.3 **Standard Checks in AIDE**

Directive	Description
p	Permissions
i	inode
n	Number of links
u	User
g	Group
s	Size
b	Block count
m	mtime
a	atime
c	ctime
S	Check for growing size

Table 14.4 **Explanation of Some Standard Checks**

Check Name	Explanation
inode	The inode is a data structure that holds information about a given file in Linux. The inode contains information such as the location of the file, the permissions, the owner and group information, and many other useful bits.
Number of links	Links are akin to shortcuts in the Windows world. This type of check looks to see how many links exist to the given file.
mtime	The mtime of a file is the time when the file was last modified.
atime	The atime of a file is the time when the file was last accessed.
ctime	The ctime of a file is the time when the file was created.

Table 14.5 **Grouped Checks in AIDE**

Directive	Definition
R	p+ftype+i+l+n+u+g+s+m+c+md5
L	p+ftype+i+l+n+u+g
E	Empty group
>	Growing logfile p+u+g+i+n+S

Table 14.6 **Checksum Checks in AIDE**

Directive	Definition
md5	md5 checksum
sha1	sha1 checksum
sha256	sha256 checksum
sha512	sha512 checksum
rmd160	rmd160 checksum
tiger	tiger checksum
haval	haval checksum
gost	gost checksum
crc32	crc32 checksum

Finally, checksums utilize cryptographic checksums of the files, as explained earlier in the chapter and defined in Table 14.6.

The differences in the various checksum check types can be explained simply as the differences in the cryptographic algorithms used to create the checksums. I'll leave it up to you to do further research on the types of cryptographic algorithms used by AIDE. I recommend *Applied Cryptography*, by Bruce Schneier, as a great reference for this purpose.

Summary

This chapter looked at filesystem integrity and how it can help your system security by ensuring that files haven't been unexpectedly altered. The chapter began with a look at how checksums are used to check files. The chapter continued with an in-depth look at one filesystem integrity software package, AIDE. You saw how to install, configure, and use AIDE on your system.

IV

Appendices

A

Security Resources

This appendix lists some common sources of security-related notices, information, tools, updates, and patches currently on the Internet. Many more sites exist, and new sites pop up every day—consider this list a starting point, not a complete list. The appendix also serves as a general reference section for this book.

Security Information Sources

Security information of all kinds—notices and alerts, whitepapers, tutorials, and so on—can be found in the following sources:

BugTraq:
http://www.securityfocus.com/archive/1

CERT Coordination Center:
https://www.us-cert.gov

Internet Engineering Task Force (IETF):
http://www.ietf.org/

Packet Storm:
http://packetstormsecurity.org/

RFC Editor:
http://www.rfc-editor.org/

SANS Institute:
http://www.sans.org/

Security Focus:
http://www.securityfocus.com/

Reference Papers and FAQs

Some useful reference papers, some of which were cited within the book, can be found on these sites:

"Help Defeat Denial of Service Attacks: Step-by-Step":
http://www.sans.org/dosstep/

"Internet Firewalls: Frequently Asked Questions":
http://www.interhack.net/pubs/fwfaq/

"Service Name and Transport Protocol Port Number Registry" (IANA):
http://www.iana.org/assignments/port-numbers

Firewall Examples and Support Scripts

A firewall for a standalone system is described in Chapter 5, "Building and Installing a Standalone Firewall." The standalone example is optimized in Chapter 6, "Firewall Optimization." The same example is extended in Chapter 7, "Packet Forwarding," to function as either a gateway or a choke firewall, with a full set of firewall rules applied to both the external public interface and the internal local network interface. The gateway serves as the link between the Internet and a DMZ network containing public servers. The choke serves as the link between a private LAN and the DMZ.

The sample firewalls are presented piecemeal in Chapters 5, 6, and 7. This appendix presents the same firewall examples as they would appear in a firewall script.

`iptables` Firewall for a Standalone System from Chapter 5

Chapter 5 covers the application protocols and firewall rules for the types of services most likely to be used on an individual, standalone Linux box. Additionally, both client and server rules are presented for services that not everyone will use. This section first presents the `iptables` script and then the `nftables` script.

The complete `iptables` firewall script, as it would appear in `/etc/rc.d/rc.firewall` or `/etc/init.d/firewall`, follows:

```
#!/bin/sh

/sbin/modprobe ip_conntrack_ftp

CONNECTION_TRACKING="1"
ACCEPT_AUTH="0"
SSH_SERVER="0"
FTP_SERVER="0"
WEB_SERVER="0"
SSL_SERVER="0"
DHCP_CLIENT="1"
```

```
IPT="/sbin/iptables"                      # Location of iptables on your system
INTERNET="eth0"                           # Internet-connected interface
LOOPBACK_INTERFACE="lo"                   # However your system names it
IPADDR="my.ip.address"                    # Your IP address
SUBNET_BASE="my.subnet.base"              # ISP network segment base address
SUBNET_BROADCAST="my.subnet.bcast"        # Network segment broadcast address
MY_ISP="my.isp.address.range"             # ISP server & NOC address range

NAMESERVER="isp.name.server.1"            # Address of a remote name server
POP_SERVER="isp.pop.server"               # Address of a remote pop server
MAIL_SERVER="isp.mail.server"             # Address of a remote mail gateway
NEWS_SERVER="isp.news.server"             # Address of a remote news server
TIME_SERVER="some.time.server"            # Address of a remote time server
DHCP_SERVER="isp.dhcp.server"             # Address of your ISP dhcp server

LOOPBACK="127.0.0.0/8"                     # Reserved loopback address range
CLASS_A="10.0.0.0/8"                       # Class A private networks
CLASS_B="172.16.0.0/12"                    # Class B private networks
CLASS_C="192.168.0.0/16"                   # Class C private networks
CLASS_D_MULTICAST="224.0.0.0/4"            # Class D multicast addresses
CLASS_E_RESERVED_NET="240.0.0.0/5"         # Class E reserved addresses
BROADCAST_SRC="0.0.0.0"                    # Broadcast source address
BROADCAST_DEST="255.255.255.255"           # Broadcast destination address

PRIVPORTS="0:1023"                         # Well-known, privileged port range
UNPRIVPORTS="1024:65535"                   # Unprivileged port range

SSH_PORTS="1024:65535"

###############################################################

# Enable broadcast echo Protection
echo 1 > /proc/sys/net/ipv4/icmp_echo_ignore_broadcasts

# Disable Source Routed Packets
for f in /proc/sys/net/ipv4/conf/*/accept_source_route; do
    echo 0 > $f
done

# Enable TCP SYN Cookie Protection
echo 1 > /proc/sys/net/ipv4/tcp_syncookies

# Disable ICMP Redirect Acceptance
for f in /proc/sys/net/ipv4/conf/*/accept_redirects; do
    echo 0 > $f
done

# Don't send Redirect Messages
for f in /proc/sys/net/ipv4/conf/*/send_redirects; do
    echo 0 > $f
done

# Drop Spoofed Packets coming in on an interface, which, if replied to,
# would result in the reply going out a different interface.
for f in /proc/sys/net/ipv4/conf/*/rp_filter; do
    echo 1 > $f
done
```

```
# Log packets with impossible addresses.
for f in /proc/sys/net/ipv4/conf/*/log_martians; do
    echo 1 > $f
done

##################################################################

# Remove any existing rules from all chains
$IPT --flush
$IPT -t nat --flush
$IPT -t mangle --flush
$IPT -X
$IPT -t nat -X
$IPT -t mangle -X
$IPT --policy INPUT    ACCEPT
$IPT --policy OUTPUT   ACCEPT
$IPT --policy FORWARD ACCEPT
$IPT -t nat --policy PREROUTING   ACCEPT
$IPT -t nat --policy OUTPUT ACCEPT
$IPT -t nat --policy POSTROUTING ACCEPT
$IPT -t mangle --policy PREROUTING ACCEPT
$IPT -t mangle --policy OUTPUT ACCEPT
if [ "$1" = "stop" ]
then
echo "Firewall completely stopped!  WARNING: THIS HOST HAS NO FIREWALL RUNNING."
exit 0
fi
# Unlimited traffic on the loopback interface
$IPT -A INPUT  -i lo -j ACCEPT
$IPT -A OUTPUT -o lo -j ACCEPT

# Set the default policy to drop
$IPT --policy INPUT    DROP
$IPT --policy OUTPUT   DROP
$IPT --policy FORWARD DROP

##################################################################
# Stealth Scans and TCP State Flags
# All of the bits are cleared
$IPT -A INPUT -p tcp --tcp-flags ALL NONE -j DROP
# SYN and FIN are both set
$IPT -A INPUT -p tcp --tcp-flags SYN,FIN SYN,FIN -j DROP
# SYN and RST are both set
$IPT -A INPUT -p tcp --tcp-flags SYN,RST SYN,RST -j DROP
# FIN and RST are both set
$IPT -A INPUT -p tcp --tcp-flags FIN,RST FIN,RST -j DROP
# FIN is the only bit set, without the expected accompanying ACK
$IPT -A INPUT -p tcp --tcp-flags ACK,FIN FIN -j DROP
# PSH is the only bit set, without the expected accompanying ACK
$IPT -A INPUT -p tcp --tcp-flags ACK,PSH PSH -j DROP
# URG is the only bit set, without the expected accompanying ACK
$IPT -A INPUT -p tcp --tcp-flags ACK,URG URG -j DROP

##################################################################
# Using Connection State to Bypass Rule Checking
```

```
if [ "$CONNECTION_TRACKING" = "1" ]; then
    $IPT -A INPUT   -m state --state ESTABLISHED,RELATED -j ACCEPT
    $IPT -A OUTPUT -m state --state ESTABLISHED,RELATED -j ACCEPT

    $IPT -A INPUT -m state --state INVALID -j LOG \
            --log-prefix "INVALID input: "
    $IPT -A INPUT -m state --state INVALID -j DROP

    $IPT -A OUTPUT -m state --state INVALID -j LOG \
            --log-prefix "INVALID output: "
    $IPT -A OUTPUT -m state --state INVALID -j DROP
fi

##############################################################
# Source Address Spoofing and Other Bad Addresses

# Refuse spoofed packets pretending to be from
# the external interface's IP address
$IPT -A INPUT   -i $INTERNET -s $IPADDR -j DROP

# Refuse packets claiming to be from a Class A private network
$IPT -A INPUT   -i $INTERNET -s $CLASS_A -j DROP

# Refuse packets claiming to be from a Class B private network
$IPT -A INPUT   -i $INTERNET -s $CLASS_B -j DROP

# Refuse packets claiming to be from a Class C private network
$IPT -A INPUT   -i $INTERNET -s $CLASS_C -j DROP
# Refuse packets claiming to be from the loopback interface
$IPT -A INPUT   -i $INTERNET -s $LOOPBACK -j DROP

# Refuse malformed broadcast packets
$IPT -A INPUT   -i $INTERNET -s $BROADCAST_DEST -j LOG
$IPT -A INPUT   -i $INTERNET -s $BROADCAST_DEST -j DROP

$IPT -A INPUT   -i $INTERNET -d $BROADCAST_SRC  -j LOG
$IPT -A INPUT   -i $INTERNET -d $BROADCAST_SRC  -j DROP

if [ "$DHCP_CLIENT" = "0" ]; then
    # Refuse directed broadcasts
    # Used to map networks and in Denial of Service attacks
    $IPT -A INPUT -i $INTERNET -d $SUBNET_BASE -j DROP
    $IPT -A INPUT -i $INTERNET -d $SUBNET_BROADCAST -j DROP

    # Refuse limited broadcasts
    $IPT -A INPUT -i $INTERNET -d $BROADCAST_DEST -j DROP
fi

# Refuse Class D multicast addresses
# illegal as a source address
$IPT -A INPUT -i $INTERNET -s $CLASS_D_MULTICAST -j DROP

$IPT -A INPUT -i $INTERNET ! -p UDP -d $CLASS_D_MULTICAST -j DROP

$IPT -A INPUT   -i $INTERNET -p udp -d $CLASS_D_MULTICAST -j ACCEPT
```

```
# Refuse Class E reserved IP addresses
$IPT -A INPUT  -i $INTERNET -s $CLASS_E_RESERVED_NET -j DROP

if [ "$DHCP_CLIENT" = "1" ]; then
    $IPT -A INPUT  -i $INTERNET -p udp \
            -s $BROADCAST_SRC --sport 67 \
            -d $BROADCAST_DEST --dport 68 -j ACCEPT
fi

# refuse addresses defined as reserved by the IANA
# 0.*.*.*          - Can't be blocked unilaterally with DHCP
# 169.254.0.0/16   - Link Local Networks
# 192.0.2.0/24     - TEST-NET

$IPT -A INPUT -i $INTERNET -s 0.0.0.0/8 -j DROP
$IPT -A INPUT -i $INTERNET -s 169.254.0.0/16 -j DROP
$IPT -A INPUT -i $INTERNET -s 192.0.2.0/24 -j DROP

###############################################################
# DNS Name Server

# DNS Forwarding Name Server or client requests

if [ "$CONNECTION_TRACKING" = "1" ]; then
    $IPT -A OUTPUT -o $INTERNET -p udp \
            -s $IPADDR --sport $UNPRIVPORTS \
            -d $NAMESERVER --dport 53 \
            -m state --state NEW -j ACCEPT
fi

$IPT -A OUTPUT -o $INTERNET -p udp \
        -s $IPADDR --sport $UNPRIVPORTS \
        -d $NAMESERVER --dport 53 -j ACCEPT

$IPT -A INPUT  -i $INTERNET -p udp \
        -s $NAMESERVER --sport 53 \
        -d $IPADDR --dport $UNPRIVPORTS -j ACCEPT

#..........................................................
# TCP is used for large responses

if [ "$CONNECTION_TRACKING" = "1" ]; then
    $IPT -A OUTPUT -o $INTERNET -p tcp \
            -s $IPADDR --sport $UNPRIVPORTS \
            -d $NAMESERVER --dport 53 \
            -m state --state NEW -j ACCEPT
fi

$IPT -A OUTPUT -o $INTERNET -p tcp \
        -s $IPADDR --sport $UNPRIVPORTS \
        -d $NAMESERVER --dport 53 -j ACCEPT

$IPT -A INPUT -i $INTERNET -p tcp ! --syn \
        -s $NAMESERVER --sport 53 \
        -d $IPADDR --dport $UNPRIVPORTS -j ACCEPT
```

```
#...............................................................
# DNS Caching Name Server (local server to primary server)

if [ "$CONNECTION_TRACKING" = "1" ]; then
    $IPT -A OUTPUT -o $INTERNET -p udp \
            -s $IPADDR --sport 53 \
            -d $NAMESERVER --dport 53 \
            -m state --state NEW -j ACCEPT
fi

$IPT -A OUTPUT -o $INTERNET -p udp \
        -s $IPADDR --sport 53 \
        -d $NAMESERVER --dport 53 -j ACCEPT

$IPT -A INPUT  -i $INTERNET -p udp \
        -s $NAMESERVER --sport 53 \
        -d $IPADDR --dport 53 -j ACCEPT

#...............................................................
# Incoming Remote Client Requests to Local Servers


if [ "$ACCEPT_AUTH" = "1" ]; then
    if [ "$CONNECTION_TRACKING" = "1" ]; then
    $IPT -A INPUT  -i $INTERNET -p tcp \
            --sport $UNPRIVPORTS \
            -d $IPADDR --dport 113 \
            -m state --state NEW -j ACCEPT
    fi

$IPT -A INPUT  -i $INTERNET -p tcp \
        --sport $UNPRIVPORTS \
        -d $IPADDR --dport 113 -j ACCEPT

$IPT -A OUTPUT -o $INTERNET -p tcp ! --syn \
        -s $IPADDR --sport 113 \
        --dport $UNPRIVPORTS -j ACCEPT
else
$IPT -A INPUT -i $INTERNET -p tcp \
        --sport $UNPRIVPORTS \
        -d $IPADDR --dport 113 -j REJECT --reject-with tcp-reset
fi

################################################################
# Sending Mail to Any External Mail Server
# Use "-d $MAIL_SERVER" if an ISP mail gateway is used instead

if [ "$CONNECTION_TRACKING" = "1" ]; then
    $IPT -A OUTPUT -o $INTERNET -p tcp \
            -s $IPADDR --sport $UNPRIVPORTS \
            --dport 25 -m state --state NEW -j ACCEPT
fi

$IPT -A OUTPUT -o $INTERNET -p tcp \
        -s $IPADDR --sport $UNPRIVPORTS \
        --dport 25 -j ACCEPT
```

```
$IPT -A INPUT -i $INTERNET -p tcp ! --syn \
        --sport 25 \
        -d $IPADDR --dport $UNPRIVPORTS -j ACCEPT

###############################################################
# Retrieving Mail as a POP Client (TCP Port 110)

if [ "$CONNECTION_TRACKING" = "1" ]; then
    $IPT -A OUTPUT -o $INTERNET -p tcp \
            -s $IPADDR --sport $UNPRIVPORTS \
            -d $POP_SERVER --dport 110 -m state --state NEW -j ACCEPT
fi

$IPT -A OUTPUT -o $INTERNET -p tcp \
        -s $IPADDR --sport $UNPRIVPORTS \
        -d $POP_SERVER --dport 110 -j ACCEPT

$IPT -A INPUT -i $INTERNET -p tcp ! --syn \
        -s $POP_SERVER --sport 110 \
        -d $IPADDR --dport $UNPRIVPORTS -j ACCEPT

###############################################################
# ssh (TCP Port 22)

# Outgoing Local Client Requests to Remote Servers

if [ "$CONNECTION_TRACKING" = "1" ]; then
    $IPT -A OUTPUT -o $INTERNET -p tcp \
            -s $IPADDR --sport $SSH_PORTS \
            --dport 22 -m state --state NEW -j ACCEPT
fi

$IPT -A OUTPUT -o $INTERNET -p tcp \
        -s $IPADDR --sport $SSH_PORTS \
        --dport 22 -j ACCEPT

$IPT -A INPUT -i $INTERNET -p tcp ! --syn \
        --sport 22 \
        -d $IPADDR --dport $SSH_PORTS -j ACCEPT

#.............................................................
# Incoming Remote Client Requests to Local Servers

if [ "$SSH_SERVER" = "1" ]; then
    if [ "$CONNECTION_TRACKING" = "1" ]; then
    $IPT -A INPUT   -i $INTERNET -p tcp \
            --sport $SSH_PORTS \
            -d $IPADDR --dport 22 \
            -m state --state NEW -j ACCEPT
    fi

$IPT -A INPUT   -i $INTERNET -p tcp \
        --sport $SSH_PORTS \
        -d $IPADDR --dport 22 -j ACCEPT
```

```
$IPT -A OUTPUT -o $INTERNET -p tcp ! --syn \
        -s $IPADDR --sport 22 \
        --dport $SSH_PORTS -j ACCEPT
fi

##################################################################
# ftp (TCP Ports 21, 20)

# Outgoing Local Client Requests to Remote Servers

# Outgoing Control Connection to Port 21
if [ "$CONNECTION_TRACKING" = "1" ]; then
    $IPT -A OUTPUT -o $INTERNET -p tcp \
            -s $IPADDR --sport $UNPRIVPORTS \
            --dport 21 -m state --state NEW -j ACCEPT
fi

$IPT -A OUTPUT -o $INTERNET -p tcp \
        -s $IPADDR --sport $UNPRIVPORTS \
        --dport 21 -j ACCEPT

$IPT -A INPUT -i $INTERNET -p tcp ! --syn \
        --sport 21 \
        -d $IPADDR --dport $UNPRIVPORTS -j ACCEPT

# Incoming Port Mode Data Channel Connection from Port 20
if [ "$CONNECTION_TRACKING" = "1" ]; then
    # This rule is not necessary if the ip_conntrack_ftp
    # module is used.
    $IPT -A INPUT  -i $INTERNET -p tcp \
            --sport 20 \
            -d $IPADDR --dport $UNPRIVPORTS \
            -m state --state NEW -j ACCEPT
fi

$IPT -A INPUT  -i $INTERNET -p tcp \
        --sport 20 \
        -d $IPADDR --dport $UNPRIVPORTS -j ACCEPT

$IPT -A OUTPUT -o $INTERNET -p tcp ! --syn \
        -s $IPADDR --sport $UNPRIVPORTS \
        --dport 20 -j ACCEPT

# Outgoing Passive Mode Data Channel Connection Between Unprivileged Ports
if [ "$CONNECTION_TRACKING" = "1" ]; then
    # This rule is not necessary if the ip_conntrack_ftp
    # module is used.
    $IPT -A OUTPUT -o $INTERNET -p tcp \
            -s $IPADDR --sport $UNPRIVPORTS \
            --dport $UNPRIVPORTS -m state --state NEW -j ACCEPT
fi

    $IPT -A OUTPUT -o $INTERNET -p tcp \
            -s $IPADDR --sport $UNPRIVPORTS \
            --dport $UNPRIVPORTS -j ACCEPT
```

```
    $IPT -A INPUT -i $INTERNET -p tcp ! --syn \
            --sport $UNPRIVPORTS \
            -d $IPADDR --dport $UNPRIVPORTS -j ACCEPT

#...........................................................
# Incoming Remote Client Requests to Local Servers

if [ "$FTP_SERVER" = "1" ]; then

    # Incoming Control Connection to Port 21
    if [ "$CONNECTION_TRACKING" = "1" ]; then
    $IPT -A INPUT  -i $INTERNET -p tcp \
            --sport $UNPRIVPORTS \
            -d $IPADDR --dport 21 \
            -m state --state NEW -j ACCEPT
    fi

$IPT -A INPUT  -i $INTERNET -p tcp \
        --sport $UNPRIVPORTS \
        -d $IPADDR --dport 21 -j ACCEPT

$IPT -A OUTPUT -o $INTERNET -p tcp ! --syn \
        -s $IPADDR --sport 21 \
        --dport $UNPRIVPORTS -j ACCEPT

    # Outgoing Port Mode Data Channel Connection to Port 20
    if [ "$CONNECTION_TRACKING" = "1" ]; then
    $IPT -A OUTPUT -o $INTERNET -p tcp \
            -s $IPADDR --sport 20\
            --dport $UNPRIVPORTS -m state --state NEW -j ACCEPT
    fi

$IPT -A OUTPUT -o $INTERNET -p tcp \
        -s $IPADDR --sport 20 \
        --dport $UNPRIVPORTS -j ACCEPT

$IPT -A INPUT -i $INTERNET -p tcp ! --syn \
        --sport $UNPRIVPORTS \
        -d $IPADDR --dport 20 -j ACCEPT

    # Incoming Passive Mode Data Channel Connection Between Unprivileged Ports
if [ "$CONNECTION_TRACKING" = "1" ]; then
    $IPT -A INPUT  -i $INTERNET -p tcp \
            --sport $UNPRIVPORTS \
            -d $IPADDR --dport $UNPRIVPORTS \
            -m state --state NEW -j ACCEPT
    fi

$IPT -A INPUT  -i $INTERNET -p tcp \
        --sport $UNPRIVPORTS \
        -d $IPADDR --dport $UNPRIVPORTS -j ACCEPT

$IPT -A OUTPUT -o $INTERNET -p tcp ! --syn \
        -s $IPADDR --sport $UNPRIVPORTS \
        --dport $UNPRIVPORTS -j ACCEPT
fi
```

```
###############################################################
# HTTP Web Traffic (TCP Port 80)

# Outgoing Local Client Requests to Remote Servers

if [ "$CONNECTION_TRACKING" = "1" ]; then
    $IPT -A OUTPUT -o $INTERNET -p tcp \
            -s $IPADDR --sport $UNPRIVPORTS \
            --dport 80 -m state --state NEW -j ACCEPT
fi

$IPT -A OUTPUT -o $INTERNET -p tcp \
        -s $IPADDR --sport $UNPRIVPORTS \
        --dport 80 -j ACCEPT

$IPT -A INPUT -i $INTERNET -p tcp ! --syn \
        --sport 80 \
        -d $IPADDR --dport $UNPRIVPORTS -j ACCEPT

#.............................................................
# Incoming Remote Client Requests to Local Servers

if [ "$WEB_SERVER" = "1" ]; then
    if [ "$CONNECTION_TRACKING" = "1" ]; then
    $IPT -A INPUT  -i $INTERNET -p tcp \
            --sport $UNPRIVPORTS \
            -d $IPADDR --dport 80 \
            -m state --state NEW -j ACCEPT
fi

$IPT -A INPUT  -i $INTERNET -p tcp \
        --sport $UNPRIVPORTS \
        -d $IPADDR --dport 80 -j ACCEPT

$IPT -A OUTPUT -o $INTERNET -p tcp ! --syn \
        -s $IPADDR --sport 80 \
        --dport $UNPRIVPORTS -j ACCEPT
fi

###############################################################
# SSL Web Traffic (TCP Port 443)

# Outgoing Local Client Requests to Remote Servers

if [ "$CONNECTION_TRACKING" = "1" ]; then
    $IPT -A OUTPUT -o $INTERNET -p tcp \
            -s $IPADDR --sport $UNPRIVPORTS \
            --dport 443 -m state --state NEW -j ACCEPT
fi

$IPT -A OUTPUT -o $INTERNET -p tcp \
        -s $IPADDR --sport $UNPRIVPORTS \
        --dport 443 -j ACCEPT

$IPT -A INPUT -i $INTERNET -p tcp ! --syn \
        --sport 443 \
        -d $IPADDR --dport $UNPRIVPORTS -j ACCEPT
```

```
#.......................................................
# Incoming Remote Client Requests to Local Servers

if [ "$SSL_SERVER" = "1" ]; then
    if [ "$CONNECTION_TRACKING" = "1" ]; then
    $IPT -A INPUT  -i $INTERNET -p tcp \
            --sport $UNPRIVPORTS \
            -d $IPADDR --dport 443 \
            -m state --state NEW -j ACCEPT
fi

$IPT -A INPUT  -i $INTERNET -p tcp \
        --sport $UNPRIVPORTS \
        -d $IPADDR --dport 443 -j ACCEPT

$IPT -A OUTPUT -o $INTERNET -p tcp ! --syn \
        -s $IPADDR --sport 443 \
        --dport $UNPRIVPORTS -j ACCEPT
fi

#################################################################
# whois (TCP Port 43)

# Outgoing Local Client Requests to Remote Servers

if [ "$CONNECTION_TRACKING" = "1" ]; then
    $IPT -A OUTPUT -o $INTERNET -p tcp \
            -s $IPADDR --sport $UNPRIVPORTS \
            --dport 43 -m state --state NEW -j ACCEPT
fi

$IPT -A OUTPUT -o $INTERNET -p tcp \
        -s $IPADDR --sport $UNPRIVPORTS \
        --dport 43 -j ACCEPT

$IPT -A INPUT -i $INTERNET -p tcp ! --syn \
        --sport 43 \
        -d $IPADDR --dport $UNPRIVPORTS -j ACCEPT


#################################################################
# Accessing Remote Network Time Servers (UDP 123)
# Note: Some client and servers use source port 123
# when querying a remote server on destination port 123.

if [ "$CONNECTION_TRACKING" = "1" ]; then
    $IPT -A OUTPUT -o $INTERNET -p udp \
            -s $IPADDR --sport $UNPRIVPORTS \
            -d $TIME_SERVER --dport 123 \
            -m state --state NEW -j ACCEPT
fi

$IPT -A OUTPUT -o $INTERNET -p udp \
        -s $IPADDR --sport $UNPRIVPORTS \
        -d $TIME_SERVER --dport 123 -j ACCEPT
```

```
$IPT -A INPUT  -i $INTERNET -p udp \
        -s $TIME_SERVER --sport 123 \
        -d $IPADDR --dport $UNPRIVPORTS -j ACCEPT

###############################################################
# Accessing Your ISP's DHCP Server (UDP Ports 67, 68)

# Some broadcast packets are explicitly ignored by the firewall.
# Others are dropped by the default policy.
# DHCP tests must precede broadcast-related rules, as DHCP relies
# on broadcast traffic initially.

if [ "$DHCP_CLIENT" = "1" ]; then
    # Initialization or rebinding: No lease or Lease time expired.

$IPT -A OUTPUT -o $INTERNET -p udp \
        -s $BROADCAST_SRC --sport 68 \
        -d $BROADCAST_DEST --dport 67 -j ACCEPT

    # Incoming DHCPOFFER from available DHCP servers

$IPT -A INPUT  -i $INTERNET -p udp \
        -s $BROADCAST_SRC --sport 67 \
        -d $BROADCAST_DEST --dport 68 -j ACCEPT

    # Fall back to initialization
    # The client knows its server, but has either lost its lease,
    # or else needs to reconfirm the IP address after rebooting.

$IPT -A OUTPUT -o $INTERNET -p udp \
        -s $BROADCAST_SRC --sport 68 \
        -d $DHCP_SERVER --dport 67 -j ACCEPT

$IPT -A INPUT  -i $INTERNET -p udp \
        -s $DHCP_SERVER --sport 67 \
        -d $BROADCAST_DEST --dport 68 -j ACCEPT


    # As a result of the above, we're supposed to change our IP
    # address with this message, which is addressed to our new
    # address before the dhcp client has received the update.
    # Depending on the server implementation, the destination address
    # can be the new IP address, the subnet address, or the limited
    # broadcast address.

    # If the network subnet address is used as the destination,
    # the next rule must allow incoming packets destined to the
    # subnet address, and the rule must precede any general rules
    # that block such incoming broadcast packets.

$IPT -A INPUT  -i $INTERNET -p udp \
        -s $DHCP_SERVER --sport 67 \
        --dport 68 -j ACCEPT

    # Lease renewal
```

```
$IPT -A OUTPUT -o $INTERNET -p udp \
        -s $IPADDR --sport 68 \
        -d $DHCP_SERVER --dport 67 -j ACCEPT
$IPT -A INPUT  -i $INTERNET -p udp \
        -s $DHCP_SERVER --sport 67 \
        -d $IPADDR --dport 68 -j ACCEPT

    # Refuse directed broadcasts
    # Used to map networks and in Denial of Service attacks
    iptables -A INPUT -i $INTERNET -d $SUBNET_BASE -j DROP
    iptables -A INPUT -i $INTERNET -d $SUBNET_BROADCAST -j DROP

    # Refuse limited broadcasts
    iptables -A INPUT -i $INTERNET -d $BROADCAST_DEST -j DROP

fi
##################################################################
# ICMP Control and Status Messages

# Log and drop initial ICMP fragments
$IPT -A INPUT  -i $INTERNET --fragment -p icmp -j LOG \
        --log-prefix "Fragmented ICMP: "

$IPT -A INPUT  -i $INTERNET --fragment -p icmp -j DROP

$IPT -A INPUT  -i $INTERNET -p icmp \
        --icmp-type source-quench -d $IPADDR -j ACCEPT

$IPT -A OUTPUT -o $INTERNET -p icmp \
        -s $IPADDR --icmp-type source-quench -j ACCEPT

$IPT -A INPUT  -i $INTERNET -p icmp \
        --icmp-type parameter-problem -d $IPADDR -j ACCEPT

$IPT -A OUTPUT -o $INTERNET -p icmp \
        -s $IPADDR --icmp-type parameter-problem -j ACCEPT

$IPT -A INPUT  -i $INTERNET -p icmp \
        --icmp-type destination-unreachable -d $IPADDR -j ACCEPT

$IPT -A OUTPUT -o $INTERNET -p icmp \
        -s $IPADDR --icmp-type fragmentation-needed -j ACCEPT

# Don't log dropped outgoing ICMP error messages
$IPT -A OUTPUT -o $INTERNET -p icmp \
        -s $IPADDR --icmp-type destination-unreachable -j DROP

# Intermediate traceroute responses
$IPT -A INPUT  -i $INTERNET -p icmp \
        --icmp-type time-exceeded -d $IPADDR -j ACCEPT

# Allow outgoing pings to anywhere
if [ "$CONNECTION_TRACKING" = "1" ]; then
    $IPT -A OUTPUT -o $INTERNET -p icmp \
            -s $IPADDR --icmp-type echo-request \
            -m state --state NEW -j ACCEPT
fi
```

```
$IPT -A OUTPUT -o $INTERNET -p icmp \
        -s $IPADDR --icmp-type echo-request -j ACCEPT

$IPT -A INPUT  -i $INTERNET -p icmp \
        --icmp-type echo-reply -d $IPADDR -j ACCEPT

# Allow incoming pings from trusted hosts
if [ "$CONNECTION_TRACKING" = "1" ]; then
    $IPT -A INPUT  -i $INTERNET -p icmp \
            -s $MY_ISP --icmp-type echo-request -d $IPADDR \
            -m state --state NEW -j ACCEPT
fi

$IPT -A INPUT  -i $INTERNET -p icmp \
        -s $MY_ISP --icmp-type echo-request -d $IPADDR -j ACCEPT

$IPT -A OUTPUT -o $INTERNET -p icmp \
        -s $IPADDR --icmp-type echo-reply -d $MY_ISP -j ACCEPT

###############################################################
# Logging Dropped Packets
$IPT -A INPUT -i $INTERNET -p tcp \
        -d $IPADDR -j LOG

$IPT -A OUTPUT -o $INTERNET -j LOG

exit 0
```

`nftables` Firewall for a Standalone System from Chapter 5

This section contains an `nftables` script based on the example shown in Chapter 5. The script relies on the `setup-tables` file from that chapter, which it expects to find in the same directory. Here are the contents of the `setup-tables` file:

```
table filter {
        chain input {
                type filter hook input priority 0;
        }
        chain output {
                type filter hook output priority 0;
        }
}
```

Here is the firewall script:

```
#!/bin/sh


NFT="/usr/local/sbin/nft"         # Location of nft on your system
INTERNET="eth0"                   # Internet-connected interface
LOOPBACK_INTERFACE="lo"           # However your system names it
IPADDR="my.ip.address"            # Your IP address
MY_ISP="my.isp.address.range"     # ISP server & NOC address range
SUBNET_BASE="my.subnet.base"      # Your subnet's network address
```

```
SUBNET_BROADCAST="my.subnet.bcast"   # Your subnet's broadcast address
LOOPBACK="127.0.0.0/8"               # Reserved loopback address range
NAMESERVER="isp.name.server.1"       # Address of a remote name server
SMTP_GATEWAY="isp.smtp.server"       # Address of a remote mail gateway
POP_SERVER="isp.pop.server"          # Address of a remote pop server
IMAP_SERVER="isp.imap.server"        # Address of a remote imap server
TIME_SERVER="time.nist.gov"          # Address of a remote NTP server
CLASS_A="10.0.0.0/8"                 # Class A private networks
CLASS_B="172.16.0.0/12"              # Class B private networks
CLASS_C="192.168.0.0/16"             # Class C private networks
CLASS_D_MULTICAST="224.0.0.0/4"      # Class D multicast addresses
CLASS_E_RESERVED_NET="240.0.0.0/5"   # Class E reserved addresses
BROADCAST_SRC="0.0.0.0"              # Broadcast source address
BROADCAST_DEST="255.255.255.255"     # Broadcast destination address
PRIVPORTS="0-1023"                   # Well-known, privileged port range
UNPRIVPORTS="1024-65535"             # Unprivileged port range

for i in '$NFT list tables | awk '{print $2}''
do
        echo "Flushing ${i}"
        $NFT flush table ${i}
        for j in '$NFT list table ${i} | grep chain | awk '{print $2}''
        do
                echo "...Deleting chain ${j} from table ${i}"
                $NFT delete chain ${i} ${j}
        done
        echo "Deleting ${i}"
        $NFT delete table ${i}
done

if [ "$1" = "stop" ]
then
echo "Firewall completely stopped!  WARNING: THIS HOST HAS NO FIREWALL RUNNING."
exit 0
fi

$NFT -f setup-tables

#loopback
$NFT add rule filter input iifname lo accept
$NFT add rule filter output oifname lo accept

#connection state
$NFT add rule filter input ct state established,related accept
$NFT add rule filter input ct state invalid log prefix \"INVALID input: \" limit
➥rate 3/second drop
$NFT add rule filter output ct state established,related accept
$NFT add rule filter output ct state invalid log prefix \"INVALID output: \"
➥limit rate 3/second drop

#source address spoofing
$NFT add rule filter input iif $INTERNET ip saddr $IPADDR

#invalid addresses
$NFT add rule filter input iif $INTERNET ip saddr $CLASS_A drop
$NFT add rule filter input iif $INTERNET ip saddr $CLASS_B drop
$NFT add rule filter input iif $INTERNET ip saddr $CLASS_C drop
$NFT add rule filter input iif $INTERNET ip saddr $LOOPBACK drop
```

```
#broadcast src and dest
$NFT add rule filter input iif $INTERNET ip saddr $BROADCAST_DEST log limit rate
➥3/second drop
$NFT add rule filter input iif $INTERNET ip saddr $BROADCAST_SRC log limit rate
➥3/second drop

#directed broadcast
$NFT add rule filter input iif $INTERNET ip daddr $SUBNET_BASE drop
$NFT add rule filter input iif $INTERNET ip daddr $SUBNET_BROADCAST drop

#limited broadcast
$NFT add rule filter input iif $INTERNET ip daddr $BROADCAST_DEST drop

#multicast
$NFT add rule filter input iif $INTERNET ip saddr $CLASS_D_MULTICAST drop
$NFT add rule filter input iif $INTERNET ip daddr $CLASS_D_MULTICAST ip protocol
➥!= udp drop
$NFT add rule filter input iif $INTERNET ip daddr $CLASS_D_MULTICAST ip protocol
➥udp accept

#class e
$NFT add rule filter input iif $INTERNET ip saddr $CLASS_E_RESERVED_NET drop

#x windows
XWINDOW_PORTS="6000-6063"
$NFT add rule filter output oif $INTERNET ct state new tcp dport $XWINDOW_PORTS
➥reject
$NFT add rule filter input iif $INTERNET ct state new tcp dport $XWINDOW_PORTS
➥drop

NFS_PORT="2049"                         # (TCP) NFS
SOCKS_PORT="1080"                       # (TCP) socks
OPENWINDOWS_PORT="2000"                 # (TCP) OpenWindows
SQUID_PORT="3128"                       # (TCP) squid

$NFT add rule filter output oif $INTERNET tcp dport {$NFS_PORT,$SOCKS_
➥PORT,$OPENWINDOWS_PORT,$SQUID_PORT} ct state new reject
$NFT add rule filter input iif $INTERNET tcp dport {$NFS_PORT,$SOCKS_
➥PORT,$OPENWINDOWS_PORT,$SQUID_PORT} ct state new drop

NFS_PORT="2049"                         # NFS
LOCKD_PORT="4045"                       # RPC lockd for NFS
$NFT add rule filter output oif $INTERNET udp dport {$NFS_PORT,$LOCKD_PORT}
➥reject
$NFT add rule filter input iif $INTERNET udp dport {$NFS_PORT,$LOCKD_PORT} drop

#DNS
$NFT add rule filter output oif $INTERNET ip saddr $IPADDR udp sport $UNPRIVPORTS
➥ip daddr $NAMESERVER udp dport 53 ct state new accept
$NFT add rule filter input iif $INTERNET ip daddr $IPADDR udp dport $UNPRIVPORTS
➥ip saddr $NAMESERVER udp sport 53 accept

#tcp dns
$NFT add rule filter output oif $INTERNET ip saddr $IPADDR tcp sport $UNPRIVPORTS
➥ip daddr $NAMESERVER tcp dport 53 ct state new accept
$NFT add rule filter input iif $INTERNET ip daddr $IPADDR tcp dport $UNPRIVPORTS
➥ip saddr $NAMESERVER tcp sport 53 tcp flags != syn accept
```

```
#tcp smtp
$NFT add rule filter output oif $INTERNET ip daddr $SMTP_GATEWAY tcp dport 25 ip
➥saddr $IPADDR tcp sport $UNPRIVPORTS accept
$NFT add rule filter input iif $INTERNET ip saddr $SMTP_GATEWAY tcp sport 25 ip
➥daddr $IPADDR tcp dport $UNPRIVPORTS tcp flags != syn accept

$NFT add rule filter output oif $INTERNET ip saddr $IPADDR tcp sport $UNPRIVPORTS
➥tcp dport 25 accept
$NFT add rule filter input iif $INTERNET ip daddr $IPADDR tcp sport 25 tcp dport
➥$UNPRIVPORTS tcp flags != syn accept
$NFT add rule filter input iif $INTERNET tcp sport $UNPRIVPORTS ip daddr $IPADDR
➥tcp dport 25 accept
$NFT add rule filter output oif $INTERNET tcp sport 25 ip saddr $IPADDR tcp dport
➥$UNPRIVPORTS tcp flags != syn accept

#tcp pop3
$NFT add rule filter output oif $INTERNET ip saddr $IPADDR ip daddr $POP_SERVER
➥tcp sport $UNPRIVPORTS tcp dport 110 accept
$NFT add rule filter input iif $INTERNET ip saddr $POP_SERVER tcp sport 110 ip
➥daddr $IPADDR tcp dport $UNPRIVPORTS tcp flags != syn accept

#tcp imaps
$NFT add rule filter output oif $INTERNET ip saddr $IPADDR tcp sport $UNPRIVPORTS
➥ip daddr $IMAP_SERVER tcp dport 993 accept
$NFT add rule filter input iif $INTERNET ip saddr $IMAP_SERVER tcp sport 993 ip
➥daddr $IPADDR tcp dport $UNPRIVPORTS tcp flags != syn accept

#allowing clients to connect to your IMAPs server
$NFT add rule filter input iif $INTERNET ip saddr 0/0 tcp sport $UNPRIVPORTS ip
➥daddr $IPADDR tcp dport 993 accept
$NFT add rule filter output oif $INTERNET ip saddr $IPADDR tcp sport 993 ip daddr
➥0/0 tcp dport $UNPRIVPORTS tcp flags != syn accept

#ssh
SSH_PORTS="1020-65535"
$NFT add rule filter output oif $INTERNET ip saddr $IPADDR tcp sport $SSH_PORTS
➥tcp dport 22 accept
$NFT add rule filter input iif $INTERNET tcp sport 22 ip daddr $IPADDR tcp dport
➥$SSH_PORTS tcp flags != syn accept
$NFT add rule filter input iif $INTERNET tcp sport $SSH_PORTS ip daddr $IPADDR
➥tcp dport 22 accept
$NFT add rule filter output oif $INTERNET ip saddr $IPADDR tcp sport 22 tcp dport
➥$SSH_PORTS tcp flags != syn accept

#ftp
$NFT add rule filter output oif $INTERNET ip saddr $IPADDR tcp sport $UNPRIVPORTS
➥tcp dport 21 accept
$NFT add rule filter input iif $INTERNET ip daddr $IPADDR tcp sport 21 tcp dport
➥$UNPRIVPORTS accept
#assume use of ct state module for ftp

#dhcp (this machine does dhcp on two interfaces, so need more rules)
$NFT add rule filter output oif $INTERNET ip saddr $BROADCAST_SRC udp sport 67-68
➥ip daddr $BROADCAST_DEST udp dport 67-68 accept
$NFT add rule filter input iif $INTERNET udp sport 67-68 udp dport 67-68 accept
$NFT add rule filter output udp sport 67-68 udp dport 67-68 accept
$NFT add rule filter input udp sport 67-68 udp dport 67-68 accept
```

```
#ntp
$NFT add rule filter output oif $INTERNET ip saddr $IPADDR udp sport $UNPRIVPORTS
➥ip daddr $TIME_SERVER udp dport 123 accept
$NFT add rule filter input iif $INTERNET ip saddr $TIME_SERVER udp sport 123 ip
➥daddr $IPADDR udp dport $UNPRIVPORTS accept

#log anything that made it this far
$NFT add rule filter input log
$NFT add rule filter output log

#default policy:
$NFT add rule filter input drop
$NFT add rule filter output reject
```

Optimized `iptables` Firewall from Chapter 6

For most systems on DSL, cable modem, and lower-speed leased line connections, the chances are good that the Linux network code can handle packets faster than the network connection can. Particularly because firewall rules are order dependent and difficult to construct, organizing the rules for readability is probably a bigger win than organizing for speed.

In addition to general rule ordering, `iptables` supports user-defined rule lists, or chains, that you can use to optimize your firewall rules. Passing a packet from one chain to another based on values in the packet header provides a means to selectively test the packet against a subset of the INPUT, OUTPUT, or FORWARD rules rather than testing the packet against every rule in the list until a match is found.

Based on these particular scripts, an input packet from an NTP time server must be tested against numerous input rules in the unoptimized firewall script before the packet matches its ACCEPT rule. Using user-defined chains to optimize the firewall, the same input packet is tested against far fewer rules before matching its ACCEPT rule. With the addition of connection state tracking, the same input packet is tested against only a handful of rules before matching its ACCEPT rule.

With user-defined chains, rules are used to pass packets between chains, as well as to define under what conditions the packet is accepted or dropped. If a packet doesn't match any rule in the user-defined chain, control returns to the calling chain. If the packet doesn't match a top-level chain selection rule, the packet isn't passed to that chain for testing against the chain's rules. The packet is simply tested against the next chain selection rule.

Following is the Chapter 5 firewall script, optimized with user-defined chains:

```
#!/bin/sh

/sbin/modprobe ip_conntrack_ftp

CONNECTION_TRACKING="1"
ACCEPT_AUTH="0"
DHCP_CLIENT="0"
IPT="/sbin/iptables"              # Location of iptables on your system
INTERNET="eth0"                   # Internet-connected interface
```

```
        LOOPBACK_INTERFACE="lo"                      # However your system names it
        IPADDR="my.ip.address"                       # Your IP address
        SUBNET_BASE="network.address"                # ISP network segment base address
        SUBNET_BROADCAST="directed.broadcast"  # Network segment broadcast address
        MY_ISP="my.isp.address.range"                # ISP server & NOC address range

        NAMESERVER_1="isp.name.server.1"             # Address of a remote name server
        NAMESERVER_2="isp.name.server.2"             # Address of a remote name server
        NAMESERVER_3="isp.name.server.3"             # Address of a remote name server
        POP_SERVER="isp.pop.server"                  # Address of a remote pop server
        MAIL_SERVER="isp.mail.server"                # Address of a remote mail gateway
        NEWS_SERVER="isp.news.server"                # Address of a remote news server
        TIME_SERVER="some.timne.server"              # Address of a remote time server
        DHCP_SERVER="isp.dhcp.server"                # Address of your ISP dhcp server
        SSH_CLIENT="some.ssh.client"

        LOOPBACK="127.0.0.0/8"                        # Reserved loopback address range
        CLASS_A="10.0.0.0/8"                          # Class A private networks
        CLASS_B="172.16.0.0/12"                       # Class B private networks
        CLASS_C="192.168.0.0/16"                      # Class C private networks
        CLASS_D_MULTICAST="224.0.0.0/4"               # Class D multicast addresses
        CLASS_E_RESERVED_NET="240.0.0.0/5"            # Class E reserved addresses
        BROADCAST_SRC="0.0.0.0"                       # Broadcast source address
        BROADCAST_DEST="255.255.255.255"              # Broadcast destination address

        PRIVPORTS="0:1023"                            # Well-known, privileged port range
        UNPRIVPORTS="1024:65535"                      # Unprivileged port range

        # Traceroute usually uses -S 32769:65535 -D 33434:33523
        TRACEROUTE_SRC_PORTS="32769:65535"
        TRACEROUTE_DEST_PORTS="33434:33523"


        USER_CHAINS="EXT-input                        EXT-output \
                    tcp-state-flags                   connection-tracking  \
                    source-address-check              destination-address-check  \
                    local-dns-server-query            remote-dns-server-response  \
                    local-tcp-client-request          remote-tcp-server-response \
                    remote-tcp-client-request         local-tcp-server-response \
                    local-udp-client-request          remote-udp-server-response \
                    local-dhcp-client-query           remote-dhcp-server-response \
                    EXT-icmp-out                      EXT-icmp-in \
                    EXT-log-in                        EXT-log-out \
                    log-tcp-state"

##################################################################

# Enable broadcast echo Protection
echo 1 > /proc/sys/net/ipv4/icmp_echo_ignore_broadcasts

# Disable Source Routed Packets
for f in /proc/sys/net/ipv4/conf/*/accept_source_route; do
    echo 0 > $f
done

# Enable TCP SYN Cookie Protection
echo 1 > /proc/sys/net/ipv4/tcp_syncookies
```

```
# Disable ICMP Redirect Acceptance
for f in /proc/sys/net/ipv4/conf/*/accept_redirects; do
    echo 0 > $f
done

# Don't send Redirect Messages
for f in /proc/sys/net/ipv4/conf/*/send_redirects; do
    echo 0 > $f
done

# Drop Spoofed Packets coming in on an interface, which, if replied to,
# would result in the reply going out a different interface.
for f in /proc/sys/net/ipv4/conf/*/rp_filter; do
    echo 1 > $f
done

# Log packets with impossible addresses.
for f in /proc/sys/net/ipv4/conf/*/log_martians; do
    echo 1 > $f
done

###############################################################

# Remove any existing rules from all chains
$IPT --flush
$IPT -t nat --flush
$IPT -t mangle --flush
$IPT -X
$IPT -t nat -X
$IPT -t mangle -X

$IPT --policy INPUT    ACCEPT
$IPT --policy OUTPUT   ACCEPT
$IPT --policy FORWARD ACCEPT
$IPT -t nat --policy PREROUTING  ACCEPT
$IPT -t nat --policy OUTPUT ACCEPT
$IPT -t nat --policy POSTROUTING ACCEPT
$IPT -t mangle --policy PREROUTING ACCEPT
$IPT -t mangle --policy OUTPUT ACCEPT
if [ "$1" = "stop" ]
then
echo "Firewall completely stopped!  WARNING: THIS HOST HAS NO FIREWALL RUNNING."
exit 0
fi

# Unlimited traffic on the loopback interface
$IPT -A INPUT   -i lo -j ACCEPT
$IPT -A OUTPUT -o lo -j ACCEPT

# Set the default policy to drop
$IPT --policy INPUT DROP
$IPT --policy OUTPUT DROP
$IPT --policy FORWARD DROP

# Create the user-defined chains
for i in $USER_CHAINS; do
    $IPT -N $i
done
```

```
#################################################################
# DNS Caching Name Server (query to remote, primary server)

$IPT -A EXT-output -p udp --sport 53 --dport 53 \
        -j local-dns-server-query

$IPT -A EXT-input -p udp --sport 53 --dport 53 \
        -j remote-dns-server-response

# DNS Caching Name Server (query to remote server over TCP)

$IPT -A EXT-output -p tcp \
        --sport $UNPRIVPORTS --dport 53 \
        -j local-dns-server-query

$IPT -A EXT-input -p tcp ! --syn \
        --sport 53 --dport $UNPRIVPORTS \
        -j remote-dns-server-response

#################################################################
# DNS Forwarding Name Server or client requests

if [ "$CONNECTION_TRACKING" = "1" ]; then
    $IPT -A local-dns-server-query \
            -d $NAMESERVER_1 \
            -m state --state NEW -j ACCEPT

    $IPT -A local-dns-server-query \
            -d $NAMESERVER_2 \
            -m state --state NEW -j ACCEPT

    $IPT -A local-dns-server-query \
            -d $NAMESERVER_3 \
            -m state --state NEW -j ACCEPT
fi

$IPT -A local-dns-server-query \
        -d $NAMESERVER_1 -j ACCEPT

$IPT -A local-dns-server-query \
        -d $NAMESERVER_2 -j ACCEPT

$IPT -A local-dns-server-query \
        -d $NAMESERVER_3 -j ACCEPT

# DNS server responses to local requests

$IPT -A remote-dns-server-response \
        -s $NAMESERVER_1 -j ACCEPT

$IPT -A remote-dns-server-response \
        -s $NAMESERVER_2 -j ACCEPT

$IPT -A remote-dns-server-response \
        -s $NAMESERVER_3 -j ACCEPT
```

```
#################################################################
# Local TCP client, remote server

$IPT -A EXT-output -p tcp \
        --sport $UNPRIVPORTS \
        -j local-tcp-client-request

$IPT -A EXT-input -p tcp ! --syn \
        --dport $UNPRIVPORTS \
        -j remote-tcp-server-response

#################################################################
# Local TCP client output and remote server input chains

# SSH client

if [ "$CONNECTION_TRACKING" = "1" ]; then
    $IPT -A local-tcp-client-request -p tcp \
            -d <selected host> --dport 22 \
            -m state --state NEW \
            -j ACCEPT
fi

$IPT -A local-tcp-client-request -p tcp \
        -d <selected host> --dport 22 \
        -j ACCEPT

$IPT -A remote-tcp-server-response -p tcp ! --syn \
        -s <selected host> --sport 22  \
        -j ACCEPT

#...............................................................
# Client rules for HTTP, HTTPS, AUTH, and FTP control requests

if [ "$CONNECTION_TRACKING" = "1" ]; then
    $IPT -A local-tcp-client-request -p tcp \
            -m multiport --destination-port 80,443,21 \
            --syn -m state --state NEW \
            -j ACCEPT
fi

$IPT -A local-tcp-client-request -p tcp \
        -m multiport --destination-port 80,443,21 \
        -j ACCEPT

$IPT -A remote-tcp-server-response -p tcp \
        -m multiport --source-port 80,443,21  ! --syn \
        -j ACCEPT

#...............................................................
# POP client

if [ "$CONNECTION_TRACKING" = "1" ]; then
    $IPT -A local-tcp-client-request -p tcp \
            -d $POP_SERVER --dport 110 \
            -m state --state NEW \
            -j ACCEPT
fi
```

```
$IPT -A local-tcp-client-request -p tcp \
        -d $POP_SERVER --dport 110 \
        -j ACCEPT

$IPT -A remote-tcp-server-response -p tcp ! --syn \
        -s $POP_SERVER --sport 110  \
        -j ACCEPT
#.......................................................................
# SMTP mail client

if [ "$CONNECTION_TRACKING" = "1" ]; then
    $IPT -A local-tcp-client-request -p tcp \
            -d $MAIL_SERVER --dport 25 \
            -m state --state NEW \
            -j ACCEPT
fi

$IPT -A local-tcp-client-request -p tcp \
        -d $MAIL_SERVER --dport 25 \
        -j ACCEPT

$IPT -A remote-tcp-server-response -p tcp ! --syn \
        -s $MAIL_SERVER --sport 25  \
        -j ACCEPT

#.......................................................................
# Usenet news client

if [ "$CONNECTION_TRACKING" = "1" ]; then
    $IPT -A local-tcp-client-request -p tcp \
            -d $NEWS_SERVER --dport 119 \
            -m state --state NEW \
            -j ACCEPT
fi
$IPT -A local-tcp-client-request -p tcp \
        -d $NEWS_SERVER --dport 119 \
        -j ACCEPT

$IPT -A remote-tcp-server-response -p tcp ! --syn \
        -s $NEWS_SERVER --sport 119  \
        -j ACCEPT

#.......................................................................
# FTP client - passive mode data channel connection

if [ "$CONNECTION_TRACKING" = "1" ]; then
    $IPT -A local-tcp-client-request -p tcp \
            --dport $UNPRIVPORTS \
            -m state --state NEW \
            -j ACCEPT
fi

$IPT -A local-tcp-client-request -p tcp \
        --dport $UNPRIVPORTS -j ACCEPT

$IPT -A remote-tcp-server-response -p tcp  ! --syn \
        --sport $UNPRIVPORTS -j ACCEPT
```

```
################################################################
# Local TCP server, remote client

$IPT -A EXT-input -p tcp \
        --sport $UNPRIVPORTS \
        -j remote-tcp-client-request

$IPT -A EXT-output -p tcp ! --syn \
        --dport $UNPRIVPORTS \
        -j local-tcp-server-response

# Kludge for incoming FTP data channel connections
# from remote servers using port mode.
# The state modules treat this connection as RELATED
# if the ip_conntrack_ftp module is loaded.

$IPT -A EXT-input -p tcp \
        --sport 20 --dport $UNPRIVPORTS \
        -j ACCEPT

$IPT -A EXT-output -p tcp ! --syn \
        --sport $UNPRIVPORTS --dport 20 \
        -j ACCEPT


################################################################
# Remote TCP client input and local server output chains

# SSH server

if [ "$CONNECTION_TRACKING" = "1" ]; then
    $IPT -A remote-tcp-client-request -p tcp \
            -s <selected host> --destination-port 22 \
            -m state --state NEW \
            -j ACCEPT
fi

$IPT -A remote-tcp-client-request -p tcp \
        -s <selected host> --destination-port 22 \
        -j ACCEPT

$IPT -A local-tcp-server-response -p tcp  ! --syn \
        --source-port 22 -d <selected host> \
        -j ACCEPT

#..............................................................
# AUTH identd server

if [ "$ACCEPT_AUTH" = "0" ]; then
    $IPT -A remote-tcp-client-request -p tcp \
        --destination-port 113 \
        -j REJECT --reject-with tcp-reset
else
    $IPT -A remote-tcp-client-request -p tcp \
            --destination-port 113 \
            -j ACCEPT
```

```
        $IPT -A local-tcp-server-response -p tcp  ! --syn \
                --source-port 113 \
                -j ACCEPT
fi

##############################################################
# Local UDP client, remote server

$IPT -A EXT-output -p udp \
        --sport $UNPRIVPORTS \
        -j local-udp-client-request

$IPT -A EXT-input -p udp \
        --dport $UNPRIVPORTS \
        -j remote-udp-server-response

##############################################################
# NTP time client

if [ "$CONNECTION_TRACKING" = "1" ]; then
    $IPT -A local-udp-client-request -p udp \
            -d $TIME_SERVER --dport 123 \
            -m state --state NEW \
            -j ACCEPT
fi
$IPT -A local-udp-client-request -p udp \
        -d $TIME_SERVER --dport 123 \
        -j ACCEPT

$IPT -A remote-udp-server-response -p udp \
        -s $TIME_SERVER --sport 123 \
        -j ACCEPT

##############################################################
# ICMP

$IPT -A EXT-input -p icmp -j EXT-icmp-in

$IPT -A EXT-output -p icmp -j EXT-icmp-out

##############################################################
# ICMP traffic

# Log and drop initial ICMP fragments
$IPT -A EXT-icmp-in --fragment -j LOG \
        --log-prefix "Fragmented incoming ICMP: "

$IPT -A EXT-icmp-in --fragment -j DROP

$IPT -A EXT-icmp-out --fragment -j LOG \
        --log-prefix "Fragmented outgoing ICMP: "

$IPT -A EXT-icmp-out --fragment -j DROP

# Outgoing ping
```

```
if [ "$CONNECTION_TRACKING" = "1" ]; then
    $IPT -A EXT-icmp-out -p icmp \
            --icmp-type echo-request \
            -m state --state NEW \
            -j ACCEPT
fi

$IPT -A EXT-icmp-out -p icmp \
        --icmp-type echo-request -j ACCEPT

$IPT -A EXT-icmp-in -p icmp \
        --icmp-type echo-reply -j ACCEPT

# Incoming ping

if [ "$CONNECTION_TRACKING" = "1" ]; then
    $IPT -A EXT-icmp-in -p icmp \
            -s $MY_ISP  \
            --icmp-type echo-request \
            -m state --state NEW \
            -j ACCEPT
fi

$IPT -A EXT-icmp-in -p icmp \
        --icmp-type echo-request \
        -s $MY_ISP -j ACCEPT

$IPT -A EXT-icmp-out -p icmp \
        --icmp-type echo-reply \
        -d $MY_ISP -j ACCEPT

# Destination Unreachable Type 3
$IPT -A EXT-icmp-out -p icmp \
        --icmp-type fragmentation-needed -j ACCEPT

$IPT -A EXT-icmp-in -p icmp \
        --icmp-type destination-unreachable -j ACCEPT

# Parameter Problem
$IPT -A EXT-icmp-out -p icmp \
        --icmp-type parameter-problem -j ACCEPT

$IPT -A EXT-icmp-in -p icmp \
        --icmp-type parameter-problem -j ACCEPT

# Time Exceeded
$IPT -A EXT-icmp-in -p icmp \
        --icmp-type time-exceeded -j ACCEPT

# Source Quench
$IPT -A EXT-icmp-out -p icmp \
        --icmp-type source-quench -j ACCEPT

###############################################################
# TCP State Flags

# All of the bits are cleared
$IPT -A tcp-state-flags -p tcp --tcp-flags ALL NONE -j log-tcp-state
```

```
# SYN and FIN are both set
$IPT -A tcp-state-flags -p tcp --tcp-flags SYN,FIN SYN,FIN -j log-tcp-state

# SYN and RST are both set
$IPT -A tcp-state-flags -p tcp --tcp-flags SYN,RST SYN,RST -j log-tcp-state

# FIN and RST are both set
$IPT -A tcp-state-flags -p tcp --tcp-flags FIN,RST FIN,RST -j log-tcp-state

# FIN is the only bit set, without the expected accompanying ACK
$IPT -A tcp-state-flags -p tcp --tcp-flags ACK,FIN FIN -j log-tcp-state

# PSH is the only bit set, without the expected accompanying ACK
$IPT -A tcp-state-flags -p tcp --tcp-flags ACK,PSH PSH -j log-tcp-state

# URG is the only bit set, without the expected accompanying ACK
$IPT -A tcp-state-flags -p tcp --tcp-flags ACK,URG URG -j log-tcp-state

###############################################################
# Log and drop TCP packets with bad state combinations

$IPT -A log-tcp-state -p tcp -j LOG \
        --log-prefix "Illegal TCP state: " \
        --log-ip-options --log-tcp-options

$IPT -A log-tcp-state -j DROP

###############################################################
# Bypass rule checking for ESTABLISHED exchanges

if [ "$CONNECTION_TRACKING" = "1" ]; then
    # Bypass the firewall filters for established exchanges
    $IPT -A connection-tracking -m state \
            --state ESTABLISHED,RELATED \
            -j ACCEPT

    $IPT -A connection-tracking -m state --state INVALID \
            -j LOG --log-prefix "INVALID packet: "
    $IPT -A connection-tracking -m state --state INVALID -j DROP
fi

###############################################################
# DHCP traffic

# Some broadcast packets are explicitly ignored by the firewall.
# Others are dropped by the default policy.
# DHCP tests must precede broadcast-related rules, as DHCP relies
# on broadcast traffic initially.

if [ "$DHCP_CLIENT" = "1" ]; then

    # Initialization or rebinding: No lease or Lease time expired.

    $IPT -A local-dhcp-client-query \
            -s $BROADCAST_SRC \
            -d $BROADCAST_DEST -j ACCEPT

    # Incoming DHCPOFFER from available DHCP servers
```

```
        $IPT -A remote-dhcp-server-response \
                -s $BROADCAST_SRC \
                -d $BROADCAST_DEST -j ACCEPT

        # Fall back to initialization
        # The client knows its server, but has either lost its lease,
        # or else needs to reconfirm the IP address after rebooting.

        $IPT -A local-dhcp-client-query \
                -s $BROADCAST_SRC \
                -d $DHCP_SERVER -j ACCEPT

        $IPT -A remote-dhcp-server-response \
                -s $DHCP_SERVER \
                -d $BROADCAST_DEST -j ACCEPT

        # As a result of the above, we're supposed to change our IP
        # address with this message, which is addressed to our new
        # address before the dhcp client has received the update.
        # Depending on the server implementation, the destination address
        # can be the new IP address, the subnet address, or the limited
        # broadcast address.

        # If the network subnet address is used as the destination,
        # the next rule must allow incoming packets destined to the
        # subnet address, and the rule must precede any general rules
        # that block such incoming broadcast packets.

        $IPT -A remote-dhcp-server-response \
                -s $DHCP_SERVER -j ACCEPT

        # Lease renewal

        $IPT -A local-dhcp-client-query \
                -s $IPADDR \
                -d $DHCP_SERVER -j ACCEPT
fi
##################################################################
# Source Address Spoof Checks

# Drop packets pretending to be originating from the receiving interface
$IPT -A source-address-check -s $IPADDR -j DROP

# Refuse packets claiming to be from private networks

$IPT -A source-address-check -s $CLASS_A -j DROP
$IPT -A source-address-check -s $CLASS_B -j DROP
$IPT -A source-address-check -s $CLASS_C -j DROP
$IPT -A source-address-check -s $CLASS_D_MULTICAST -j DROP
$IPT -A source-address-check -s $CLASS_E_RESERVED_NET -j DROP
$IPT -A source-address-check -s $LOOPBACK  -j DROP

$IPT -A source-address-check -s 0.0.0.0/8 -j DROP
$IPT -A source-address-check -s 169.254.0.0/16 -j DROP
$IPT -A source-address-check -s 192.0.2.0/24 -j DROP
```

```
###############################################################
# Bad Destination Address and Port Checks

# Block directed broadcasts from the Internet

$IPT -A destination-address-check -d $BROADCAST_DEST -j DROP
$IPT -A destination-address-check -d $SUBNET_BASE -j DROP
$IPT -A destination-address-check -d $SUBNET_BROADCAST -j DROP
$IPT -A destination-address-check ! -p udp \
         -d $CLASS_D_MULTICAST -j DROP

###############################################################
# Logging Rules Prior to Dropping by the Default Policy

# ICMP rules

$IPT -A EXT-log-in -p icmp \
        ! --icmp-type echo-request -m limit -j LOG

# TCP rules

$IPT -A EXT-log-in -p tcp \
        --dport 0:19 -j LOG

# Skip ftp, telnet, ssh
$IPT -A EXT-log-in -p tcp \
        --dport 24 -j LOG

# Skip smtp
$IPT -A EXT-log-in -p tcp \
        --dport 26:78 -j LOG

# Skip finger, www
$IPT -A EXT-log-in -p tcp \
        --dport 81:109 -j LOG

# Skip pop-3, sunrpc
$IPT -A EXT-log-in -p tcp \
        --dport 112:136 -j LOG

# Skip NetBIOS
$IPT -A EXT-log-in -p tcp \
        --dport 140:142 -j LOG

# Skip imap
$IPT -A EXT-log-in -p tcp \
        --dport 144:442 -j LOG

# Skip secure_web/SSL
$IPT -A EXT-log-in -p tcp \
        --dport 444:65535 -j LOG

#UDP rules

$IPT -A EXT-log-in -p udp \
        --dport 0:110 -j LOG
```

```
# Skip sunrpc
$IPT -A EXT-log-in -p udp \
        --dport 112:160 -j LOG

# Skip snmp
$IPT -A EXT-log-in -p udp \
        --dport 163:634 -j LOG

# Skip NFS mountd
$IPT -A EXT-log-in -p udp \
        --dport 636:5631 -j LOG

# Skip pcAnywhere
$IPT -A EXT-log-in -p udp \
        --dport 5633:31336 -j LOG

# Skip traceroute's default ports
$IPT -A EXT-log-in -p udp \
        --sport $TRACEROUTE_SRC_PORTS \
        --dport $TRACEROUTE_DEST_PORTS -j LOG

# Skip the rest
$IPT -A EXT-log-in -p udp \
        --dport 33434:65535 -j LOG

# Outgoing Packets

# Don't log rejected outgoing ICMP destination-unreachable packets
$IPT -A EXT-log-out -p icmp \
        --icmp-type destination-unreachable -j DROP

$IPT -A EXT-log-out -j LOG

###############################################################
# Install the User-defined Chains on the built-in
# INPUT and OUTPUT chains

# If TCP: Check for common stealth scan TCP state patterns
$IPT -A INPUT  -p tcp -j tcp-state-flags
$IPT -A OUTPUT -p tcp -j tcp-state-flags

if [ "$CONNECTION_TRACKING" = "1" ]; then
    # Bypass the firewall filters for established exchanges
    $IPT -A INPUT  -j connection-tracking
    $IPT -A OUTPUT -j connection-tracking
fi

if [ "$DHCP_CLIENT" = "1" ]; then
    $IPT -A INPUT  -i $INTERNET -p udp \
            --sport 67 --dport 68 -j remote-dhcp-server-response
    $IPT -A OUTPUT -o $INTERNET -p udp \
            --sport 68 --dport 67 -j local-dhcp-client-query
fi

# Test for illegal source and destination addresses in incoming packets
$IPT -A INPUT  ! -p tcp -j source-address-check
$IPT -A INPUT  -p tcp --syn -j source-address-check
$IPT -A INPUT  -j destination-address-check
```

```
# Test for illegal destination addresses in outgoing packets
$IPT -A OUTPUT -j destination-address-check

# Begin standard firewall tests for packets addressed to this host
$IPT -A INPUT -i $INTERNET -d $IPADDR -j EXT-input

# Multicast traffic
#### CHOOSE WHETHER TO DROP OR ACCEPT!
$IPT -A INPUT  -i $INTERNET -p udp -d $CLASS_D_MULTICAST -j [ DROP | ACCEPT ]
$IPT -A OUTPUT -o $INTERNET -p udp -s $IPADDR -d $CLASS_D_MULTICAST \
-j [ DROP | ACCEPT ]

# Begin standard firewall tests for packets sent from this host.
# Source address spoofing by this host is not allowed due to the
# test on source address in this rule.
$IPT -A OUTPUT -o $INTERNET -s $IPADDR -j EXT-output

# Log anything of interest that fell through,
# before the default policy drops the packet.
$IPT -A INPUT  -j EXT-log-in
$IPT -A OUTPUT -j EXT-log-out

exit 0
```

nftables **Firewall from Chapter 6**

Recall that in Chapter 6 we built an optimized nftables firewall that used several different files for declaring variables and building rules. This section shows the contents of each of those files. The only one that needs to be executed is the main rc.firewall. The remainder need to be in the same directory.

Here are the rc.firewall contents:

```
#!/bin/sh

NFT="/usr/local/sbin/nft"              # Location of nft on your system

# Enable broadcast echo Protection
echo 1 > /proc/sys/net/ipv4/icmp_echo_ignore_broadcasts
# Disable Source Routed Packets
for f in /proc/sys/net/ipv4/conf/*/accept_source_route; do
    echo 0 > $f
done
# Enable TCP SYN Cookie Protection
echo 1 > /proc/sys/net/ipv4/tcp_syncookies
# Disable ICMP Redirect Acceptance
for f in /proc/sys/net/ipv4/conf/*/accept_redirects; do
    echo 0 > $f
done

# Don't send Redirect Messages
for f in /proc/sys/net/ipv4/conf/*/send_redirects; do
    echo 0 > $f
done
# Drop Spoofed Packets coming in on an interface, which, if replied to,
# would result in the reply going out a different interface.
```

```
for f in /proc/sys/net/ipv4/conf/*/rp_filter; do
    echo 1 > $f
done
# Log packets with impossible addresses.
for f in /proc/sys/net/ipv4/conf/*/log_martians; do
    echo 1 > $f
done

for i in '$NFT list tables | awk '{print $2}''
do
        echo "Flushing ${i}"
        $NFT flush table ${i}
        for j in '$NFT list table ${i} | grep chain | awk '{print $2}''
        do
                echo "...Deleting chain ${j} from table ${i}"
                $NFT delete chain ${i} ${j}
        done
        echo "Deleting ${i}"
        $NFT delete table ${i}
done

if [ "$1" = "stop" ]
then
echo "Firewall completely stopped!  WARNING: THIS HOST HAS NO FIREWALL RUNNING."
exit 0
fi
$NFT -f setup-tables
$NFT -f localhost-policy
$NFT -f connectionstate-policy

$NFT -f invalid-policy
$NFT -f dns-policy

$NFT -f tcp-client-policy
$NFT -f tcp-server-policy

$NFT -f icmp-policy

$NFT -f log-policy
#default drop
$NFT -f default-policy
```

Here are the contents of nft-vars:

```
define int_loopback = lo
define int_internet = ethN
define ip_external =
define subnet_external =
define subnet_bcast =
define net_loopback = 127.0.0.0/8
define net_class_a = 10.0.0.0/8
define net_class_b = 172.16.0.0/16
define net_class_c = 192.168.0.0/16
define net_class_d = 224.0.0.0/4
define net_class_e = 240.0.0.0/5
define broadcast_src = 0.0.0.0
define broadcast_dest = 255.255.255.255
```

```
define ports_priv = 0-1023
define ports_unpriv = 1024-65535

define nameserver_1 =
define nameserver_2 =
define nameserver_3 =

define server_smtp =
```

Here are the contents of `connectionstate-policy`:

```
table filter {
      chain input {
            ct state established,related accept
            ct state invalid log prefix "INVALID input: " limit rate 3/second
            ➥drop
      }
      chain output {
            ct state established,related accept
            ct state invalid log prefix "INVALID output: " limit rate
            ➥3/second drop
      }
}
```

Here are the contents of `default-policy`:

```
table filter {
      chain input {
            drop
      }
      chain output {
            drop
      }
}
table nat {
      chain postrouting {
            drop
      }
      chain prerouting {
            drop
      }
}
```

Here are the contents of `dns-policy`:

```
include "nft-vars"
table filter {
      chain input {
            ip daddr { $nameserver_1,$nameserver_2,$nameserver_3 } udp sport
            ➥53 udp dport 53 accept
            ip daddr { $nameserver_1,$nameserver_2,$nameserver_3 } tcp sport
            ➥53 tcp dport $ports_unpriv accept
            ip daddr { $nameserver_1,$nameserver_2,$nameserver_3 } udp sport
            ➥53 udp dport $ports_unpriv accept
      }
      chain output {
            ip daddr { $nameserver_1,$nameserver_2,$nameserver_3 } udp sport
            ➥53 udp dport 53 accept
```

```
                        ip daddr { $nameserver_1,$nameserver_2,$nameserver_3 } tcp sport
➥$ports_unpriv tcp dport 53 accept
                        ip daddr { $nameserver_1,$nameserver_2,$nameserver_3 } udp sport
➥$ports_unpriv udp dport 53 accept
        }
}
```

Here are the contents of `icmp-policy`:

```
include "nft-vars"
table filter {
        chain input {
                icmp type { echo-reply,destination-unreachable,parameter-
➥problem,source-quench,time-exceeded} accept
        }
        chain output {
                icmp type { echo-request,parameter-problem,source-quench} accept
        }
}
```

Here are the contents of `invalid-policy`:

```
include "nft-vars"
table filter {
        chain input {
                iif $int_internet ip saddr $ip_external drop
                iif $int_internet ip saddr $net_class_a drop
                iif $int_internet ip saddr $net_class_b drop
                iif $int_internet ip saddr $net_class_c drop
                iif $int_internet ip protocol udp ip daddr $net_class_d accept
                iif $int_internet ip saddr $net_class_e drop
                iif $int_internet ip saddr $net_loopback drop
                iif $int_internet ip daddr $broadcast_dest drop
        }
        chain output {
        }
}
```

Here are the contents of `localhost-policy`:

```
include "nft-vars"
table filter {
        chain input {
                iifname $int_loopback accept
        }
        chain output {
                oifname $int_loopback accept
        }
}
```

Here are the contents of `log-policy`:

```
include "nft-vars"
table filter {
        chain input {
                log prefix "INPUT packet dropped: " limit rate 3/second
        }
```

```
        chain output {
                log prefix "OUTPUT packet dropped: " limit rate 3/second
        }
}
```

Here are the contents of setup-tables:

```
include "nft-vars"
table filter {
        chain input {
                type filter hook input priority 0;
        }
        chain output {
                type filter hook output priority 0;
        }
}
```

Here are the contents of tcp-client-policy:

```
include "nft-vars"
table filter {
        chain input {
        }
        chain output {
                tcp dport {21,22,80,110,143,993,995,443} tcp sport $ports_unpriv
                ➥accept
                ip daddr $server_smtp tcp dport 25 tcp sport $ports_unpriv accept
        }
}
```

Here are the contents of tcp-server-policy:

```
include "nft-vars"
table filter {
        chain input {
                #CHOOSE WHETHER TO ACCEPT OR DROP!
                ip daddr $ip_external tcp sport $ports_unpriv tcp dport {22} [
                ➥accept | drop ]
        }
        chain output {
        }
}
```

C

Glossary

This glossary defines terms and acronyms used in the book. Multiword terms are alphabetized on the major noun in the term, followed by a comma and the rest of the term.

ACCEPT A firewall-filtering rule decision to pass a packet through to its next destination.

accept-everything-by-default policy A policy that accepts all packets that don't match a firewall rule in the chain. Therefore, most firewall rules are DENY rules defining the exceptions to the default ACCEPT policy.

ACK The TCP flag that acknowledges receipt of a previously received TCP segment.

application-level gateway *See also* proxy, application-level. Often referred to as ALG, application-level (or layer) gateway is an overloaded term. In firewall terms, ALG often refers to application-specific support modules that inspect application payload for embedded addresses and ports, and that recognize secondary streams associated with the session.

AUTH TCP service port 113, associated with the identd user authentication server.

authentication The process of determining that an entity is who or what it claims to be.

authorization The process of determining what services and resources an entity can use.

bastion *See* firewall, bastion.

BIND Berkeley Internet Name Domain, the Berkeley implementation of the DNS protocol.

BOOTP Bootstrap Protocol, which is used by diskless workstations to discover their IP address and the location of the boot server, and to initiate the system download over TFTP before booting. BOOTP was developed to replace RARP.

BOOTPC UDP service port 68, associated with the BOOTP and DHCP clients.

bootpd The BOOTP server program.

BOOTPS UDP service port 67, associated with the BOOTP and DHCP servers.

border router A device to route packets that resides on the edge or boundary of a network.

broadcast An IP packet that is addressed and sent to all interfaces connected to the same network or subnet.

CERT Computer Emergency Response Team, an information coordination center and Internet security emergency prevention center formed at the Software Engineering Institute of Carnegie Mellon University after the Internet Worm incident in 1988.

chain The list of rules defining which packets can come in and which can go out through a network interface.

checksum A number produced by performing some arithmetic computation on the numeric value of each byte in a file or packet. If the file is changed, or the packet corrupted, a second checksum produced for the same object will not match the original checksum.

choke *See* firewall, choke.

chroot Both a program and a system call that defines a directory to be the root of the filesystem, and that then executes a program to run confined to that virtual filesystem.

circuit gateway *See* proxy, circuit-level.

class, network address Historically, one of five classes of network addresses. An IPv4 address is a 32-bit value. The address space is divided into Class A through Class E addresses, depending on the value of the first 4 most significant bits in the 32-bit value. The Class A network address space maps 128 separate networks, each addressing more than 16 million hosts. The Class B network address space maps 16,384 networks, each addressing up to 64,534 hosts. The Class C network address space maps about 2 million networks, each addressing up to 254 hosts. Class D is used for multicast addresses. Class E is reserved for unspecified or experimental purposes. The network classes have largely become an artifact with the introduction of CIDR. People refer to them out of familiarity and because their byte-boundary characteristics make them convenient to use in examples.

Classless Inter-Domain Routing CIDR replaces the concept of network address classes for space allocation with the concept of variable-length network fields. A conceptual extension of the idea of variable-length subnet masks, CIDR is intended to improve router table scalability and to solve the allocation problems caused by the exhaustion of the classful address space for midsize organizations.

client/server model The model for distributed network services, in which a centralized program, a server, provides a service to remote client programs requesting that service, whether the service is receiving a copy of a web page, downloading a file from a central repository, performing a database lookup, sending or receiving electronic mail, performing some kind of computation on client-supplied data, or establishing human communication connections between two or more people.

daemon A basic system services server running in the background.

DARPA Defense Advanced Research Projects Agency.

Datalink layer In the OSI reference model, the second layer, which represents point-to-point data signal delivery between two adjacent network devices, such as the delivery of an Ethernet frame from a computer to an external router. (In the TCP/IP reference model, this functionality is included as part of the first layer, the subnet layer.)

default policy A policy for a firewall rule set—whether for an INPUT chain, an OUTPUT chain, or a FORWARD chain in the filter table—that defines a packet's disposition when the packet doesn't match any rule in the set. *See also* accept-everything-by-default policy and deny-everything-by-default policy.

denial-of-service (DoS) attack An attack based on the idea of sending unexpected data or flooding a system with packets to disrupt or seriously degrade service, tie up local servers to the extent that legitimate requests can't be honored, or, in the worst case, crash a system or systems altogether.

deny-everything-by-default policy A policy that silently drops all packets that don't match a firewall rule in the chain. Most firewall rules are ACCEPT rules defining the exceptions to the default DENY policy.

DHCP Dynamic Host Configuration Protocol, which is used to dynamically assign IP addresses and provide server and router information to clients without registered IP addresses. DHCP was developed to replace BOOTP.

DMZ The demilitarized zone, a perimeter network containing machines hosting public services, separated from a local, private network. The less secure public servers are isolated from the private LAN.

DNS Domain Name Service, a global Internet database service primarily providing host-to-IP and IP-to-host mapping.

DROP A firewall-filtering rule decision to silently drop a packet without returning any notification to the sender. DROP is identical to DENY in earlier Linux firewall technologies.

dual-homed A computer that has two network interfaces. *See also* multihomed.

dynamically assigned address IP address temporarily assigned to a client network interface by a central server, such as a DHCP server.

Ethernet frame Over an Ethernet network, IP datagrams are encapsulated in Ethernet frames.

filter, firewall A firewall packet-filtering rule defining the characteristics of the packet's IP and transport headers, which, if matched, determines whether the packet is to be allowed through the network interface or is to be dropped. Filters are defined in terms of such fields as a packet's source and destination addresses, source and destination ports, protocol type, TCP connection state, and ICMP message type.

finger A user information lookup program.

firewall A device or group of devices that enforces an access control policy between networks.

firewall, bastion Frequently, a firewall that has two or more network interfaces and is the gateway or connection point between those networks, most typically between a local site and the Internet. Because a bastion firewall is the single point of connection between networks, the bastion is secured to the greatest extent possible. More generally, a bastion is a firewall that remote sites have direct access to, whether that host connects networks or protects a server that provides public services.

firewall, choke A LAN firewall that has two or more network interfaces and is the gateway or connection point between those networks. One side connects to a DMZ perimeter network between the choke firewall and a bastion gateway firewall. The other network interface connects to an internal, private LAN.

firewall, dual-homed A single-host, gateway firewall that either requires local users to specifically connect to the firewall machine to access the Internet or proxies all remote services accessible to the site. In a dual-homed gateway firewall system, no traffic is allowed to pass between the LAN and the Internet.

firewall, screened-host Almost identical to a dual-homed firewall, the single-host firewall does not sit directly between the Internet and the local network. The screened-host firewall is separated from the public network by an intermediate router and a packet filter. Local users must either specifically connect to the firewall machine to access the Internet or go through proxies on the firewall machine. The screening router ensures that all traffic between networks, or at least specific kinds of traffic, goes through the screened host. The difference between the screened-host firewall and the dual-host firewall is primarily in the location of the firewall within the local network.

firewall, screened-subnet A firewall system incorporating a gateway firewall, a DMZ network housing public servers, and an internal choke firewall that screens the LAN from both the DMZ and direct Internet access. Public services are not hosted from the choke firewall.

flooding, packet A denial-of-service attack in which the victim host or network is sent more packets of a given type than the victim can accommodate.

forward To route packets from one network to another in the process of delivering a packet from one computer to another.

fragment An IP packet containing a piece of a TCP segment.

FTP File Transfer Protocol. The protocol and programs used to copy files between networked computers.

FTP, anonymous FTP service accessible to any client that requests the service.

FTP, authenticated FTP service accessible to predefined accounts, which must be authenticated before using the service.

gateway A computer or program serving as either the conduit or the termination point and relay between two networks.

hosts.allow, hosts.deny TCP wrappers' configuration files are `/etc/hosts.allow` and `/etc/hosts.deny`.

HOWTO In addition to the standard man pages, Linux includes user-supplied online documentation on numerous topics, in many languages and in multiple formats. The HOWTO documents are coordinated and maintained by the Linux Documentation Project.

HTTP Hypertext Transfer Protocol, used by web servers and browsers.

hub A hardware signal repeater used to physically connect multiple network segments, extend the distance of a physical network, or connect network segments of different physical types.

IANA Internet Assigned Numbers Authority.

ICMP Internet Control Message Protocol. A Network-layer IP status and control message.

identd The user authentication (AUTH) server.

IMAP Internet Message Access Protocol, used to retrieve mail from mail hosts running an IMAP server.

inetd A network superserver that listens for incoming connections to service ports used by servers that it manages. When a connection request arrives, `inetd` starts a copy of the request server to handle the connection. By default, `inetd` has been replaced by an extended version called `xinetd`.

IP datagram An IP Network-layer packet.

ipchains With the introduction of the newer implementation of the IPFW firewall mechanism in Linux, the firewall administration program that replaced `ipfwadm`. `iptables` is supplied with an `ipchains` compatibility module for sites that want to continue using their existing firewall scripts.

IPFW IP firewall mechanism, now replaced by Netfilter.

ipfwadm Before the introduction of `ipchains`, the Linux IPFW firewall administration program. `iptables` is supplied with an `ipfwadm` compatibility module for sites that want to continue using their existing firewall scripts.

iptables The firewall administration program beginning in the 2.4 series kernel.

klogd The kernel logging daemon that collects operating-system error and status messages from the kernel message buffers and, in conjunction with `syslogd`, writes the messages to a system log file.

LAN Local area network.

localhost The symbolic name often given to a machine's loopback interface in `/etc/hosts`.

loopback interface A special software network interface used by the system to deliver locally generated network messages destined to the local machine, bypassing the hardware network interface and associated network driver.

man page The standard Linux online documentation format. Manual pages are written for almost all user and system administration programs, as well as system calls, library calls, device types, and system file formats.

masquerading The process of replacing an outgoing packet's local source address with that of the firewall or gateway machine so that the LAN's IP addresses remain hidden. In the IPFW firewall mechanism, masquerading referred to the source NAT functionality implemented in Linux. In Netfilter, masquerading refers to a specialized form of source NAT for use with connections that are dynamically assigned temporary IP addresses that tend to change with each connection.

MD5 A cryptographic checksum algorithm used to ensure data integrity by creating digital signatures, called message digests, of objects.

MTU Maximum Transmission Unit, the maximum packet size based on the underlying network.

multicast An IP packet specially addressed to a Class D multicast IP address. Multicast clients are registered with the intermediate routers to receive packets addressed to a particular multicast address.

multihomed A computer that has two or more network interfaces. *See also* dual-homed.

name server, primary An authoritative server for a domain or a zone of the domain space. The server maintains a complete database of hostnames and IP addresses for this zone.

name server, secondary A backup or peer to a primary name server.

NAT Network Address Translation, the process of replacing a packet's source or destination address with that of some other network interface. NAT is primarily intended to allow traffic between incompatible network address spaces, such as between the Internet and a LAN that is assigned private addresses internally.

Netfilter The firewall mechanism included beginning with the Linux 2.4 kernel.

nft The administration program for an `nftables` firewall.

nftables The firewall mechanism included beginning with the Linux 3.13 kernel.

netstat A program that reports various kinds of network status based on the various network-related kernel tables.

Network layer In the OSI reference model, the third layer, which represents end-to-end communication between two computers, such as routing and delivery of an IP datagram from a source computer to some external destination computer. In the TCP/IP reference model, this is referred to as the second layer, the Internet layer.

NFS Network File System, used to share filesystems between networked computers.

Nmap A network security auditing (that is, port-scanning) tool that includes many of the newer scanning techniques in use today.

NNTP Network News Transfer Protocol, used by Usenet.

NTP Network Time Protocol, used by `ntpd` and `ntpdate`.

OSI (Open System Interconnection) reference model A seven-layer model developed by the International Organization for Standardization (ISO) to provide a framework or guide for network interconnection standards.

OSPF The Open Shortest Path First routing protocol for TCP/IP, which is the most commonly used routing protocol today.

packet An IP network datagram.

packet filtering *See* firewall.

PATH The shell environmental variable defining which directories the shell should search for unqualified executable commands and in which order the shell should search those directories.

peer-to-peer A communication mode used for communication between two server programs. A peer-to-peer communication protocol is often, but not always, different from the protocol used to communicate between the server and a client.

Physical layer In the OSI reference model, the first layer, which represents the physical medium used to carry the signals between two adjacent network devices, such as copper wire, optical fiber, packet radio, or infrared. In the TCP/IP reference model, this is included as part of the first layer, the subnet layer.

PID Process ID, which is a process's unique numeric identifier on the system, usually associated with the process's slot in the system process table.

ping A simple network-analysis tool used to determine whether a remote host is reachable and responding. `ping` sends an ICMP echo request message. The recipient host returns an ICMP echo reply message in response.

POP Post Office Protocol, used to retrieve mail from mail hosts running a POP server.

port In TCP or UDP, the numeric designator of a particular network communication channel. Port assignments are managed by IANA. Some ports are assigned to particular application communication protocols as part of the protocol standard. Some ports are registered as being associated with a particular service by convention. Some ports are unassigned and free to be dynamically assigned for use by clients and user programs:

- **Privileged**—A port in the range from 0 to 1023. Many of these ports are assigned to application protocols by international standard. On a Linux system, access to the privileged ports requires system-level privilege.

- **Unprivileged**—A port in the range from 1024 to 65535. Some of these ports are registered for use by certain programs by convention. Any port in this range can be used by a client program to establish a connection with a networked server.

port scan A probe of all or a set of a host computer's service ports, typically service ports that are often associated with security vulnerabilities.

portmap An RPC manager daemon, used to map between a particular RPC service number that a client is requesting to access and the service port to which the associated server is bound.

probe To send some kind of packet to a service port on a host computer. The purpose of a probe is to determine whether a response is generated from the target host.

proxy A program that creates and maintains a network connection on behalf of another program, providing an application-level conduit between a client and a server. The actual client and server have no direct communication. The proxy appears to be the server to the client program and appears to be the client to the server program. Application proxies generally are categorized as application gateways or circuit gateways.

proxy, application-level A proxy server for a particular service. Application-level gateway proxies understand the particular application protocol that they proxy for. The proxy is capable of inspecting the application payload and making decisions based on information at the Application level, instead of making decisions merely at the IP and Transport levels.

proxy, circuit-level A proxy server that can be implemented either as separate applications for each service being proxied or as a single generalized connection relay. A circuit-level proxy doesn't have any specific knowledge about the application protocols.

The proxy makes decisions based on the same IP and transport information that a packet-filtering firewall does, with the possible addition of some amount of user authentication functionality.

QoS Quality of Service.

RARP Reverse Address Resolution Protocol, developed to enable diskless machines to ask servers for their IP address based on their MAC hardware address.

REJECT A firewall-filtering rule decision to drop a packet and return an error message to the sender.

resolver The client side of DNS. The resolver is implemented as library code that is linked to programs requiring network access. The DNS client configuration file is `/etc/resolv.conf`.

RFC Request for Comments, a note or memo published through the Internet Society or the Internet Engineering Task Force. Some RFCs become standards. RFCs typically concern a topic related to the Internet or the TCP/IP protocol suite.

RIP Routing Information Protocol, an older routing protocol still in use today, especially within a large LAN. The `routed` daemon uses RIP.

RPC Remote procedure call.

rule *See* firewall and filter, firewall.

runlevel A booting and system state concept taken from System V UNIX. A system normally operates at one of runlevels 2, 3, or 5. Runlevel 3 is the default, normal, multiuser system state. Runlevel 2 is similar to runlevel 3, without `xinetd`, `portmap`, or NFS services running. Runlevel 5 is the same as runlevel 3, with the addition of the X Window Display Manager, which presents an X-based login and host-selection screen.

screened host *See* firewall, screened-host.

screened subnet *See* firewall, screened-subnet.

script An ASCII file that can contain either shell or Linux program commands. These scripts are interpreted by shell programs such as sh, csh, bash, zsh, or ksh, or by programs such as perl, awk, or sed.

segment, TCP A TCP message.

setgid A program that, when executed, assumes the group ID of the program's owner rather than the group ID of the process running the program.

setuid A program that, when executed, assumes the user ID of the program's owner rather than the user ID of the process running the program.

shell A command interpreter, such as sh, csh, bash, zsh, and ksh.

SMTP Simple Mail Transfer Protocol, used to exchange mail between mail servers and between mail programs and mail servers.

SNMP Simple Network Management Protocol, used to manage network device configuration from a remote workstation.

socket The unique network connection point defined by the pairing of an IP address with a particular TCP or UDP service port.

SOCKS A circuit gateway proxy package available from NEC.

spoofing, source address Forging the source address in an IP packet header so that it appears to be that of some other address.

SSH Secure Shell protocol, used for authenticated, encrypted network connections.

SSL Secure Socket Layer protocol, used for encrypted communication. SSL is most commonly used by web servers and browsers for exchanging personal information for e-commerce.

statically assigned address Permanently assigned, hard-coded IP addresses, whether publicly registered addresses or private class addresses.

subnet layer In the TCP/IP reference model, the first layer, which represents both the physical media used to carry the signals between two adjacent network devices and point-to-point data signal delivery between two adjacent network devices, such as the delivery of an Ethernet frame from a computer to an external router.

SYN The TCP connection synchronization request flag. A `SYN` message is the first message sent from a program seeking to open a connection with another networked program.

syslog.conf The system-logging daemon's configuration file.

syslogd The system-logging daemon, which collects error and status messages generated by system programs that post messages using the `syslog()` system call.

TCP Transmission Control Protocol, used for reliable, ongoing network connections between two programs.

TCP/IP reference model An informal network communication model developed when TCP/IP became the de facto standard for Internet communication among UNIX machines during the late 1970s and early 1980s. Rather than being a formal, academic ideal, the TCP/IP reference model is based on what manufacturers and developers finally came to agree on for communication across the Internet.

tcp_wrapper An authorization scheme used to control which local services are available to which remote hosts on the network.

TFTP Trivial File Transfer Protocol, the protocol used to download a boot image to a diskless workstation or router. The protocol is a UDP-based, simplified version of FTP.

three-way handshake The TCP connection establishment protocol. When a client program sends its first message to a server, the connection request message, the SYN flag is set and accompanied by a synchronization sequence number that the client will use as the starting point to number all the rest of the messages that the client will send. The server responds with an acknowledgment (ACK) to the SYN message, along with its own synchronization request (SYN). The server includes the client's sequence number incremented by the number of contiguous data bytes received, plus 1. The purpose of the acknowledgment is to acknowledge the message to which the client referred by its sequence number. As with the client's first message, the SYN flag is accompanied by a synchronization sequence number. The server is passing along its own starting sequence number for its half of the connection. The client responds with an ACK of the server's SYN-ACK, incrementing the server's sequence number by the number of contiguous data bytes received, plus 1 to indicate receipt of the message. The connection is established.

TOS Type of Service, the field in the IP packet header that was intended to provide a hint of the preferred routing policy or packet-routing preference.

traceroute A network analysis tool used to determine the path from one computer to another across the network.

Transport layer In the OSI reference model, the fourth layer, which represents end-to-end communication between two programs, such as the delivery of a packet from a client program to a server program. In the TCP/IP reference model, this is referred to as the third layer, also the Transport layer. However, the TCP/IP Layer 3 Transport-level abstraction includes the concept of the OSI Layer 5 Session layer, which includes the concepts of an orderly and synchronized exchange of messages.

TTL Time to Live, an IP packet header field that is a maximum count of the number of routers the packet can pass through before reaching its destination.

UDP User Datagram Protocol, used to send individual network messages between programs, without any guarantee of delivery or delivery order.

unicast An IP packet sent point to point, from one computer's network interface to another's.

UUCP UNIX-to-UNIX Copy Protocol.

world-readable Filesystem objects—files, directories, and entire filesystems—that are readable by any account or program on the system.

world-writable Filesystem objects—files, directories, and entire filesystems—that are writable by any account or program on the system.

X Windows The Linux graphical user interface window display system.

D

GNU Free Documentation License[1]

Version 1.3, 3 November 2008

0. Preamble

The purpose of this License is to make a manual, textbook, or other functional and useful document "free" in the sense of freedom: to assure everyone the effective freedom to copy and redistribute it, with or without modifying it, either commercially or noncommercially. Secondarily, this License preserves for the author and publisher a way to get credit for their work, while not being considered responsible for modifications made by others.

This License is a kind of "copyleft," which means that derivative works of the document must themselves be free in the same sense. It complements the GNU General Public License, which is a copyleft license designed for free software.

We have designed this License in order to use it for manuals for free software, because free software needs free documentation: a free program should come with manuals providing the same freedoms that the software does. But this License is not limited to software manuals; it can be used for any textual work, regardless of subject matter or whether it is published as a printed book. We recommend this License principally for works whose purpose is instruction or reference.

1. Applicability and Definitions

This License applies to any manual or other work, in any medium, that contains a notice placed by the copyright holder saying it can be distributed under the terms of this License. Such a notice grants a world-wide, royalty-free license, unlimited in duration, to use that work under the conditions stated herein. The "Document," below, refers to any such manual or work. Any member of the public is a licensee, and is addressed as "you." You accept the license if you copy, modify or distribute the work in a way requiring permission under copyright law.

---

1. Copyright © 2000, 2001, 2002, 2007, 2008 Free Software Foundation, Inc. <http://fsf.org/>

Everyone is permitted to copy and distribute verbatim copies of this license document, but changing it is not allowed.

A "Modified Version" of the Document means any work containing the Document or a portion of it, either copied verbatim, or with modifications and/or translated into another language.

A "Secondary Section" is a named appendix or a front-matter section of the Document that deals exclusively with the relationship of the publishers or authors of the Document to the Document's overall subject (or to related matters) and contains nothing that could fall directly within that overall subject. (Thus, if the Document is in part a textbook of mathematics, a Secondary Section may not explain any mathematics.) The relationship could be a matter of historical connection with the subject or with related matters, or of legal, commercial, philosophical, ethical or political position regarding them.

The "Invariant Sections" are certain Secondary Sections whose titles are designated, as being those of Invariant Sections, in the notice that says that the Document is released under this License. If a section does not fit the above definition of Secondary then it is not allowed to be designated as Invariant. The Document may contain zero Invariant Sections. If the Document does not identify any Invariant Sections then there are none.

The "Cover Texts" are certain short passages of text that are listed, as Front-Cover Texts or Back-Cover Texts, in the notice that says that the Document is released under this License. A Front-Cover Text may be at most 5 words, and a Back-Cover Text may be at most 25 words.

A "Transparent" copy of the Document means a machine-readable copy, represented in a format whose specification is available to the general public, that is suitable for revising the document straightforwardly with generic text editors or (for images composed of pixels) generic paint programs or (for drawings) some widely available drawing editor, and that is suitable for input to text formatters or for automatic translation to a variety of formats suitable for input to text formatters. A copy made in an otherwise Transparent file format whose markup, or absence of markup, has been arranged to thwart or discourage subsequent modification by readers is not Transparent. An image format is not Transparent if used for any substantial amount of text. A copy that is not "Transparent" is called "Opaque."

Examples of suitable formats for Transparent copies include plain ASCII without markup, Texinfo input format, LaTeX input format, SGML or XML using a publicly available DTD, and standard-conforming simple HTML, PostScript or PDF designed for human modification. Examples of transparent image formats include PNG, XCF and JPG. Opaque formats include proprietary formats that can be read and edited only by proprietary word processors, SGML or XML for which the DTD and/or processing tools are not generally available, and the machine-generated HTML, PostScript or PDF produced by some word processors for output purposes only.

The "Title Page" means, for a printed book, the title page itself, plus such following pages as are needed to hold, legibly, the material this License requires to appear in the title page. For works in formats which do not have any title page as such, "Title Page" means the text near the most prominent appearance of the work's title, preceding the beginning of the body of the text.

The "publisher" means any person or entity that distributes copies of the Document to the public.

A section "Entitled XYZ" means a named subunit of the Document whose title either is precisely XYZ or contains XYZ in parentheses following text that translates XYZ in another language. (Here XYZ stands for a specific section name mentioned below, such as "Acknowledgements," "Dedications," "Endorsements," or "History.") To "Preserve the Title" of such a section when you modify the Document means that it remains a section "Entitled XYZ" according to this definition.

The Document may include Warranty Disclaimers next to the notice which states that this License applies to the Document. These Warranty Disclaimers are considered to be included by reference in this License, but only as regards disclaiming warranties: any other implication that these Warranty Disclaimers may have is void and has no effect on the meaning of this License.

2. Verbatim Copying

You may copy and distribute the Document in any medium, either commercially or non-commercially, provided that this License, the copyright notices, and the license notice saying this License applies to the Document are reproduced in all copies, and that you add no other conditions whatsoever to those of this License. You may not use technical measures to obstruct or control the reading or further copying of the copies you make or distribute. However, you may accept compensation in exchange for copies. If you distribute a large enough number of copies you must also follow the conditions in section 3.

You may also lend copies, under the same conditions stated above, and you may publicly display copies.

3. Copying in Quantity

If you publish printed copies (or copies in media that commonly have printed covers) of the Document, numbering more than 100, and the Document's license notice requires Cover Texts, you must enclose the copies in covers that carry, clearly and legibly, all these Cover Texts: Front-Cover Texts on the front cover, and Back-Cover Texts on the back cover. Both covers must also clearly and legibly identify you as the publisher of these copies. The front cover must present the full title with all words of the title equally prominent and visible. You may add other material on the covers in addition. Copying with changes limited to the covers, as long as they preserve the title of the Document and satisfy these conditions, can be treated as verbatim copying in other respects.

If the required texts for either cover are too voluminous to fit legibly, you should put the first ones listed (as many as fit reasonably) on the actual cover, and continue the rest onto adjacent pages.

If you publish or distribute Opaque copies of the Document numbering more than 100, you must either include a machine-readable Transparent copy along with each Opaque copy, or state in or with each Opaque copy a computer-network location from which the general network-using public has access to download using public-standard network protocols a complete Transparent copy of the Document, free of added material.

If you use the latter option, you must take reasonably prudent steps, when you begin distribution of Opaque copies in quantity, to ensure that this Transparent copy will remain thus accessible at the stated location until at least one year after the last time you distribute an Opaque copy (directly or through your agents or retailers) of that edition to the public.

It is requested, but not required, that you contact the authors of the Document well before redistributing any large number of copies, to give them a chance to provide you with an updated version of the Document.

4. Modifications

You may copy and distribute a Modified Version of the Document under the conditions of sections 2 and 3 above, provided that you release the Modified Version under precisely this License, with the Modified Version filling the role of the Document, thus licensing distribution and modification of the Modified Version to whoever possesses a copy of it. In addition, you must do these things in the Modified Version:

- A. Use in the Title Page (and on the covers, if any) a title distinct from that of the Document, and from those of previous versions (which should, if there were any, be listed in the History section of the Document). You may use the same title as a previous version if the original publisher of that version gives permission.

- B. List on the Title Page, as authors, one or more persons or entities responsible for authorship of the modifications in the Modified Version, together with at least five of the principal authors of the Document (all of its principal authors, if it has fewer than five), unless they release you from this requirement.

- C. State on the Title page the name of the publisher of the Modified Version, as the publisher.

- D. Preserve all the copyright notices of the Document.

- E. Add an appropriate copyright notice for your modifications adjacent to the other copyright notices.

- F. Include, immediately after the copyright notices, a license notice giving the public permission to use the Modified Version under the terms of this License, in the form shown in the Addendum below.

- G. Preserve in that license notice the full lists of Invariant Sections and required Cover Texts given in the Document's license notice.

- H. Include an unaltered copy of this License.

- I. Preserve the section Entitled "History," Preserve its Title, and add to it an item stating at least the title, year, new authors, and publisher of the Modified Version as given on the Title Page. If there is no section Entitled "History" in the Document, create one stating the title, year, authors, and publisher of the Document as given on its Title Page, then add an item describing the Modified Version as stated in the previous sentence.

- J. Preserve the network location, if any, given in the Document for public access to a Transparent copy of the Document, and likewise the network locations given in the Document for previous versions it was based on. These may be placed in the "History" section. You may omit a network location for a work that was published at least four years before the Document itself, or if the original publisher of the version it refers to gives permission.

- K. For any section Entitled "Acknowledgements" or "Dedications," Preserve the Title of the section, and preserve in the section all the substance and tone of each of the contributor acknowledgements and/or dedications given therein.

- L. Preserve all the Invariant Sections of the Document, unaltered in their text and in their titles. Section numbers or the equivalent are not considered part of the section titles.

- M. Delete any section Entitled "Endorsements." Such a section may not be included in the Modified Version.

- N. Do not retitle any existing section to be Entitled "Endorsements" or to conflict in title with any Invariant Section.

- O. Preserve any Warranty Disclaimers.

If the Modified Version includes new front-matter sections or appendices that qualify as Secondary Sections and contain no material copied from the Document, you may at your option designate some or all of these sections as invariant. To do this, add their titles to the list of Invariant Sections in the Modified Version's license notice. These titles must be distinct from any other section titles.

You may add a section Entitled "Endorsements," provided it contains nothing but endorsements of your Modified Version by various parties—for example, statements of peer review or that the text has been approved by an organization as the authoritative definition of a standard.

You may add a passage of up to five words as a Front-Cover Text, and a passage of up to 25 words as a Back-Cover Text, to the end of the list of Cover Texts in the Modified Version. Only one passage of Front-Cover Text and one of Back-Cover Text may be added by (or through arrangements made by) any one entity. If the Document already includes a cover text for the same cover, previously added by you or by arrangement made by the same entity you are acting on behalf of, you may not add another; but you may replace the old one, on explicit permission from the previous publisher that added the old one.

The author(s) and publisher(s) of the Document do not by this License give permission to use their names for publicity for or to assert or imply endorsement of any Modified Version.

5. Combining Documents

You may combine the Document with other documents released under this License, under the terms defined in section 4 above for modified versions, provided that you include in the combination all of the Invariant Sections of all of the original documents, unmodified, and list them all as Invariant Sections of your combined work in its license notice, and that you preserve all their Warranty Disclaimers.

The combined work need only contain one copy of this License, and multiple identical Invariant Sections may be replaced with a single copy. If there are multiple Invariant Sections with the same name but different contents, make the title of each such section unique by adding at the end of it, in parentheses, the name of the original author or publisher of that section if known, or else a unique number. Make the same adjustment to the section titles in the list of Invariant Sections in the license notice of the combined work.

In the combination, you must combine any sections Entitled "History" in the various original documents, forming one section Entitled "History"; likewise combine any sections Entitled "Acknowledgements," and any sections Entitled "Dedications." You must delete all sections Entitled "Endorsements."

6. Collections of Documents

You may make a collection consisting of the Document and other documents released under this License, and replace the individual copies of this License in the various documents with a single copy that is included in the collection, provided that you follow the rules of this License for verbatim copying of each of the documents in all other respects.

You may extract a single document from such a collection, and distribute it individually under this License, provided you insert a copy of this License into the extracted document, and follow this License in all other respects regarding verbatim copying of that document.

7. Aggregation with Independent Works

A compilation of the Document or its derivatives with other separate and independent documents or works, in or on a volume of a storage or distribution medium, is called an "aggregate" if the copyright resulting from the compilation is not used to limit the legal rights of the compilation's users beyond what the individual works permit. When the Document is included in an aggregate, this License does not apply to the other works in the aggregate which are not themselves derivative works of the Document.

If the Cover Text requirement of section 3 is applicable to these copies of the Document, then if the Document is less than one half of the entire aggregate, the Document's Cover Texts may be placed on covers that bracket the Document within the aggregate, or the electronic equivalent of covers if the Document is in electronic form. Otherwise they must appear on printed covers that bracket the whole aggregate.

8. Translation

Translation is considered a kind of modification, so you may distribute translations of the Document under the terms of section 4. Replacing Invariant Sections with translations requires special permission from their copyright holders, but you may include translations of some or all Invariant Sections in addition to the original versions of these Invariant Sections. You may include a translation of this License, and all the license notices in the Document, and any Warranty Disclaimers, provided that you also include the original English version of this License and the original versions of those notices and disclaimers. In case of a disagreement between the translation and the original version of this License or a notice or disclaimer, the original version will prevail.

If a section in the Document is Entitled "Acknowledgements," "Dedications," or "History," the requirement (section 4) to Preserve its Title (section 1) will typically require changing the actual title.

9. Termination

You may not copy, modify, sublicense, or distribute the Document except as expressly provided under this License. Any attempt otherwise to copy, modify, sublicense, or distribute it is void, and will automatically terminate your rights under this License.

However, if you cease all violation of this License, then your license from a particular copyright holder is reinstated (a) provisionally, unless and until the copyright holder explicitly and finally terminates your license, and (b) permanently, if the copyright holder fails to notify you of the violation by some reasonable means prior to 60 days after the cessation.

Moreover, your license from a particular copyright holder is reinstated permanently if the copyright holder notifies you of the violation by some reasonable means, this is the first time you have received notice of violation of this License (for any work) from that copyright holder, and you cure the violation prior to 30 days after your receipt of the notice.

Termination of your rights under this section does not terminate the licenses of parties who have received copies or rights from you under this License. If your rights have been terminated and not permanently reinstated, receipt of a copy of some or all of the same material does not give you any rights to use it.

10. Future Revisions of this License

The Free Software Foundation may publish new, revised versions of the GNU Free Documentation License from time to time. Such new versions will be similar in spirit to the present version, but may differ in detail to address new problems or concerns. See http://www.gnu.org/copyleft/.

Each version of the License is given a distinguishing version number. If the Document specifies that a particular numbered version of this License "or any later version" applies to it, you have the option of following the terms and conditions either of that specified version or of any later version that has been published (not as a draft) by the Free Software Foundation. If the Document does not specify a version number of this License, you may choose any version ever published (not as a draft) by the Free Software Foundation. If the

Document specifies that a proxy can decide which future versions of this License can be used, that proxy's public statement of acceptance of a version permanently authorizes you to choose that version for the Document.

11. Relicensing

"Massive Multiauthor Collaboration Site" (or "MMC Site") means any World Wide Web server that publishes copyrightable works and also provides prominent facilities for anybody to edit those works. A public wiki that anybody can edit is an example of such a server. A "Massive Multiauthor Collaboration" (or "MMC") contained in the site means any set of copyrightable works thus published on the MMC site.

"CC-BY-SA" means the Creative Commons Attribution-Share Alike 3.0 license published by Creative Commons Corporation, a not-for-profit corporation with a principal place of business in San Francisco, California, as well as future copyleft versions of that license published by that same organization.

"Incorporate" means to publish or republish a Document, in whole or in part, as part of another Document.

An MMC is "eligible for relicensing" if it is licensed under this License, and if all works that were first published under this License somewhere other than this MMC, and subsequently incorporated in whole or in part into the MMC, (1) had no cover texts or invariant sections, and (2) were thus incorporated prior to November 1, 2008.

The operator of an MMC Site may republish an MMC contained in the site under CC-BY-SA on the same site at any time before August 1, 2009, provided the MMC is eligible for relicensing.

Index

C

E

M

Q

R

U

informIT.com THE TRUSTED TECHNOLOGY LEARNING SOURCE

PEARSON **InformIT** is a brand of Pearson and the online presence for the world's leading technology publishers. It's your source for reliable and qualified content and knowledge, providing access to the leading brands, authors, and contributors from the tech community.

↟Addison-Wesley **Cisco Press** **IBM Press** Microsoft Press

PEARSON IT CERTIFICATION **PRENTICE HALL** **que** **SAMS** **vmware PRESS**

LearnIT at InformIT

Looking for a book, eBook, or training video on a new technology? Seeking timely and relevant information and tutorials. Looking for expert opinions, advice, and tips? **InformIT has a solution.**

- Learn about new releases and special promotions by subscribing to a wide variety of monthly newsletters. Visit **informit.com/newsletters**.

- FREE Podcasts from experts at **informit.com/podcasts**.

- Read the latest author articles and sample chapters at **informit.com/articles**.

- Access thousands of books and videos in the Safari Books Online digital library. **safari.informit.com**.

- Get Advice and tips from expert blogs at **informit.com/blogs**.

Visit **informit.com** to find out all the ways you can access the hottest technology content.

Are you part of the IT crowd?

Connect with Pearson authors and editors via RSS feeds, Facebook, Twitter, YouTube and more! Visit **informit.com/socialconnect**.

REGISTER

THIS PRODUCT

informit.com/register

Register the Addison-Wesley, Exam Cram, Prentice Hall, Que, and Sams products you own to unlock great benefits.

To begin the registration process, simply go to **informit.com/register** to sign in or create an account. You will then be prompted to enter the 10- or 13-digit ISBN that appears on the back cover of your product.

Registering your products can unlock the following benefits:

- Access to supplemental content, including bonus chapters, source code, or project files.
- A coupon to be used on your next purchase.

Registration benefits vary by product. Benefits will be listed on your Account page under Registered Products.

About InformIT — THE TRUSTED TECHNOLOGY LEARNING SOURCE

INFORMIT IS HOME TO THE LEADING TECHNOLOGY PUBLISHING IMPRINTS Addison-Wesley Professional, Cisco Press, Exam Cram, IBM Press, Prentice Hall Professional, Que, and Sams. Here you will gain access to quality and trusted content and resources from the authors, creators, innovators, and leaders of technology. Whether you're looking for a book on a new technology, a helpful article, timely newsletters, or access to the Safari Books Online digital library, InformIT has a solution for you.

THE TRUSTED TECHNOLOGY LEARNING SOURCE

Addison-Wesley | Cisco Press | Exam Cram
IBM Press | Que | Prentice Hall | Sams

SAFARI BOOKS ONLINE